PENGUIN BOOKS

THE PENGUIN HISTORY OF BRITAIN
GENERAL EDITOR: DAVID CANNADINE

BRITAIN AFTER ROME

Robin Fleming is the author of *Kings and Lords in Conquest England* and *Domesday Book and the Law*. She is Professor of Medieval History at Boston College and has received grants and fellowships from the Institute for Advanced Study at Princeton and the Radcliffe Institute at Harvard University, and a Guggenheim Fellowship. She is a Fellow of the London Society of Antiquaries.

THE PENGUIN HISTORY OF BRITAIN

General Editor: David Cannadine

* already published

ROBIN FLEMING

Britain after Rome

The Fall and Rise,
400–1070

PENGUIN BOOKS

PENGUIN BOOKS

Published by the Penguin Group
Penguin Books Ltd, 80 Strand, London WC2R ORL, England
Penguin Group (USA) Inc., 375 Hudson Street, New York, New York 10014, USA
Penguin Group (Canada), 90 Eglinton Avenue East, Suite 700, Toronto, Ontario,
Canada M4P 2Y3 (a division of Pearson Penguin Canada Inc.)
Penguin Ireland, 25 St Stephen's Green, Dublin 2, Ireland (a division of Penguin Books Ltd)
Penguin Group (Australia), 250 Camberwell Road, Camberwell, Victoria 3124, Australia
(a division of Pearson Australia Group Pty Ltd)
Penguin Books India Pvt Ltd, 11 Community Centre, Panchsheel Park,
New Delhi – 110 017, India
Penguin Group (NZ), 67 Apollo Drive, Rosedale, Auckland 0632, New Zealand
(a division of Pearson New Zealand Ltd)
Penguin Books (South Africa) (Pty) Ltd, 24 Sturdee Avenue, Rosebank, Johannesburg 2196,
South Africa

Penguin Books Ltd, Registered Offices: 80 Strand, London WC2R ORL, England

www.penguin.com

First published by Allen Lane 2010
Published in Penguin Books 2011

017

Copyright © Robin Fleming, 2010
All rights reserved

The moral right of the author has been asserted

Typeset by Jouve (UK), Milton Keynes

Printed and bound in Great Britain by Clays Ltd, Elcograf S.p.A.

ISBN: 978-0-140-14823-7

www.greenpenguin.co.uk

Για την Ελένη, την Κλειώ, τη Λιλή και φυσικά, τον Σταύρο.

Your pier-glass or extensive surface of polished steel made to be rubbed by a housemaid, will be minutely and multitudinously scratched in all directions; but place now against it a lighted candle as a centre of illumination, and lo! the scratches will seem to arrange themselves in a fine series of concentric circles around that little sun. It is demonstrable that the scratches are going everywhere impartially, and it is only your candle which produces the flattering illusion of a concentric arrangement, its light falling with an exclusive optical selection. These things are a parable.

George Eliot, *Middlemarch*

Contents

Acknowledgements

One of the (many) pleasures of finishing a book is writing the acknowledgements. First, I would like to express my heartfelt thanks to a number of people and institutions for financial support, including funds for research trips and research assistants and for time off to write. At Boston College, Patricia De Leeuw, Lynn Johnson, David Quigley, Joe Quinn and Peter Weiler have been enormously helpful. The early chapters of this book were written thanks to the generosity of the John Simon Guggenheim Memorial Trust and the School of Historical Studies at The Institute for Advanced Study in Princeton. I owe special thanks to Giles Constable and Caroline Bynum for selecting me for the George William Cottrell, Jr. Endowed Membership. It is also a pleasure to acknowledge the good company and sound advice of my friends and colleagues there – Julie Barreau, Stephen Bensch, Constance Bouchard, Celia Chazelle, Angela Creager, Susanne Ebbinghaus, Josh Fogel, Kit French, Joan Judge, Christina Kraus, Nino Luraghi, Elisabeth Mégier, Peter Morgan, Leslie Peirce and Morton White. The final gruelling months spent finishing this book have been supported by the Radcliffe Institute for Advanced Study at Harvard University, a blissfully luxurious and stimulating refuge.

Libraries and librarians have, of course, been crucially important for my project. The librarians and staff at Boston College's O'Neill Library, particularly the heroic members of its Inter-Library Loan Department, have been very helpful, as were the wonderful people at the library of the Institute for Advanced Study. The staff at Tozzer Library, Harvard University's Anthropology Library, have not only provided me with access to the best organized collection (at least for my purposes) in the world, but they have, over the years, kindly provided me with a study carrel as well.

I also owe thanks to a multitude of historians. David Bates, Julia Crick, Wendy Davies, Sarah Hamilton, John Gillingham, Alessandra Massari, Nancy Netzer, Robert Schneider and Elisabeth van Houts have all, at one time or another, invited me to write articles or chapters, and each of these undertakings gave me both the excuse and the opportunity to rethink the ways I write history and to explore different kinds of non-textual evidence. Richard Abels, Katherine French, Chris Lewis and Bruce O'Brien have read, discussed and commented on many of this book's chapters and ideas. A host of past and present graduate students have also helped me think through my period's and its evidence's conundrums – Lisabeth Buchelt, Tracey-Anne Cooper, Kylie Dodson, Regan Eby, Josh Graboff, Jessie Ostrom, Mark Mullane, Chris Riedel, Christine Senecal, Sally Shockro, Karine Ugé, and especially Alecia Arceo, David Crane, Andrew Lowerre and Austin Mason, who share my interest in the material world. I owe special thanks to two of my former graduate students, Mary Frances Giandrea and Patricia Halpin, with whom I co-authored an article in 2001, the writing of which marks the moment I fell into the great, gaping maw of material culture.

The Boston College undergraduates in my 'Romans and Barbarians' course and my undergraduate material culture seminar have (unbeknownst to them) helped me clarify many of the arguments found in this book; and two undergraduate research assistants, Henry Saglio and Mike Kitson, worked hard on the book's bibliographies. My colleagues at Boston College – both B.C.'s historians and its medievalist – have been a source of support and inspiration as well, especially Prasannan Parthasarathi, Nancy Netzer and Peter Weiler, all of whom, in their own ways, are curious, as scholars, about the same issues as am I.

I am deeply grateful to my editor at Penguin, Simon Winder, not only for his Job-like patience, but for his superb advice and enthusiasm, and to David Cannadine, who asked me to write this book in the first place. I would also like to thank Elizabeth Stratford for her extraordinary copy-editing. Last and certainly not least, I am eternally indebted to Stavros Macrakis, whose companionship, culinary virtuosity, curiosity, elephantine memory, patience and love of *The Elements of Style* and *Fowler's Modern English Usage* have not only made this a better book, but have made the years spent writing it such happy ones.

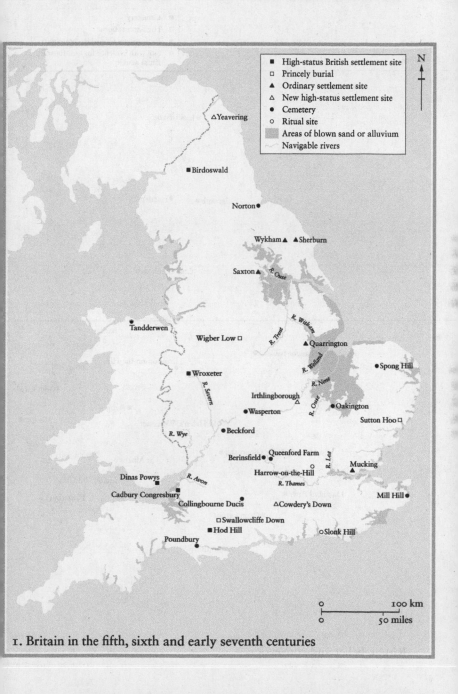

Legend:
- ■ High-status British settlement site
- □ Princely burial
- ▲ Ordinary settlement site
- △ New high-status settlement site
- ● Cemetery
- ○ Ritual site
- ▒ Areas of blown sand or alluvium
- Navigable rivers

N

△ Yeavering

■ Birdoswald

Norton ●

Wykham ▲ ● Sherburn

Saxton ▲ *R. Ouse*

● Tandderwen

Wigber Low □ *R. Trent* *R. Witham*

■ Wroxeter *R. Severn* ▲ Quarrington

R. Welland ● Spong Hill

R. Nene

Irthlingborough △ *R. Ouse*

● Wasperton ● Oakington

R. Wye Sutton Hoo □

● Beckford

Berinsfield ● ● Queenford Farm *R. Lea* ▲ Mucking

Dinas Powys ■ *R. Avon* Harrow-on-the-Hill ○

Cadbury Congresbury ■ *R. Thames*

Collingbourne Ducis ● △ Cowdery's Down Mill Hill ●

□ Swallowcliffe Down

■ Hod Hill ○ Slonk Hill

Poundbury ●

0 — 100 km
0 — 50 miles

1. Britain in the fifth, sixth and early seventh centuries

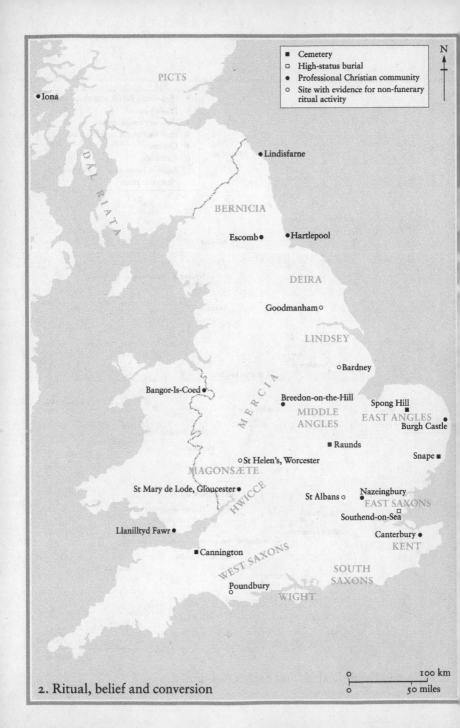

2. Ritual, belief and conversion

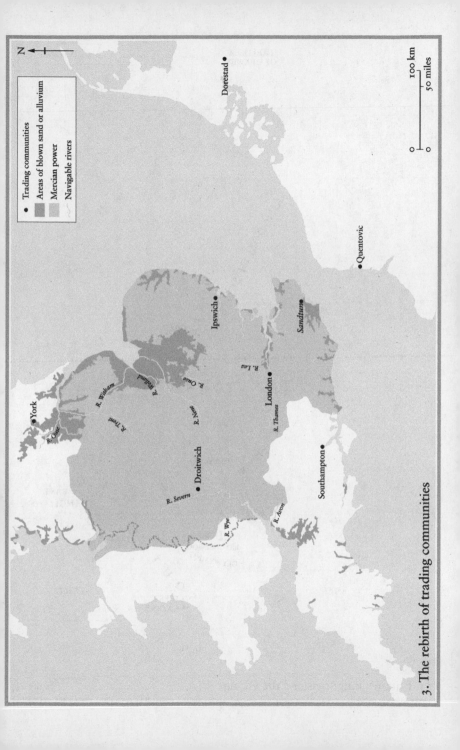

3. The rebirth of trading communities

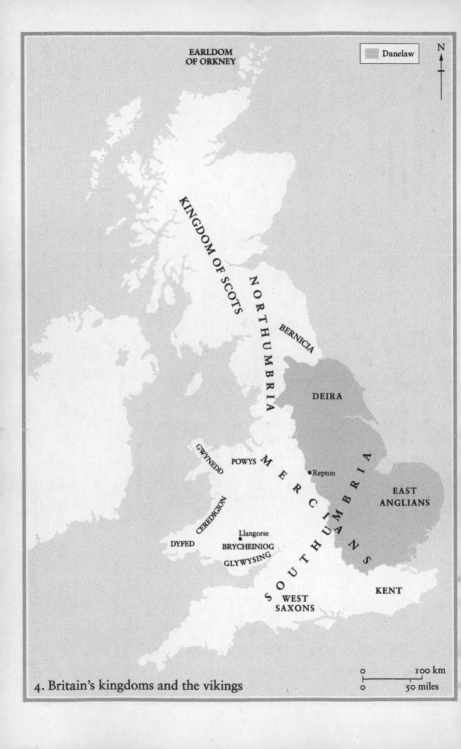

4. Britain's kingdoms and the vikings

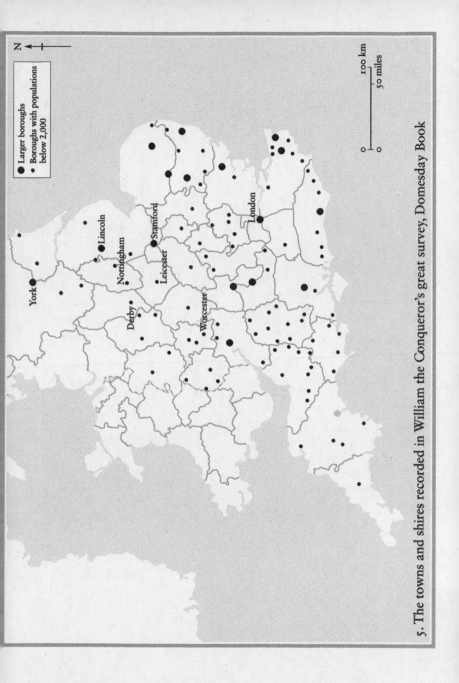

5. The towns and shires recorded in William the Conqueror's great survey, Domesday Book

Introduction

This is a book about the people of early medieval Britain and the communities in which they lived. It is also a narrative history, one that sets out to tell the story of these people's lives. Named individuals – St Columba, Edgar the Peaceable, Hywel Dda, Æthelred the Unready – are almost always the focus of the narrative histories of this period, and they drive the action. These people's lives and careers, though, because of the thinness and ambiguities of our written sources, are often desperately hard to reconstruct; and many historians have spent their careers undertaking the hard work of creating meaningful life-stories out of the few disparate facts known about them. When we let people like these loose in our narrative histories, they (alongside our often lengthy discussions about what we can and cannot say about them) tend to take up all the space, and as a result there is little space left for the hundreds of thousands of nameless individuals who lived and died alongside the likes of King Offa and Harold Godwineson. Because I wanted to make room for these other people in the story I am going to tell, better-known figures are not much present in this book; indeed, readers will find fewer named individuals and specific events in the pages that follow than they would in most narrative histories. But they will also find many more historical actors than they would normally find in a narrative history of this period.

In part, the reason I chose to write the book this way is pragmatic. There are many excellent political accounts of the period, written by very good historians, so the need for yet another treatment along similar lines is hardly pressing. But there are also more philosophical reasons that led me to construct my narrative the way I did. Having lived through eight years of the presidency of George W. Bush, I am more willing that I used to be to concede that people at the top can have dramatic effects on the lives of individuals and on the societies in which they live. Nonetheless, the slow, steady, faceless and eventless trends that we find hundreds of thousand of people ascribing to and participating in – in our own times, the widespread adoption of smart-phones and Facebook, the turn away from tobacco, readily available birth-control, meat-eating possible seven days a week, and the (for some) irresistible tug of fundamentalism – not only shape whole societies and cultures, but have profound impacts on the lived experience, not just of prime ministers and presidents, but of the rest of us as well. Because I have long suspected that the same holds true for the more distant past, I wanted to write a history which included lots of people doing the kinds of things that lots of people did in the early Middle Ages, and which placed these actors and activities (rather than kings and political events) at the heart of the story. In short, the founding contention of this book is that the aggregate of the actions, beliefs and tribulations of whole generations of individuals shaped lives and changed societies in very profound ways in early medieval Britain; indeed, they did so more fundamentally than the actions of the people whose names we happen know. Now that I have completed the book, I find that I have written a history in much the same spirit as Brian Harrison's recent volume, *Seeking a Role: The United Kingdom 1951–70*. In it, he begins by telling us that his book's 'focus will rest less upon a single political chronology than upon the far less familiar and usually distinct chronologies of non-political change, whose long-term effects are often no less revolutionary for being gradual and even sometimes unrecognized while in progress. In no society do politicians and government administrators dominate day-to-day life.' I, too, think 'the usually distinct chronologies of non-political change' should drive our narrative, rather than be relegated, as they so often are, to the kinds of separate but equal histories we find them in, generally in those 'companion volumes' that offer chapters on women's history, social history, agrarian history and economic history, in order to supplement the 'real history' of kings and kingdoms.

Both the difficulties of finding nameless people to populate my history and the joys of piecing together their lives stem from the nature of the evidence. Texts deal almost exclusively with kings and churchmen, and they report on these people's world from their own very specific and particular points of view. So, if we want to witness the ways a handful of households in the sixth century persuaded others to render agricultural surpluses to them, or to catch glimpses of the early seventh-century traders busy reintroducing urban life into Britain, or to investigate the ways some ninth-century Picts became vikings, we have to put aside our copies of the Anglo-Saxon Chronicle and look instead to the mountains of contemporary material evidence excavated by archaeologists. A few historians in the last couple of decades have not only mastered this kind of evidence, but have developed an enviable talent for using it. But most historians, it must be said, pay little attention to it. And yet the discoveries unearthed by archaeologists in the past thirty years are profoundly transformative, not least because they are so often at odds with our texts. It is vitally important, therefore, that material evidence be scrutinized, understood and internalized, not only by archaeologists, but by historians as well, and we need to master it to understand, emend and reimagine the particular piece of the past in which we work.

Material evidence also, at times, demands different chronologies from those our texts suggest, something that I have found both sobering and liberating. One of the most important things its use has taught me is that we need to begin the history of the early Middle Ages when Roman Britain is at its height rather than after its fall; when we ignore the fact of Rome, we tend to ignore Britain's large, native population, and this is profoundly distorting. Of course, we can only factor in Roman Britain if we are willing to consider material evidence, because hardly any contemporary texts survive which describe it. Similarly, the neat division drawn in our texts between the pagan and Christian periods seems to have been much less clear to those who were actually living in the period, and many practices still breezily described as 'pagan' by historians – like grave-goods burial and barrow burial – continued for generations to be valued by Christians from 'better' sorts of families. Material culture also calls into question some of the political and 'ethnic' boundaries which historians have traditionally drawn from texts and which often dominate the ways we think about the period.

Of course, whether material or textual, the evidence we have is the evidence we have, which means that it is not necessarily the evidence we would like. I had hoped, for example, to focus less on the English, say, than on the Picts or the Welsh, since there is more material evidence for these two groups than textual. But material evidence, like textual evidence, is uneven both across Britain and across time, and this continues to determine whom we can write about. Material evidence is also as treacherous as any text, and it requires careful handling. If we historians hope to incorporate it into our analyses, we must do the hard work of reading up on *all* the material evidence, not just an iconic object or site, and we have to read more than those convenient little summaries found at the ends of excavation reports. In short, we need to learn to 'read' material evidence the way we 'read' texts, that is, carefully, thoughtfully and imaginatively.

Many years ago, when David Cannadine invited me to write this book, he laid down three inviolable rules. First, there were to be no footnotes. Second, there would be no discussion of historiography. Third and finally, I was to write a book that general readers, undergraduates, graduate students and professional historians could all profit from. I have done my best. Of course, the interpretations set forth in this book are utterly dependent on the research of hundreds of archaeologists and historians. In the Further Reading section, I have tried to suggest what I think are the most fundamental readings for each chapter's topic, and then to extend this list, as a way of acknowledging this book's intellectual debts. The section relating to this introduction, moreover, includes six short 'suggested reading' lists. The first is a selection of books for those who would like a better understanding of the political narrative, and the second provides a small selection of basic, important and readable books that treat the period more thematically. The third section offers suggestions for books and articles on particular classes of material evidence, which provide useful introductions for readers who are interested in learning more. The fourth contains a few pieces that deal specifically with material culture itself, as well as discussions of the ways historians might use it. The fifth and sixth sections comprise ten books and ten articles that treat material evidence and the material world (everything from bugs to fish bones) in interesting, original and exciting ways, and all are 'good to think with'. These are here to provide historians and general readers who want a taste of the possibilities and varieties of material evidence with an entrée into a literature that may not be familiar. I hope readers are curious enough to find and read all of these works. Each one made me think differently about the past, and all constitute the kind of work that made me want to write a different kind of narrative history.

I

The Rise and Fall of Late Antique Britain: The Second to Early Fifth Century

The Rome that fell in Britain at the beginning of the fifth century was only a distant relative of the Rome that had conquered and colonized it. Late antique Britain, the Britain thriving in the hundred years before the fall, was the child of a series of economic circumstances and political crises that had played themselves out not in Britain, but in Gaul, in Italy and along Rome's easternmost frontiers. The third century had been a hard one for much of the empire, a period characterized outside of Britain by alarming barbarian incursions, incessant civil war, endless military coups and ferocious inflation. By the time the empire once again stabilized, around the turn of the fourth century, it had undergone a stunning administrative revolution, and its culture and society were quite remade. Its emperors were now powerful military strongmen, its cities were overrun with professional administrators, and its rich were incomparably richer than they had been four generations earlier in the golden days of the principate, when Roman emperors, at least in theory, had been considered 'first among equals'. This new Rome, the Rome of the more despotic dominate (from the Latin *dominus*, or 'lord'), shaped Britain in its last, Roman century, and it formed a society there that was at once less classical and more Roman than it had been before.

ROMAN BRITAIN'S FIRST ECONOMY

Since Britain itself was spared most of the political upheavals and barbarian invasions of the third century, the changes it underwent were driven to a large extent by economic dislocations that came about through prolonged and painful transformations in the structures of empire. Before the troubles began, classical-style cities had flourished in

Britain. Although they were built on a smaller scale (London at its peak had a population of something like 30,000 to Rome's 1 million), British towns had many of the same amenities – precise grid-planned streets, aqueducts, baths, forums, even amphitheatres. These planned towns, founded in the early days of the principate, were less lavish than urban communities in other parts of the empire, but they, too, had marble-faced buildings, tiled roofs and public monuments. Urban communities in Britain, especially London, grew and prospered because they were centres of massive international commerce. The volume of trade to Britain in the second century and the distances over which copious amounts of modestly valued goods travelled to get there are breathtaking; indeed, levels of trade were greater then than at any other time during the next 1,500 years. The huge numbers of amphorae that arrived at the docks of London filled with olive oil from Spain or wine from Palestine and the mountains of red Samian tableware from Gaul testify to the scale and scope of this trade. Some of it was stimulated by networks of taxation and exploitation used to transfer wealth from the conquered province and bring it back to the core of the empire. The consumer habits and Romanizing tastes of a small, native elite also encouraged this cosmopolitan trade. Yet Britain itself was hardly a wealthy province, and, left on its own, would never have attracted commerce from across the Roman world. What Britain did have, however, was an exceptionally large army; and it is clear that the bulk of the province's trade was fuelled by enormous amounts of revenue spent by imperial administrators on the British garrison and by the systems of transport used to supply it.

The army stationed in northern Britain was very large, more than 40,000 men at its height, or about an eighth of the imperial army. This level of garrisoning required the expenditure of something on the order of a sixteenth of the total imperial budget each year, although Britain itself was only one of forty Roman provinces. An army of this size required not only immense outlays of state funding, but constant provisioning with a wide range of goods – food (in particular grain), clothing, arms, transport animals, building materials – some supplied by local communities, but much brought from further afield. During the height of the principate, the army contracted supply agents and transporters from provinces across the Channel to provision it with much of the food and *matériel* it needed. These commodities, as well as goods for indigenous British markets, followed inland waterways across Gaul to the Rhine and then on into Britain. It would have been less costly for traders catering to civilian markets in Britain to ship their goods via the Atlantic sea lanes, unless the more expensive inland routes were subsidized in some way; and this, indeed, seems to have been the case. We know from the excavations of shipwrecks that imported manufactured goods – like the pottery, glass and metalwork so pervasive in second-century Britain's archaeological record – constituted only a portion of the total cargoes of most ships supplying the military, and that their bulk was made up of raw materials and food. It appears, therefore, that enterprising *negotiatores* took advantage of the space left over, once military supplies were loaded, and used the extra room for luxury goods, which they then sold to Roman administrators, soldiers with cash and sophisticated provincials. The transportation of these latter items was therefore free, silently absorbed into the cost of military supply. These accidental and ad hoc arrangements that grew out of imperial expansion enabled the inner, richer provinces of the empire to recover the costs of conquest, which they had paid for with their taxes, via this subsidized trade.

Britain's economy of massive governmental expenditure and privileged Continental trade created immense amounts of wealth throughout the century and a half they were in operation, but how much these profits were enjoyed by the British and how much by imperial administrators and Continental traders and suppliers is hard to say. The majority of Britannia's rural settlements – both prosperous households and less well-to-do farmsteads – remained resolutely un-Roman during these years. It looks, therefore, as if most of the benefits of the principate's glorious long-distance trade were reaped by those who policed, administered and did business in Britain, but whose origins lay elsewhere.

This system, which produced extraordinary wealth and allowed for Britain's initial urbanization, could not, however, be sustained. The beginning of the third century witnessed the last major military campaigns in Britain. This, combined with the rise of a series of new threats along the Rhine, the Danube and the Persian frontiers, led to a notable reduction of troops in Britain to something like half their former strength. Once this happened, the dominant patterns of trade and expenditure, upon which so much of Romanized life in Britain depended, were impossible to sustain. Military contracts changed, so the parasitical trade in Continental goods went into crisis. Barbarian incursions across Gaul and northern Italy in the 230s, 240s and 250s also disrupted inter-provincial trade. These invasions, along with periodic civil war, meant that goods were increasingly at risk as they moved across the western empire, and this added to their cost. Coastal piracy, which had arisen a century and a half earlier with the high volume of Channel shipping, grew during the crisis, and soon after the turn of the century expensive coastal forts at Reculver, in Kent, and Brancaster, on the Norfolk shore, had to be built; and by the middle of the century additional forts joined these two. Under the combined troubles of shattered peace and diminished military transports, Continental import producers failed.

As British markets created around soldiers shrank, producers and towns in the central provinces of the empire, whose economies were organized around imperial expansion, faltered. Both Gaul's Samian pottery industry and the Spanish olive oil industry, whose products were so ubiquitous in second-century Britain, fell victim to these disruptions, and traces of both very nearly vanished from Britain's archaeological record during the early third century. The economies of cities on the Continent like Amiens, moreover, whose prosperity was founded on the British trade, were in tatters; and some of the richest agricultural regions in the ancient world – places like Tuscany and Picardy – whose great estates had once grown rich on the cross-Channel trade, also went into decline.

Under these circumstances, towns in Britain underwent dramatic transformations. London, as the most important of Roman Britain's international ports, was especially hard hit by the restructuring of imperial trade and defence. Its decline began in the later second century, just as these processes were beginning to make themselves felt, and its slide continued into the third century. During this period there was a startling reduction in building density within the city. At one time London had been a crowded place, but by 300 CE perhaps as many as two-thirds of London's early second-century buildings had been dismantled, and they were not replaced. At the dawn of the fourth century there was no longer a public bath within the city and its forum had gone out of use; and its basilica, which was once the largest building in north-west Europe, had been demolished. At the same time, London's suburbs shrank precipitously as did a number of roadside settlements nearby, especially those situated along Watling Street, the major overland route from the port of London to Britain's northern frontier. These changes are directly linked to declining international trade and shrinking military presence and are reflected by London's and its suburb Southwark's shrinking warehouse districts. It can also be seen in the decline of London's hinterland, which had, when the city was at its second-century height, been heavily engaged in the production of basic goods for the army. Salt production in Kent and Essex and iron production in the eastern Weald had boomed in the first and second centuries because of the demands of military procurement, but both declined dramatically in the third, after the reduction of troops along Britain's northern frontier. At the same time, many villas in Kent and Surrey, doubtless the country homes of families who had prospered in London's good times, were deserted in the second half of the third century. In this way, the old institutions of parasitic trade and army supply collapsed, killing off much of London's commercial life.

Organized urban life, however, hardly disappeared during this period, and London remained resolutely a city. There is good evidence that London's derelict buildings were demolished in an organized fashion, rather than left vacant and ruinous; and it looks very much as if large areas within the city walls, within a couple of generations of the beginning of the economic crisis, were transformed from crowded industrial neighbourhoods into market gardens, orchards and waste grounds used for rubbish dumping. Luxurious town houses were eventually built as well, in spacious and serene new neighbourhoods that had once housed craftsmen, traders and the working poor. And at the very end of the third century imperial workmen broke ground for an enormous new palace and administrative complex. In this new London of the later empire, private houses were more important than public monuments; *otium*, leisure, more important than industry; imperial bureaucrats more important than traders. This was a stunning transformation from the early, crowded city with its cramped shops, packed tenements and dearth of open spaces.

Changes like the ones found in London are evident in other 'public towns' (a term used to describe towns with important administrative functions) whose early prosperity was yoked to imperial expansion. Colchester, although still quite a large place after the third century, was both smaller than it had been and very much different in character. It had a number of new, impressive government buildings: major storage facilities to house levies raised from the grain tax; a huge new administrative complex; and an impressive new temple and newly strengthened defences – all of which point to the central administrative role of late antique Colchester within Roman Britain. But the glorious public buildings that had graced the city in the second century – its public baths, its forum and its theatre – were gone. And, like London, Colchester was a strangely under-populated place with cultivated areas inside its walls and luxurious houses set within elaborate gardens. The picture, then, in fourth-century Colchester is of a city without the commercial vitality of the first and second centuries, and without the old, Mediterranean-style public life centred on the forum and the baths. Instead we find a town organized around the needs of imperial taxation, and encompassing the offices, storehouses and mansions of the dominate's elite.

York, too, followed this same pattern. Early York was both an army town and a cosmopolitan place. There are funerary inscriptions dating from the second century commemorating people who had travelled to York from south-eastern France, Sardinia and Greece but who had died in the city; and a number of York's Roman-period skeletons betray North African origins. There is also extensive evidence from second- and early third-century York for goods flooding in from across the Roman world alongside high levels of local manufacturing. But there are few traces of either after *c.* 300. Still, there were lovely houses in fourth-century York and some major state building projects. Clearly, York's livelihood in the fourth century, like London's and Colchester's, was rooted in its administrative functions and elegant mansions. This was not classical urbanism.

THE RISE OF ROMAN BRITAIN'S SECOND ECONOMY

The metamorphosis of Britain's public towns over the course of a hard third century is only one of a host of developments that signal the rise of a new economy, one that was considerably smaller than the economy that had operated at the height of the principate. The transition from the old economy to the new was slow and periodically painful, and it took much of the third century. With the coming of the crisis, imports, as we have seen, grew scarce. Nonetheless, local goods only gradually came to take the place of Continental products. Some imported commodities, in particular agricultural produce, could never be replicated in rainy Britain, so local and permanent substitutions were found. Beer drinking, by and large, replaced wine drinking; lard and butter, olive oil; candles and braziers, oil lamps. Other Continental products, however, were eventually supplanted by closer indigenous facsimiles. Excavated ceramics illustrate the ways in which British producers were eventually able to provide quantities of Roman-style tableware and make up for failed Continental supplies. It took much of the third century, though, for British potters to achieve this. Samian ware was no longer available after the 230s, but local British surrogates – the fine wares of Oxfordshire, the Nene valley and the New Forest – were not much evident before the end of the century. Indeed, modest amounts of pottery had been produced in these regions during the second century, but, like organized Continental kilns, Britain's pottery producers had gone into decline sometime after 200. The slow gearing up of local replacement industries suggests that there were fairly serious economic and material dislocations in Britain during the third century, even though Britain itself had avoided many of the bloodier aspects of the crisis. Other evidence points in the same direction. Both new construction and repairs to existing structures were rare in the third century, and few luxury mosaics were installed during this period. By the year 300, however, construction, rebuilding and redecoration projects were going on across lowland Britain. At the same time, large-scale, Romano-British production of well-made tableware and more utilitarian coarse wares was now in full gear. Thus, within a couple of generations local producers were able to fill the gap left by the waning of the old economy, and prosperity returned to Britain.

The new economy, however, was different in essential ways from the one it replaced. This is most clearly seen in ceramic production, because pottery makes up such a large part of the archaeological record. The Romano-British pottery industry was vastly different from its earlier Continental progenitor. Its pots were traded mostly within Britain, and the few that moved to the Continent were marketed in a narrow band along the coast. Provincial kilns, moreover, never made the amphorae that were once so common in Britain. This is because amphorae were not traded per se, but were exchanged, rather, for the more valuable commodities shipped within them. Since Britain produced neither wine nor olive oil, and since tableware, cooking pots and domestic storage vessels were of lower value than the goods transported within amphorae, their production and exchange could never generate the wealth of second-century commerce. Yet the blossoming of the British tableware industry did bring good fortune to British potters, traders and entrepreneurs. To a large degree, this is because the pottery market had broadened during this period within Britain itself. The pottery fashioned in organized, British kilns was now finding its way, for the first time, into the most unpretentious of lowland Britain's rural sites, as were modest amounts of other manufactured goods, such as nails. Bronze coins, too, were now regularly lost on humble farmsteads; lost because they were more frequently used by the people living there. Indeed, it was really only in the last forty years of the third century that large numbers of low-value coins came to circulate in Britain and function as everyday currency. So it was only now that the bulk of Britain's population – its British peasantry – was entangled in the money economy (although non-monetary exchange practices doubtless continued) and had lives cluttered with mass-produced, Roman-style goods. Taken together, the evidence from late Roman Britain paints a picture of flourishing provincial production of low-value goods for a large and essentially British market. Such an economy was predicated on a crowd of humble people willing and able to spend a few bronze coins for goods they had not made themselves. These changes betray not only profound economic shifts, but crucial cultural ones. British producers were now capable, as they had never been before, of creating Romanized goods for a largely native market. They could now manufacture, replicate and sell their own, home-grown versions of *romanitas*, and there were many eager to purchase it.

As this new provincial economy emerged, so too did an exceptionally wealthy, highly Romanized elite. The families that came to dominate life in late Roman Britain were doubtless the scions of Britain's ancient tribal elites. Yet by the late Roman period these fair-skinned, blue-eyed Celts had internalized the manners, the values and the Latin of Rome's senatorial aristocracy, and they had come to lead the same pampered lives as the great in Gaul, in Italy and in Roman North Africa.

The new rich and the old public towns soon developed an interesting symbiotic relationship in the brave new world of the dominate. Although it is clear that Britain's gracious deindustrialized cities no longer sat at the heart of the economy, they nonetheless remained alluring places, continuing to act as centres of social and cultural life for those Britons whose grand fortunes and absolute acculturation had solidified during the period of economic transition. Perhaps 500 villas were built, improved or elaborated upon by the British elite in late antiquity, and the vast majority lay in or very near one of Britain's lowland cities. Most important towns in the fourth century had at least a dozen such residences within their walls, a few of which even had the barns, paddocks and corn-dryers of rural villas. Some of these would have housed imperial administrators, but most belonged to native oligarchs, who chose to live at least part of each year in comfortable urban enclaves. Other wealthy families built their chief residences within a half-day's journey of such places. Villas were especially thick on the ground around Cirencester, Gloucester and Silchester, but they were found in great knots outside most southern and eastern towns. Although none of the musings of the British gentlemen who lived in this magnificence survive, Decimus Magnus Ausonius (c. 310–94), a contemporary Gallo-Roman, praised both his own town, Bordeaux, and his villa, writing: 'my estate does not lie far from town, nor is it right next to it, thus it rids me of town crowds but allows me to benefit from its advantages. And so, whenever satiety moves me to change my seat, I pass from one to the other, enjoying country and town by turns.' Ausonius' joy in his villa was bound up with its proximity to one of these lovely, economically declining late Roman towns.

The juxtaposition of late Roman villas and public towns is at first glance a puzzle, since towns were in many ways so much less than they had been a hundred years earlier. Our written evidence for late Roman Britain is so poor that we do not know the name of a single villa owner, nor is there a scrap of written evidence describing the connections between such a person and a local town, but we can make some guesses. Well-heeled Britons in the late third or early fourth century could not have been attracted to public towns for economic reasons, because their economies were in decline. They could not have been drawn to them for their public amenities, because in many places these were gone. And they could not have longed to travel to town to compete with their peers in that costly ancient pastime of civic patronage, because few in the age of the dominate still participated in this. Moreover, the collective activities that had once taken place in the forums and basilicas of classical cities could no longer have been important, since these spaces had often ceased to be maintained. And since the most extravagant urban houses were now built with their own baths and private places of worship, the old, communal rituals centred on public baths and temples must have been in decline as well. It is almost as if a town's public life, as the community shrank economically, underwent a quiet privatization and retreated into the houses of the very rich. Now, one had to be invited in to mingle with the political classes; one had to be a friend, a kinsman, a client to socialize among the fountains and hand-laid floors. These private spaces came to dominate the life of important Britons in late antiquity, and with their delicately painted frescos and tessellated corridors they established an impenetrable barrier between the *honestiores*, the 'better people', and the lower orders; between those who had access to these impressively decorated rooms, and therefore power, and those who did not.

Urban wealth underwent a similar transformation between the second and the fourth centuries; in a sense, wealth, like public life, was co-opted during the third century by the Romanized native oligarchy. Because public towns had ceased to act as significant marketplaces and centres of manufacturing, they no longer produced the wealth they once had. Yet cities and their immediate environs were sites of great prosperity because the rich had moved in. Thus urban wealth and power were both reconstituted along the same lines: they had been hijacked by the Romanized British elite.

Deepening social stratification alongside the phenomenal prosperity of the few marked not only urban life but rural life as well. The rise of the luxury villa during this period is symptomatic of the concentration of wealth into fewer hands and the increasing success of the chosen few in controlling ever more land and labour. The middle range of fourth-century villas was distinguished by their comfort, size and grace; indeed, they would be unmatched in Britain until the eighteenth century and the rise of the great country house. These villas were conspicuously different from the muddy farmsteads inhabited by most people in Britain, but even they were modest in comparison to the seven or eight palatial houses that were constructed during this time by the very rich. Many owners of grand establishments built impressive rooms within their houses in which to overawe clients or tenants and reinforce social relations that emphasized hierarchy. Box, in Wiltshire, for example, had an elaborate apsidal room that dominated the whole structure. It looks very much like an audience hall, a seat of dominal power in which private justice could be dispensed to dependants and tenants, and where the lower orders might be reminded of their places. The principal room at Woodchester, near Stroud in Gloucestershire, built sometime between 325 and 350, measured a breathtaking 760 square metres. This room was too large to function as a private chamber and is better understood as a backdrop for lordship, one built to underscore and prop up hierarchical relations in rural Britain. Other villas were designed to implement lordship in a different way. At Chedworth, in Gloucestershire, for example, a small room was built back by the kitchen and the latrines, one that could not be entered through the house. It was in this room that archaeologists discovered most of the coins found on the site. Both the room's location and the coins suggest that this was where tenants, entering by the back door, came to pay their rents and dues.

The new, more private forms of expenditure and politics embraced by fourth-century elites required not only great wealth but an appreciative audience, and the whole system fed on the admiration of friends and followers. Villas during this period developed elaborate spaces that served as great entertainment rooms, not for subordinates, but for friends and allies. One of Woodchester's two dining suites was not only heated and decorated to impress, but one end of the room had a dais for high-table dining: so even among intimates there was hierarchy. The mosaic floors, especially, were laid to impress. The scenes depicted on many exhibit a highly cultivated appreciation of Latin literature, in particular Virgil and Ovid, as well as familiarity with more arcane religious and philosophical teachings. Most of these mosaics were eclectic in their themes and resolutely pagan, and they displayed a kind of bookish conservatism that the well-known Italian Symmachus and his reactionary fourth-century circle would have admired. Such scenes were not simply installed for the pleasure of a villa's proprietor, but were there to impress or overawe those who walked across them. This need of the wealthy to parade their riches may also explain why late antique villas were often built so near one another.

Because lavish private display lay at the heart of aristocratic life, it drove the rich to collect and flaunt not only their sumptuous mosaics, but gorgeous wall paintings, extraordinary gardens (complete with water features and herb-beds), jewellery (official imperial belt-sets for men and elaborate body chains for women), beautifully decorated silver plate, deluxe manuscripts and magnificent clothing. All these things – the floors, the jewellery, the silver dishes – were the crucial social markers of their age (the Rolexes, Bentleys and first-class tickets of the period), and they were essential elements of power. Such esoterica, however, would have been impossible to procure in a ragged little market town. Indeed, we know that the most accomplished mosaics of the period were the creations of well-known urban workshops. The clusters of villas located near or in public towns stimulated high-end craft production there. Such luxuries, however, although costly, could only generate a fraction of the wealth created by the old imperial commerce, and they were certainly not stimulating enough to return the public towns to the centre of Roman Britain's economy. These towns, throughout the late antique period, remained the locus of wealth and power, but they no longer drove the economy.

Both British elites and public towns had been refashioned, and both were emblematic of the new Rome. Yet much of the rest of British society had also been remade in the crucible of the third century. The most productive British kilns, for example, were now ensconced in areas that once lay at the margins of the economy; indeed, the potteries closest to public towns failed, while those at some distance flourished. The shift of the economy from the core to the periphery, and from public towns to less classically urban, or even rural sites, is symptomatic of much else in late antiquity.

The clearest example of the economic triumph of the periphery during this period is the burgeoning of a class of unpretentious little communities known as 'small towns'. In an earlier age small towns had been insignificant in the economy, but by 300 they were fixed at its very heart. Unlike the public towns, implanted in the first century by Roman soldiers and administrators, these settlements developed organically and on their own. There were seventy or eighty by the later Roman period, most sited within 15 kilometres of one another. All grew up along Roman roads, most at the junction of more than one road, and many sat near important river crossings. Their ubiquity and their locations embedded them in local trade, agriculture and manufacturing networks, rather than making them part of some wider, more cosmopolitan world. The goods and services they provided, the markets held within them and the pools of labour they housed made them central places for peasants and local farmers, as well as for the managers of great rural estates.

Like most of their clientele, small towns were often a little ramshackle. Most straggled along some major road in an unfocused way, and they usually lacked the carefully laid out streets of Britain's more self-consciously classical towns. Baths, aqueducts, forums and heated buildings were almost never found in small towns, and the rich usually chose to live somewhere else. Indeed, it was the very features that small towns lacked that made cities cities to those who had internalized classical culture. Ausonius, when describing Bordeaux, wrote of just these things: 'Within her, you may marvel at streets clearly laid out, at houses regularly / plotted out, at spacious boulevards which uphold their name . . .' Still, life in most small towns was modestly Roman, albeit Roman with a thick British overlay. The architecture of such towns tended to be a hybrid of native and classical. Temples and cult centres in small towns, for example, with the dramatic exception of Bath, usually looked more British than Mediterranean. There was a circular shrine at Worcester; Neatham had a surfeit of votive wells; and Shiptonthorpe, in East Yorkshire, had a communal watering hole for livestock that also served as the site of infant burials and animal sacrifice. These places were a far cry from temples in the city of Rome. Secular structures, on the other hand, were almost always rectangular rather than round, and were therefore Roman in form; but they were usually built with timber and thatch, that is, from native materials.

The most obvious Roman buildings in small towns would have been grubbier manifestations of empire than those found in cities – a staging post for the imperial postal system, or a state granary, acting as a collection point for the late Roman tax in-kind, the *annona militaris*. Some small towns – Dorchester-on-Thames, Water Newton, Catterick – may have housed a few soldiers as well, to guard state storehouses or to act as official escorts for imperial transports. But the intrusion of the larger Roman state into these communities was usually limited to annual tax collection and the housing of a few imperial officials in the un-citied backwaters of the province.

The overwhelming majority of small town structures took the form of strip-buildings, which functioned simultaneously as houses and workshops. Each strip-building had a large front section facing the street and opened to it, which could be closed to passers-by with shutters. Thus the front portion could serve as commercial space and provide ateliers for pewter-, bone-, leather-, glass- and metal-workers or working areas for bakers and builders. The backs of these buildings functioned as small, sometimes comfortable living quarters. The plots on which they sat, like the structures themselves, were long at the sides and narrow towards the street, and many had cobbled yards, animal pens, vegetable patches, even ovens at their backs. Late Roman small towns would not therefore have looked so very different from the small towns of late medieval England, with their narrow tenements, their crowd of street frontages and their kitchen gardens.

Besides general manufacturing, some small towns were closely tied to extractive industries: Charterhouse grew up around the lead and silver mining of the Mendips, Middlewich prospered from salt mining, and Chichester grew rich from iron extracted from the western Weald. These communities were also intimately involved in agriculture and food production. Godmanchester, for example, contained hay-racks, corn-drying ovens, threshing floors and granaries. Ox-goads have been excavated at Alchester and Shepton Mallet, turf cutters at Great Chesterton, reaping-hooks at Dorchester-on-Thames. Small towns were also the sites of both seasonal and permanent markets. A number had large, cobbled squares – sometimes found in association with temples – where open markets were held. The lead weights used by merchants and traders, along with copious quantities of bronze coins, have been excavated at such sites.

Like public towns, the most successful small towns had defences enclosing their centres, and, unlike more humble settlements, the best of them had a public building or two, a handful of masonry structures, perhaps even an elaborate cult centre. And a few of the more affluent small towns, in particular Bath and Water Newton, had a concentration of villas outside their walls. But most were characterized not by grand houses or governmental buildings, but by forges, shops and barns. They supplied traders, peasants, imperial officials, even the occasional Christian bishop with places to stay, with repair shops and with pools of day labourers and skilled artisans. Between their markets, granaries and craftsmen, and because of their locations, small towns lay at the centre of exchange networks that turned the agriculture of the Romano-British countryside into cash, into taxes and into manufactured goods; and it was here that products were distributed to native peasants and farmers.

It was here that rustics learned the necessity of money, here that they were seduced by a local and slightly idiosyncratic version of the empire's material culture. These communities, then, were rarely grand and seldom attracted the rich and the powerful. But, like rural kilns, they sat at the centre of the late Roman economy, and what prosperity there was in Britain came, in large part, from them.

Good times also came from agriculture, which was undergoing a quiet revolution of its own. The owners of many country estates during this period made considerable investments in their rural properties, constructing new buildings, paying for novel technologies and experimenting with crops. The result of this lavishing of labour, capital and thought on the countryside was increasing crop yields and growing rural manufacturing. The proprietor of the late Roman villa of Gatcombe, 6.5 kilometres west of Bristol, for example, laid out a highly organized zone dedicated to production sometime around 275. A group of Gatcombe's outbuildings were devoted to the milling and storing of grain and the large-scale baking of bread. Another cluster included a slaughterhouse, a cold-storage area for meat and a bone-working shop. Yet another set of buildings was dedicated to iron smelting, iron smithing and pewter working. Gatcombe was erected all at one time, at what must have been considerable expense, and it operated for a century. It was part of a thoughtfully laid out and carefully managed estate on which much effort and capital had been expended, and it was a place dedicated to large-scale agricultural and craft production.

Gatcombe's industrial zone is only one example of the ways in which the countryside was being reorganized in late antiquity. A whole array of changes evident in rural Britain suggests a systemic restructuring of rural life. Like so much else in this period, the new landscape was at once marked by growing social differentiation and higher levels of Romanization. The great country houses of the elite were stark symbols of the hardening lines between rich and poor, between oligarchs and peasants. But modest farms, too, became more Roman during this period. Barton Court Farm, in Oxfordshire, was not an elegant establishment like Chedworth or Box, yet it was more prosperous and more efficiently farmed in the fourth century than it had been at any other time in its history. Unlike high-status villa sites, there was little sign here of extravagance or conspicuous consumption: there were no elaborately heated buildings or stunning mosaics, and no grand audience hall. Still, life was good and modestly Roman. Those who lived here in the fourth century spiced their food with the decidedly un-British coriander, dill and poppy. They ate better cuts of meat than their progenitors had done, and they now consumed quantities of oysters brought up the Thames from the sea. More goods produced off-site were found at Barton Court Farm from the fourth century than from any other period: a little window glass, a few lovely glass vessels, some pottery, a quantity of ironwork, a surfeit of coins. All of this suggests a farm that was mostly self-sufficient, but one that produced a surplus its proprietor used to purchase a more comfortable and more Roman life.

Less well-to-do sites than Barton Court Farm were also quietly transformed in the later third and early fourth centuries. Farmsteads like Butcombe, in Somerset, and peasant communities like Catsgore, in Gloucestershire, witnessed the wholesale reorganization of buildings, enclosures and fields; and coins and mass-produced ceramics were now found in much greater quantities at sites like these. Similarly, a quite ordinary farmstead at Rayne, in Essex, had a few amenities in the fourth century that would not have been out of place at a villa. By the late Roman period, moreover, peasants across lowland Britain were eating a more Roman diet than they had a century earlier. People on low-status rural sites had begun to incorporate Roman herbs like coriander and Roman fruits like apples into their diet, all Roman imports, and the butchery techniques used in these places now involved heavy chopping tools cutting through the bones of joints, rather than the older, traditional sharp-knife butchery. The fruits, herbs and styles of butchering had probably first been brought to Britain by the imperial army, and by the late antique period these things were firmly established among the peasantry. Food is an intimate part of culture, one resistant to change, yet it had been altered even among the poor by the fourth century through long centuries of colonization. Even in thoroughly unacculturated backwaters – places like south-western Britain, north Wales and the Pennines – where people continued in the fourth century to live in the traditional roundhouses of the pre-Roman Iron Age – Romanized goods had become part of daily life.

Driving this Romanization and small-scale prosperity were subtle agricultural shifts. There were few agricultural innovations in the first two centuries of Roman rule: although the scale of farming, its organization and specialization increased, many patterns established in the late pre-Roman Iron Age – field systems, settlement patterns, building styles, agricultural implements – endured. Yet all of these things changed quite dramatically in the late third and early fourth centuries. There was, for example, a shift in cropping. The cultivation of all cereals was more intensive now, including spelt, long the staple grain-crop of the Roman empire. Most importantly, bread wheat (*Triticum aestivum*) was cultivated in great quantity. The appearance of bread wheat in Britain during this period is a critical development in agrarian history, since it was to become *the* staple crop of most people living in Britain. This was also a great period for the creation of hay meadows and increased hay cultivation. These changes are the result of a host of agricultural innovations establishing themselves from the late third century onwards, including the use of a heavier plough and larger, imported ploughing animals, which allowed for the exploitation of the fertile, but heavy, clay soils; the appearance of long scythes, which improved harvesting; a more extensive use of metal in ploughs and harvesting equipment; more deep cultivation and mouldboard ploughing; the rise of crop-rotation regimens; and intensive manuring. There was also a proliferation in the fourth century of barns and granaries with raised floors and corn-dryers for the drying or malting of grain. There was more use of masonry in farm buildings. There were more enclosures, paddocks and wells for livestock. All of these changes required considerable investments of capital and labour, and all led to greater efficiency in the handling, processing and storage of food.

THE LIVING AND THE DEAD
IN LATE ANTIQUE BRITAIN

How did the gross and impersonal changes in economy, in settlement and in technology manifest themselves in the lives of individuals? How did average men and women live their lives in this new world of small towns, booming kilns and improved farming? No texts survive to answer these questions, but the contours of work, of health and of sorrow can be read in the skeletons excavated from the outsized burial grounds of the period. At Poundbury, one of Dorchester's extramural cemeteries, the remains of nearly 1,200 fourth-century Britons have been excavated, and they tell us things worth knowing about life in

Britain's last Roman century. Although many buried at Poundbury lived out their days in fourth-century Dorchester, others probably came from communities and farms in the surrounding countryside, even, perhaps, from the nearby villas of Frampton and Hinton St Mary. So they tell us both about urban and rural life, about the rich and the poor.

In spite of its modest prosperity, late Roman Britain was not Paradise. Those interred at Poundbury had led peaceful lives, but the days of most were spent in hard physical labour. Although a single infant buried there may have died from battering, there is no other evidence of violence. The injuries most people suffered were those of wear and strain, sustained over long years of grinding labour. Adults, judging from the state of their joints, lived with the nagging aches of arthritis and sore backs. The spines and shoulders of Poundbury's men were those of people engaged in heavy work from early adolescence to what passed in the fourth century for old age. Their joints showed the wear of digging and lifting, of driving carts and working ploughs. Women, for their part, lived with aching knees. The state of their legs suggests that they spent long hours squatting, probably while grinding corn at rotary querns. Men and women, therefore, were set apart by the labours they performed each day and by their small physical agonies.

Children died in great numbers around Poundbury; not newborns so much as toddlers. The babies who survived early childhood often lived through adolescence, but death again took many, both men and women, in their early twenties and thirties. Indeed, about half of all those who reached the age of 5 died between the ages of 20 and 45. Still, there were a few old people in Dorchester, some well into their eighties when they died. So the communities that buried their dead at Poundbury were full of children and adolescents; they had many 20-year-olds, fewer people in their thirties, and still fewer in their forties.

Infectious disease doubtless played a part in these heartbreakingly early deaths. There were periodic outbreaks of smallpox around Dorchester, and a few suffered from tuberculosis. For the most part, though, the brevity of their lives was the result of long-term, low-grade malnutrition, not from starvation, but rather from a flawed diet. Children grew slowly (the growth of young children lagged two years behind those of comparable age today), and puberty came late; and those who lived to adulthood had light bones and poor teeth. These are classic signs of poor nutrition. Lead, infant feeding practices and scurvy may have been major culprits in this. Stomach maladies like diarrhoea could also compromise health, because they led to the poor absorption of nutrients from food and brought on a host of more serious complaints: gout, osteoporosis, leg ulcers and infertility were all likely common catastrophes in fourth-century Dorset. The people buried at Poundbury also suffered from parasites, in particular roundworm and whipworm, which could result in dysentery. This, in turn, produced chronic malnutrition and anaemia, especially among young children. The people eventually buried at Poundbury, like many others in Roman Britain, must have been uncomfortable and in pain. Everyone must have been a little cranky from stomach ailments, from arthritis and from gout, and ill-tempered because of head lice. These were also people habitually saddened by the deaths of their children and their friends, not from the calamity of plague, but rather from mystifying ill health brought on by dietary troubles, microbes and parasites no one knew existed.

At Poundbury, we can also garner some notion of what ordinary Roman Britons looked like. The population buried there was exceptionally homogenous in features and stature. Almost to a person, the people of Poundbury had smaller heads and shorter facial heights than Britain's modern population, yet they also had large, powerful jaws, and would appear heavily jowled to us. Very nearly every man stood between 1.63 and 1.73 metres (only one was over 1.83 metres tall and one under 1.52 metres), and most women were between 1.57 and 1.65 metres. The hair of a few was preserved because their coffins had been packed with plaster. This rare survival suggests that hair in and around Poundbury was neatly combed and dressed with oil. The men wore their hair long at the neck and combed forward from the crowns of their heads. One older man had dyed his hair with henna, and combed it to cover his bald spot! The women wore their hair coiled or braided in buns and twists, and the coif of one woman was so elaborate that she could not have done it without help. This woman was not the only person buried at Poundbury who looks like a member of the elite. A number of men and women clustered in family groups were buried in a more elaborate fashion than most. Some were laid to rest in lead coffins, others inside mausoleums. Most of these people were especially tall and robust, and they would have stood out physically in and around Poundbury. A number of men in this group, moreover, exhibited signs of a condition known as diffuse idiopathic skeletal hyperostosis, something which in modern populations signals adult-onset diabetes or obesity. And two of them, as we know from an analysis of stable isotopes trapped in their bones, were among the only people buried in the cemetery to have eaten seafood, or perhaps fish sauce, which would have been an expensive delicacy in fourth-century Britain. Their bones, moreover, did not exhibit the same patterns of wear and tear as those of most people buried in the cemetery. These may be the remains of the especially well-nourished, clean-water-drinking members of the villa-owning elite.

The funerary rights with which these dead were laid to rest had much in common with those used across the Roman world. Like many in the empire, Britons had abandoned cremation by the fourth century for inhumation: they now preferred carefully aligned burials (what archaeologists call 'oriented graves') in extensive and carefully regulated suburban cemeteries, and they buried their loved ones with few, if any, grave goods. These empire-wide fashions were first adopted in British towns, like so many other things Roman, and like other practices, these rites gradually percolated into the countryside. Burial in late Roman Britain was like much else in life: it was increasingly Romanized, it was embraced by more and more people and it steadily infiltrated rural areas. We can see exogenous practices, such as plaster-packed coffins, which originated in North Africa, or overtly Christian rites from far-off Palestine, making their first appearance in cosmopolitan places like London or York, then moving out to small towns, to villas, and finally to rural burial sites. In similar fashion, many Britons were now buried with Charon's obol, a coin placed in the hand or the mouth to pay passage across the River Styx. This practice began in earnest in Britain after 260, at just that moment when the use of low-value currency exploded in Britain, suggesting a new attitude not only towards death, but towards money. Like so much else in Roman Britain, however, native practices amended and modified foreign rites. Rural traditions indigenous to Britain, such as the puzzling decapitation burial, in which the head was removed after death and laid carefully between the feet, or the less gruesome shoe-burials, in which the deceased's hobnailed boots were carefully placed inside or near the coffin, gradually made their way into urban cemeteries. Thus burial was like much else in late antiquity: broadly Roman, broadly imperial practices were appropriated by Britons of all social classes, then modified by local rites and practices. Here we can also see locally produced, but essentially Roman, objects – hobnailed boots, ceramic pots, low-value currency – gradually incorporated into British funerary practice at all levels of society, in much the same way they had been adopted in life.

The years from around 290 to 360 were the high-water mark of *romanitas* in Britain, and in many ways these years constitute the most Roman moment in British history. Roman culture, the Roman state and Roman goods were embraced or imposed, to varying degrees, both in public and in small towns, in palatial villas and on peasant farmsteads. Most people had some access to the profusion of British-produced Roman-style goods of the period – goods created in a Roman economy founded on mass production, and dependent upon organized industries, networks of local markets, an abundance of low-value currency and, of course, peace. In these seventy or eighty years Britain had much in common with the localized provincial societies that were cropping up everywhere within the empire. Late antique societies across the Roman world – not only in Britain, but in Egypt, Cappadocia, North Africa and elsewhere – were marked by idiosyncratic and local variations of standard Roman themes. The stamp-decorated vessels made in fourth-century Britain, for example, developed at the same moment as the stamped wares of Tunisia and the eastern Mediterranean. Fourth-century Romano-British pottery was therefore both distinctly British and recognizably late Roman in its design and production. Or again, the emperor Diocletian's great administrative palace complex, built along the coast at Split, was roughly contemporary to that begun in London, but never finished, by an imperial rival named Allectus; so Britain's political culture, with its pretenders and its grand palaces, although geographically at a great distance from the centre, shared much with it. Even Britain's curious public towns were not so very different from other cities of the period. Ostia, for example, one of the great commercial centres of Italy in the second century, had lost much of its economic vigour by the fourth, but it was filled with grand residences; and the fourth-century orator Libanius described towns in Gaul as places where 'oxen were yoked, furrows drawn, the seed set. The corn grew, was reaped and threshed all inside the city gates.' Britain's dead, laid to rest in lead or nailed coffins, in oriented graves in great extramural grave-yards, were close cousins, in spite of their hobnailed boots and the occasional dismembered dog, to the dead found across the Channel or even across the Mediterranean. Britain, although less thoroughly integrated economically into the empire than it had been in the second century and less strategically important, and although less recognizably classical, was thoroughly late Roman; indeed, it was as Roman in the fourth century as any other place on the planet.

IMPLOSION

Britain could have continued like this for centuries, with its modest economy and organized industry, its small urban communities and quirky, Romanizing culture. But its prosperity was founded on the ability of a substantial part of the population to purchase and sell copious amounts of low-value goods, both agricultural and manufactured, and it could do so only if there was a dense network of small towns providing ready access to flourishing markets. But a series of small disasters, each one compounding the effects of the last, ruined the late Roman economy by fracturing the peace and by requiring more resources for defence than either Britain or the empire as a whole could afford. Once these problems began to compound, towns, commerce and even the structures of rural life were undermined, and Britain declined rapidly; indeed, its economy, robust in 350, eroded so swiftly in the half century centring on 400 that Britain not only fell out of the empire but lost everything that made it Roman.

Britain's troubles began quietly, almost imperceptibly, with the odd incursion from north of Hadrian's Wall and the occasional raid along the coast. For Britain, it was not so much Germanic peoples as loosely affiliated tribes and federations native to the British Isles themselves that began making forays into Roman territory. In particular, it was the 'Painted People', the Picts, of highland Scotland and the *Scotti* of Ireland who were increasingly restive. Raiders from the far side of the frontiers had long beset the empire, but Britain, blessed with the sea and protected by Hadrian's Wall, was less troubled in the third and early fourth centuries than most places. New or improved defences along the coast and at Hadrian's Wall dating from the early decades of the fourth century, however, do suggest that Britain was beginning to have more trouble with barbarians than it had had in the past, and there was a flurry of military building in the 330s, which may have been in response to increasing pressures along the frontier. Still, what incursions there were were isolated events in the beginning and were only locally troubling. Indeed, as we have seen, the last years of the third century and the first half of the fourth constituted the apogee of Roman Britain. Raiding, however, intensified: early in 343 the problem was so grave that the emperor Constans and an expeditionary force chanced a risky Channel crossing in midwinter to shore up Britain's defences. After the frontier had been stabilized and a new set of improvements began along Hadrian's Wall and to the forts along the east coast of Britain, peace returned. Episodic raiding doubtless continued, but it was not until 360 that Britain once again faced a serious incursion. In this year the Picts and the Scots embarked on a full season of hit-and-run raids. As in 343, the danger was acute, and Rome's greatest general was sent to Britain with a large field army. Then in 367 Britain faced a much more serious threat, a bona fide invasion, described by the Roman historian Ammianus Marcellinus (c. 330–c. 390) as a 'Barbarian Conspiracy', in which the Picts, the Scots and the Attacotti from the Outer Isles raided Britain in concert, while Saxons and Franks attacked the coast of Gaul. Hadrian's Wall was overrun and defences along the North Sea collapsed. Once again, Britain's own garrison had to be supplemented with troops brought in from afar, and it took two years for the commanding general to restore order and rid Britain of the small war bands and motley groups of army deserters who roamed the countryside, absconding with cattle, loot and British captives. In 396–8 there was another terrible invasion by the Picts, Scots and Saxon sea raiders. This incursion required Stilicho, the emperor's great Vandal *magister militum*, to lead yet another expeditionary force to Britain. But when Italy itself was threatened in 401, Stilicho quickly removed much-needed troops from Britain for Rome's own defence. The fourth century witnessed persistent raiding by Picts and Scots, which accelerated as the century progressed, and the peace was punctuated four times by increasingly organized and damaging incursions. No raid, no single invasion was enough to destroy late antique life and culture in Britain, but over the decades their effects were slowly but inexorably compounded.

At the same time as Britain's barbarian neighbours grew more restive, the internal politics of the later empire spilled over into Britain, intensifying its troubles. Imperial politics, bloody and all-consuming in the 340s and 350s, drew in many of Britain's great landowners, military officers and civilian officials. In 353, after a British imperial pretender was defeated on the Continent, there was a terrible political purge in Britain. Then from 383 to 388 the Spanish military commander of Britain, Magnus Maximus, established himself as the head of a breakaway western empire with its capital at Trier. His imperial aspirations and eventually fatal difficulties led him to withdraw troops from Britain and to tax the territories subject to him heavily in order to pay for his Continental adventures. In this way a number of Britain's most important families and imperial administrators were ruined and Britain's increasingly necessary troops diverted.

The purges, the corrosive politics and the barbarians began to make necessary extraordinary levels of expenditure for defence. Most public towns and many small towns had had earthen ramparts for a century or more and some had stone walls, but it was probably after the 'Barbarian Conspiracy' that masonry walls were constructed by many communities, and that sturdy towers, a standard feature of late Roman urban defence across the empire, were added to town walls. Labour and funds were also expended on repairing and modifying Hadrian's Wall. Inscriptions found along the Wall record that towns hundreds of kilometres to the south provided gangs of labourers at what must have been enormous effort and expense. Because military costs were mounting across the West there was little state aid for such projects, so local communities had to shoulder much of the burden themselves. If the rich in Britain were able to evade their taxes as successfully as the rich did on the Continent during this period, these expenditures would have fallen increasingly on more ordinary people, and this, in turn, would have compromised their ability to buy goods. The building campaigns undertaken in the aftermath of the 'Barbarian Conspiracy', moreover, taxed the resources of Britons at the very moment their lives had been ruptured by war and at a time when they could ill afford it.

The picture, especially from the 340s on, is of periodic but serious raiding, primarily by Irish and Pictish adventurers, distracting imperial politics and increasing demands on expenditure for defence. In these circumstances, where one problem exacerbated other troubles, the economy of Roman Britain unravelled. It was not the incursions alone or the civil wars or the high cost of defence that shattered the economy but the three combined. The erosion began gently and only gradually worsened. At some point in the late 360s or early 370s, however, a line was crossed, and the economy of Roman Britain and its culture entered into a terminal decline, one that would have been unimaginable a generation earlier.

From the 360s, the things that made Britain Roman – its genteel villas and highly Romanized elite, its economy of mass production, local commerce and heavy coin use, its urban communities, its association with the greater Roman world – faltered, then ceased. The great villas of fourth-century Britain began to fail in the 360s. Some still flourished: Hucclecote Villa had new mosaics laid during this period, and lavish rooms were being built at a villa in Chedworth. Most country houses, however, were showing signs of hard wear and spiralling decline. A wing of the villa at Kings Weston, Avon, for example, was destroyed by fire around this time. Although the house remained occupied, the damaged rooms were never repaired, and overnight the villa changed from grand to shabby. The principal rooms of a number of other villas were falling down in the 360s and 370s or being converted into kitchens, barns or corn-dryers, which can only mean that the kind of life that used to go on in these rooms – the grand dinner-parties, the highly choreographed rituals of lordship and clientage – were disappearing. Without narrative sources to recount the story of this decline it is difficult to know what happened. A few villas may have been destroyed by raiders, but it is likely that most were simply the victims of the usual disasters of ancient life – accidental fire, poor engineering, subsidence – and when calamity struck after the economy began to fail no one could afford repairs. It may also be that the frenetic spending of the rich on their country estates over the course of three or four generations helped to precipitate their end. Huge amounts of capital, which produced nothing but social standing, were tied up in country houses, and some families may have impoverished themselves in their pursuit of the good life. This certainly happened in Gaul, where our written evidence is better. Ausonius' grandson, Paulinus of Pellas, for example, although the scion of a grand Gallo-Roman family, lost everything during the period of the fall. As a young man, and as heir to a great estate, Paulinus' only interest, so he confessed in old age, was in luxury,

> in my house and in my life so that at each season
> the rooms where I lived were always comfortable.
> My own table was richly and handsomely set;
> my servants were not only young but numerous;

the place was furnished with taste and variety;
the silver was valued more for price than for weight;
many skilled workmen were there to fill my requests;
many well-bred, well-trained horses filled my stables
and there were carriages to take me where I wished ...

But when the invasions and politics of the late empire intensified in
Gaul, he lost most of his estates.

Finally, I decided to live in Marseilles ...
I had only a small property which was part
of my family estate. There was no new income
there to raise new hopes, there were no fields being ploughed
and no vineyards – which are that city's wealth – were mine.
All that I have is a small house in the city with a near-by
    garden. It is humble indeed.
Though there are a few vines and some fruit trees, there is
no land that seems worth the care of cultivation.
Still, I was persuaded to till the fallow land
which was really quite small, and build a little house
in a rocky place so that I would not reduce
the amount of usable soil. To purchase things
that only money buys, I planned to let out land.
At the time I still had slaves to manage my house
and I still possessed the strength of my active years.
But after that, when the fickle world changed my luck,
I was finally broken both by the loss of land
and by the weakness that came on me with old age.
I was a wanderer, poor and without family.

(trans. Harold Isbell)

In Britain there is some indication that smaller estates failed before
the greatest ones, and that sometime mid-century large villas began
acquiring distressed estates. Although this would have allowed a few
families enormous short-term gains, it was disastrous in the long run,
since the prosperity of all Britons, even the richest, was founded on
broad local markets and modest, but widespread prosperity.

More inauspicious than the failure of villa estates was the collapse of
organized industry. The pottery industry began to exhibit signs of strain

in the middle of the century. Although there was no change in the number of kilns, from *c.* 350 the range of vessels and decorative motifs was dramatically curtailed. Large amounts of pottery were still produced, but sometime in the 370s the great Romano-British kilns of the New Forest and Oxfordshire went into steep decline, and within a single generation of 400 pottery became a lost art, and large parts of Britain became aceramic. *Circa* 350, iron production in the Weald plummeted to something like a quarter of its early fourth-century level, and by 410 Wealden iron production had ceased. Ironwork and pots were not cherished by the rich, but were, rather, the unconscious and necessary objects of everyday life. Nails, for example, seem like such trivial things, but once they were gone Britain became a harder place. They grew scarce in the 370s, and by the 390s nails for coffins and hobnailed boots were simply no longer available, so the British slipped in the mud and buried the people they loved directly in the cold, hard ground. Pottery and metalwork leave clear impressions in the archaeological record, but more perishable manufactured goods – worked leather, wood, foodstuff – doubtless met similar fates.

Collapsing estates and dying industry helped to topple towns. It was the suburbs, the areas outside town walls, that foundered first. Excavated suburbs have produced significantly less pottery and coins from mid-century levels on, and both coin finds and pottery sherds almost disappear from these areas after *c.* 370. Since suburbs had been vital centres of manufacturing and commerce, their decline and abandonment is ominous. Although these crumbling suburbs lay outside town walls, there is not a scrap of evidence to suggest that they were destroyed by raiders. Their collapse instead was the product of systemic economic troubles, and their failure is evidence that Britain could no longer sustain a large craft population.

Areas within urban defences atrophied more slowly: their own terminal decline generally began a decade or so after that of the suburbs. But infrastructure began to fail mid-century. At Canterbury, the sewers started clogging up around 350, and a thick layer of silt began to form in the city's baths and on its streets. At the same time frontages of buildings started to encroach upon the public roads of both Canterbury and York, something no earlier civic authority would have allowed. Sewers, water supplies and roads were fundamental aspects of urban life in Britain's public towns. Their decline suggests a critical lack of resources and a weakening of local magistrates. Nevertheless, urban life persisted to the end of the century in most places and in some for a decade or two longer. At Bath, for example, although temples were being dismantled, the town's late fourth-century streets show heavy wear, and one was recobbled six times between the mid-fourth and the early fifth centuries. So, although temples in Bath were crumbling, its streets were still heavily travelled and its magistrates sufficiently organized to make the most crucial repairs. Similarly, Cirencester's late Roman walls were repaired and maintained into the early fifth century, and its forum was also scrupulously clean, kept clear of the rubbish one would expect to find in a tatty, dying town. But the forum's stone floor was in very bad state, its once-impressive sandstone slabs worn paper thin. In Cirencester, therefore, civic life was sufficiently organized at the end of the century to keep the marketplace tidy and make emergency repairs to town defences, but not enough to resurface the forum. In Canterbury, Bath, Cirencester and elsewhere repairs to roads and walls, coupled with a dearth of coin and pottery finds, suggest that organized but impoverished communal life continued in the face of economic collapse.

At some point in the early fifth century, though, urban life died completely, and all of Britain's towns, public and small, simply ceased to exist. The archaeology that supports this is often eloquent, even moving. The ruined and empty city of York, for example, reverted back to marshland in the fifth century. Fossils of beetles whose habitat was a world of high grass and reeds have been found in the early fifth-century earth and debris that blanketed the moribund city. Froghoppers, creatures native to England's wetlands, are also found in fifth-century levels, but are unknown in Roman deposits from York. Field mice, too, and water voles, weasels and shrews returned to the ruined city, and lived their watery lives in the decaying streets and ruined town houses now reclaimed by marsh. Within the walled city of Canterbury, archaeologists have excavated a strange early fifth-century burial. Roman burials, of course, are found in great suburban cemeteries like Poundbury. Romans had exceptionally strong taboos against human burial within towns, and there were rigorously enforced laws that upheld a strict apartheid between the living and the dead. So any burial within the walls of Canterbury represents a serious break with past traditions and suggests a failure of urban authority and a breach of long-standing cultural inhibitions. But the burial itself is stranger still. It was of a whole family – a man, a woman and two young children, as well as two dogs. They were buried together with great care in a pit lined with grass. The parents were seated. The woman held one child in her lap, and the other lay at her feet. The dogs were laid across the father. One child had died from a blow to the head, and although the cause of death for the others cannot be determined, given the child's crushed skull it is likely that all were victims of violence. Their burial in a single pit within a dying town is not a standard Roman burial by any means; but the people themselves were Romanized Britons. They were buried with late Roman bronze and silver jewellery, with Roman glass and keys. This and the violence which preceded their burial suggest extraordinary and terrible events in a town that was no longer a town, and points not to barbarian invaders, but to disorder, collapse and cultural breakdown.

By 420 Britain's villas had been abandoned. Its towns were mostly empty, its organized industries dead, its connections with the larger Roman world severed: and all with hardly an Angle or a Saxon in sight.

2

Life among the Ruins: The Fifth and Early Sixth Centuries

In the year 420 there were still people in Britain who had been born in a world shaped by the structures of empire, people whose early lives had been ordered by Rome's material culture, men and women whose universe had been given meaning by the shared assumptions of antiquity. There were tens of thousands left in 420 who had come of age playing in dusty, small-town streets, whose childhood dinners were served on pewter and glass, who had stood by the graves of grandparents and baby brothers dug in the great municipal cemeteries edging every town. There were middle-aged men who had been raised in heated villas. There were grandmothers whose fathers had paid taxes and whose mothers had bought cooking pots at local markets. Perhaps as many as a quarter of all those alive in 420 were conditioned by this world, had been formed by it and had become the people they were in some ways because of it. But, although there were Romanized Britons, by 420 there was no longer a Roman Britain in which to live.

Beyond this, new groups of people had begun settling in Britain, people who had never before lived within the confines of the Roman world. It was within a decade or so of 420 that Germanic peoples from across the Channel began making their way to Britain, mostly in small family groups, a boat-load or two at a time. Most had never used coins or seen a town. A few may have laboured on Roman estates or fought in imperial armies, but most, so far as we can tell, had not. These people began to settle along the east coast of Britain, particularly in East Anglia and Kent, but they could also be found establishing themselves up river valleys in the eastern half of Britain. Along the west coast of Britain there were now Irish immigrants. These people had a longer shared history with the British. They had been raiding Romano-British settlements for a hundred years, but now, as the Roman state receded, they were coming to stay.

What did the British (as historians call the people in this period whose ancestors had been Romano-British) make of these newcomers? How did they and their new neighbours survive? What kind of society did they cobble together from the ruins of antiquity? These are exceptionally difficult questions to answer. Only two contemporary texts survive that give brief glimpses of life among the ruins, the writings of the Briton St Patrick, and a *vita*, that is, a biography, of a bishop from Gaul, a man named Germanus, who had travelled to Britain on Church business. Most other early medieval texts describing fifth-century Britain were written long after the fact. They were based on unreliable oral tradition or imaginative reconstruction and all are better indications of the age in which they were composed than the period they describe. Beyond the poverty of texts, there is the paucity of personalities. We know the names of only a handful of people who lived in Britain during this century: Patrick's father, Calpornius, who had a little villa in the far north; a British magnate named Elafius, whose child was cured by St Germanus; the Irishman Cunorix, who was commemorated with a crudely inscribed stone. For these three at least we have names, but we know nothing else about their lives. Because there are, for all intents and purposes, no texts and no ready narrative for the half-dozen or so generations after Rome's collapse, we are absolutely dependent on the evidence of archaeology, which tends to be inarticulate about the lives of known individuals and mute on specific events. Still, material remains tell us things that few early medieval texts can – about the nature of the economy, about the subtle signs of social distinction and hierarchy, about the physical hardships of agrarian life. By studying the evidence uncovered by archaeologists, especially in conjunction with the extraordinary testimony of the British landscape and its early place names, some of this century's lost history is revealed.

THREE BRITISH COMMUNITIES

The Roman empire had both required and created surpluses. The state, the army, written administration and the leisured lives of the upper classes were all founded on excess production. Yet when the Roman state withdrew from Britain and the economy collapsed there were no longer organized and interlinked markets. There was no tax, no money economy, no mass production of goods. As a result, surpluses had fewer uses and became increasingly difficult both to create and to store. As markets, money and surpluses disappeared, so, too, did basic elements of Roman material culture. Roman sites, particularly those of the fourth century, are littered with the remains of substantial buildings, coins and broken and discarded manufactured goods, and excavators find scatters of everyday objects lying in broad swaths around every farmstead and villa. Fifth-century settlements, on the other hand, are practically invisible, so rare had ceramics and metalwork become, so inconsequential their buildings. One of the results of this is that all places in Britain, compared with their fourth-century progenitors, now looked impoverished. But this dreary sameness disguised very real differences between one settlement and the next, because the unifying forces of state and culture, which had given all Roman small towns, all villas and all hamlets a kind of comforting similarity, had vanished; and beneath their dreary dilapidation settlements began to diverge, as local communities and individuals struggled and improvised in the fragmented universe of the fifth century.

Many people in the late fourth and early fifth centuries were on the move. Towns, both public and small, lost their entire populations, and most villas were abandoned. It is harder to know what was happening to rural farmsteads and hamlets, but there does seem to have been some shifting in population there as well, as people realized the unsuitability of traditional sites in the face of collapse; and those places that remained occupied were sometimes radically reconfigured. Where these people went and how they reordered their local societies depended very much on what remained to be used.

In the West Country, some left their homes and moved into ancient hillforts, which were built long before the Roman conquest and had been abandoned for centuries. One such hillfort, Cadbury Congresbury in Somerset, was reoccupied in the second half of the fifth century, and it became home to a British community for five or six generations. The site of the new community was an impressive, multi-vallate hillfort. It provided its new settlers with a ready-made enclosure for themselves and their livestock and with security from both brigands and competing British communities.

The people who first resettled the hillfort were culturally Romano-British, but they had only an impoverished, residual version of fourth-century material culture. They seem to have arrived with pack-loads of possessions, possessions that bespoke *romanitas*. During the early years at Cadbury Congresbury, they used fast-wheel, mass-produced Romano-British pottery. They also had a little glass, and there was dressed, Roman-style building stone at the site. But compared to fourth-century settlements in the neighbourhood, Cadbury Congres-bury's first fifth-century inhabitants had little. Most of the pots, the glass and the dressed stone were being used there in the second half of the fifth century, but they had been produced fifty or even a hundred years earlier. Some things unearthed at the hillfort – the glass and some of the brooches, for example – may have been cherished family heir-looms or prized personal possessions, their longevity guaranteed by sen-timent. But other objects look as if they had been looted from abandoned sites. Dressed stone, for example, was robbed from derelict buildings in the neighbourhood, and some of the glass and pottery may have come from picking through the ruins of local villas. The world was full of such places in the fifth century. One in Gaul is described in the *Life of St Germanus* (although the story itself was cribbed from Pliny). One winter's evening, so we are told, the saint and his party, exhausted from travel, came across a house, abandoned, overgrown with brambles and its roof fallen in: and 'among what had once been a great many rooms', only one was habitable. According to the locals, the place was haunted by the ghosts of evil men. Places like this were a major feature of low-land Britain after Rome's collapse, and they could be ransacked for things needed by people, but which they could no longer fabricate on their own. Some of the pottery at Cadbury Congresbury, however, came from another source: it was probably salvaged from nearby third-century cemeteries, places where cremation burials lay, and where pots could be dug up, emptied of their human ash and then used for cooking or hauling water. The presence of such material at Cadbury Congres-bury and other resettled hillforts points to people clinging to the mater-ial culture of their forebears no matter how grim the undertaking, no matter how great the humiliations of scavenging.

The society forming at Cadbury Congresbury, though, rapidly evolved from this final Roman phase into something quite different. The mix of people who had moved into the hillfort – refugees from defunct urban communities, villa owners and their peasants, communities surrounding temple complexes, small farmers – had resided in different worlds before the fall, but they now lived in a new place, in a single community, and under these circumstances and in the face of catastrophic collapse their little society moved rapidly from late antique to early medieval. Within a generation of the hillfort's reoccupation, and quite possibly from its inception, some individual, family or clique was in charge. Indeed, claiming such an impressive site in the first place may have been the way some person or group moved to assert authority in the neighbourhood. By *c.* 500 serious refortification work was under way at the hillfort, and an impressive watchtower, reminiscent of late Roman military architecture, was built from timber and sod. Over the course of Cadbury Congresbury's second life, as many as two hundred structures were also built, and this points to a large number of labourers and considerable resources and organization. The buildings themselves were quite varied. None were of mortared stone, a lost art in fifth-century Britain, but there was a large timber longhouse, doubtless the residence of some great man and his kin. Other structures at Cadbury Congresbury, however, were closely related to the modest roundhouses of the pre-Roman Iron Age, a vernacular building style that continued throughout the Roman period in rural backwaters, and one that was now reasserting itself in the face of the de-skilling of more Romanized populations. The mix of Roman-style watchtowers, longhouses and simple roundhouses reveals a community in which some were in charge and others did what they were told. Jewellery, which began to be made on the site a generation or two after resettlement, suggests this as well: craftsmen who worked there were using gold, copper, silvered bronze and glass, fine materials that only a very few would have had the means to acquire.

For a seventy-five-year period, from the later fifth to the middle of the sixth century, there was also regular, probably annual trade conducted between traders from Byzantium and a handful of communities settled in reoccupied hillforts in western Britain, including Cadbury Congresbury. Here and elsewhere – most famously at Tintagel in Cornwall and Dinas Powys in Glamorgan – archaeologists have recovered sherds of fifth- and sixth-century tableware and amphorae from the Aegean, the eastern Mediterranean, North Africa and perhaps southern Spain, the latter of which had been used as containers for wine or olive oil. These extraordinary finds bespeak the resumption of a microscopic but significant long-distance trade in which merchants and sailors found it worth their while to cross the whole of the Mediterranean and then brave the western sea routes to Britain, a round trip of some 10,000 kilometres. Whoever controlled the community at Cadbury Congresbury, in the wilds of the lost colony, must have had something Greek-speaking traders wanted very badly. What they probably had was tin, a rarity in Europe and a commodity known in late antiquity as 'the British metal'. It was a crucial ingredient in the making of bronze, a much-used alloy in the period. In return for this, and whatever else they had worth trading, a thin trickle of Roman goods once again came into the hands of some of the hillfort's inhabitants. Infrequent though these contacts may have been, this exchange allowed the most important members of the community to reassert their *romanitas* and to underscore their superior position within the society of the rebuilt hillfort. During great feasts and celebrations held in their timber hall, they ate beef taken from the large herds of cattle they now controlled, dined on Roman tableware and drank rare Greek wine. This was hardly the good life as described by Ausonius, but it was the continuation of a political style that was centuries old by Roman Britain's fall, a social strategy of marking one's grand status by connecting oneself to Rome and things Roman.

Far to the north, another community was coalescing within Birdoswald, a second-century military fort on Hadrian's Wall. Like Cadbury Congresbury, Birdoswald was an ancient site, but unlike the hillfort it was occupied before, during and after the fall. In the late antique period Birdoswald's garrison, like garrisons across the Roman world, was small. Here as elsewhere, soldiers were local boys, probably recruited from communities scattered between the rivers Tyne and Esk. These 'Roman' soldiers would have married local girls, and their sons, during the dominate, would have been compelled to follow in their fathers' footsteps. Garrisons like these ceased to receive pay and supplies in the first decade of the fifth century; yet the community at the fort persisted. In the early years of the fifth century soldiers may have continued receiving supplies from local communities in return for policing and military service, at least as long as the institutions of local Roman government and the power of local magistrates remained intact. But, like Cadbury Congresbury, Birdoswald's little world was rapidly transformed.

The evolution of Birdoswald's early third-century granaries is emblematic of changes undergone by the community itself. As long as the garrison was large and military supply networks were in operation, stone storehouses were needed for the unit's share of the *annona milit-aris*. But by the late fourth century, with the shrinking of the garrison, most of the communal granaries fell into disuse. One was abandoned and quarried. Another was changed from a storehouse into some sort of grand domestic building, with a new, solid floor laid and hearths installed at one end. In its new incarnation the old granary was not divided and it would have been difficult to heat, so it is clear that it was not modified for common domestic use. Moreover, the most impressive late Roman objects excavated at Birdoswald – a gold earring and a glass ring – were found near the new hearths. All of this suggests that the granary had some high-status, quasi-private function: perhaps it acted as an assembly building for the garrison and as a residence for its com-mander, who would have been not only a military man, but a *patronus*, whom people in the area could petition for favours or protection. This was a combination of attributes seen elsewhere in the late Roman empire, and such a person would have had authority, not only over the men who served him, but over civilians as well.

The transformations which began at Birdoswald before the fall continued well beyond the withdrawal of the Roman state. By *c.* 420, however, a number of buildings within the fort, including the granary-cum-assembly-hall, could no longer be maintained. As buildings began to fail, they were simply abandoned, and the people living or working in them moved on to more stable structures. For a generation or so people lived in the slowly collapsing ruins. At some point in the mid-fifth century the half-standing, half-ruinous imperial buildings began to be incorporated into hybrid structures, part stone, part timber, as lean-tos were propped against standing walls, and as more solid timber structures were built incorporating the remains of ancient buildings. By *c.* 470 those living in the fort were dismantling standing Roman walls, and building new structures within the fort from scratch, entirely from timber. Even the ancient layout of the fort and the alignments of its old buildings and roads now ceased to influence the placement of new struc-tures. At this time, a timber hall was raised, a prototype of the early medieval hall. It probably had thick turf walls and a thatched roof, and it was very large. The hall was an impressive building, placed squarely on the old Roman road which had run through the south portal of the fort's main gate, a gate that still stood. The hall, therefore, was backed by an impressive piece of late imperial architecture, and it would have been the first thing people entering Birdoswald would have seen. It looks like the residence of a great man.

All this suggests that the descendants of the late Roman military garrison housed at Birdoswald cohered as a community for a hundred years after Rome's fall, and that a hereditary commander and the grandsons of late Roman conscripts managed to maintain possession of their fort, perhaps as an armed community with deeply entrenched military traditions. In his *Gothic Wars*, the great sixth-century Byzantine historian Procopius, describing some of the local garrisons in Gaul, may have also coincidentally captured the people of Birdoswald:

> Roman soldiers . . . stationed on the frontiers of Gaul to serve as guards . . . handed down to their offspring all the customs of their fathers . . . Even today they are clearly recognized as belonging to the legions to which they were assigned in ancient times, and they carry their own standards when they enter battle . . . And they preserve the dress of the Romans in every particular, even down to their shoes.

There are hints that another military establishment may have similarly persevered at Cirencester, so perhaps such communities were commonplace in fifth-century Britain. In any case, we know from the analysis of ancient pollen that the land along Hadrian's Wall did not return to scrub until the sixth century, which suggests that the pastoral economy of late Roman Cumbria continued alongside the fort community. But Birdoswald's excavators found no trace of industry, no evidence of long-distance trade, and it seems that the settlement failed, a full century after the Roman state's withdrawal, sometime before the mid-sixth century.

We can glimpse a third British community coalescing in the ruins of Wroxeter (or *Viroconium Cornoviorum*, as it was called in the Roman period), a once-prosperous public town. The basilica of the city's baths, which has been excavated, was not only still heavily used around the year 400, but continued to receive repairs. Within a generation or so, however, people ceased to maintain it. Sometime mid-century, when it became too dilapidated to use, the building was stripped of its roof and colonnades, but its walls were left standing as an open, floorless shell. Within, it looks as if some sort of open-air market, perhaps a seasonal one, was held, accompanied by a few lean-to stalls and a set of heavily used latrines. These developments suggest some faint continuation of civic organization. The market site was demolished in turn, along with a cobbled street running beside it, and the detritus hauled away. It was replaced by a number of timber structures, one of them very grand. This last reworking of the site sometime in the late fifth century required massive amounts of labour, and perhaps a year's work. With this change the site ceased in any way to be public or urban. Nonetheless, Wroxeter continued as an important place, having been rescued, hijacked or otherwise taken over by a man powerful enough to privatize one of the old Roman city's most public spaces, and someone familiar enough with fourth-century genteel architecture to have built, where the town's basilica once lay, a great timber house that had as its inspiration a Roman-style winged-corridor villa. The residence itself, its construction in the ruins of a Roman town and its siting on the old baths' basilica are all obvious assertions of *romanitas*. Although the town itself had lost its economic and civic functions, it was able to continue as a central place because it had become the seat of a central person. It can be argued that a powerful figure within Wroxeter society emerged in the second half of the fifth century as the leader of the community, and that he took over whatever public functions he could, perhaps gaining authority, not only over the ruined city, but over its ancient territory as well.

Life also apparently continued in the south-western corner of the old city, where the church of St Andrew's can be found today. The church still incorporates early medieval stonework within its fabric, but its foundation is likely to date from earlier, the fourth or fifth century. The orientation of St Andrew's is also odd: the church is aligned 23 degrees north of east, the same alignment as a major Roman road, traces of which still run alongside the church. In the late Roman period the road ran from a crossing on the River Severn and linked the ford to the town's main thoroughfare. The road must have been intact and important when the first church was built, since it dictated its orientation. That there could be a Christian community in late Roman Wroxeter is hardly surprising. From the time of Constantine the Great, Christianity was the empire's favoured religion. It may well be that the community evolving at Wroxeter found itself, by the late fifth century, thoroughly Christian, headed by a descendant of the old villa-owning elite and in control of the ancient administrative territory surrounding the town. All three features, in equal measure, were important relics of Wroxeter's Roman past and enduring components of its early medieval future. It is hard to decide which is more startling – the continuity or the lack of it.

THE NEW NEIGHBOURS

What we have seen in western Britain is evidence for the development of a series of small-scale, politically independent, socially stratified little worlds, each one founded on a different piece of the past – the pre-Roman Iron Age, the imperial army, late antique urban life. Each of these places was also subject to catastrophic economic and political reversals, the privatization of state power, material impoverishment and the rapid mutation of social structures. The groups with whom the people of Cadbury Congresbury, Birdoswald and Wroxeter were coming into contact during the fifth century, and the groups with whom they were most likely to compete, were other organized British communities, or Irish elites, who were beginning to establish a foothold in western Britain at just this time. But there is little archaeological evidence from places like these for any relations, hostile or otherwise, between their British inhabitants and newcomers from the Continent. The communities we have examined must have evolved in response to imperial collapse rather than Germanic invasion.

Nonetheless, it is at just this time, around 420, that Germanic-speaking immigrants were beginning to make their way to eastern Britain. Here, few traces of organized British communities have been found. There was probably one centred on Lincoln and another at St Albans, and there were certainly others in the far north-east, but it does seem that there were fewer in eastern than in western Britain. Why organized, hierarchical British communities were not forming and/or persevering at the same rate in the east as in the west is unclear; but it is certainly the case overall that regions in Britain which were less thoroughly Romanized in the fourth century were better able to maintain some pretensions of *romanitas* after the fall than were more thoroughly Romanized parts of it. Perhaps the places most dependent on Roman economic structures and state institutions were the least able to cope after their unravellings. Whatever the case, beginning in the generation on either side of 420, and far to the east of Birdoswald, Wroxeter and Cadbury Congresbury, Germanic immigrants were beginning to make their way to Britain. Most were from northern Germany, Frisia or southern Scandinavia (the eighth-century historian the Venerable Bede tells us, famously, that they were Saxons, Angles and Jutes), and they met the ancient definition of barbarian: they spoke neither Greek nor Latin, and they were newly arrived from beyond the empire's frontiers. This set them apart from many thousands of ethnic Germans settled, from the third century on, on the continent of Europe along Rome's frontiers or in Roman imperial territory. By the fifth century this latter group of men and women had had long experience with the late antique state and Roman ways of life. Many, for example, were buried with official, imperial-issue, bronze belt-sets and late Roman crossbow brooches. Germans they may have been, but in the fourth and fifth centuries they had cosy relations with the imperial state and its army.

In contrast, most of what the people washing up on Britain's shores knew about Rome was second-hand at best: certainly, few possessed any of the paraphernalia of imperial service. Their arrival, moreover, seems ad hoc and unplanned. When the fifth-century Gallo-Roman gentleman Sidonius Apollinaris wrote about Saxon pirates operating off the coast of Gaul, he spoke of single boats stitched together from animal skins rather than menacing fleets, and he tells us that every man acted as both captain and crew. This well describes most of the earliest Germanic-speaking people who came to Britain. They, too, for the most part, seemed uninterested in or incapable of conquering anybody or anything. They wanted land to farm, and they must have hoped for woods where their swine could forage. A few peasant-farmers arrived in the south-east and in East Anglia in the first decades of the fifth century; these earliest settlers were then followed by larger-scale migrations beginning sometime mid-century; and immigrants were still braving the seas with their children and their household goods in the middle of the sixth century. The arrival of these people in Britain, therefore, did not constitute a single, dramatic moment, and their coming cannot be characterized as an invasion. Rather, the *adventus Anglorum*, the 'coming of the English', as Bede called it, should be seen as a long historical process rather than a single historical event.

But, given the nature of the immigrants, it seems unlikely that the few organized British communities there were in eastern Britain had much to do with their new neighbours. Although there is considerable evidence from the early fifth century for immigrant farmers and their small-scale settlements, there is little to suggest roving bands of Germanic warriors. A handful of men from the Continent may well have been recruited in the early fifth century as mercenaries by organized

Romano-British groups or strongmen. Gildas, a British churchman writing in the middle of the sixth century, certainly believed that this had happened, and he wrote of the hiring by a British 'tyrant' of 'three keels', that is, three ships-full of Germanic warriors, to bolster his regime. Gildas goes on to tell us that this ill-fated policy led to the swamping of Britain by the Saxons, who soon put native peoples to the sword. Aside from Gildas's story, however – a tale satisfying in the mid-sixth century not, perhaps, because it was accurate, but because it provided an explanation for why there were so many Englishmen in Gildas's own day – there is only the slightest evidence for this. Dozens of late Roman hoards have been found in Britain, mostly east and south of the rivers Severn and Humber. A number include beautifully worked silver plate, caches of precious-metal spoons, intricate open-work gold jewellery and high-value coinage, and one easy explanation would be their burial by Roman Britons on the run from Germanic war bands. But a closer examination of these hoards suggests that many were buried in response to the hardboiled politics of the fourth-century empire rather than barbarian invasion. The Mildenhall Treasure, for example, with its Bacchic plates, covered bowls and a silver platter weighing more than 8 kilograms, was probably deposited in the 360s by a wealthy family who had backed the wrong imperial faction; and the Thetford Hoard, with its cache of finger rings and buckles, may represent the treasury of a sanctuary dedicated to the pagan god Faunus, a hoard probably hidden in the 380s as a result of the emperor Theodosius' campaign against pagan cults. Even hoards secreted away after 400, like the great treasure recovered at Hoxne, were as likely concealed from competing British groups as from newly arrived immigrants.

Better evidence for Germanic warriors in early fifth-century Britain comes from the rare stray find, like the two early fifth-century Continental brooches recovered from the slopes of Hod Hill, an Iron Age hillfort in Dorset. Dorset in the fifth century lay far to the west of any 'Anglo-Saxon'-style cemeteries, but Hod Hill may have been reoccupied during this period by Romanized Britons in much the same way as Cadbury Congresbury had been. It could just be that the Germanic brooches found at Hod Hill belonged to foreigners used as muscle by the local Roman population. Similarly, two *tutulus* brooches, little pins that look like miniature shield bosses and which had come from the northern Rhineland, were buried in the first decades of the fifth century on a body laid to rest in one of London's extramural cemeteries. Perhaps this person, too, was the wife of a foreign ally, part of a mercenary group hired by people living in the ruins of the dying city. Yet finds like these can be counted on the fingers of two hands. The overwhelming preponderance of fifth-century evidence relates to Germanic immigrants who farmed rather than fought, and to newcomers whose little communities were comprised, not of battle-hardened warriors, but of pregnant women, small children and hard-labouring men.

The lives these people led in the early years are difficult to reconstruct because their numbers were small and their worldly possessions meagre, but we can catch glimpses of two groups of early incomers: one, men and women newly settled near Beckford, in Herefordshire; and the other, people building their lives on a gravel terrace above the Thames estuary at Mucking, in Essex. The few things members of these two groups left behind, including their own bones, give us some sense of the lives led by early peasant-pioneers. Two early cemeteries excavated at Beckford contained the remains of a handful of people who died in the fifth century, along with a scatter of their grave goods and dress ornaments. It seems that there was very little pottery in late fifth-century Beckford, and what there was was shoddily made; and the cloth used for their clothing was not of notably high quality. The ankle joints of many of the adolescents and adults, both male and female, reveal people who spent long hours squatting during rest and indicate that there were few stools or benches in the houses in which they lived. And their teeth were very worn from coarse food, either because their grinding querns were poor, or because ash and grit got into their food from being cooked directly on the hearth, without pots or pans. Every day without cooking pots or decent grinding stones, well-made cloth or the simplest furnishings would have been hard.

Things around Beckford in the early years, however, may have been unusually hard. The early settlers at Mucking, so far as we can tell, were better off. We also know more about them, too, because both their settlement and their cemeteries have been found and excavated. Like Beckford, the settlement at Mucking was founded in the fifth century, and it, like other migration-period settlements, cannot be described as a village. Unlike later village communities, Mucking's houses and outbuildings were not organized around a permanent set of property boundaries, nor were they built along a coherent network of tracks or roadways. Instead, they formed a cluster of undefended farmsteads that straggled along the gravel terrace and shifted over time as families died out or expanded. It also looks as if most households at Mucking farmed on their own. Close kin, dependants and friends may well have built dwellings near one another, but overall each small family group seems to have worked and lived on fairly independent, fairly dispersed farmsteads. And, unlike later villages, Mucking and other early hamlets were never surrounded by common fields cultivated by communal labour. Like the institution of the village, the development of the open-field system is centuries later than the age of migration.

Like many other early English settlements, Mucking stood on marginal land, perhaps because the most fertile fields in the neighbourhood were already being worked by others. There were no elaborate dwellings within Mucking either, and no one place that seems to have been more important in the settlement than others. The impressive longhouses and commodious farmyards found in contemporary Germanic settlements on the Continent are absent from Mucking as well, and this suggests smaller, less extended households and less command of labour. It looks, then, as if people in Mucking, unlike members of the British communities examined earlier, all lived in much the same way, with no very rich households and no very poor ones. Mucking's graves, however, reveal more social differentiation than its houses. Several men, for example, were buried with swords, although the vast majority were not, and a couple of the women had fine brooches. In spite of modest differences in grave goods, there were no 'princely' graves at Mucking, that is, no startlingly wealthy burials that outmatched all the rest. Early migration-period cemeteries across England are much the same as Mucking's, so it is not that this community alone lacked richly buried dead: everywhere did.

One of the things that made Mucking different from Beckford, and from most other fifth-century settlements that have been discovered, was its size. Across the centuries of its existence Mucking had a population of eighty or ninety people, who lived there in nine or ten households, each with its own small, hall-like house and each with a sunken-floored outbuilding or two. Most of the other early settlements that have been excavated were smaller, usually hamlets with twenty or thirty souls, divided among four or five families. Even Mucking, though, at ninety-strong, presents a stark contrast to Roman settlements. A hundred years earlier there had been towns and cities as well as farms and villas, and there had been places large enough to accommodate strangers and nodding acquaintances, not just cousins. But by the mid-fifth century there were no big places, only small ones, and everyone's universe of familiars was highly circumscribed. Such places, even the outsized Mucking, would have been genetically unviable and would have required the out-marrying of daughters and the in-marrying of wives. Indeed, it may well be through women that the culture of the newcomers, whose origins were mixed and whose material culture was diverse, began to homogenize, at least locally, over the first few generations.

Beckford, Mucking and hundreds of similar contemporary settlements were linked by neither a money nor a market economy. They had no large-scale, organized manufacturing and no pools of skilled labour. Still, the agriculture in which these communities engaged must have produced some small surpluses. Everyone had knives or brooches, but only a few living in the fifth century would have had the requisite skills to make them. Women, moreover, often wore strings of glass beads or stunning brooches which had been brought to families by new brides or acquired to broadcast a household's prosperity. A few people got hold of even rarer goods – stemmed, soda-glass beakers, for example, or wooden-staved, bronze-ringed buckets. The economy, then, was mostly one of subsistence agriculture, but there were some small surpluses; enough, in any case, to support a few craftsmen and some exchange of goods. Access to well-to-do brides and exotic objects would have been limited to a handful in every neighbourhood, and this, in turn, suggests some small measure of social differentiation and hierarchy. What Mucking and other fifth-century English sites betray, then, is broadly equal, but internally ranked communities: each settlement was much like its neighbours in terms of its resources, its look and its size, but within each place there were modest social differences. There was no aristocracy in such hamlets, no warrior class. But locally important individuals, perhaps the most powerful members of each family, were given more elaborate burials and had a clutch of valuable possessions because they had some edge over their familiars. There is nothing, however, to suggest that the children of those who had more also had more in the next generation; little evidence that the modest inequalities found in one generation were reproduced in exactly the same way thirty years on.

IMMIGRANTS, INDIGENES
AND THE FIRST 'ANGLO-SAXONS'

By the later fifth century, settlements like the ones at Beckford and Mucking were spreading rapidly across eastern England. Here, the vast majority of migration-period sites came into existence sometime after *c*. 470 but before *c*. 520. It was in these decades that Germanic migration changed from a trickle to a flood. Still, the communities being founded in eastern England during this period were not big enough, organized enough, socially stratified enough or wealthy enough to compete with communities like Wroxeter, Birdoswald or Cadbury Congresbury. So where were the British in eastern England? And for that matter, where were all Bede's Angles, Saxons and Jutes, those presumably easily identifiable, homogeneous ethnic groups whose archaeologically visible remains can be traced back to clear-cut, homogeneous peoples from the Continent?

To answer these questions, we must investigate, as best we can, the identities of the inhabitants of fifth-century eastern Britain. Our clearest view of these people comes from the region's migration-period cemeteries, places usually found at some distance from the now-defunct Roman towns and their derelict burial places. In eastern England's new cemeteries, a series of novel and starkly un-Roman mortuary practices came to prevail. The most dramatic of these was the reappearance of the funeral pyre. Cremation had once been a common rite in the Roman world, but it had gone out of fashion in the third century. Now, once again, in the fifth century and beyond, clothed bodies were placed on pyres and burned. Then the ashes and the half-melted buckles and brooches that were left from the fire were scooped up into handmade pots, which were then buried in communal cemeteries, some of them containing thousands of such urns. Other corpses, however, were placed unburned in the ground and accompanied by an assortment of possessions. Both rites – cremation and grave-goods inhumation – were establishing themselves in eastern England in the fifth century, often in the very same cemeteries.

Inhumations, in particular, provide us with vast amounts of evidence for what is otherwise an elusive century. In late antiquity, as we have seen, a few objects – a pot, a crossbow brooch, or a pair of hobnail boots, perhaps a coin or two – were sometimes buried with the corpse, although by the mid-fourth century many graves, including those excavated at Poundbury, were empty of everything but coffined bodies. The fifth-century dead, however, were dealt with differently. Like most Roman dead, they were fully clothed, but now they were adorned with brooches and other kinds of jewellery new to Britain, and their graves were supplied with a different assortment of objects than those chosen before the fall. Fifth-century inhumations were rarely coffined either, although some were cist burials, that is, graves carefully lined with stones. These differences between fourth- and fifth-century burials were, in some ways, simply a consequence of the failure of the Romano-British economy – both organized production and cities had foundered: there were no new coins to place in dead women's hands, no sawmills to cut planks for coffins, no crowd of townspeople seeking to bury their kith and kin.

Not all fifth-century funerary practices, however, were dictated by collapse. Some represent active choice, and they signal profound transformations in people's views of themselves and their world. Women, for example, were now regularly kitted out with a whole new set of grave goods – bronze pendants in the shape of tiny buckets, long metal objects dangling from their girdles and little bags worn on their belts. Men, on the other hand, were sometimes interred with weapons, mostly spears, but sometimes shields or swords. We should not, however, label the men buried with weapons 'warriors'. A single spear, or even a spear and shield, hardly denotes membership of some kind of closed military brotherhood. Hare killing, boar hunting or self-protection are as likely signalled as organized warfare. Besides, elderly men, even those with healed axe or sword wounds, were not often buried with weapons, so these objects cannot have marked out fighters from everyone else.

Both the changes in women's grave goods and men's attest to more than a remade material culture: they hint at the mutation of ideologies and social practices. Weapons, for example, are never found in late Roman provincial cemeteries, even those a stone's throw from Roman military camps. Weapons' determined association with dead men in fifth-century England and women's habitual burial with girdle-hangers were apparently newly minted ways of proclaiming gender identity, and increasingly, towards the end of the fifth century, they were also coming to signal social status as well. Profound cultural shifts were also marked by the very make-up of the new burial communities. A host of infants and toddlers are often found in late Roman cemeteries, but they are scarce in migration-era burial places, not because babies had ceased to die, but because most groups chose not to bury them with the rest of their dead. This is a breath-catching break with fourth-century Romano-British practices, and it betrays a sea change in attitudes towards babies, towards burial and perhaps even towards the very notion of what made a person a person.

Although it is easy to differentiate between fifth-century 'Anglo-Saxon' cemeteries and fourth-century Romano-British ones, each fifth-century cemetery was, nonetheless, different; and even those a single valley apart display remarkable heterogeneity. As we have already seen, for example, some communities in fifth-century England buried their loved ones, while others chose the funeral pyre. Some settlements buried their dead with no one else's, but others banded together to create cemeteries for congeries of people residing in the area. In some cemeteries the dead were accompanied by little pots filled with the ashes of cremated dogs or horses, but in others tree branches were placed in the grave. Sometimes family relationships determined the layout of cemeteries, but elsewhere it seems that age or gender was the guiding principle. Indeed, judging from the diversity of customs surrounding death, ritual practice and social values must have varied considerably from one hamlet to the next.

Similarly, because the fifth-century dead were buried in their clothes, we know that the costumes of the living were quite localized. Although cloth rarely survives in graves, many of the metal fasteners that kept clothes together – the ubiquitous buckles, brooches and dress pins of the period – remain. Like funerary rites, these dress accessories changed dramatically between the late fourth century and the beginning of the sixth, and in the new cemeteries we find both alien jewellery and novel ways of wearing it. Women in eastern England now typically wore a pair of brooches to the grave – one pinned to each shoulder, and often with a string or two of brightly coloured beads festooned between the two. North of the Thames, women regularly wore a third brooch between their breasts, probably to fasten a cloak or shawl. These brooches came in an astonishing variety of shapes and sizes. There were cruciform, square-headed and long-small brooches, equal-armed and supporting-arm brooches, and radiate-, bird- and disc-brooches. Each class of brooch was decorated with a variety of designs and knobs and fashioned using an array of techniques. Some were tinned and others gilded. Sometimes designs were punched; other times they were cast.

This wide assortment of brooches tells us something about the origins of English immigrants. Very early brooches with exact Continental parallels, for example, point towards the regions from which immigrants were coming. Small, plain cruciform brooches, like the ones excavated at Sarre and Howletts in Kent, for example, have also turned up in Jutland in early fifth-century contexts, and equal-armed brooches, like the one found at Hod Hill, look like those worn between the Elbe and the Weser in north-western Germany. Fifth-century brooches found in some Cambridgeshire graves are close relatives to examples excavated in and around present-day Hanover, in Lower Saxony, and others which have turned up in Oxfordshire are very like those that were worn in fifth-century western Saxony. Brooches like these, with exact Continental analogues, may well have been the very ones worn by women who had braved a Channel crossing and had come as part of that first, straggling migration. Nonetheless, we cannot assume that the people in whose graves these brooches were buried were themselves immigrants. Many of our earliest examples are very worn: some had even lost their pins and had to be stitched onto the dresses of the dead. These brooches look as if they had been deposited in the ground decades after they were made, and they could either represent prized family heirlooms used to honour the dead or battered, old pieces that no one minded burying.

Many early English brooches, however, have no exact Continental parallels. Long-small brooches are found nowhere but in England, and they may represent homely imitations of fancier square-headed brooches, the earliest of which seem to have come from Scandinavia. Nor are the disc-brooches so often recovered from early cemeteries in the Upper Thames Valley found on the Continent. These and another early brooch type, the quoit-style brooch, developed out of indigenous Romano-British metal-working traditions. It seems, therefore, that some communities brought with them and wore the jewellery of their homelands and went to some pains to replicate it once they had settled in England. Others, however, within a generation or two were creating distinctly insular pieces, many with clear links to old-style Continental forms, but which were, nonetheless, unmistakably 'English'.

In spite of the strong links most fifth-century metalwork has to well-provenanced Continental pieces, what brooches do not reveal is a set of clear-cut origins and watertight ethnic identities for the members of communities in whose cemeteries they were uncovered. Although it is true that particular types of brooches are more often found in some neighbourhoods than others, it would be unwise to see specific regions in the fifth century as impermeable enclaves of particular Continental 'tribes', enceintes impervious to other peoples or cultures. Regions in which a particular brooch style was most common almost always overlapped with areas in which another kind of brooch dominated. And women buried with brooches that have been labelled 'Anglian' or 'Saxon' were habitually accompanied in their graves by an assortment of other objects, the origins of which lay elsewhere. Indeed, few burials in eastern England and no cemeteries conform exactly with contemporary Continental ones. The earliest cemeteries in Kent, for example, where Jutish-style brooches abound, are nonetheless different from those found in Jutland, and careful comparison between the two regions' cemeteries suggests that funerary rights and styles of dress often differed dramatically in the homeland and the new land. Using brooches or any other class of artefact to establish strict 'tribal' affiliations for the people with whom they were buried therefore seems unwise. Indeed, try as we might, we cannot identify the material culture of a discrete, autonomous ethnic group in fifth-century eastern Britain, because distinctive ethnic identities had probably not yet coalesced.

The brooches worn by women in fifth- and early sixth-century Britain, then, were a mongrel assortment: some had clear antecedents, others were subtle mutations of older or fancier forms, and still others were unique to Britain. Together they suggest that the old, Continental-style jewellery was rethought, abandoned or remade in England from the very start, probably in much the same way that less tangible pieces of people's lives – their songs, their language, their tastes – were changing. Surely this is because small groups and individuals were coming into contact with all sorts of strangers in the early days – immigrant families from some other part of north-west Europe, communities that had established themselves a generation or two earlier, even British-speakers still residing in the neighbourhood: and what this confusion of brooches suggests is that people living and dying in eastern England in the generations after 420 were cobbling together distinctive little cultures all their own out of this cacophony of peoples and circumstances, and that these cultures were heterogeneous, highly localized and very fluid. In the end, the most interesting thing about burial and dress in fifth- and early sixth-century England is their variety; that they sometimes differed not only from region to region or from cemetery to cemetery, but from grave to grave and from mother-in-law to daughter-in-law. The baffling array of brooches and other grave furnishings also illustrates how different the material culture of groups in England could be, even those living within a kilometre or two of one another; and this, in turn, suggests that the women who wore these things were each part of a highly local, very particular little universe. Given the wild diversity of this period's material culture and funerary habits, it looks as if the first century of settlers did not migrate in large, 'tribal' groups, each with its own homogeneous material culture, ethnic costumes and funerary habits, which they then replicated in Britain. Rather, there were dozens of subtly different and idiosyncratic little societies, each one noticeable for its variety and its rapid transformation.

Although there were no well-formed regional identities in fifth-century England based on Continental affiliations – like Bede's famous assertion that the people who settled the Isle of Wight were Jutes and those who settled Northumbria were Angles – and although there was no single 'Anglo-Saxon' culture in fifth-century England, it is, nonetheless, clear that social practices and objects new to Britain were coming to shape people's lives in eastern England, and they were increasingly doing so as the sixth century drew nearer.

It is, of course, tempting, when confronted with the period's novel burial sites, funerary rites, dress fashions and artefact types, and with the disappearance of Romano-British burial practices and objects, to argue that Germanic invaders drove out or exterminated the native population. Our evidence, however, cries out for some other explanation. Above all else, common sense tells us that one of the results of the collapse of the Roman state and its economy was that British people ceased to have much metalwork, pottery or masonry; and because of this these things are hard for archaeologists to find. Painstaking excavations of early migration-period sites, moreover, have uncovered few signs of political or military organization among the first immigrants. Indeed, there is tantalizing evidence that the grandchildren and great-grandchildren of Roman Britons persisted in eastern England, and that they often lived with their new neighbours in a state of peace, not war.

Although many brooch-wearers would have had parents or

grandparents who had been born across the sea, British women living in areas settled by outlanders may have acquired a taste for Germanic-style metalwork, especially in neighbourhoods where modes of Romano-British production were so interrupted that the newfangled brooches were the only ones available. This may, for example, lie behind the jewellery buried with a group of women eventually laid to rest in a cemetery at Mill Hill, near Deal, in Kent. A number sported a single brooch at their necks, and their dresses, when they were buried, were cinched in at the waist with belts that had large, showy buckles. These are fourth-century, Romano-British fashions. Other women at Mill Hill, however, rather than wearing a single brooch or the more usual pair, wore five or six at a time, pinned in lines down the fronts of their dresses from neck to waist in a manner that no Germanic woman on the Continent every did. One woman was even wearing a brooch pinned to her headdress. Many of these dress fasteners were Continental in origin or fashioned according to traditional Continental tastes, but the unorthodox ways in which some women at Mill Hill displayed them suggests that they were either unfamiliar with the subtleties of Germanic dress or did not care, and that they were following their own local and highly idiosyncratic ideas about how to dress. The men's grave goods at Mill Hill, on the other hand, were more conventionally 'Germanic'. It may just be that the communities who carried out burials at Mill Hill were made up, in part, of immigrant men and their native wives, some of whom continued to dress in a fashion akin to that of their fourth-century ancestors, and others, who, when given Continental jewellery by their husbands, pinned it on themselves in inventive new ways.

Roman objects, too, were still finding their ways into the new cemeteries, and this material and its ritual interment is worth pondering, because it may, in some instances, signal continuity in cultural practices and population. Nonetheless, we must be careful not to ascribe a single meaning to this practice. Take, for example, an elderly woman unearthed at Alton, in Hampshire. She was somewhere between 60 and 80 when she died, and those who buried her decked her out in a remarkable get-up. She had a necklace made from Romano-British glass beads, perforated Roman coins and a Roman fibula brooch that was centuries old when buried with her. She also had strange, D-shaped, buckle-like brooches on her shoulders. Who was she? A remarkably stubborn cultural conservative, clinging a century after Rome's collapse to family heirlooms and boring her neighbours with claims of British ancestry? Or had all four of her grandparents been born on the Continent, and had she simply stumbled on a little hoard of Roman goods and decided to wear them? Perhaps she was too poor or too unimportant to warrant burial with anything other than a collection of old junk. Alas, we shall never know the story that lay behind her jewellery. What we can say, however, is that, whether she was a native or not, she was using Roman objects in ways that no Romano-British woman would ever have done. A little bronze-plated Roman theatre ticket was found in another Alton woman's grave, and this, alongside the first burial, suggests that women in and around Alton liked to poke around derelict Roman sites in their spare time in search of little treasures. In other cemeteries, however, we find Roman material deployed in a more strictly orthodox manner. A man buried at Collingbourne Ducis, in Wiltshire, for example, not only lay on his belly in the grave, a practice of enormous antiquity in Britain, and not only was he wearing a late Roman, gilded disc-brooch, but the brooch was pinned at his shoulder just as it would have been a century earlier. So here not only do we have a man buried with a Roman object, but it was being used in proper Roman fashion. Although he was placed in the grave with fewer Roman goods than the Alton woman, this man's connection to the Roman past seems more profound.

In spite of the hazards of interpretation, it does look as if there are all sorts of subtle indications of Britishness found in 'Anglo-Saxon' cemeteries. Almost every large, early 'Anglo-Saxon' cemetery contains graves that are entirely devoid of grave goods and dug in strict alignment, the way many late Roman graves had been. Some of these could well be the graves of poorer members of the community or adolescents without households of their own, but some may represent the burials of British people, who shared local cemeteries with their immigrant neighbours, but who continued to bury in a traditional late Roman manner. A small number of early 'Anglo-Saxon' graves also contain single coins found in or near the hands of the dead, perhaps a continuation of the Roman practice of Charon's obol. Interestingly, however, a significant number of the coins found in migration-period graves are inscribed with a *chi rho*, the Greek monogram for Christ. Again, this suggests the possibility of a British population as well as the survival of a kind of folk Christianity after Rome's fall. Cist burials, a common grave type in the later Roman period, continued as a dominant custom in places like eastern

Yorkshire, although many such burials now included Continental-style metalwork. This suggests that British people either carried on with this tradition, fall or no fall, or that the newcomers had taken up the indigenous rite, having learned it from the locals. Romano-British women in the fourth century had worn bracelets, sometimes more than one, a fashion not followed by Germanic peoples in the putative homelands of the 'Anglo-Saxons'. Nonetheless, substantial numbers of women and children in fifth- and early sixth-century 'Anglo-Saxon' cemeteries were buried with bracelets, suggesting the survival of a British fashion among the women and children in some communities. And some people buried in the fifth century with 'Anglo-Saxon' grave goods were nonetheless wearing textiles which had been manufactured using Romano-British rather than 'Anglo-Saxon' techniques. Each of these practices extended back into the Roman period, and all continued into the fifth century and beyond in cemeteries that are described as 'Anglo-Saxon'.

The meaning of these ancient 'British' or 'Roman' practices (if that is, indeed, what they sometimes were) doubtless shifted over time. In the early fifth century they may have represented dogged adherence to time-worn traditions. By the early sixth century, however, these customs could have been freighted with entirely new meanings and embraced by people whose great-great grandparents had been born in north-west Germany. This mix of endogenous and exotic burial practices and dress probably signals both the newcomers' adoption of some aspects of indigenous culture and the British people's assimilation of new practices and objects. Indeed, by the end of the fifth century it seems as if ancestry in eastern Britain was becoming uncoupled from material culture. This can be seen in the remarkable example of two neighbouring cemeteries in Oxfordshire, one at Queenford Farm and the other less than a kilometre away at Berinsfield. During the fourth century Romano-British people had buried their dead in the Roman manner at the cemetery at Queenford Farm. In the fifth century a brand-new cemetery at nearby Berinsfield came to be the place where 'Anglo-Saxons', following more Continental rites, buried their dead. Yet some of the people buried in these two cemeteries had remarkably similar teeth. Eleven epigenetic traits manifest in teeth – little ridges, wrinkles and cusps that are genetically determined – were present at nearly the same rate in each cemetery, and this can only mean that the two burial groups were related. So it looks as if culture, rather than population, had shifted. In the fourth century people in the neighbourhood were buried at Queenford Farm in quite typical Romano-British fashion, but in the fifth century some of their descendants had begun to be buried in the new cemetery at Berinsfield using the seductive rites and material culture of their immigrant neighbours. Regardless of their meanings, the continuation of a few visible fourth-century traditions into the fifth century and beyond suggests that Germanic migration and settlement took place in a peopled landscape, and that the descendants of the men and women early immigrants had encountered were still there generations on.

Rare evidence from Yorkshire may actually provide us with glimpses of a handful of hybrid communities, places where the beginnings of such cultural adaptation and accommodation were taking place. In the mid-fourth century the people living on an isolated farmstead near Saxton, in the Vale of Pickering, were not very Romanized; but they, like everyone else, were implicated in the broader imperial economy. Indeed, here, at the end of an unpromising little trackway in the northernmost reaches of the empire, there were pots from Gaul. Some 150 years later, people still lived on the farmstead. They were probably the descendants of its fourth-century proprietors, since there was never a break in habitation. Now, however, the people living here were using new-style 'Anglo-Saxon' pottery, and at least one woman was wearing a pair of little metal hooks-and-eyes called 'wrist-clasps' on her sleeves, a fashion introduced into Britain from south-western Norway. A few kilometres away, hamlets in Wykham and Sherburn also show signs of unbroken settlement across the great divide of 400, but sometime in the fifth century Germanic-style, sunken-featured buildings known as *grubenhäuser* joined these settlements' indigenous roundhouses; and Germanic-style ceramics and worked bone began to be used, not only by the people with the *grubenhäuser*, but by those living in the roundhouses as well. Further afield, at Quarrington, near Sleaford in Lincolnshire, people in the fifth century were building both roundhouses and rectangular structures, wearing Romano-British style twisted-metal bracelets and using 'Anglo-Saxon' pottery.

The fifth century's landscape and environment, like its burials and material culture, similarly suggests dislocations, continuities and comings together. As we have seen, the Roman institutions of the army, the state, the town and the villa had vanished from Britain by 420, so systems designed to supply markets with food and peasants with surpluses for rents and taxes withered away. But farmers still farmed, crops still grew and herds still grazed. What had changed were the social institutions within which agriculture was now practised. Sometimes large landowners during the Roman period had organized their labour forces to build and maintain extensive systems of drainage ditches, which they also used to define estate boundaries. The fate of such ditches in the fifth century hints that the power of landlords had faltered in much of eastern England sometime between the late fourth century and the early fifth, and this waning of the chosen few's power over the many's labour is etched in the landscape. At Barton Court Farm, in Oxfordshire, the labour-hungry drainage system, so crucial for the cultivation of the fertile, waterlogged lands running along the first gravel terrace of the Thames, became so weed-choked and silt-clogged that it ceased to function, and the land had to be abandoned, although the fields on the drier, less ditch-dependent second terrace continued under the plough. North of the River Humber, ditches were also going to rack and ruin. Farmlands once marked off by ditches dug three feet deep or more were now sometimes bounded, instead, by less labour-intensive fences. Ditch-making and maintenance require prodigious amounts of labour ruthlessly organized, but once the institutions that buttressed landlord's rights had disappeared it must have been difficult for villa stewards to muster the necessary gangs of workers. Still, Roman field systems and boundaries endured in some places. On the Gwent Levels, for example, a grid of highly organized fields, probably first grubbed out by Roman legionaries stationed at Caerleon, successfully persevered, and it survives to this day. This must be because old, imperial landholding rights and property boundaries were maintained there even as Rome receded. More typically, as at Yaxley in Sussex, important Roman boundaries and tracks continued to mark and divide the landscape, but the lesser boundaries radiating out from them vanished, in part, no doubt, because they had become obscured by the lack of upkeep and the fall of landlords.

What was being raised on fifth-century fields, many of which had been cleared and exploited since the Iron Age, was sometimes the same as in Roman times. The remains of cattle and sheep, for example, excavated from migration-period sites are the cattle and sheep of Roman Britain, not northern Germany. The bones of domestic quadrupeds are, moreover, found in different ratios in eastern England than they are on the Continent. On Continental sites a much larger percentage of cattle and horse bones are found and fewer pigs and sheep. So even in areas heavily settled by immigrants, British herds still grazed, and the meat served up at mealtimes differed from the meat back home in Jutland or the Lower Rhine. At the same time, however, the mix of domestic animal bones found on fifth-century sites is different from those found on sites of the late Roman period, so it is not as if British eating and farming carried on unchanged. For one thing, pigs became an increasingly important meat source, probably because they are indiscriminate eaters and astonishing weight gainers, virtues that would have endeared them to pioneers trying to get through their first few winters. Herds were also more vigorously culled, probably because people found it harder now to over-winter animals.

Although immigrants would have grown up planting barley, oats and bread wheat, some, in the early days after coming to Britain, raised spelt, a staple of the Roman diet, and a crop already established in the fields they had begun to farm. Pollen from the now-rare weed *Camelina alyssum*, a pretty little pest that grew in flax fields in Roman Britain, has been found both in late Roman and in early medieval levels of settlement sites, suggesting that flax, fall or no fall, continued to be grown in the same fields across the fourth and fifth centuries. On the other hand, there are indications that fifth-century British communities were cultivating new crops. At the post-Roman British settlement established among the graves and mausoleums of the late Roman cemetery at Poundbury, which was examined in some detail in the last chapter, free-threshing bread wheat was being grown for the first time. Like so much else, however, the range of cultivated plants contracted. Culinary herbs like coriander and fennel, medicinal plants like opium poppy, vegetables like cucumber and turnips, and fruits like apples, damsons and plums ceased to be cultivated. And exotic rarities like stone pine, mulberry and box, which had been carefully nursed in the gardens of the great in the Roman period, disappeared from Britain altogether.

The evidence of place names tells much the same story. An unreflective use of place names might tempt one to argue a fire-and-sword fate for many British, since so few of the place names used while the Roman empire flourished survived, and since so many are Germanic in origin. But the renaming of the landscape is more complicated than it first appears, and England's place names, like its cemeteries, cannot in actual fact be used as evidence that the British were driven wholesale from eastern England. Certainly, the loss of Romano-British place names cannot be explained by the loss of British population. Although few in number, many more British place names survive today in eastern England, where Germanic settlement was heaviest and earliest, than in the west, where we know that the English did not begin to settle until the eighth century. Even in Cornwall and Wales, places where Celtic languages continued to be spoken into the modern era, much of the landscape is dominated by English place names.

People living in Roman Britain, so far as we can tell, favoured topographical names for their settlements. The names they chose – *Canonum*, 'place on the reedy river', *Maglona*, 'high place', or *Uxelodunum*, 'high fort' – were physical descriptions of the landscape in which each place sat. This habit continued long after the fall in British-speaking communities. But early Germanic immigrants, too, as far as we can tell, named the places of their world descriptively, and the few places whose early names we know – both Old English and British – bear similar descriptive names, names like 'blue hill' or 'clearing in the woods'. From the ninth century on, however, both Welsh-speakers (who spoke a language that developed in the early Middle Ages out of the British vernacular of the Romano-British period) and English-speakers (who spoke a relative of the Germanic languages used by fifth- and sixth-century immigrants from the Continent) began to rename the land. Old topographical names were no longer satisfactory, and they were replaced with habitative place names, names in England that often have elements like *-tun* and in Wales words like *trefi*, combined with a personal name. What these new-style place names were proclaiming was lords' rights to land. This style of naming places arose in a world populated by elites whose power was derived from the ownership of land. But this was not the world of the fifth and sixth centuries, and what we see on maps of England today are not the names of fifth- and sixth-century Germanic settlers, but those chosen by people living there in the ninth century and beyond. Most early place names, both English and British, disappeared not during the period of English migration but rather three or four hundred years later. And when the English landscape was renamed, most people, regardless of the origins of their long-dead ancestors, spoke English; and so the names they chose, the majority of which are still in use, were English.

In actual fact, a study of fifth- and sixth-century names suggests a long and peaceful coexistence between British- and English-speakers. A number of early English place names, for example, include Latin elements. *Portus* is the Latin word for harbour. In the south-east of England, before Rome's fall, one of the big channel harbours was called *Portus Adurni*. An English chronicler writing in the ninth century explained that Portsmouth (which was what *Portus Adurni* was now called) acquired its name because 'Port and his two sons ... came to Britain with two ships at the place which is called *Portes mutha*'. This early medieval etymology required the invention of a fictitious barbarian warlord named Port to explain the genesis of the name, when people had ceased to remember that *port* meant 'harbour' and that the place had been called *Port*-something for eight hundred years. In actual fact, the only way 'port' could have survived as part of this place's name was if English newcomers had learned what the place was called from their British neighbours. Similarly, an ancient hillfort overlooking the Roman wall fort of Vindolanda is called Barcombe, an Anglicized version of *Vercovicium*, the Latin name for Housesteads, one fort down Hadrian's Wall from Vindolanda. Perhaps the people living at Vindolanda and Housesteads moved together to Barcombe once the imperial government stopped sending supplies. A hundred years later, as immigrants began to settle in the area, and as local people began to adopt the newcomers' material culture and language, the Roman place name survived.

Other place names tell similar stories. Many of the great landscape features of Britain – its most important rivers, like the Thames, the Avon and the Severn, its highest foothills, like the Malvern Hills and Pennines, and its largest forests, like the forests of Arden and Wyre – have British rather than Old English names. Immigrant communities settled up and down these major features must have learned from their British-speaking neighbours what they were called.

Other place names are hybrids, part English and part British. Doverdale in Worcestershire is one such name: it has been fashioned from the Old English word for valley and a British-language river name. Or there is Charnwood, a name cobbled together from the British 'rock' and the English 'wood'. Other hybrids are little redundancies, like Breedon, in Leicestershire, which takes its first syllable from the Welsh *bre* and its second from the English *dun*. It means 'hill-hill'. From Bede we learn of a similar place name, a monastery in a spot called *Inderawudu*, or 'wood wood'. Such hybrids are the relics of conversations struck up during the migration period between people speaking different tongues but living at the edge of the same woods and farming on the rise of the same slopes, people who could not comprehend one another's languages, but who were looking at the same rivers and forests and asking, as best they could, 'What do you call this place?' Early place names, then, rather than suggesting the wholesale slaughter or displacement of the native, British population, show it settled nearby.

Evidence from the fifth century, meagre, sketchy and enigmatic though it is, suggests something very different than invading Anglo-Saxon warriors putting Romano-British people to the sword. Some communities in the west, like Birdoswald, Wroxeter and Cadbury Congresbury, were able to carry on attenuated forms of Roman life, but many places, especially in the east, could not. The picture that emerges is one of incoming migrants without much social hierarchy and certainly without a warrior aristocracy. These people came to a Britain ruined by economic and political catastrophes not of their own making. When they began to arrive, *c.* 420, in small family groups, they often settled in places with the descendants of Romano-British peasants nearby, people whose landlords had fallen or disappeared, who paid no taxes and who no longer had access to mass-produced Roman goods. At times, the newcomers and the old-timers may have come to blows, but there is considerable evidence to suggest that more often than not they talked to one another and settled next to one another. Indeed, British peasants may have preferred immigrant agriculturists as neighbours to omnivorous villa owners or voracious imperial tax collectors. The newcomers and the natives married one another's womenfolk, and they were buried in the same new cemeteries. Roman material culture was dead and gone in eastern Britain in the fifth century, and many British seem to have adopted that of the newcomers, whose numbers were significant by the year 500, but who were never so many that they outnumbered the indigenes. It is at places like Wroxeter that Latin, Christianity, old families and tales of late Roman usurpers would have been alive and well. But in the eastern half of Britain, it looks very much as if the descendants of the Romano-British were experimenting with barbarian material culture, all the while exposing the immigrants to their own habits and social practices. In doing so, British people and immigrants alike began to devise novel identities. Over the course of the next century, these new solidarities would begin to coalesce into a nascent Englishness. But we must remember: this new sense of Englishness was not the result of conquest or colonization, but rather of settlement, accommodation and acculturation. And it was as much the invention of British as of Germanic-speaking people.

In the sixth century new and broader identities – based on social distinction, on large-scale ethnicities and on territory – would come to produce the kinds of people and social structures described by Bede – broad ethnic groups like the English and the Welsh, politically self-conscious affinities like the West Saxons or the 'men of Kent', nobles like Imma and Guthlac, and princely dynasties like the *Wuffingas* and the *Oiscingas*. None of these, however, were present yet in the first century after the fall.

3

Making Peoples, Making Class: The Late Fifth and Sixth Centuries

The Venerable Bede, writing in the eighth century, describes an England whose earliest Germanic settlers arrived with full-blown identities, identities derived from the Continental 'tribes' from which they sprang. He asserts that the English

> came from three very powerful Germanic tribes, the Saxons, the Angles and the Jutes. The people of Kent and the inhabitants of the Isle of Wight are of Jutish origin as are those opposite the Isle of Wight, that part of the kingdom of Wessex which is still today called the nation of the Jutes. From the Saxon country, that is, the district now known as Old Saxony, came the East Saxons, the South Saxons and the West Saxons. Besides this, from the country of the Angles, that is, the land between the kingdoms of the Jutes and the Saxons, which is called *Angulus*, came the East Angles, the Middle Angles, the Mercians and all the Northumbrian race (that is, those people who dwell north of the Humber) as well as the other Anglian tribes.

The archaeological remains of the fifth century, of course, call into question Bede's neat cataloguing of England's earliest immigrants. Although it confirms that he was correct, for example, in assigning some of England's settlers to homelands in Jutland and Saxony, we now know that there were many other groups – Franks and Norwegians to name but two – whom Bede failed to mention. We also know that the people coming together in fifth-century Britain were a real ethnic stew, hailing from across the whole of north-west Europe and, indeed, from elsewhere in Britain and Ireland, and that they were embracing a wide spectrum of social practices and material culture, the origins of which were mixed. It seems likely, therefore, that the fifth-century England detailed by Bede, a world of well-defined communities of Angles, Saxons and Jutes, was an anachronistic confection, one that mirrored Bede's present, with its robust and all-important groups claiming descent from these very three peoples.

The archaeology of the sixth century, however, is a different matter; indeed, it demonstrates that the broad cultural groups described by Bede were, in fact, beginning to coalesce. If the story of the fifth century is about the replacement of an overarching state and culture with hundreds of local, improvised societies; if it is about the erosion of older and larger identities and the forging of new, small-scale ones; then the story of the sixth century is about the creation of yet another set of broader identities – identities based first on social distinction and then on regional differences. How, in the five or six generations between *c.* 475 and *c.* 600, did individuals and groups go about making themselves distinct from others around them? How did they express their solidarity with people they believed to be like themselves? And what were the circumstances that allowed for, perhaps even demanded, the enlargement and elaboration of particular identities? To begin to answer these questions we must first try to understand the ways individuals thought about themselves in relation to others and how they showed the world who they were.

CONSTRUCTING IDENTITIES

A cemetery at Wasperton, in Warwickshire, used from the late Roman period to the seventh century, was a place where, by the late fifth century, we can see both indigenous British people and newcomers burying their dead. Because burial plots were maintained in this cemetery, the burial practices used by the different groups who controlled the plots allow us to witness the starkly different rites taking place in Wasperton *c.* 500. The family or group of families who were burying their dead in the south-east corner of the cemetery had long lived in the neighbourhood, and they continued to dispose of their dead in ways that would have been familiar to members of British communities living further west, using rites that harked back to the late Roman period. But there were also newcomers burying at Wasperton by this time. Room had been made for them in the cemetery, in spite of the fact that they were using different rites, including cremation and inhumation with the kinds of grave goods we think of as 'Anglo-Saxon'. Yet after a generation or two, the newcomers and the old-timers were burying in much the same fashion, probably because they had spent many years doing the kinds of things that neighbours often do – talking together on long summer evenings, helping one another at harvest time, marrying one another's daughters and doting over the same grandchildren. So by the middle of the sixth century we can see that the funerary rituals being used at Wasperton, far from being biologically determined, were the result of active choice. Here, the descendants of Romano-British people were making radically different statements about who they were than their grandparents would have done. Nonetheless, sixth-century Wasperton burials, grave goods or no, were only distant approximations of the first immigrant burials found there. So in a very real sense, all the people in Wasperton, wherever their great-grandparents had lived, were signalling identities which, in so far as they were expressed in funerary practices, were novel.

The adoption, adaptation and traditionalism moulding funerary rites were part of a wider set of strategies used by small groups and individuals to make claims about who they were, who they were related to and what their histories were. Like funerary rites, humble, everyday objects broadcast information about the identities of their users to anyone who saw them. The type of cooking vessel a woman carried or the weave of her cloak telegraphed information about who she was. People almost certainly also engaged in a wide range of archaeologically invisible actions and ideologies – slang, religious beliefs, personal names, hairstyles – to mark themselves as particular kinds of people, like or unlike others with whom they came into contact. These identities, needless to say, were not genetically determined, but were, rather, social and cultural constructions. People of Continental, Germanic ancestry were not programmed to act like Germans any more than people of British ancestry were compelled by their genes to act British.

Identity, however, is never a simple, unitary proposition. In the early sixth century a man could simultaneously be the son of British parents who had adopted the material culture of his new neighbours, the *paterfamilias* of an extended household, a person beholden to a more respected local headman, a husband married into a prosperous immigrant family and a devotee of a cult that embraced cremation. Each of these identities would have been expressed materially – in clothes fasteners, in burial rites, in food preparation or in architecture. Thus, vestigial remnants of individuals' and settlements' compound and complex identities are present in the archaeological record.

Unfortunately for us, however, culture, identity, origins and the objects of everyday life are knotted together in the archaeological remains of the sixth century in such a way that it is nearly impossible, a millennium and a half on, to disentangle them and to understand absolutely what, in this mess of recoverable things, was used to signify who and what a person was. The meaning of things, of habits and of actions, however, would have been clearer to contemporaries. They would have been able to discern important marks of identity in the same ways we do today. We know, for example, that Marmite-eating signals Britishness and root-beer drinking marks Americans, but that the use of salt and pepper does little to distinguish between the two nationalities. Similarly, people in sixth-century Britain would have taken the measure of a person by perceiving the crucial signifiers of his or her identity and by filtering out the noise of everything else.

Each person, moreover, had his or her own unique bundle of identities. Sixth-century individuals living in the same hamlet or dying within a single household had much in common. They walked the same hills and gossiped with the same neighbours. They had the same cousins and in-laws. They wept at the same funerals. As a result of their shared sense of people and place, they had overlapping communal and familial identities. Nonetheless, even those living in a single, tight-knit community also had divergent identities. Men and women in the sixth century, for example, even those living under the same roof, led very different lives. Women spent long hours in damp weaving sheds working at their looms, and they bore and tended children. Men (so we know from their skeletons) had lifetimes of hard labour, and they got into fights. More women died young: more men spent part of their adult lives as widowers. One of the consequences of these disparate experiences was that in some ways poor and prosperous women, women living north of the River Humber and south of the River Thames, British-speaking women and English-speaking girls, had more in common with one another than with their own brothers and husbands.

In other ways, however, an individual's place within his or her community and household transcended gender or communal identity, especially as we move forward in time. Rank, for example, would have gone a long way in determining friendships and marital options. Well-to-do farmers in the early sixth century, who led their extended households and settlements, may have sought to marry their daughters to the sons of similarly prosperous fathers, even if they had to travel some distance to do so. In the case of the wealthiest people burying at Mill Hill, in eastern Kent, they would have had to journey 15, even 20 kilometres to settlements near Buckland, Bifrons or Lyminge in order to find similar garnet-brooch- and sword-burying families. Most sixth-century cemeteries, moreover, include the graves of one or two women with unusual jewellery, jewellery more typically worn in neighbouring regions. Some of this metalwork doubtless arrived in the packs of itinerant traders or craftsmen, but some must have come pinned to the dresses of brides married by their families to distant acquaintances. Over the course of a couple of generations people like these built broad networks of kith and kin and had daughters married and settled 15 kilometres to the north and 15 kilometres to the south and granddaughters living even further afield. The geographic reach of such people created different kinds of families and experiences for them, and they must have been different kinds of people than lower-ranked members of their communities, who lived in more circumscribed worlds. During the sixth century these high-status networks and identities would be transformative.

THE ORIGINS OF SOCIAL STRATIFICATION

Social and economic inequalities were on the rise in eastern Britain from the last quarter of the fifth century. These inequalities, of course, had been present at the level of the household and the hamlet from the very beginning. Ranked societies, like the one so evident at Mucking, are not egalitarian societies: even in 450 some people bullied or bossed, and others did as they were told. In ranked societies, though, individuals are unable to divert an inordinate share of the material resources and labour of their communities towards their own or their families' uses. But social inequalities, alongside the economic inequalities that came to buttress them, grew and hardened over the course of the sixth century and became permanently inscribed in the settlements and landscapes of eastern Britain. By the mid-sixth century in many parts of eastern Britain there were no longer simply two or three heads of household in every hamlet or a headman here or there with a few extra resources. Now there were whole families who owned considerably more than other people, and there were individuals born to wealth.

The move from a ranked society to a profoundly hierarchical one must in some ways have been a by-product of migration. Often, in the modern world, the descendants of immigrants who arrive first have an edge, within a couple of generations, over late-comers from the same home communities. It is possible that some of the fifth century's first immigrants came to enjoy similar advantages. Those who arrived early may have encouraged others from home to follow. It was they who could teach friends and relatives about good routes and promising destinations. It was these people who were in a position to lend a hand to those who had just arrived. Over the course of a few decades, members of these first families (some of whom could, of course, have married into local British families) would have garnered a mountain of gratitude for all the favours they had done. Something like this may have happened in the area around Spong Hill, in Norfolk, where a cemetery was established. Many of Spong Hill's earliest cremations are apparently of people who came to England from the same part of what is now Schleswig-Holstein. It seems likely that the social networks that stretched between immigrants and their families across the North Sea siphoned several generations of migrants from one region on the Continent into another in Norfolk. Nonetheless, a number of those living near Spong Hill, including the potters who produced its cemetery's cremation urns, probably hailed from elsewhere on the Continent, so people in the area there were of mixed origins. But judging from the number of immigrants whose families originated in the same part of the world, it looks as though early families settled in the region encouraged old neighbours and kinsfolk to join them in Britain. Their grandchildren, two generations on, may have sat, because of their families' place at the beginning of a chain of migration, at the apex of some of the most extensive social networks in the region. This, in turn, would have given them an edge in social competition.

Immigrants in the modern world often maintain close contacts with their home communities, and, indeed, some return annually. It looks as if this, too, happened in fifth- and sixth-century Britain, and this so-called circular migration may have also shaped social relations in the sixth century and beyond. It is unlikely, for example, that immigrant settlements would have been entirely self-sufficient in their first few years. If none of those building their farmsteads together were smiths or if no one knew how to make glass beakers, it may have been necessary for someone to return home and either fetch these things or encourage craftspeople or pedlars to visit them with their wares. We know that something like this must have occurred, because from the very beginning of the migration period, the metalwork worn or made in England was profoundly influenced by changing fashions across the Channel: for this to have happened there had to be fairly persistent toing and froing across the sea. Those who made the annual journey, or who had close ties to people who did, would have had better access to status-enhancing commodities, a decided advantage in a world with only the most basic systems of production and exchange.

Good luck and bad, too, would have contributed to individuals' and communities' standing in a period when social differentiation was on the rise. At a time when people lived so close to the margin, a single rainless summer, a few weeks of child-killing measles or the death of cattle could wreck the hopes of an entire hamlet for decades, and it is clear from the bones of the sixth-century dead that some communities were dogged by misfortune. Nearly 40 per cent of the skeletons excavated from the sixth-century cemetery at Oakington, in Cambridgeshire, for example, show signs of malnutrition or serious childhood illness. At Mill Hill, in Kent, on the other hand, only a small percentage of the population showed similar signs of ill health. Clearly childhood disease and hunger struck different places in different ways, but a community that lost most of its children would have had a grimmer future than one in which they had all been spared. In the later fifth and sixth centuries, when individuals and families were scrambling for resources and social position, a hungry year or a dearth of household labour could ruin a family, indeed could wreck a whole community, for generations.

A story in Adomnán's *Life of Columba*, the life and miracles of the Irish holy man St Columba (521–97), who evangelized among the Picts of Scotland, illustrates for us the consequences of healthy herds and grandchildren, if not in sixth-century Britain, then in sixth-century Ireland:

> Nesán, though he was a very poor man, rejoiced on one occasion to receive
> St Columba as his guest. When the saint had enjoyed one night's hospitality
> from Nesán, as far as his means would stretch, he asked how many cows

he owned. 'Five,' said Nesán. 'Bring them to me', said St Columba, 'so that I may bless them.' They were brought, and St Columba blessed them, raising his holy hand and said: 'From this day on your little herd of five cows will grow until you have one hundred and five cows.' Since Nesán was a layman with a wife and children, St Columba made this addition to his benediction, saying: 'Your seed will be blessed in your sons and grandsons . . .' There was also a rich man called Vigen who was very tight-fisted, and who looked down on St Columba, and would not receive him as a guest. About this man the saint made quite the opposite prophecy, saying: 'The riches of this miser, who has rejected Christ in the pilgrim visitors, will from henceforth be diminished little by little until there is nothing. He himself will be a beggar, and his son will run from house to house with a half-empty bag. A rival will strike him with an axe and he will die in the trench of a threshing-floor.' All of these things were fulfilled according to the saint's prophecies as they concerned the two men.

The reasons, then, for social stratification are numerous and complex, and different individuals and groups would have won or lost status during this period because of the way a set of highly local and very particular circumstances played themselves out among various social groups, be they families, settlements or burial communities. But whatever special stories lay behind specific triumphs or defeats, the results were similar: by the mid-sixth century, a few people had more of everything – resources, alliances, access – than their grandparents or most of their contemporaries had had. The widening chasm between the socially inferior, who made up the bulk of England's population, and the socially blessed, who never constituted more than a small minority, was doubtless signalled in a hundred ways, but from the vantage point of the twenty-first century we can see it best in the period's cemeteries and settlements.

The new inequality is most evident in the creeping inegalitarianism of sixth-century funerary practices. As we have seen, in the fifth century burials were far from uniform. A dead person's gender and stage of life had a noticeable impact on his or her burial, and this practice produced some of the variations found within individual cemeteries. Young children, for example, were usually buried without grave goods or with mere tokens, perhaps a bead or two, or a knife. Individuals who died in late adolescence, on the other hand, were sometimes accorded a portion of the same goods as those found with dead adults. Adults, for their part, were given gender-specific grave goods. Women were often accompanied by clothes fasteners, strings of beads and belts hung with bags and girdle-hangers, while men sometimes had spears, or shields and spears. Nonetheless, more than half of all adults buried in fifth-century eastern Britain had neither jewellery nor weapons. Early on and in some places, a dearth of grave goods may reflect a continuation of the late Roman practice of unaccompanied inhumation. Elsewhere, however, mourners perhaps felt that the squandering of useful or personal items was inappropriate for anyone other than the couple who headed an extended household.

Differences in age and gender continued to mark sixth-century burials, but the portion of individuals who were now accorded male or female grave-sets changed. The statistics look something like this: before c. 525, just under a third of all inhumed adult women were buried with clothes fasteners, jewellery and/or girdle-hangers. For the next hundred years over half were. Then, in the seventh century, female-specific grave goods once again became more restricted, and were only accorded to something like a quarter of all women. For men the trend, at least in the beginning, moved in the opposite direction. Over 40 per cent of all men inhumed before 525 were buried with spears. From 525 to 625 only about a third were, and for the rest of the seventh century less than a fifth were honoured in this way. Thus it seems that weapon-burials became slowly and inexorably more restricted, either because fewer men were deemed worthy of the rite or because fewer people were willing or able to assert a particular kind of identity when burying their dead kinsmen. This in turn suggests that male social status was reorganized during the course of the sixth century, and that marks of higher social standing were becoming steadily and consistently more exclusive. During the same period, however, at least until the first decades of the seventh century, relatively large numbers of dead women were placed in the ground with grave goods. It may well be that women's identities as important people within their own households, and perhaps as wives and as the mothers of young children, continued to be expressed in sixth-century funerary practices, but that men's ranking, as expressed in death, was no longer based on their place within the household, but rather within a larger social arena, such as the settlement or the locality. At the same time, however, precious objects – gold-and-garnet jewellery, necklaces comprised of amber beads, exquisitely crafted square-headed brooches – came to find their way into the graves of a minority of sixth-century women. So although substantial numbers of dead women were accorded grave goods in the sixth century, only a minority were buried with such exotica. In short, high social status was registered in the funerary rites of both men and women in the sixth century, but it was registered in different ways.

The narrowing of the group of people accorded gender-specific or exotic grave goods happened at different times in different places, and indeed, in some neighbourhoods, the transformation took a very long time. At the relatively modest sixth-century cemetery excavated at Norton, Cleveland, for example, a handful of graves stood out from all the rest. One woman buried there wore a pair of punched, spiral silver bracelets, a rare find north of the River Humber, and only one man at Norton was buried with a small, single-edged weapon called a seax, another rarity in the north during this period. Nonetheless, many women at Norton were placed in their graves with good brooches, and a number of men were accompanied by spears or spears and shields. In Norton, then, it looks as if household rank was as crucial in the sixth century as it had been in the fifth for determining how both men and women were laid to rest. What the graves at Norton and similar cemeteries may witness, even at the end of the sixth century, is old-fashioned, ranked communities, places resistant to the establishment of stark social hierarchies.

Elsewhere, however, the difference between richly buried individuals and everyone else intensified, and it was manifest not only in the more parsimonious granting of gendered burial-sets, but in the occasional bestowal of opulent grave goods. At Buckland, near Dover in Kent, for example, 260 broadly sixth-century graves were excavated in the 1990s, and a number contained extraordinary objects. One woman, for example, wore a gold brocade headband and a pendant made from an old Roman intaglio. Her body was also adorned with two silver and three gilt brooches, all set with garnets, and a long necklace strung with glass and amber beads and hung with gold and silver pendants. Much of this woman's finery came from abroad, and it must have looked as impressive to contemporaries as it does to us. The most imposing man interred in this part of the cemetery was buried with a sword, a spear and a shield, as well as a fancy, bronze-studded belt and a pair of scales. These are stunning assemblages, but there were several dozen graves nearby similarly equipped with lavish arrays of grave goods and dress accessories. Yet amid all this splendour lay large numbers of people buried with only a single knife or buckle; indeed, a full third of the people interred in this part of the cemetery had no grave goods at all.

This glaring gulf between especially rich graves and unaccompanied ones was new in the sixth century, and it was particularly evident in eastern Kent, a region where rich graves now typically contained objects that were either made by Franks or were Frankish-inspired. It is clear from the profusion of Frankish-style objects in Kentish graves that high-status families were now in regular contact with Franks. These Franks were a barbarian group which had come together as a people and settled in Gaul a century and a half before the collapse of the western empire, and, over the course of this period, had become quite Romanized; indeed, they have aptly been described as 'Roman Barbarians'. After the fall, the Franks became the dominant political group in Gaul, and it is their name that comes to mark the region, first, in the early Middle Ages, as Francia, and later, as France. In spite of the dramatic changes in political circumstances and leadership witnessed in fifth- and sixth-century Gaul, many components of Roman culture and economy persevered here, in ways that they did not in Britain. Indeed, not only did written administration and the state survive, but so too did old Gallo-Roman elite families, Christianity, Latin, a money economy and towns. Even vestiges of Roman modes of industrial-scale production were present in the sixth and early seventh centuries in kingdoms now ruled by Franks. The Franks, although hardly Romans in the classical sense, nonetheless ruled a very hierarchical society, one that produced copious amounts of jewellery, gold coins, wine, ceramics and textiles, which English people in contact with them began to use to mark or make claims about their own high status. Indeed, judging from sixth-century Kentish burials, it looks as if Kentish families of means were increasingly coming to model their own burial practices and dress on those of the Franks, whom they must have admired, in part, because they seemed so 'Roman'.

In other places, English families were coming into contact with quite different groups of emulation-worthy foreigners. On either side of the River Humber, for example, would-be elites were rubbing shoulders with a better sort of people from western Norway, people, like the Franks, with a tradition of elegantly costumed women and a highly articulated social hierarchy, and whom local English families began to emulate. And in places like northern Lincolnshire, ambitious individuals who were culturally English had dealings with British elites and they began acquiring and flaunting beautiful hanging bowls and penannular brooches made in British contexts. Such contacts with sophisticated outsiders, be they Frankish, Norwegian or British, were exploited during this period by ambitious English families, who deployed some of the jewellery and styles of dress used by more politically and economically advanced outsiders as ways of marking themselves as different from, or better than, their own less successful kinsmen and neighbours.

Other practices pioneered in the sixth century similarly suggest that some families were establishing themselves as special, privileged and different. In the fifth century, as we have seen, children went to their graves with little. Nonetheless, we occasionally come across idiosyncratic children's burials. At Loveden Hill, in Lincolnshire, for example, a dead 5-year-old was found in the arms of an elderly man and the two had a lame old dog buried at their feet. The composition of this grave, however, was the result of archaeologically visible sentiment, not vast expenditure. In the sixth and seventh centuries, though, a handful of youngsters were buried with impressive collections of objects. Three of the nineteen children found in the cemetery at Finglesham, in Kent, for example, had stunning objects with them. One was buried in a coffin with a necklace hung with glass beads and coin pendants, a ceramic bottle and flagon, a purse and a fancy chatelaine, objects usually the preserve of grown women. Since children rarely garner elevated social status on their own merits, burials like these reflect a society in which entire families, even their youngest members, are thought to be special, and where prominent kin groups believe that it is sometimes crucial, for the maintenance or enhancement of their social standing, to provide even their youngest members with elaborate send-offs. So the appearance of costly child burials in sixth-century England discloses the development of the heritability of high status and the notion that it belonged not only to those who had earned or arrogated it, but to their offspring as well.

The sixth century's inegalitarian burials mirrored living inequalities. The wearing of well-crafted precious-metal jewellery by a privileged family's most prominent womenfolk was one of the many things in this period that came to broadcast and then reinforce social differences between neighbours. Triple strings of beads, which sometimes included amber from the Baltic, or brooches, which were embellished with garnets from India, were sported in the sixth century by an exclusive little club, women whose families and friends could tap into networks of trade and gift exchange that ranged across the whole of Europe. Similarly, a number of women wore immense, intricately patterned square-headed brooches. The most ostentatious of these measured more than 15 centimetres in length, and the humble could have spotted them from 100 metres away. And people could probably hear women with elaborate sets of rings, bars and keys dangling from their belts as they walked along. Showy female trappings were far from subtle, and they clearly distinguished the have-mores from the have-lesses.

Both the wearing of exotica and the burying of it came to be the standard modus operandi for privileged families in sixth-century eastern Britain, and this display formed part of a complex of practices deployed to underline their hierarchical claims. This performance played simultaneously to two very different audiences. On the one hand, the wearing of such finery signalled people's place in the world to others like themselves and revealed to their would-be equals that they participated in the same rarefied networks of friendship and exchange; it corroborated that they were the kinds of people who received gifts from well-connected men or had craftsmen working at their beck and call. This display of social distinction was actively deployed by some to concoct a new social identity, one that transcended household and hamlet and linked similarly resourced people across wide stretches of territory. The wearers of this finery, although living at some distance from one another, were coming to share costumes, tastes, funerary rites and social strategies, and this can only mean that new, self-conscious affinities were emerging based on social standing. The meeting of such people was probably occasional rather than constant, but given how much they were emulating one another, their encounters must have been of great importance. Simultaneously, such practices of fancy dress and fancy burial defined these people against all the rest. This was particularly true for the wilful destruction of wealth in burial, a practice which must often have been aimed at socially inferior neighbours rather than more distant social equals, since so many funerals in the sixth century took place in little local cemeteries, and were, therefore, rituals performed for exceptionally circumscribed audiences. Funerary displays were sometimes witnessed by small, socially mixed groups, more likely comprised of one's labouring neighbours than one's important associates residing a couple of days' journey away.

The people who had the wherewithal to acquire bronze girdle-hangers or garnet-inlaid brooches also began, in the sixth century, to reside in a new kind of settlement. One has been excavated at Cowdery's Down, near Basingstoke in Hampshire. Cowdery's Down was first laid out sometime in the middle of the sixth century. Across the whole of its hundred-year occupation the site was divided into two compounds, each with its own set of wattle-fenced buildings, and each half, perhaps, constituting the home of an extended household. There were also a number of structures outside the two enclosures, including a succession of major timber buildings, one of which the site's excavators have interpreted as a communal hall, used either for feasting or as the residence of whoever was in charge. Another building outside the wattle fences may have had a ritual function. It was very large – more than 12 metres long and 6 metres wide – and it was built next to a strange, circular pit in which the jaw of a boar and the carcass of a cow had been interred. Overall, the buildings on the site look high status. Certainly, they were bigger than any found at Mucking or hamlets like it dating to the previous century, and the use of timber at Cowdery's Down was profligate. Indeed, its builders must have controlled considerable labour for the felling of trees, the making of boards, and the hauling of raw materials. Cowdery's Down, especially in its later decades, was also more organized than places like Mucking, and planning clearly lay behind its various and increasingly elaborate rebuildings. Little evidence, though, has been found here for the messy business of food production – butchery, grain threshing and the like – so this may well have been a place to which people in the neighbourhood rendered butchered sheep, cattle carcasses and cereals processed nearer their own homes to their betters.

Sites like Cowdery's Down were made possible by a radical restructuring of the countryside and its settlements. For every grand place like Cowdery's Down, controlled by an exotica-wearing proprietor, there had to be a dozen or more ramshackle hamlets like Mucking, whose inhabitants were linked to it by a web of social obligations requiring them to render up food and labour services to the people who resided there. The laws of an English king named Ine, written in the last decade of the seventh century, give some indication of the kinds and amounts of tribute people living at places like Mucking were, perhaps, beginning to render to places like Cowdery's Down in the sixth century: 'ten vats of honey, three hundred loaves, twelve ambers of Welsh ale, thirty of clear ale, two full-grown cows or ten wethers, ten geese, twenty hens, ten cheeses, an amber of butter, five salmon, twenty pounds of fodder and one hundred eels.' A thoughtful study of sites like the one at Cowdery's Down in the context of their ancient landscapes allows us to see the dim outlines of a hierarchy of settlements developing – that is, grand places linked to humble ones – something absent in eastern Britain since the fall of Rome. High-status settlements, not only that discovered at Cowdery's Down, but that found at Yeavering in the Tweed Valley in Northumberland, are identifiable by the remains of imposing timber halls and odd ritual monuments; but such sites are also found in relatively close proximity to other, less grand places like Thirlings, a hamlet made up of craft workshops, storage sheds, animal enclosures and modest houses.

Cowdery's Down, abandoned sometime in the seventh century, lies on the boundaries of two early medieval estates, one of which is Basing, an early place name meaning 'the settlement of the people of Basa'. One wonders if a Basa ever resided here, and if some of Basa's people provided him with food and labour.

COMPETITIVE EMULATION AND THE
BIRTH OF REGIONAL IDENTITIES

The rise of elite identities in sixth-century Britain stimulated the formation of regional ones. As newly minted, high-status families began to stitch together broad social networks, they created face-to-face communities comprised of local grandees settled at some distance from one another. These people, who were beginning to live alike and bury alike, were also pioneering a more uniform material culture, which was disseminated among people like themselves through gift exchange, marriage and emulation. Indeed, judging from the spread of fairly homogeneous styles of brooches and metalwork decoration across whole regions, it looks as if Bede's Angles, Saxons and Jutes were now, at last, beginning to emerge.

It is in the costumes of sixth-century women that we can best see the beginnings of carefully articulated, geographically extensive regional identities. Kent is a case in point. Judging from their graves, women here (or at least women of means) were now dressing in belted skirts and short jackets, a costume that followed Frankish fashions more closely than anywhere else in Britain. Kentish women also deployed a wide range of Frankish-style clothes fasteners, including types rarely found elsewhere in Britain – garnet-set pins, for example, in the form of rosettes or little brooches fashioned in the shape of birds. Kentish women also deployed brooches in the same manner that Frankish women did, pinning them, for example, to their belts or using them to fasten their jackets. Ready-to-use cut-and-polished garnets, a mainstay of Frankish metalwork, were also ubiquitous in Kent. So, too, were linen clothes, in particular those made from tabby-woven linen, a simple weave of weft and warp, a standard feature of Frankish dress. Nor is it surprising, given the dominance of Frankish fashions here, that Kentish women's tastes in jewellery changed in lock-step with styles current in Francia.

In spite of their enthusiasm for things Frankish, however, Kentish women did more than simply dress themselves as Franks. They eschewed earrings, hairpins and gaiters, all important elements of female dress across the Channel, and they embraced accessories from other places. They were fond, for example, of small square-headed brooches and gold bracteates, that is, wafer-thin pendants ornamented with abstract beasts and faces: these were Scandinavian-inspired objects. And, although women in Kent wore and were buried with Frank-like objects, they were as often Kentish-made as Frankish imports and were, therefore, subtly crafted for insular tastes. Kentish women, then, were hardly perfect facsimiles of Frankish women, and they would have stood out as much in northern Francia as they did in East Anglia or Northumbria. Clearly, sixth-century women in eastern Kent deliberately selected from a range of Frankish goods, chose some over others, augmented them with a few accessories popular in Scandinavia, combined them with locally made crafts, and, out of this mélange, developed a regional costume all their own. By the middle of the sixth century wealthy women living in hamlets near Mill Hill, Finglesham and Canterbury were all dressing in similar ways, and their filiations to other important people in Kent would have been unmistakable.

At the same time that Kentish women were pioneering a regional costume, women living on either side of the River Humber and in Norfolk were doing the same. Here, women began to sew metal clasps on the ends of their sleeves and use them to hook their split cuffs together. Wrist-clasps, which survive, unlike cloth, because they are metal, provide evidence that women in the north were beginning to wear long-sleeved undergarments, something their counterparts in Kent did not do. The well-to-do in Scandinavia had long used wrist-clasps, but the particular form adopted in England came from western Norway. Both the sleeved dresses and the clasps themselves imply the coming of a new group of well-clad Norwegian women to northern England, doubtless in the company of Norwegian men, and that these newcomers were the kind of people that others wished to emulate. The adoption of wrist-clasps began *c.* 475, and the fashion spread across the north and east of England with astonishing rapidity: in perhaps as little as a single generation they became a standard accessory for well-heeled women in Yorkshire, Lincolnshire and Norfolk. As a result, by the early sixth century, it looks as if the wearing of a Norwegian-like costume signalled affiliation to other similarly dressed people in the region. The 'wrist-clasp habit' was taken up by women from striving families, regardless of where their grandparents had been born, and it was widely adopted in areas that Bede would later describe as 'Anglian'. The history of wrist-clasps hints that 'Anglian' material culture, including styles of dress, did not date from the first century of migration nor did it stem from the putative homeland of the Angles, but rather developed in England itself three or four generations after the *adventus* began.

Thus it seems that standard regional styles of dress began to appear in the very late fifth or early sixth century and were first deployed as social markers. Originally, the wearing of garnet-radiate brooches in Kent or silvered wrist-clasps in Norfolk signalled their wearers' and their kin's affiliations with other families who had access to similar luxuries. With several generations of intermarriage and gift exchange, and through the tireless trafficking of itinerant craftsmen and pedlars, these styles of dress were disseminated, improved upon, and copied across wide swaths of eastern Britain. As a result, by the middle of the sixth century, when members of elite households encountered individuals who were their social equals and who hailed from the same region, they found people dressed like themselves. Costumes were doubtless only one of many shared practices: prosperous families within broad regions could well have sung common songs, participated in similar ritual observances or subscribed to the same myths and legends.

Regions where such outward signs of homogeneity developed had advantages over areas where they did not. Solidarities and alliances fostered conformity, and behind them lay close-knit networks of prominent families. When members of distinguished households encountered top families from other regions, their differences could be underscored. Thus these identities could be manipulated, with similarities between peoples enhanced or differences purposefully exaggerated.

Although there can be little doubt that regional costumes sprang up first among socially prominent families, it is also clear that women from lesser households sometimes emulated the sartorial habits of their social betters. There is interesting evidence suggesting that individuals and families without the requisite connections or economic resources for fancy jewellery sometimes did what they could to outfit themselves in similar costumes. Women from families successful in their pursuit of high social status and surpluses often wore long, elegant girdle-hangers on their belts alongside sieves and imported crystal balls suspended from slings. But some women from families on the wrong side of emerging social hierarchies copied these fashions as best they could. Without the wherewithal for bronze or craftsmen, some, judging by their graves, seem to have scrounged around derelict Roman sites looking for large iron spoons. When found, their handles would be knocked off, and the bowls hung on women's belts in imitation of the imported sieves. Old Roman keys and the hardware from ancient harnesses were also looted and suspended from poorer women's girdles, and oak apples were used in place of imported crystal balls. Here, we can see the seductive tug of high-status material culture, and the attempt by some women, perhaps those from some striving, middle rank, to use simulated high-status objects and counterfeit fashions to approximate the dress of their social betters.

What made such emulation possible, perhaps even socially worthwhile, was the fact that English elites, despite their increasing advantages, lived in close proximity to everyone else, and they were still far from forming a completely exclusive, watertight caste. This made them different from the Romano-British rich of the early fourth century, who had managed to establish a vast social distance between themselves and everyone else, successfully cordoning themselves off through the use of bailiffs, state tax collectors and hundred-room villas. One of the consequences of the remoteness of this earlier elite, however, was that few heard their hypercorrect Latin or witnessed their elegant dinner-parties. Elite families in the first half of the sixth century, on the other hand, were more intimate with their social inferiors. As members of the new would-be elite were busy carving out novel social identities for themselves marked by dress, burial, language or cult, their proximity allowed others to study and ape them. People in the neighbourhood who admired or envied them could, after a fashion, learn their manners of speech or copy their dress. So through emulation the use of regionally specific material culture and social practices extended downwards, broadening participation in newly forming regional identities.

One of the occasions on which the high and the low are likely to have met in this period was during feasting, a social practice necessitated by the constraints of the early medieval economy. Cattle in the early Middle Ages were smaller than their modern descendants, and a good-sized cow would have only weighed something on the order of 450 kilograms. Still, when slaughtered, skinned and butchered it provided an intimidating amount of meat, perhaps as much as 200 kilograms. Without food markets, refrigeration or bulk salt trade, it would have been impossible for a single household to sell, preserve or consume so much flesh. The slaughter of a cow therefore not only provided the pretext for, but the necessity of, communal feasting, an event that would have included people from widely different social circles. Bede describes one such occasion in his story of the seventh-century poet Cædmon. Cædmon was the servant of an estate manager, or reeve, who was, in turn, the servant of an abbess; so Cædmon hardly sat at the pinnacle of local society. Indeed, according to Bede, he often slept in the barn with the cattle. Cædmon, then, was an undistinguished man. Nonetheless, he regularly attended feasts, and like all who came he was expected to sing for the crowd and play the harp. During these occasions he may not have been served the choicest cuts of beef: in early Ireland we know that the distribution of meat was hierarchical, and that lower-status members of the community were fed the meat from legs or heads, while more important men ate choicer cuts. But regardless of what Cædmon ate on these occasions, we can see that communal feasting included more than a great man and his important retainers. At moments like these, humble people could observe their betters at close range and learn their manners, their language and their dress. Such social proximity helped transform local, elite practices into regional ones.

Distinct regional cultures organized around developing social hierarchies did not, however, evolve at the same pace across all of eastern Britain. Regional costumes, for example, were slow to emerge in some places. Sixth-century Cambridgeshire is a case in point. The burials excavated at Edix Hill suggest that women living here in the first half of the sixth century were wearing four fairly distinct costumes, and that they continued to do so until 560 or 570, at which point female dress suddenly became more homogeneous. Only generations after this development in Kent and Northumbria did female dress in Cambridgeshire become regionalized. This, in turn, suggests that larger identities in Cambridgeshire were slow to evolve, perhaps helping to explain why no early kingdom developed here.

Regional identities, moreover, could take generations to sort out, and members of isolated farming communities would adopt one style of dress and then another, in part because of shifting trade patterns, but also because those they were emulating changed over the generations, as elites formed and as power shifted among them. In the first half of the sixth century, for example, women living near the River Avon dressed more like people settled to the east, but sometime mid-century their tastes, their access to metalwork or their cultural affinities changed, and they began to dress more like women living in the Upper Thames Valley. Even regions that showed early, relatively cohesive sets of material culture, and which must have been bound together by networks of kinship and exchange, sometimes came apart. The River Humber, for example, formed an important boundary in Bede's day, but a century before his birth it looks as if the lands on either side of the river's estuary were inhabited by people who had much in common. Indeed, before the eighth century no surviving text distinguished between Northumbrians and Southumbrians; instead, the people living on either side of the estuary were sometimes referred to as the *Humbrenses*, so perhaps the peoples of east Yorkshire and northern Lincolnshire shared the beginnings of an early, but ill-fated regional identity.

LIFE IN THE WEST

In western Britain, unlike eastern Britain, social differentiation survived Rome's fall, and it continued in the fifth century and beyond to shape communities like those at Wroxeter and Cadbury Congresbury. Proof of hierarchy and inequality, however, is different here than in the eastern half of Britain, because significant components of late antique culture – Christianity, literacy, Latinity, even personal names – lingered in the west, and this continuity played a fundamental role in the formation of our evidence. The perseverance of the late Roman practice of unaccompanied inhumation throughout Wales and the West Country, for example, robs us of the metalwork jewellery that is our principal source of information for fifth- and sixth-century eastern Britain. Although the old Roman cemetery just outside the east gate of the ancient *civitas* capital of *Venta Silurum* (the modern-day Caerwent, in Monmouthshire) has an extraordinary run of burials dating from the fourth or early fifth century to the tenth, none includes the kinds of grave goods found in early East Anglian or Kentish burials, so their contents cannot be used to calibrate social differences between contemporaries. Similarly, the thousand or so graves excavated at Llandough, in Glamorgan, probably date to this same long period. They lay in the shadow of a church dedicated to St Dochdwy, an elusive fifth-century figure whose memory lives on in the name of Llandough itself, which means 'the enclosure of Dochdwy'. As at Caerwent, the dead here were placed in the ground without weapons or jewellery (with the exception of two people who wore knives on their belts), so we cannot begin to speculate if some, in life, had been wealthier or more socially prominent than others. Many of the Llandough graves, however, like early graves elsewhere in Wales, contained small, white quartz stones, which mourners may have placed there, inspired by words found in Revelation 2: 17: 'To him that overcometh will I give to eat of the hidden manna, and will give him a white stone, and in the stone a new name written, which no man knoweth, saving he that receiveth it.' The burials at Llandough, then, like those outside of Caerwent, testify to perhaps twenty generations of broadly similar mortuary rites, to a Christianity sustained in spite of Roman Britain's fall, and to the enduring efficacy of holy places. But these cemeteries tell us little about social hierarchies or economic inequalities.

Christianity and steadfast Roman traditions, however, did more than deny us precious grave goods: they ensured that we have texts. We know both from a sixth-century harangue, *The Ruin of Britain*, written by the British churchman Gildas, and from the seventh-century traditions preserved in the *Life of St Samson*, that there were people in western

Britain who, because of their birth, their occupations or their kindred, were better than other people. Gildas, for example, tells us that there were kings in Britain, and he decried them for 'exalting to the stars ... their military companions'. The stories which make up the poem Y Gododdin were first sung in the north of Britain in the seventh century, and they recount how people like these marshalled material culture to mark their superiority. In the poem we read descriptions of the accoutrements of power – shields with polychrome bosses and gold-filigreed decorations, horses 'the colour of swans', marten-pelt coats and amber jewellery. We hear of the 'bejewelled breasts' of kings and the wearing of 'ornaments of rank', of men riding to battle with gold torques around their necks and gleaming coats of mail. We are told of great men's slaves and personal poets, and of their drinking wine from fine glass vessels. Thus it is clear that here, as in eastern Britain, elites in the sixth century dressed and lived in particular ways, had access to rare, even exotic goods, and participated in highly restricted social practices – organized warfare, the patronage of bards, the drinking of wine – that were limited to the special few.

Many of the settlements in which people like Gildas's kings and Y Gododdin's warriors lived, sat, as Cadbury Congresbury did, atop ancient hillforts or on rocky promontories. A number have been identified in Wales: Dinas Powys and Hen Gastell in Glamorgan, Coygan Camp in Carmarthenshire, Degannwy and Dinas Emrys in Caernarfonshire, Dinorben in Denbighshire, and Carew Castle and Gateholm in Pembrokeshire. Each of these sites has produced a range of artefacts that archaeologists now see as evidence for a high-status settlement, in particular ceramics and glass from the Mediterranean or Francia and the remnants of precious-metal smithing. Sites like these were usually, but not always, fortified. Longley Bank in Dyfed, for example, was not; nonetheless, smiths here crafted brooches from silver, copper and bronze, and diners sometimes ate their meals on imported ceramics, including tableware that had come all the way from Asia Minor. A few of these sites have produced evidence of fourth-century occupation; others have not.

There is a possibility that some of the people who controlled places like these, in the fifth and sixth centuries, were descended from distinguished Romano-British families. There is some indication that although villa houses had long been abandoned by the sixth century, a few of the great estates surrounding them were still intact. The earliest documented gifts of land to the Church at Llandaff, for example, which date to the second half of the sixth century, are measured in *unciae*, a Roman unit of about 200 hectares. Several of the properties given were as many as three or four *unciae*, that is, 600 to 800 hectares, monstrous blocks of land that may well have their origins in late antiquity. A string of early donations, moreover, ranged along the Roman road running between Abergavenny and Kenchester, further suggesting that these estates may have been organized during the period when the road served as a major artery for the Roman state.

There is also evidence that two of the sixth century's emerging kingdoms owed something to late antique institutions. The kingdom of Gwent, for example, took its name from the ancient *civitas* capital *Venta Silurum*. The kingdom was up and running by the turn of the sixth century, because St Samson of Dol, a man at the peak of his career in the third quarter of the sixth century, had a grandfather who had served the 'king of *Ventia*'. The persistence of the name *Venta* is suggestive, and it may be that those who wielded power over at least some of the former town's hinterland in the century after Rome's collapse had grandfathers who served as magistrates during the fourth century and would have grandsons who became kings in the sixth. To the north-west there were kings in Ergyng. This polity took its name from the Roman small town *Ariconium* (Weston-under-Penyard, Herefordshire). Indeed, a memory of the kingdom is still fossilized in the name Archenfield. The naming of these early medieval polities after Roman towns, the presence of oversized estates and the durability of Roman measurements suggest that people with power here cared about the Roman past and perhaps owed the very conception of the territories they ruled and the lands they controlled to Roman administrative traditions. Still, vital components of Roman political culture disappeared in this period. No British ruler minted coins. None gave their followers the belt-sets and crossbow brooches that had been the insignia of officialdom in the late Roman world.

Some people in western Britain during this period also memorialized their notable dead with inscriptions carved on standing stones. This epigraphical habit in part stems from a continuation of the late fourth-century, empire-wide practice of Christian commemoration, a habit that endured and spread in the fifth, sixth and seventh centuries in north-western and south-western Wales, the Isle of Man, southern Scotland

and south-western England. Dozens of these stones point to the perpetuation of *romanitas*. Many are inscribed, for example, not in the hypercorrect language of classical literature, but rather the vulgar Latin of everyday, late Roman usage, proof that some households in western Britain had not just learned their Latin from books, but continued, after Rome's collapse, to speak it. The choice of vocabulary also gives one pause. One late sixth-century inscription praised a man because he was 'an example to all his fellow citizens'. Another was erected in honour of a man who was a 'citizen of Gwynedd and cousin of Maglos the Magistrate'. Here, then, is evidence that, in spite of imperial collapse, Roman notions of citizenship and public office still had some currency in western Britain, and were occasionally deployed to impart glory on the people they were used to describe. One fifth-century inscription from Whithorn, in Dumfries and Galloway, memorializing a man with the telling name Latinus, begins with the words 'we praise Thee, Lord'. Both the stone's Christianity and its Latinity underscored the *romanitas* of the dead man and its commissioner. A host of fifth- and sixth-century inscriptions also honoured people who bore Roman names: Tribunus, Aeternus, Paterninus, Florentius, and the like. One – Paulinus Marinus – even had a Roman-style *nomen* and *cognomen*.

The patrons of monuments like these were adherents of the religion of the later empire. A few carried in their heads at least some Roman political vocabulary. They had kinsmen with Roman personal names, and some spoke Latin. A handful could probably even read, although a famous North African inscription – 'here lies the body of a boy, put name here' – reminds us that not all those who commissioned or carved such memorials were literate. Graffiti – the names of three otherwise unknown individuals called Paternus, Coliavus and Artogno – written on a slate at Tintagel sometime before 550, and probably the work of two or three of these men, suggests, though, that there were still laymen in Britain who could write their own names and knew their Latin declensions. Some in sixth-century western Britain, moreover, could not only read and write but had mastered a very high degree of Latinity. The Latin of Gildas's *The Ruin of Britain*, for example, unlike the Latin of inscribed stones, is book-learned, and it testifies that it was still possible in early sixth-century western Britain for a man to receive a good, late Roman education in grammar and rhetoric. This is because Gildas deployed the same baroque late antique style embraced by fifth-century *literati* like Sidonius Apollinaris, a skill that required an intensive, Roman-style education and a good library. Gildas himself read widely. He had an intimate familiarity with the work of the important Church Father St Jerome, the hagiography of the Gallo-Roman bishop Sulpicius Severus, and the late antique Christian historians Rufinus and Orosius, as well as the monastic innovator John Cassian. But he also knew the classical-period poet Virgil, and there are distant echoes throughout his work of Virgil's *Aeneid*.

What we have evidence for in the western half of Britain, especially in Wales, is a few early kingdoms which took their names from important Roman towns, the continued use of some Roman political vocabulary, the possible survival of a handful of very large estates, communities of Latin-speakers and Latin-readers, a few high-status settlements and an elite who deployed a standard set of material culture to mark their elevated social status. It is not clear how each of these things stood in relation to the others, but it is at least possible that a few descendants of local Romano-British gentlemen emerged from the fifth century still holding family estates, still speaking Latin and still in control of administrative districts that bore some relationship to Roman ones. But they were now living in non-Roman, high-status sites, using new forms of material culture and participating in novel rituals of social display.

Not all of those living and prospering in western Britain, however, wished to claim Roman antecedents, and others had no historical grounds to do so. Alongside the descendants of Romano-British gentlemen were the grandchildren of barely Romanized British peasants, and people whose ancestors had been imperial clients living outside the bounds of the empire. There were also Irish settlers. All these people lived in a broad cultural zone stretching from the tip of Cornwall up through western Scotland, and they were a kind of mirror image of the variegated populations and communities coming together in the eastern half of Britain. In western Britain, however, newcomers had come down from Scotland or had crossed the Irish Sea, and rather than speaking a Germanic language, they spoke the ancestor of Gaelic. So it looks as if western Britain, like eastern Britain, was still broadly British, but that there was enough immigration to be transformative. Certainly, by the end of the sixth century it was home to a mixed population.

The names of some early kingdoms – *Dumnonia* (still preserved in the name Devon), *Demetia* (or the kingdom of Dyfed) and *Gododdin* (in Lothian) – have their origins in British tribal names that pre-date Roman colonization. One fifth-century inscription from Gwynedd, moreover, commemorates a man described as 'an Ordovician', yet another pre-Roman Iron Age tribal group settled in north-central Wales. It seems that some people in the sixth century were still asserting these identities. Groups who had lived on the far side of Hadrian's Wall in the third century may have also moved into the former Roman provinces. A group of northern Britons from south-eastern Scotland, for example, known collectively as the Votadini, may have settled in Gwynedd in the generation on either side of 400. A ninth-century historian believed this to be true, and there is some slight evidence to back his claim. For one thing, British heroes from the far north were celebrated in seventh-century Welsh poetry, and this may be because northern Britons had brought these tales with them into Wales. Beyond this, an early cemetery excavated at Tandderwen, in Clwyd, was bounded by a square-ditched enclosure, a practice more common in early Scotland, and one that might have been introduced into Wales by northern British newcomers.

There was also a substantial Irish migration up and down Britain's western seaboard, which paralleled Germanic settlement in the east. Large numbers of Irish place names are found on the south-western peninsula of Wales and in Anglesey. As in eastern Britain, these place names cannot be used to argue wholesale population displacement, but they do point to the homeland and language of incoming settlers. A series of inscribed stones also adds to our knowledge of these people. Besides Latin-language inscriptions, many fifth- and sixth-century stones bear Irish-language inscriptions, written in ogham, a script which had been deployed by Irish elites in southern Ireland since the fourth century to memorialize their dead and make claims to land. The appearance of similar inscriptions in fifth- and sixth-century western Britain suggests that men from Ireland's ogham-inscribing classes had become important players in parts of Britain. Other stones of the period are bilingual, deploying both Latin and Irish. Ogham and/or bilingual inscriptions and Irish place names are thickest on the ground in northern Pembrokeshire, but they are also quite common in central Pembrokeshire, Cardiganshire, Devon and Cornwall. There is also a small concentration in Brycheniog, and a handful in northern Wales. Like place names, they mark areas in which the Irish were inserting themselves.

Like the Latin inscriptions, the ogham and bilingual stones tell us things worth knowing about the names and pretensions of western Britain's new, memorializing elites. First and foremost, the appearance of ogham inscriptions witnesses the arrival of elite Irishmen, who were making claims to land. These inscriptions, however, also point towards communities and households which created solidarities based on similar levels of wealth and power rather than ancestry or language. Seen at the highest levels, Vortipor, Gildas's adulterous, sin-stained 'tyrant of the Demetae', was perhaps memorialized both in Latin and in Irish on a stone carved 'in memory of Vortipor Protector'. Why would the followers of a man who had appropriated a Roman title once used by the head of the praetorian guard, who lived in a Christian milieu, who bore a British name, and who led a group of people who called themselves after a pre-Roman Iron Age British tribe, have included an ogham inscription on his memorial, unless some of the important people around him were Irish-speakers? Another pair of inscriptions allows us to see these changes occurring over time. The first probably dates to the second half of the fifth century, and it was carved in honour of a certain 'Clutorigus son of Paulinus Marinus from Latium'. The second, later inscription, found a dozen kilometres away, commemorates 'Maglicunas son of Clutorigus'. It seems that these two stones record the names of a grandfather (Paulinus Marinus), a father (Clutorigus) and a son (Maglicunas). The language of the first stone is Latin, but the second memorial is bilingual and includes a Hibernicized version of Maglicunas's name. Thus we have a grandfather with a very Roman *nomen* and *cognomen*, who may have been born in Latium in Italy. His son Clutorigus was known by a British name, and his grandson spent enough time in the company of Irishmen that it was deemed appropriate, when he died, to commemorate him both in Latin and in Irish. We seem to be moving inexorably from a more or less Roman world to a world of bilingual or even trilingual households, places where formerly Romanized elites and Irishmen cooperated and made common cause to gain or solidify control over bits of territory.

Such miscegenation is often witnessed in the inscriptions of western Britain. The one reading 'Cantiorix lies here, citizen of Gwynedd and cousin of Maglos the Magistrate' associates Roman titles, concepts and language with Irish personal names. Even sites with clear Romano-British cultural affinities and a long way from the Irish Sea seem to have hosted a few Irishmen. Someone at Wroxeter, in landlocked Shropshire, for example, had a stone inscribed in the late fifth century in honour of the memory of an Irishman named Cunorix Macus Maqui Coline. The artisan who inscribed the stone apparently knew no Irish, but he did his best, when confronted with this outlandish name – which means something like 'Hound-king son of the holly' – to fashion it into Latin capitals. In any case, the mix of languages, of names and of titles paints the picture of a world where members of the commemorating classes operated in some sort of bilingual or trilingual milieu, in mixed communities, with mixed cultural and, indeed, genetic legacies. This evidence points not so much towards watertight ethnic groups, spearheaded by war bands, seeking to take land from people speaking different languages, as towards mixed groups of elites, whose great-grandparents had lived in quite different worlds, but who now, in post-Roman Britain, intermarried and colluded with one another in their bid to fill the power vacuum left by Rome.

4

Elites, Kingdoms and a Brand-New Past: The Later Sixth and Seventh Centuries

As we have seen, people in the early Middle Ages often went to their graves as fair approximations of their living selves. Dead men, for example, were not buried in female clothing, and women were almost never placed in the ground with weapons, so living identities rooted in gender seem to have survived death and followed individuals to the grave. Similarly, hard-luck families with bare barns and empty bellies did not have the wherewithal to provide their dead with rare or precious-metal objects, so it seems unlikely that those buried with amethyst beads or garnet brooches were poor people, posed in death as prosperous ones. Still, we must always remember that the dead did not bury themselves, and that they were represented in their graves as particular kinds of social beings by the friends and families who oversaw their funerals. Some deaths, moreover, are more disruptive than others. The demise of a charismatic head of household or a wife who had yet to produce an heir could both imperil a family's place in the world and threaten the social order in a score of neighbouring hamlets. Under these circumstances, well-heeled survivors must have sometimes felt obliged to make excessive claims about the departed in order to put forth hyperbolic assertions about themselves. As a result, particularly unsettling deaths could occasion profligate outlays on grave goods and funerals, and they may stand behind some of the period's richest burials. Similarly, if an important member of an esteemed family had recently received an extravagant funeral, both admirers and adversaries may have felt obliged to treat their own dead in similar fashion. Thus in seventh-century Derbyshire elaborate, treasure-filled barrow burials became ubiquitous, and it is hard to believe that the popularity of this practice was not spurred on by some combination of faithful emulation and anxious competition. Over the course of the later sixth and seventh centuries, it looks as if conspicuous, even ruinously elaborate burials grew increasingly irresistible to people of means, because elite households at just this time were hoping to improve their positions in local society by out-competing rivals, by inveigling followers and by ensuring that the last generation's gains were inherited by the next.

In the later sixth and seventh centuries, both with the help of extravagant burials and a series of other strategies, some families managed both to territorialize their authority and to make it heritable. In this period, too, the social distance so carefully cultivated by high-ranking members of local communities became a permanent feature of English society, and aristocratic social identity came to be bound up in warrior identity. Finally, and perhaps most importantly, it is in this period that kings and kingdoms finally emerged in the English-speaking regions of Britain.

BUILDING A USABLE PAST

One of the pervasive features of English society from the later sixth century was its leading families' obsession with the past and their aggressive and thoroughgoing efforts to reimagine it. As we have seen, there is little fifth-century evidence from the eastern half of Britain for elite families or high-status settlements, and it seems that most of those in the later sixth century who were in a position to live large and bury rich, like parvenus everywhere, worked hard to shore up their novel privileges by claiming (and doubtless believing) that they had always had them. To assert, as elite families now seemed to be doing, that their control over other people's labour and surpluses was legitimate, they put forth claims that social differentiation was traditional; and, because inequalities had been part of the world since time out of mind, their special rights were natural and heritable. This ideology of the permanence of privilege manifested itself during this period in the creation of origin legends and their epic retellings, in genealogical memories, in burial fashions, in the co-opting of ritual landscapes and in the embracing of a kind of barbarizing, heroicizing, high-status material culture. A culture-wide reconfiguration of the past along all these fronts during the later sixth and the seventh centuries helped create a brand-new present founded on ideas about the past which, although factually incorrect, were eminently usable.

Our clearest view of this remaking of the past comes, unsurprisingly, from texts. Written culture, however, was not introduced into England until the turn of the seventh century, so none of the texts preserving tales of conquest and colonization date to the period of settlement. The Anglo-Saxon Chronicle's retrospective annals for the *adventus*, for example, were only compiled in the later ninth century. As they stand, they consist of a dozen stripped-down little tales of small-scale invasions led by Germanic war leaders, all of whom were victorious against the British, established kingdoms and founded dynasties. The Chronicle tells us that in 495

> two chieftains, Cerdic and his son Cynric, came with five ships to Britain at the place which is called *Cerdicesora*, and they fought against the Britons on the same day.
>
> 501. In this year Port and his two sons Bieda and Mægla came to Britain with two ships at the place which is called Portsmouth, and there they killed a British man of very high rank . . .
>
> 514. In this year the West Saxons came into Britain with three ships at the place which is called *Cerdicesora*, and Stuf and Wihtgar [the alleged founders of the dynasty established on the Isle of Wight] fought against the Britons and put them to flight.
>
> 519. In this year Cerdic and Cynric succeeded to the [West Saxon] kingdom . . .

In each of these annals, as is so often the case with the Chronicle and other early English sources, a pair or triad of named warriors sails to Britain in two or three or five ships. Founding pairs are endlessly invoked in early accounts of all sorts of peoples, including the Romans' own Romulus and Remus, and one suspects that what we are reading here are tales of archetypal legendary heroes rather than flesh-and-blood historical figures. Beyond their highly conventionalized appearances, a number of the Chronicle's early conquerors also played starring roles in 'just so' stories revolving around how particular places got their names. Portsmouth, according to the Chronicle, took its name from Port, and the Isle of Wight was named for Wihtgar. In actual fact, both place names originated in the Roman period, so Port and Wihtgar look like pure inventions, back-formations slipped into the dynastic rememberings of leading men in later centuries as proof that their families' founders were so important that their names were fossilized in the very landscape. Cerdic, moreover, one of the two dynastic founders appearing above in the annals for 519, bears a British personal name, a highly unlikely state of affairs for a man allegedly born in Saxony. Other English conquerors are equally improbable. Hengist and Horsa, the putative founders of the Kentish royal dynasty, whose adventures are lovingly detailed in Bede's history and lay at the heart of an elaborate story related by the author of the ninth-century *Historia Brittonum*, or *History of the Britons*, have names that mean 'stallion' and 'horse', and are thus more likely to be figures of myth than of history. So too is Oisc, sometimes Hengist's son, sometimes his grandson, whose name means 'god'.

The Chronicle's epic reimagining of Britain's settlement by Germanic war leaders seems to reflect a series of ideologically charged traditions beginning to develop in the second half of the sixth century in the households of a score of men who were coming, at just this time, to see themselves as the heads of important local dynasties and as rulers who justly commanded the surpluses and loyalty of others. Although the Anglo-Saxon Chronicle's stories were written down in the late ninth century, elaborate royal genealogies were being committed to parchment in the later eighth century, and they preserve the names of many of the Chronicle's legendary heroes. Thus stories were circulating about them at least a century before the making of the Chronicle. Careful analysis of the earliest set of genealogies, a compilation known as the 'Anglian Collection', makes clear that beyond a few generations the pedigrees recorded were polite fictions governed by the exigencies of eighth-century politics. Indeed, the earliest genuine historical figures recorded in them for kingdoms like East Anglia and Mercia date to the last quarter of the sixth century, and this may suggest that royal dynasties were indeed beginning to emerge at just this time. Bede, whose own history predates the 'Anglian Collection' by a few decades, also details the descent of living kings, so royal pedigrees were clearly cultivated in his day. Bede, moreover, was as interested as the Anglo-Saxon Chronicle in inscribing dynastic founders onto the landscape, writing, for example, that the spot where Horsa died was still marked with 'a monument distinguished by his name'. The Chronicle's association of landscape features with royal pedigrees had a long pedigree of its own. Finally, some of the assertions made by both Bede and the genealogies smack of pre-Christian and, therefore, pre-seventh-century origins. The god Woden is the originating ancestor of choice in most of the genealogies, something not likely to have been invented out of nothing in a Christian milieu. Another, slightly later genealogical collection relates that the kings of the East Saxons traced their origins back to a relatively obscure Old Saxon god called Seaxnot, a flourish more likely dating to the pagan than the Christian period.

Given the different stories swirling around Hengist and Horsa, the equine founders of the Kentish royal dynasty, in a variety of eighth- and ninth-century sources, including legends circulating among the British, it seems that some of these putative founders were characters with lives of their own in cycles of heroic tales popular in aristocratic households. There is also some evidence that early versions of tales preserved in *Beowulf* were known. The author of one eighth-century saint's life, for example, claimed that the kings of Mercia sprang from the same line as some of the Danish heroes of that poem, and it looks as if East Anglian kings were making similar assertions. Such tales of conquest and consolidation, and of kings and the warriors who followed them, valorized elites and certainly made more interesting listening than stories of a great-grandfather's canny stockmanship or his mean-spirited exploitation of luckless neighbours. What later texts and their prehistories suggest is that by 600 some households fancied that their ancestors had arrived in England as war leaders and that they had sprung from the gods. In short, the emerging party line was that soon after their arrival, these households' founders won many of the rights and privileges now enjoyed by their descendants.

Leading families exaggerated the longevity of their dynasties and legitimized their control over resources in other ways as well, in particular through innovative burial rites. One common and curious way living families made claims about their ancestors was through the reuse of ancient monuments as burial sites. In this, paramount households were taking advantage of a practice long embraced by other social groups. It was not uncommon, for example, in the later fifth and sixth centuries for communities without much social hierarchy to associate their dead with monuments not of their own making. The early medieval landscape was thick with stone circles and henges, long and circular barrows, Roman roads, abandoned towns and deserted villas. In the two centuries after Rome's collapse an extraordinary range of people laid claim to such sites by burying their dead in close proximity to them. This impulse was hardly novel: the living had reused ancient monuments in Britain for a thousand years. In the Bronze Age the builders of burial mounds and ritual monuments modified, emended and built around Neolithic sites; in western Scotland, people in the Iron Age visited, reused and transformed Neolithic tombs; and in Wales and the Peak District Bronze Age funerary monuments were selected for burials during the Roman period. Within a century of Rome's fall, farming communities across Britain were, in their turn, digging their cemeteries in and around Bronze Age barrows. It seems likely, given the commonplace of reuse, that the practice was deliberate rather than coincidental, and that the appropriation of ancient monuments for cemeteries was one of the many strategies communities adopted to strengthen their rights to the lands they farmed. By holding their funerals and burying their dead in the shadows of ancient barrows, many groups seemed to be moving to co-opt the past, in order to claim some sort of kinship with the original builders of mounds and to assert that families of the recent dead had tilled nearby fields since time immemorial.

Barrows continued to be used for burial in the later sixth, seventh and even eighth centuries, but some families now concocted novel funerary rites focused on them to enhance their own – rather than their communities' – status and legitimacy, an action undertaken in much the same spirit as aristocratic reworkings of the story of the *adventus*. Some of these people used Bronze Age barrows, but others chose to build new mounds that mimicked the older monuments in size and shape. At the outsized cremation cemetery at Spong Hill, in Norfolk, for example, some years after the foundation of the cemetery, a small group – no more than one or two households – began to inhume its dead at the northernmost edge of the urn field. Two of Spong Hill's earliest inhumations were centred within a pair of brand-new, purpose-built barrows surrounded by ring ditches. Each body lay in a large, labour-squandering chamber made from turf and timber. Something like fifty-five men, women and children were then buried around the two barrows. These inhumations represent a single phase in the history of the cemetery, lasting, perhaps, a couple of generations. Cremation continued at Spong Hill during this period and indeed after the inhumers had either abandoned the cemetery and had begun to bury elsewhere or had given up their anomalous rites (and, perhaps, their pretensions) and returned to cremation. Spong Hill's inhumers were precocious, building barrows as they did in the sixth century. In the seventh century, however, particularly in Kent, new barrows were being put up at the edges of many established cemeteries – some with ancient barrows and others without – and they were constructed again and again to underscore the fact that important individuals and their followers were different from *hoi polloi*.

Elsewhere, again especially in the seventh century, high-status households sometimes co-opted more distant, isolated barrows, especially those found on ridges and hilltops, to anchor burial plots used exclusively by their own households, households that now chose to bury far from the men and women whose labour must have supported them. At Wigber Low, in Derbyshire, for example, an early Bronze Age cairn, originally built as an excarnation platform for exposing the dead to scavenging animals and the elements, was transformed in the seventh century into a small family cemetery. Its name means 'Wicga's burial barrow'. In all, seven people were buried there. Two were children, three were late adolescents and the remaining two adults. All had grave goods, and altogether the site's excavators found an impressive little corpus of objects placed in the ground, including two beaver-tooth pendants set in gold, a sword, a purse and a side of beef.

Other barrows were more exclusive still, and they were used to designate the graves of lone individuals buried far even from their own close kin. The monuments chosen for isolated graves often rose up on the skyline and sat at the edges of emerging territories. A Bronze Age barrow on Swallowcliffe Down, in Wiltshire, for example, known as *Posses Hlæwe*, or 'Poss's burial mound', was one such site. The barrow sat high on the downs, and could be seen for many kilometres by those who passed through the neighbourhood on ancient trackways. Later the barrow would mark the boundary of an estate. It was opened up sometime in the seventh century and its original Bronze Age interment was replaced with the body of a young, well-dressed woman. She lay in the barrow on an elaborate wooden bed, surrounded by a stunning collection of objects – iron- and bronze-bound buckets, a small wooden casket filled with precious possessions, a pair of green, blown-glass palm cups, and a fancy pouch adorned with a large, intricately worked copper-alloy disc embellished with gold and silver foil. After her grave was sealed the ancient barrow was then remodelled. In this way the dead woman's survivors not only annexed an old, highly visible landmark, but outdid the barrow's original creators by reshaping the old mound and changing the landscape.

Other impresarios of isolated burials built brand-new barrows. At Benty Grange, in Derbyshire, for example, in one of the richest graves ever found in England, a dead man lay with his treasure under a large, purpose-built barrow. So too did the man interred at Lowbury Hill, in Berkshire: his followers built their leaders' funerary mound at the entrance of the ruins of a Romano-Celtic temple. These and the many other barrows thrown up from scratch during the period were enormously ambitious creations, and they witness the capacity of a small number of households to marshal the labour of their dependants to monumentalize their own power.

These isolated barrow burials explicitly promoted the connection between power and territory. This is because elite families apparently used barrow burials to signal the extent or boundaries of the territories they claimed. In Wessex and the Upper Thames Valley alone, eleven reused barrows have been identified, all of which lay on the boundaries of later administrative districts known as hundreds or on later estate boundaries or 'natural frontiers', and all were visible from a distance or from some major trackway. It seems likely, therefore, that the mortuary rituals surrounding such burials were connected in crucial ways to the defining of elite families' spheres of influence, helping those who had scrambled to the top of regional society to map out on the ground the lands and communities that were theirs.

Barrow burials fit neatly into the project of the genealogies and the origin myths. Some, for example, may preserve the names of the people whose bodies lay beneath them – places like Taplow, or 'Tæppa's *hlaw*', and Offlow, or 'Offa's *hlaw*', *hlaw* being the Old English word for 'barrow'. Barrow burials not only monumentalized individuals' and their households' power, but also inscribed the landscape with the names of dynastic progenitors. Barrow burials seem, therefore, to be part of the same genealogical discourse found in stories like the naming of Portsmouth. Both the 'just so' stories and the barrows were as much about the dynastic ambitions of the present as about past ancestors, and the purpose of both in the end was legitimist, a move that historians sometimes describe as 'retrospective validation'. Barrows, however, unlike genealogies and epics, broadcast assertions of dynastic longevity, rights over the labour of others and claims to territory to very wide audiences.

They spoke not just to like-minded people within elite households, but to all those moving through the landscape.

It was not just the barrows, though, but the extravagant, archaizing funerals that took place around them that created a legitimizing past. A number of long-standing English mortuary traditions were in steep decline by the beginning of the seventh century. Cremation, for example, long a dominant death rite in many parts of eastern Britain, was now receding in the face of inhumation. Similarly, weapon-burials, accorded to almost half of all men interred in early sixth-century England, were much more restricted by the seventh. Yet, in spite of the fact that large segments of the population had abandoned these rites, a handful of seventh-century dead were treated to baroque versions of them. Some of the most remarkable seventh-century barrow burials are cremations, a sign of the status now attached to the funeral pyre. The ashes of a number of late cremations, moreover, were placed, not in ceramic pots, the traditional container of choice, but rather in elegant bronze vessels from the Mediterranean, a class of imports very much restricted to the grandest households. Six such burials, which combine cremation, barrows and metal receptacles, were excavated at the most famous of all early medieval cemeteries, Sutton Hoo; and something like a dozen other elaborate, contemporary cremations are known. Similarly, in spite of the general decline of weapon-burials, a handful of extraordinary examples date to the later sixth and the seventh centuries, and a number of these were also barrow burials. The most spectacular was the Mound One ship burial at Sutton Hoo. Other graves, however, like the barrow burial at Benty Grange, also contained stunning military equipment, the like of which was never placed in the ground in earlier generations. The man buried at Benty Grange, for example, was accompanied by an astonishing iron and horn helmet, topped with a bronze and gold-gilt, polka-dot boar, which had been finished off with a bristled crest and glowing, garnet eyes. Both the late cremations and the late weapon-burials were exaggerated manifestations of older, less exclusive rites. The people orchestrating funerals like these appear, at first glance, to have overseen arch-conservative funerals harking back to archaic rituals: in actual fact, they were reconfiguring older burial traditions in radical new ways. The long and the short of all of this is that the new-fangled rites lent an aura of ancient, ancestral tradition to the funerals of people whose grandparents had been buried in no such way.

The *Beowulf* poet, although writing at least a century and a half after the English had converted to Christianity, nonetheless penned a description of one of these overwrought, faux-traditional, pagan funerals, replete with cremation pyre, weapon-burial and barrow building:

> The Geat race then reared up for him
> a funeral pyre. It was not a petty mound,
> but shining mail-coats and shields of war
> and helmets hung upon it, as he had desired.
> Then the heroes, lamenting, laid out in the middle
> their great chief, their cherished lord.
> On top of the mound the men then kindled
> the biggest of funeral-fires. Black wood-smoke
> arose from the blaze, and the roaring of flames
> mingled with weeping. The winds lay still
> as the heat at the fire's heart consumed
> the house of bone. And in heavy mood
> they uttered their sorrow at the slaughter of their lord ...
> ... Heaven swallowed the smoke.
> Then the Storm-Geat nation constructed for him
> a stronghold on the headland, so high and broad
> that seafarers might see it from afar.
> The beacon to that battle-reckless man
> they made in ten days. What remained from the fire
> they cast a wall around, of workmanship
> as fine as their wisest men could frame for it.
> They placed in the tomb both the torques and the jewels,
> all the magnificence that the men had earlier
> taken from the hoard in hostile mood.
> They left the earls' wealth in the earth's keeping,
> the gold in the dirt. It dwells there yet,
> of no more use to men than in ages before.
> Then the warriors rode around the barrow,
> twelve of them in all, athelings' sons.
> They recited a dirge to declare their grief,
> spoke of the man, mourned their king.
>
> (trans. Michael Alexander)

It is hard to know if this poem is a case of art imitating life, or rather if those hearing such descriptions were patterning their lives (and the funerals of the people they were burying) on art. Whatever their inspiration, the barrow burials, the elaborate cremations and the weapon-burials were all making uniform arguments about ancestry, dynasty and the timelessness of privilege, just as the genealogies and the origin stories were. All were important components in a novel vision of the past, one that put forth the notion that a foreign, warrior elite had come to Britain and had conquered much of it.

Arguments made on the bodies of the dead were also expounded on the bodies of the living. It is clear, for example, that some very grand individuals began, during this period, to sport brooches and other metalwork finery decorated in a novel fashion. A Danish style of interlace, known as Style II, which is comprised of knots of muscular, sinuous beasts, became a highly prized decorative motif among elite families outside Scandinavia in the sixth and seventh centuries, including the Lombards (a barbarian group settled in Italy) and the Burgundians (settled in France), who were at just this time developing notions that their peoples had sprung from Scandinavia. Indeed, the adoption of Style II by important Lombards and Burgundians occurred at the same time that churchmen were first committing these two peoples' origin myths to parchment. It looks, therefore, as if both groups, in order to underscore their Scandinavian origins, began to wear the same Style II decorated metalwork that Danish elites favoured. Thus high-status, Style II objects were part of an historicizing fashion deployed in Lombard and Burgundian court circles to shore up myths of origin. Similarly, sometime in the mid-sixth century, Style II came to the attention of members of highly elite families in parts of England, in particular Kent and Suffolk. Objects decorated in this fashion first made their way to England c. 550, and within a generation Style II had been mastered by a handful of highly skilled insular craftsmen. The style, however, was used only in the most rarefied circles, especially in eastern England, where it has been found decorating objects discovered in spectacularly rich burials at Caenby, in Lincolnshire, and in the Sutton Hoo ship burial.

The use of Style II in Kent was also exclusive, but seems to have been open not just to paramount leaders, but to those families who kept company with Kentish kings. In both East Anglia and Kent it seems that leading households, as in Lombardy and Burgundy, were arguing their descent from Scandinavian war leaders. In East Anglia at just this time, a dynasty known as the *Wuffingas*, a family that asserted Danish origins, was gaining ascendancy. It is hardly surprising, then, that the family's rise is exactly contemporary with the introduction of Style II in Suffolk. One of the *Wuffingas*, moreover, seems to have been buried under Sutton Hoo's Mound One, a grave containing a breathtaking collection of Style II objects. The use of Style II, therefore, appears rhetorical. It gave the impression that the people who decorated their bodies with objects fashioned in this manner were different from the people they ruled. It was one more part of a fictitious narrative which maintained that a foreign elite had come to England and had imposed themselves on an altogether different population.

Similarly, landscapes of the living, and not just landscapes of the dead, were annexed and amended during this period in ways which suggest that elites were moving to co-opt very ancient ritual centres, perhaps in the hopes of enhancing their status among groups who held such sites dear. The history of a pair of Bronze Age barrows at Slonk Hill, near Shoreham in Sussex, may be an example of this. The barrows here have a long, stop-start history, which suggests that the site loomed large in the imaginations of local communities for centuries. During the Roman period, for example, the site was converted into a modest Romano-Celtic cult centre, where people made animal sacrifices, offered coins to the gods and perhaps even proffered little enamelled cockerel pins, like one found during the site's excavation. It is hard to know if the locals continued to visit the site after Rome's fall, but it does look as if sometime in the sixth or seventh century someone with a ready supply of labour came to Slonk Hill and altered it once again. At this time the ring ditches of both barrows were backfilled, and the circle formed by one of the former ditches was surrounded with a square-fenced enclosure. The body of a woman was then buried in the middle of a break in the fence line, a spot that probably marked the entrance to the enclosure. The woman had been put in the ground without family or friends nearby, and the only object found in her grave was a knife, so her interment was neither a lone, high-status barrow burial nor a typical inhumation for people of middling rank, who were usually buried in communal cemeteries. Her grave, in short, is anomalous; indeed, it may represent a ritual killing. Slonk Hill looks like neither a graveyard nor a settlement: it was something else, a special site, most probably a ritual centre.

Similar 'squared-circles' can be found elsewhere in England, some with hauntingly similar anomalous burials, and it has been argued that they represent Romano-Celtic shrines reworked by early medieval pagan elites. The long histories and ritual continuities hinted at by places like Slonk Hill do not prove unchanging religious practices across the millennia, but they do suggest that generations of local people invested particular places with special meaning, and that those who wished to claim or display power in the later sixth and seventh centuries worked hard to leave their mark on such sites. This should remind us that local identities are often bound up in the landscape, and that what people believed about the land and its enigmatic monuments could be exploited, perhaps even manipulated, by men on the make, and used by them both as a means of articulating their power and as a way of constructing useful solidarities among the people they wish to rule. A handful of place names dating to this period may further illuminate sites like Slonk Hill. A few *hearg* names (an Old English word meaning 'heathen shrine' or 'sanctuary') are combined with the suffix *-ingas* (which means 'the people of' or perhaps 'the people belonging to') and a personal name. Thus the earliest textual appearance of Harrow-on-the-Hill, in Middlesex, is as *Gumeninga hergae*; and another now lost Harrow, in Surrey, was known as *Besingahearh*. We know through excavation that *hearg* sites like these were the loci of important ritual activities. The partial excavation of Harrow Hill, in Sussex, for example, uncovered large numbers of animal skulls and jaws, mostly but not exclusively those of oxen. Extrapolating the numbers for the whole site, there might be as many as a thousand skulls. Perhaps these sites, like those at Slonk Hill and Harrow Hill, were annexed in some way by men like Guma or Basa, but they remained, nonetheless, important ritual centres for the people over whom these men were working to assert their authority. They were places around which local identities could be built and sites through which authority could be asserted.

Pits filled with ox skulls, a 'squared-circle' structure with an anomalous burial and an ancient ritual centre were all present at Yeavering, in Northumberland. This was the site of an early seventh-century royal complex, and the place where the Northumbrian king Edwin and his people were converted to Christianity *c.* 627. Here, so Bede tells us, the Italian missionary Paulinus preached for thirty-six days and baptized the king's eager (and doubtless chilly) followers in the River Glen. What Bede fails to mention is that Yeavering lay in the shadow of one of the largest Iron Age hillforts north of the Humber, and that it had been shoehorned into a very old, extremely complex ritual landscape, one that included a large henge, a stone circle and a ring barrow. Although one of the most memorable passages in Bede describes the king's hall at Yeavering, it does not mention that it and the other major structures on the site were erected in a straight line between the stone circle and the barrow, and that the layout of the 'modern', seventh-century complex was thus determined by these ancient and enigmatic monuments. Given the mountain of ox heads excavated at Yeavering, alongside a human burial with a goat head (not to mention a place name that means 'the hill of the goats'), its new 'squared-circle' structure and a creepily anomalous child burial found there, it seems that the Northumbrian kings had co-opted and emended a highly wrought ritual landscape and then used it as a theatrical backdrop for newly invented ritual practices of their own. Five and a half kilometres away at Millfield, there was another, slightly later royal hall, also noted by Bede, but once again there is no mention in his history of the stunning ritual landscape in which Millfield sat. Such juxtapositions, because of their pagan associations, had to be forgotten in Bede's day, but before the conversion they were clearly exploited by England's newly minted kings to buttress connections between the present and the past, and to legitimize their hold on people and territory by asserting that their power was as timeless and historic as the ancient landscapes they now controlled.

SOCIAL AGGREGATES AND EARLY KINGDOMS

Behind elaborate burials like the one at Wigber Low and reworkings of ritual sites like Yeavering were relatively large agglomerations of peoples and territories dominated and organized by elites. The dim outlines of some of these groupings are fossilized in -*ingas* place names, which date, for the most part, to the late sixth and seventh centuries. In Sussex, for example, between Romney Marsh and the wetlands abutting Pevensey, fifteen places once included the word *Hæstingas* in their names. These settlements help us localize a group who called themselves 'the people of Hæsta'. We shall never know whether all the inhabitants of this small corner of Sussex – from the most prosperous head of household to the most impoverished swineherd – thought of themselves as 'Hæsta's people', or if it was only the members of Hæsta's and his descendants' households who did. Whatever the case, a small territory and local population coalesced here sometime in the late sixth or early seventh century around Hæsta and his followers. Similarly, a cluster of 'Roding' names in Essex marks another early agglomeration of people and/or territory, this time of the *Hrothingas*, or 'the people of Hrotha'. The valley this group claimed, one formed by a minor tributary of the River Thames, is only 8 kilometres in length, so, like the territory of the *Hæstingas* (Hastings), it is too small to dignify with the word 'kingdom'. Still, it was considerably larger than the farmlands surrounding a single hamlet.

We have no idea what English-speaking people in this period called such entities, but by the early eighth century they were often termed *regiones* (singular *regio*) in the Latin sources. Both in Sussex and Essex, and in many places in between, it looks as if congeries of families and communities came in the sixth century to be organized around important individuals. In some cases, cohering populations may have come to think of themselves as descendants of a common ancestor and to share an identity rooted in the powerfully binding myth of kinship. Elsewhere, however, elite households perhaps upheld the notion that they alone sprang from conquering progenitors. Whatever the case, the individuals around whom such solidarities formed came to claim that all of those who lived within their territories were obligated to them in some way.

The Hæstas and Hrothas of the world, who prospered mightily in a century of galloping social differentiation, came to treat the inhabitants of their *regiones* like third-class cousins or duty-burdened rustics, and to extract agricultural surplus and labour from them. The families who were on the losing end of the period's evolving hierarchies continued to practise the same mixed subsistence agriculture as their grandparents, but they were now increasingly implicated in a tangle of obligations that required them to produce some surplus and pass it on to their betters. This, for example, was apparently happening at Quarrington, in Lincolnshire. The people here can be seen changing their animal-husbandry practices during this period, perhaps because of new tribute obligations. Sometime in the later sixth or seventh century they began slaughtering large numbers of adult pigs, but these animals were being eaten elsewhere. It may be that Quarrington's farmers were giving tribute to their 'betters' in the form of hams and bacon.

Farmers like those at Quarrington were not handing over tribute because they were tenants who owed rents to their landlords, but rather because great men were coming to rule them, and the obligation of the ruled in the early Middle Ages was tribute. The easiest way for would-be rulers to gather what was owed them was to transform their residences into central places and use them as collection points for all the goods and services to which they were entitled. Places like these become visible in the archaeology from the later sixth century. Not only have excavations of high-status sites like Cowdery's Down and Yeavering revealed a constellation of profligate practices – large-scale entertaining, the building of outsized halls, elaborate ritual practices – found nowhere else, but they show that such settlements were as much sites of consumption as production. It is here that we have evidence for cattle raised by others driven in on the hoof and for grain processed elsewhere hauled in by the wagon-load. Large tracts of land and their populations came to be organized during this period into big, loose-jointed territories oriented, both socially and economically, towards important households and their halls. This is true not only in areas controlled by English elites. Such arrangements are also much in evidence in Wales and in southern Scotland, and, indeed, they seem to have been in place in these regions for some time by the time we find them in the English-culture zone.

Although lords stayed at central places scattered throughout their territories only as long as the food held out, small populations of slaves and reeves would have lived there year round, in order to deal with each season's dues and renders and to safeguard the storehouses from damp, pests and pilfering. We have some idea of what the business end of tribute centres looked like, at least in the eighth century, because archaeologists have excavated one at Higham Ferrers, in Northamptonshire, part of a complex, poly-focal settlement (that is, a quite dispersed settlement with more than one centre) probably controlled by the kings of Mercia. The suite of buildings excavated at Higham Ferrers seems to have acted as a tribute-gathering, processing-and-storage facility, servicing the king's great hall at Irthlingborough, just across the River Nene and down wind from Higham Ferrers' cattle pens and malting ovens. The compound at Higham Ferrers was surrounded by a large, keyhole-shaped enclosure, marked by a modest ditch and probably topped with a hedge or fence. The enclosure would have served as a pen for livestock driven in by local tribute-payers. There was also living accommodation within the enclosure for a small, permanent workforce, as well as storage buildings, malting ovens and a mill. There is some evidence, as well, that items of high-status exchange – things like fancy pottery and the wine it contained – passed through, but were not consumed at Higham Ferrers itself. Instead, estate workers probably stored them there, but then carted them to the hall at Irthlingborough once the king and his friends had arrived.

Although kings and their intimates constantly travelled between the various tribute centres they controlled, these settlements were permanent homes to two very different kinds of year-round residents – slaves and reeves. Slaves were permanently settled at such places to work the demesne, that is, the lands directly tilled for the great man's own use. The Old English word for 'slaves' is *wealas*, a word that also means 'foreigners' and one that came, in this period, to be used to describe the Welsh. Here is yet another piece of evidence for the growing myth of conquest: leading dynasties and their households were now asserting historic differences between themselves and the people they owned, claiming, by eliding the word for 'slave' and 'Welsh', that slaves were theirs by right of ancient conquest, and that the differences between lords and their human property rested on a fundamental ethnic distinction. Reeves, on the other hand, were free, and one of their daily tasks was the overseeing of slave-labourers. They also supervised the delivery of tribute owed by free farmers living in the surrounding territory, and they worked hard to ensure that the locals turned out, as 'custom' obliged, when their labour was needed. Reeves may have also marshalled all the freemen in the tribute centre's hinterlands when brigands or competing war bands threatened the hall's stockpile of stores. Reeves, in short, were commanding local figures, and, in the period before states and governments, they would have been the closest thing England had to royal administrators.

For every place like Irthlingborough there were still dozens of old-style, hard-working communities engaged in the dirty business of lambing, slaughtering and threshing. Some tribute-payers lived on isolated farmsteads, but most probably resided in hamlet-size communities like the one excavated at Thirlings, just 3 kilometres from Yeavering. Here, there was a collection of small houses, workshops and grain-storage buildings. Hamlets like Thirlings, where the vast majority of people who farmed and paid tribute resided year round, were often comprised of not very well organized collections of houses and outbuildings, and, as we saw with Mucking, they tended to drift over the generations as old structures grew ramshackle and new ones came to replace them. As a result, these settlements often shifted over time along bands of light, well-drained soil, which were relatively easy to plough, and, therefore, favoured by early medieval farmers. People in settlements like this produced crops and dairy products, flitches of bacon and cloth not only for themselves, but for the fancy people feasting down the road. Thus, important centres like the ones at Irthlingborough and Yeavering came to sit atop a hierarchy of settlements and at the centre of a system of provisioning, which enabled those who controlled them to siphon off food, labour and raw materials from people living in the neighbourhood.

Over the course of the sixth and seventh centuries whole archipelagos of places like Thirlings were stitched together into ingeniously administered units of production in order to provide for central households. For this to have happened, elite households must have expended considerable amounts of energy on transforming generalized notions of obligation into thoroughgoing systems of renders, systems which could guarantee that the people of their *regiones* not only gave them a share of the land's bounty, but provided them with the entire range of supplies they needed, not just meat and wheat, but goods as diverse as cheese, fodder and honey. For high-status households to function, they would have also needed commodities like wood for burning and building, oats for horses and pigs for hams and bacon. They would have required, as well, more specialized tribute – things like salt, iron and lead – from special production-oriented communities. The result of their efforts was the rise of what is sometimes called a 'landscape of obligation', one in which farmers and the communities in which they lived came to organize themselves in such a way that they could render particular kinds of goods and services at specific moments in the year. This necessitated highly choreographed agricultural regimens, traces of which are still preserved in the names of places once tied to high-status centres. *Hunatun*, for example, was a place where the lord's hounds were raised; Linacre and Flaxley were where his flax grew. The inhabitants of Laughton and Leckhampstead provided their betters with leeks; Peasenhall and Banstead with legumes. Shipton and Swanscombe rendered sheep and pigs, and Chiswick and Buttermere cheese and butter. Place names like these are often impossible to date, but some appear in early land grants and clearly reflect leading households' efforts to rationalize the agrarian activities of the people who lived within their territories. Of course, the inhabitants of such places raised the full range of crops and animals that they themselves needed to survive each year – communities in a period without a well-developed market system could not live on hunting-dogs alone – but such place names suggest local landscapes managed with an eye towards tribute time. Over the course of a couple of generations, such centrally directed activities came to bind a *regio*'s farmers together and coordinate their production. This, in turn, may have encouraged the development of hearty local identities, as all a *regio*'s inhabitants looked towards the same lord and as all participated in the same constellation of obligations centred on a single great hall. Such systematic renders created small, localized economies as well, managed with an eye towards surplus and run for the benefit of wealthy households and the places they called home.

These early territories, however, with their central households and their labour-owing farmers, were not simply the handiwork of sword-wielding elites, ruthlessly imposing their will on the countryside. Rather, the people, woodlands, springs and flocks enmeshed in local landscapes of obligation were often geographically dispersed. Above all else, it is clear from the few early territories we can still trace on the ground that they made ecological sense, and that they tended to be knitted together by ancient droveways, some of which had been used since the pre-Roman Iron Age. In western Surrey, for example, the territories of the *Woccingas* (centred on Woking) and the *Godhelmingas* (centred on Godalming) included lands in the distant sandy heaths along the borders of Hampshire and Berkshire, probably because these groups' herds fed on the good grazing found there. Thus millennia-old patterns of transhumance, which linked far-flung summer and winter pastures, helped dictate the extent and shape of early territories. In short, these territories were in some sense organic and must have been determined, in important ways, by the needs of farm families, whose survival necessitated a broad mix of resources that could only be obtained if they had access to distinct and sometimes quite distant resources. It appears, therefore, that both surplus-grabbing lords and resource-seeking farmers participated in the organization of the landscape. Both elite interventions and the agency of farm families came together in the later sixth and seventh centuries, and both worked to create England's earliest tribute-rendering territories.

Scattered evidence suggests that freemen during this period, as a matter of course, would have held single hides of land, a hide being, as Bede tells us, the amount needed to support a household. By Bede's day the hide was both very old and very widespread, so it is little wonder that elites came to harness the hide and use it as a means of assessing tribute on individual families within their territories, thus transforming the hide from an allotment of land into a measurement of liability. By the late seventh century, when gifts of large tracts of land were sometimes detailed in writing, they were carefully assessed in hides. One early king, for example, granted a religious community 'the land whose name is Farnham', which was comprised of sixty hides, 'ten of which are in Binton, two in Churt, and the rest assigned to their own places and names . . . with everything belonging to them [in] fields, woods, meadows, pasture, fisheries, rivers [and] springs'. Another early charter preserves the gift of thirty-eight hides: 'in Lidsey and Aldingbourne [there are] twelve [hides], in *Genstedesgate* ten, in Mundham eleven, on the east bank two, on the west three'. These grants, so it seems, were not so much gifts of the land itself, as a granting away of the obligations levied on the people living on their constituent hides.

We have a tribute list preserved in the laws of an early English king, written in the last decade of the seventh century, which gives some indication of the kinds and amounts of tribute people holding hides rendered to their social betters. Every ten hides, so we are told (and many territories in England during this period would have had 300 hides or more), were to provide the king with 'ten vats of honey, three hundred loaves, twelve ambers of Welsh ale, thirty of clear ale, two full-grown cows or ten wethers, ten geese, twenty hens, ten cheeses, an amber of butter, five salmon, twenty pounds of fodder and one hundred eels'. A great man in control of 300 hides, if this list is anything to go by, would have received enough food and fodder for him and his friends to live well and never labour. Other valuable resources not mentioned in the law code were also there for lords to take. According to an early saint's life, the monastery of the Irish monk and missionary St Columba harvested a ship's load of wattle from the fields of a local layman for their new guest house. This hints at the fact that farmers owed their lords a whole universe of other goods and services never mentioned in our surviving tribute lists. At the same time, however, the burdens of tribute were not all that onerous for local farmers, with some household in a hamlet perhaps delivering two or three barrels of beer each year, a few fowl and a hundred loaves of bread, while another 5 kilometres down the road would have given over a basket of eels, two wheels of cheese and a sheep.

These large organized territories – with their central places, their labouring populations and their systems of tribute – were up and running across much of Britain by the end of the sixth century, not only in those regions dominated by English-speaking elites, but in much of British-speaking Wales and Irish-speaking western Scotland. There would, of course, have been a myriad local variations within this very loose, very ad hoc system. In Kent, for example, the territories organized around central places were larger than elsewhere. In the lands encompassing modern-day Cambridgeshire such organization may have lagged behind by a generation or more, and in places like Somerset and Dorset it is likely that such territories appeared at a very early date and developed out of a British, perhaps even a late Roman milieu. Whatever their origins, once in place, both the small unit of the hide and the larger entity of the *regio* were enormously robust, and both, although transformed in significant ways, would continue into the eleventh century and beyond.

The organization of the countryside into *regiones* had fundamental political consequences. Aggressive lords of *regiones*, with a little luck and the help of a couple of dozen bloodthirsty friends, could gain control over large blocks of land, not by conquering them a single hamlet at a time, but rather by simply grabbing hold of their central places. With a single blow, a man could thus gain an entire territory, its surplus-producing population and its organized renders. This made victors, after a couple of successes, little superpowers within their neighbourhoods. Once they had tripled or quadrupled their resources, they had three or four times the resources of their rivals, bringing about an even greater likelihood of victory. Thus the inordinate power and riches of a few, so much a part of Bede's depiction of late sixth- and early seventh-century England and so evident in the profligate high-status burials of the period, need not lie at the end of two and a half centuries of slow, steady evolution. Instead, they are more likely the outcome of a hard-fought generation or two. Other actions, however, beyond raw aggression, would have led to the heavy concentration of resources into a few lucky hands. Neighbouring households, closely allied by common interests and habitual interaction, by thoughtful marriages and strategic fosterings, may have grown to think of themselves as a single kindred and thenceforth worked in unison; and men putting together smaller or poorer territories, or entering into the game a generation late, may have been flattered when asked to join a more successful enterprise as administrators, surrogates or muscle. The consolidation of resources, populations and territories was founded on cooperation as well as conflict.

By the second half of the sixth century the most successful families in the most politically precocious parts of England were beginning to adopt royal titles. Sometimes claims of kingship were made by a single head of household, but often royal appellations in this period were shared by brothers or cousins, men who lived in separate establishments, but who partitioned both the resources of their would-be kingdoms and their ruling authority. These early kings, who controlled not a single *regio*, but a dozen or more, transformed each of their tribute centres into a *villa regalis*, or royal vill (centre). Over the course of each year, kings and their households would travel on circuit to each of these *villae* and live a few weeks off the bounty they found there.

Armed with royal titles and an ideology that justified their places in the world, supplied by an organized countryside and its dependent populations and operating in a political landscape comprised of a mosaic of *regiones*, the most successful families began to build substantial kingdoms. The Tribal Hidage, a text drawn up sometime between the late seventh and late eighth centuries, provides us with an interesting, though fragmented, snapshot of early England. It lists thirty-four separate territories south of the River Humber and gives an accounting of the number of hides at which each was assessed. Most had somewhere between 300 and 600 hides and may, by the time of the writing of the text, have been incorporated into the kingdom of Mercia. Some of the entities described in the text could have begun as administrative districts created from scratch by Mercian kings in areas where *regiones* had been slow to develop. Others, however, probably began much like the territory of the *Hrothingas* – as little polities cobbled together by families who had managed to claw their way to the top of local society and who had organized small territories and their inhabitants for their own benefit. We know of other territories, not mentioned in the Tribal

Hidage, which had been subsumed into other kingdoms. Bede, for example, describes Ely, in Cambridgeshire, as a *regio*, and he tell us that the *Loidis* settled in and around Leeds, in Yorkshire, had also controlled a *regio*. These people, by Bede's day, had been incorporated into the kingdoms of East Anglia and Northumbria respectively, and more successful dynasties would have co-opted their rudimentary systems of tribute as they enlarged their kingdoms one *regio* at a time.

A handful of the entities described in the Tribal Hidage – Mercia, Wessex, East Anglia, Essex and Kent – were coming, however, by this time to be bona fide kingdoms. Each had its own royal dynasty and all played starring roles in Bede's *Ecclesiastical History*. A closer look at one of them, Mercia, helps us understand how the most successful households in England were able to construct impressive-sized kingdoms in relatively short order. Mercia was not among the earliest English kingdoms to emerge, but by the middle decades of the seventh century it was a powerhouse. Still, we know almost nothing about its beginnings, and most of the surviving texts which describe its history were written by its victims rather than its friends. Bede, for example, was born and bred in Northumbria, a kingdom much diminished by Mercian successes. As a consequence, he was so hostile to Mercia that he consulted no Mercian informants for his history and he included no stories about Mercian saints, holy women or monks. Bede does, however, provide us with the name of Mercia's first known king, Ceorl (although one wonders if the name, from the Old English *ceorl*, which means 'rustic', is a joke). Bede mentions him in a brief aside because he was the father-in-law of Edwin of Northumbria, one of Bede's great heroes. It is because of this that we not only learn that Mercia had a king by *c.* 600, but that he was important enough to marry his daughter into a leading English dynasty. By the early eighth century Mercian kings boasted that the founder of their dynasty was a man named Icel, who ruled a whole century before Ceorl. In actual fact, though, Mercian rulers are barely visible, even in Ceorl's reign, and we know almost nothing about them until the 620s, when King Penda († 655), the successor of Ceorl, came to power.

The people that Ceorl and his successors came to rule are described by Bede as 'Angles', and, indeed, before the genesis of the kingdom, those living in the Mercian heartland had developed and/or adopted a regional material culture that archaeologists describe as 'Anglian'. The brooches and costumes worn by Mercian women distinguished them from their 'Saxon' neighbours to the south. Elite English-language speakers there may also have spoken a distinctive dialect. People in the Mercian heartland, at least the kind who buried their women with 'Anglian' brooches and spoke with a Mercian lilt, would therefore have stood out had they travelled to Kent or Northumbria. This shared regional culture may have been exploited by early Mercian kings and used as evidence of a common history and a shared set of interests. By *c.* 600, these people, or at least their leaders, were calling themselves the *Mierce*, or 'the dwellers of the border lands', probably because they lived on the eastern edge of the lands controlled by sophisticated, militarized, Welsh-speaking elites.

Before its massive expansion under Penda, Mercia's kings probably controlled a core of territory in Staffordshire, Leicestershire, Nottinghamshire, southern Derbyshire and northern Warwickshire, a region encompassing perhaps forty or fifty *regiones*, an impressive aggregation of lands, peoples and rights. Bede, when describing a Mercia of the 650s, tells us that there were southern Mercians and northern Mercians – the former with 7,000 hides of land and the latter with 5,000 hides – and that the two halves of the kingdom were divided by the River Trent. We know the names of a number of important Mercian central places by the later seventh and eighth centuries, each of which sat at the centre of a large tribute-bearing territory. Some of these probably began as bundles of peoples and territories bound together by local families but, over the course of the later sixth century, had been conquered, co-opted or cajoled into joining the great Mercian enterprise. Tamworth, for example, a place in the eighth and ninth centuries at which Mercian kings often held court, lay in the centre of the ancient territory of the *Tomsætan*, 'the people settled along the River Thame', a group who may have cohered as early as the early sixth century. In the ninth century the *Tomsæti* were under an important royal official known as an ealdorman, so the district not only existed before Mercia's rise, but after its fall, and it may have developed out of a very old, highly localized identity and an early *regio*, controlled and organized by a local strongman intent on marshalling the wealth of the 'Thame sitters' for the maintenance of his own friends and family. Penkridge, another important Mercian *villa regalis* by the eighth century, sat at the heart of the territory of the *Pencersatan*, 'the people settled by the River Penk'. And

Repton, another Mercian central place, formed the heart of the territory of a group known as the *Hrepingas*. When the church at Repton was excavated a series of timber buildings predating the church were uncovered, probably a hall and storage complex, and probably the remains of an early estate centre, perhaps up and running by the reign of Ceorl.

As Mercia expanded it not only gobbled up individual *regiones*, but moved against entities that were kingdoms in their own rights. Indeed, the former kingdoms of the Hwicce, centred on Worcestershire, Gloucestershire and Warwickshire, and the Magonsæte, centred on Herefordshire, were incorporated wholesale into Mercia in the eighth century. Like Mercia, neither kingdom predates the sixth century; and like Mercia, both were made up of a patchwork of smaller territories, many with royal vills at their centres and with fifty hides of land organized for their support. When Mercia began taking over whole kingdoms like these, it expanded rapidly.

Strategic marriages could also lead to the incorporation of one kingdom into another. We know, for example, that the daughter of an East Anglian king was married to a 'prince' of the South Gyrwa, a leader of a people who had coalesced in the Fens. This marriage must have facilitated the peaceful integration of leading families there into the East Anglian coterie. At other times, however, amalgamation was accomplished by the sword. A generation after the Northumbrian kings had lost their grip on the one-time kingdom of Lindsey, members of important local families there still loathed the dynasty. When the queen of the Mercians, a niece of the long-dead Northumbrian king Oswald, translated her uncle's remains, now considered holy relics, to the Lindsey monastery of Bardney, the monks there were furious, Bede tells us, because, although they knew him to be a saint, 'nevertheless because he belonged to another kingdom and had once conquered them, they pursued him even when dead with their former hatred'. Such hard feelings, so long nursed, were the product of long and unhappy decades of bloodletting.

The inbuilt instability of this world – a world in which big kingdoms gobbled up little ones; one in which a loser's resentful, heart-sick retainers were sometimes grudgingly welcomed, as part of a truce, to live at their former enemy's hall; where the daughters of victorious kings found themselves sleeping in the beds of old antagonists because their fathers hoped to damp down enmity – is brilliantly evoked in *Beowulf*, the Old

English epic poem. In it, the great Danish king Hrothgar marries his daughter to the son of the king of the Heathobards, a man Hrothgar had butchered on the battlefield:

> [He hopes] thus to end all the feud and their fatal wars
> by means of the lady. Yet when a lord is dead
> it is seldom the slaying-spear sleeps for long –
> seldom indeed – dear though the bride may be.
>
> The lord of the Heathobards may not like it well
> at the bringing home of his bride to the hall:
> nor may it please every earl in that nation
> to have the pride and daring of Denmark at table
> – their guests resplendent in the spoil of their ancestors!
> Heathobards had treasured these trenchant, ring-patterned
> weapons until they could wield them no longer,
> having taken part in that play of the shields
> where they lost their lives and the lives of their friends.
>
> An old spear-fighter shall speak at the feast,
> eyeing the hilt-ring – his heart grows fierce
> as he remembers all the slaying of the men by the spear.
> In his dark mood he deliberately
> tries out the mettle of a man who is younger,
> awakens his war-taste in words such as these:
> 'My friend, is that not a familiar sword?
> Your father carried it forth to battle,
> – excellent metal – masked as for war
> on his last expedition . . .
> The son of one of his slayers now
> sports the weapon here, and, spurning our hall-floor,
> boasts of the killing: he carries at his side
> the prize that you should possess by right.'
>
> With such biting words of rebuke and reminder
> he taunts him at every turn; until the time comes
> when one sleeps blood-stained from the blow of a sword:
> the follower of the lady forfeits with his life
> for the actions of his father; the other contrives
> to lose himself, and lives; the land is familiar to him.
> Both sides then will break the pact
> sworn by the earls . . .

It is little wonder, in a world like this, that elites orchestrated lavish weapon- and barrow burials when the great men in their lives lay dead; that they embellished their past histories and exaggerated the antiquity of their rights; that they moved so aggressively against their competitors; that they were so often armed to the teeth.

INSIDERS AND OUTSIDERS

What were notable households like in this brave, new world? We are able to catch a few fleeting glimpses of them in Bede's history and in a small corpus of saints' lives penned in the first half of the eighth century, because so many of the period's saints belonged to aristocratic or royal families; thus when hagiographers describe their subjects' early years they often tell us about the lives led by members of high-status households. Many hagiographers, for example, hint that when a great man and his household were in residence an estate centre teemed with people. Some of these temporary residents travelled constantly with the lord's own household: others came as guests, including, sometimes, even the king himself. Indeed, during St Wilfrid's boyhood in the 630s and 640s both the 'companions' of the Northumbrian king and these men's slaves visited his father's household often enough for him to be vouched for by them when he, in turn, visited the Northumbrian king. Other visitors who arrived at an estate centre when the great man was in residence would have included local farm families settled in the hamlets and farmsteads in the region, people who came to render food and labour to their lord, to receive justice and to watch the spectacle. St Guthlac's childhood was populated with *vulgus*, 'common people', and *ruricoli*, 'country bumpkins', as well as foster brothers, who, one assumes, were the sons of his father's allies and hangers-on.

In households like these, the sons of great men were raised with the help of nursemaids. The Northumbrian holyman St Cuthbert (*c.* 634–87), for example, loved his nurse, called her 'mother', and visited her throughout his life. Young children in such households ran in little gangs, like the boy Cuthbert and his friends, who passed their days doing cartwheels and handstands, or like Guthlac and his companions, who jumped, ran and wrestled. One eighth-century writer describes boys digging foxes out of their holes and hunting hares, boys' play we can well imagine in the seventh century. By the time boys like these reached late adolescence, they were racing horses and probably participating in the feasting, storytelling and drinking that were such an important part of noble life. Some must have been hot-headed or prone to drunkenness, because there were carefully articulated social customs which forbade the drawing of weapons at places 'where men are drinking'. The boys living in such households worked, however. Cuthbert, for example, was put in charge of the flocks, and, as an adult, he knew, in bad weather, where he could take shelter, because he remembered where the summer huts of herdsmen were. Wilfrid, for his part, ministered as a boy to his father's guests.

In the hall and its surrounding buildings, a nobleman's wife might rest on a bed in her *cubiculum*, and visiting dignitaries and their entourages, when they travelled to one another's grand residences, often slept in tents. King Oswald even travelled with a pillow. Such people had clothes for special occasions, too: when young noblemen went to the royal court, they dressed in their finest garb. Households like these held elaborate feasts as well. In the autumn great men sometimes 'feasted on pig's flesh, fattened on the fruit of trees' and ate their offal, which had been cooked on spits, not by themselves, but by underlings.

The companions of the men who headed pre-eminent households, who ate, drank and fought with their lords, and who mourned their deaths, were often drawn from across Britain. Guthlac's father, for example, although a close kinsman of the Mercian king, held his chief estate in the land of the Middle Angles, a kingdom cobbled together in the middle of the seventh century by a Mercian king for his son. One imagines that here Guthlac's father entertained not only Mercian kinsmen and dignitaries but members of distinguished, locally rooted families. Guthlac himself was certainly acquainted with a whole range of people, beyond those he had grown up with. Like so many of his well-heeled contemporaries, he passed part of his youth in exile, in his case spent among the British, where he lived, no doubt, in a household as distinguished as his father's. While there, he would have been treated as a member of the household. Indeed, St Columba's biographer tells us that an exile often lived with his protector 'as one of his friends'. The Northumbrian king and saint Oswald (*c.* 604–42) spent time among the Irish, and his brother passed his exile with the Picts. The followers of another northern king and saint, Oswine († 651), came 'from almost every kingdom', and so, for that matter, did the household described in *Beowulf*. The halls of great men, then, would have been polyglot places, with Irish-, British- and English-speakers. English exiles also lived in English-speaking households. Northumbrian exiles could be found living at the Mercian or East Anglian courts, and it may have been in such households that the 'proper' English, spoken by elites across the English-language zone, emerged. Wives would have added to the mix. The king of Kent at the turn of the seventh century had a Frankish wife and a Frankish bishop in his household, as well, no doubt, as a small group of Frankish women companions; and Edwin of Northumbria's second wife, the daughter of the Kentish king Æthelbert, arrived at her soon-to-be husband's court with an entourage of Kentish ladies and priests as well as an Italian bishop. Each visit and exile, every marriage and fostering created lifelong friendships and obligations. These itinerating, fluctuating aristocratic households did not simply include important people from the locality; rather, they were cosmopolitan and multilingual communities, places with foreign exiles, wives from distant lands and foster brothers from neighbouring kingdoms.

Such households not only embraced exotic people, but they had access to exotic goods. As we have seen, British-speaking elites far to the west had lived, since Rome's fall, in high-status sites and had consumed exotic goods from across the sea. So, too, had the British- and Irish-speakers in control, respectively, of Dunadd, in Argyll, and Whithorn, in Dumfries and Galloway. Dye plants cultivated on Frankish royal estates, for example, were available in Dunadd. Some in sixth-century Whithorn ate their suppers on tableware made by Carthaginian potters, and occasionally drank from bright, turquoise-blue vessels crafted in the eastern Mediterranean. Such Byzantine wonders were rarely seen in English halls, but English lords, nonetheless, got their hands on an impressive array of prestige goods from Francia and Scandinavia. By the end of the seventh century, for example, those in control of Flixborough, in Lincolnshire, had access to a little fancy wheel-thrown pottery from the Rhineland, and by the eighth century to much more foreign pottery as well as glass and coins from Francia, Frisia and the Rhineland. Clearly, the people in charge here were integrated into extensive networks of aristocratic gift-giving and long-distance exchange.

Central people living at central places also had access to beautifully wrought precious-metal jewellery. Constant contact with elite hostages, exiles and foreign brides as well as relentless conquests and tribute-taking led to the circulation of high-status, insular objects across the whole of Britain. A few claw-beaker drinking vessels, for example, objects that were wildly popular among the English, have been uncovered at British-controlled Whithorn, although Frankish drinking cups were much more common there. Similarly, there was a growing taste among English households for 'Celtic'-style hanging bronze bowls. Irish- and English-style metalwork and claw beakers were also present at Dinas Powys, in Glamorgan, so hybrid tastes were being cultivated in southern Wales during this same period. High-status households' familiarity with the luxury goods prized by elites living in other parts of Britain led, in turn, to the production of objects that were insular hybrids. At seventh-century Dunadd, for example, artisans fashioned penannular brooches, a traditional 'Celtic'-style of jewellery, but they were embellished with large-eyed, parrot-beaked birds, a decorative flourish borrowed from the brooches worn by Northumbrian women. Such fusions, present as early as the later sixth century, would lead, by the end of the seventh, to the development of an extraordinary artistic style found across the whole of Britain that would come to be deployed on some of the most beautiful manuscripts ever made.

In short, leading households that were culturally English now, at long last, had much in common with those headed by British or Irish elites elsewhere in Britain. Perhaps this is why the seventh-century Mercian king Penda was a successful lord not only among his pagan English followers, but among his British Christian followers as well. By the later sixth century English-, Welsh- and Irish-speaking elites across Britain all controlled large tracts of land and collected tribute. All lived in militarized households and presided over steeply hierarchical societies. English people were now expressing themselves monumentally, as well, creating magnificent backdrops against which to perform their power, a practice of longer standing among Irish- and Welsh-speakers. Irish-speaking kings, whose own magnificent settlement of Dunadd, with its ogham inscription, stone footprint and perhaps rock-carved throne, would have recognized, even appreciated, Yeavering's elaborate setting for what it was. Alongside their similarities, of course, there would have been mind-numbing variation. Elites across Britain, for example, now lived in outsized residences, but Englishmen preferred rectangular timber halls and the Irish living in Scotland resided in round, drystone houses. All wore fine jewellery, but Kentish women fancied Frankish-inspired gold and garnet pieces, while the tastes of the men living at Dunadd ran to penannular brooches. Great families across Britain craved imports from across the sea, but English households were connected by trade and diplomacy to the Rhineland, Scandinavia and northern Francia, while the Welsh more often consorted with merchants, craftsmen and other visitors from south-west France and Ireland. The noble families of each locale would have appeared foreign, perhaps even barbaric, to one another. Nonetheless, those in charge of a place like Yeavering or Cowdery's Down probably had more in common with, were more interested in emulating and had a greater familiarity with Dál Riatan grandees or Welsh warriors than with ragged English boys who herded sheep in distant summer pastures or with red-faced 'Saxon' farm women who worked as hard as men.

Acculturation and accommodation are always more likely between people who inhabit similar economic, social and cultural universes, and by the end of the sixth century the elite societies of Welsh Britain, Irish Britain and English Britain looked much the same. But there is a dark side to similarity. Political competition, ideological differences and ethnic distinctions often arise between people who are much alike. These things came to take centre stage in Britain in the seventh century and have dogged the politics of the British Isles from then until the twenty-first century.

5

Belief and Ritual: The Fourth
to Seventh Century

It is all but impossible to reconstruct the religious beliefs and practices of people living in Britain in the ten generations between Rome's fall and the coming of St Augustine's mission to Kent in 597. In part, this is because early medieval Britain is so poorly served by texts, and without the direct testimony of words it is difficult to say what, exactly, it was that people believed in their heads and in their hearts about the deities who animated their worlds, or how they went about acting upon their beliefs. Our picture is further complicated by Britain's fragmentation after Rome's fall, and its attendant devolution into scores of small-scale societies. Because of this, the ways in which one group of Irish immigrants or a British household or single set of English neighbours worshipped their deities may have been quite unlike anything found fifty kilometres down the road. One of the worries, then, for historians and archaeologists, is that what little evidence we have might simply reveal eccentric local practices embraced by no more than a handful of people. Different places in these years also experienced different levels of continuity, and this meant that Romano-British paganism and late Roman Christianity were able to persevere in some places, but elsewhere, as with other aspects of *romanitas*, they simply faded away. Disparate regions also experienced both different levels of immigration and different groups of migrants, and this, too, shaped ritual practices and beliefs. Places, for example, where descendants of the old Romano-British elite were still very much in charge or where Irish immigrants – whose families at home were converting to Christianity – were settling, experienced one kind of religious history. But regions where British peasants – who adhered to some vaguely Romanized, indigenous polytheism – were living alongside migrants from Jutland had quite another. The very particular social contexts in which these comings-together took place would have also affected the preservation of old ways, the reception of new ideas and the syncretic evolution of religion, belief and ritual.

CHRISTIANS IN WESTERN BRITAIN

The diversity of religious experience and the mystery of religion's practice hold true even among the British communities of western Britain, where people over the course of the fourth, fifth and sixth centuries embraced Christianity. What this Christianity looked like, what its links were to earlier Romano-British Christianity and how it resembled the varieties of that religion practised on the Continent is difficult to say, but our evidence, slim though it is, hints at a religion that would have been familiar to Christians elsewhere in Europe.

Christianity had become the official religion of the Roman empire in the 360s, and by 391–2 public displays of paganism were illegal. During the intervening thirty years it is likely that Roman magistrates in Britain pressured communities without churches to construct them, so it is probably during these decades that churches came to be built in important public spaces in Romano-British towns. Archaeologists may have actually uncovered a few. Some have argued, for example, that churches have been found next to the Roman forums at Lincoln, Silchester and Exeter, although none of these claims is without difficulties. It may have also been in this period that pagan temples in towns, like the one excavated in Southwark, were desecrated. Important rural shrines also seem to have been Christianized in these decades. It is in the late fourth century, for example, that some individuals or groups converted the hilltop shrines at Uley, in Gloucestershire, Lamyatt Beacon, in Somerset, and Henley Wood, in Avon, from pagan sites into Christian ones. And although a few Roman-style pagan temples, like the ones at Bath, in Somerset, Woodeaton, in Oxfordshire, and Weycock Hill, in Berkshire, or native shrines, like the one at Great Dunmow, in Essex, managed to evade such treatment, there is little to suggest that the lucky, long-lived few were functioning in any organized way after 400 or 420. However, the progress of Christianity and the decline of paganism, at least among those groups and communities well supervised by imperial administrators, until Roman rule collapsed in Britain, followed the same trajectories in Britain as they did elsewhere in the Roman world.

Given all this, it is not surprising that the Christianity practised in Britain in the late fourth, fifth and sixth centuries had much in common with that practised in other parts of the Christian world. Christians in Italy, Spain and Gaul, for example, became powerfully attached during this period to the saints, whom they looked upon as spiritual patrons capable of intervening with God on their behalf. From the fourth century on, pilgrims sought out the saints at their shrines, often their tombs, and sites, therefore, regularly found in late Roman extramural cemeteries. Here, saints were visited, venerated and petitioned because it was here that their powers were thought most potent. The earliest of the special Christian dead treated in this fashion were martyrs, but missionaries, bishops and the famously pious soon joined the ranks of the saints. There is a massive amount of evidence for all of this across the Mediterranean world; for Britain, however, where so few texts survive, there are only hints. We do know that when Germanus, bishop of Auxerre, which lay in the Roman province of Gaul, travelled to Britain in 429, he visited the shrine of the British martyr St Alban, and that he took some of the saint's relics back with him to Gaul. Gildas, in an aside written a century later, mentions two other British saints, Julius and Aaron, whom he describes as *legionum urbis cives*, or 'citizens of the legionary town', probably the Roman fortress at Caerleon (Monmouthshire). A ninth-century charter mentions a *Merthir Iun et Aaron*, or 'sanctified cemetery of Julius and Aaron', at Caerleon; and in the twelfth century the chapel that sat at the edge of the old Roman fort's extramural cemetery still bore a dedication to Julius and Aaron. All this suggests that the two martyrs' tombs served as cult sites in Caerleon without interruption from the late Roman period to the high Middle Ages. So we have textual witnesses for the veneration of three British martyrs and hints that there were special tombs in extramural cemeteries.

We can supplement our sparse written accounts with material evidence. Excavations at Verulamium/St Albans, in Hertfordshire, have laid bare the long, strange history of St Alban's shrine. There was a tradition, at least four centuries old by the time St Germanus visited the saint, of ritual activity at Verulamium. Early on there was a large, Romano-Celtic temple outside the town, probably built in the first century CE, but used and elaborated for several hundred years. At its heart lay the extraordinary first-century burial of a man whose grave was filled with Roman-style drinking vessels and dress accessories, and whose body lay on an ivory couch. The temple built on top of the dead man was surrounded by a zone of pits used for ritual deposits, including a scalped, defleshed human head, animal skulls and numerous pots decorated with human faces that had been 'killed', that is, purposely broken before burial. The temple complex was associated, by road and by views, with the Roman town's intramural theatre and baths complex. As far as we can tell, by the late Roman period these public buildings could accommodate many more people than the town's population, so they must have catered not only to townspeople but to those living in the countryside, who perhaps journeyed to Verulamium a few times each year for religious festivals associated with the temple. For a half century, from the late third century to the early fourth, ritual activities around the temple slowed and then halted. Sometime in this same period, however, a new cult centre, one hill away, came to supersede the old one, this one revolving around the Christian martyr St Alban. There was already a late Roman extramural cemetery here, and it is likely that this was the location of Alban's tomb. Graves in one section of the cemetery, dating from the late Roman period, were sealed under a gravel surface at the end of the fourth century, and this part of the cemetery ceased to be used for burial. This surface shows hard wear and conscientious repair well into the fifth century. Indeed, at some point the surface was completely relaid. Coins, glass fragments and pottery shards littered the area. The site's excavators suggest that this is what we should expect to find near a shrine or church built over a martyr's grave, a place where food and drink stalls sat (hence the glass and pottery), where people made offerings (hence the coins) and came in droves on the feast of the martyr (hence the heavy wear). The tradition of a major cult in Verulamium and of the town as the focus for pilgrimage predates Alban's martyrdom by a dozen generations, so the habit of venerating a local hero here was very old. Alban, moreover, was decapitated, and thus his death fits snugly within the traditions of the head cult apparently in operation at Verulamium during the Roman period. So perhaps this new cult and this new focus of pilgrimage were syncretic with older cults and pilgrimages.

There is also evidence for an active saint's cult on the site of the extramural Roman cemetery at Poundbury, whose excavated skeletons have already been considered. In the early decades of the fifth century, as the nearby Roman town of Dorchester went into terminal decline and as the need for a suburban cemetery withered away, a small, rural settlement grew up among Poundbury's graves. The appearance of farm buildings and animal pens in the midst of a defunct cemetery seems incongruous, and one can only imagine the horror such juxtapositions would have elicited from fourth-century Britons, who were uneasy about the dead. But in the fifth century the dead, especially the notable Christian dead, were companionable neighbours, and their coddled presence is often the sign of an active saint's cult. This seems to be the case at fifth-century Poundbury, because several of the cemetery's late Roman mausoleums still stood during this later phase. These little structures determined the layout of the new settlement and began acting as the focus for other burials. The surviving mausoleums had plastered walls, painted with scenes of men carrying rods or sheaves of wheat, not inappropriate embellishments for the graves of important Christians. These buildings also show signs of continuous repair, and, indeed, modest enlargement. Their floors, moreover, were heavily worn over the years, and someone in the post-Roman period not only built crudely paved paths leading to the mausoleums, but maintained the walkways. One way of interpreting these developments is that the fourth-century mausoleums were serving in the fifth century and perhaps even in the sixth as memorial chapels for especially revered Christians: local martyrs, men and women of particular piety, or beloved priests and bishops. Although corn-dryers and farm animals seem strange neighbours for the special dead, the fact that a few mausoleums continued to stand and serve as the focus of settlement, burial and visitors suggests that a Christian community – perhaps even a community of professional religious – and a cult centred on a handful of extramural, late Roman, Christian tombs was thriving three, four, even five generations after the abandonment of the Roman town that had once buried its dead in the cemetery.

Alban was a major saint. He was the subject of an early *vita*, and his shrine not only acted as a focus for local devotion, but was a magnet for pilgrims from abroad. The saints venerated at Poundbury, on the other hand, are unknown to us, and even in their heyday their cults may never have had more than local adherents. This is hardly surprising, given the fragmented state of fifth- and sixth-century Britain. Indeed, there is evidence for hundreds of early and intensely local saints in western Britain, shadowy figures whose cults are sometimes witnessed only by single place names which combine personal names and the word -*lann*, an element meaning 'an enclosed cemetery' or 'church site'; -*lann* place names are often attached to settlements that were founded in the early Middle Ages far from centres of lay power. Originally, they seem to have been attached to places with a church or cemetery and a house or two, and perhaps a couple of clerics or a holy man to see to the spiritual needs of local people. Llansadwrn, in Anglesey, means 'church or cemetery settlement of Sadwrn', Sadwrn being the saint to whom the church is still dedicated. Interestingly, an inscribed sixth-century stone, found in the eighteenth century in Llansadwrn's churchyard, commemorates *beatus Saturninus*, the Latin version of the Welsh name Sadwrn. So perhaps Saturninus was the founder of the church here, a man who, by the time of the stone's carving, had earned the sobriquet *beatus*, 'blessed', and was venerated locally. Not all the men and women whose memories are preserved in -*lann* place names, however, would have been thought of as saints in their own lifetimes. Some were probably lay patrons, clerics or hermits, whose names came to be associated with a place, a cemetery or a church, and who only later gained reputations for sanctity.

Church dedications and holy wells, too, occasionally preserve the memories of early saints. The Cornish saint Entenin provides an interesting example. His cult is witnessed in the dedications of two small Cornish churches, St Anthony in Meneage and St Anthony in Roseland, and at a holy well, Ventontinny (from 'Entenin' and *fenten*, which means 'spring', 'well' or 'holy well'). Entenin is the Cornish rendition of the Latin name Antoninus, but, because his feast day is different from the feast days of the numerous Anthonys venerated outside Cornwall, he must have been a different man, one fêted only in this small corner of Britain.

The army of British saints represented by such obscure names – not just the Entenins, but the Hyldrens, Sadwrns and Wyllows – provide us with a glimpse of a kaleidoscopic Christianity in western Britain, a Christianity that was spreading and flourishing, but one that was also decentralized, unhomogenized and localized. The plethora of cosy neighbourhood saint cults points to an intense Christian devotion as well; a devotion not limited to professional religious or high-and-mighty laymen, but one embraced by farm families living and worshipping in remote hamlets. At the same time, it seems that the people who made the trip to Ventontinny or Poundbury practised a Christianity that, while rooted in fourth-century Roman Britain, was nonetheless 'modern'; a Christianity that kept up with post-400 currents found across the Channel, like the burgeoning preoccupation with the cult of the saints. Evidence for the cult of the saints in western Britain, then, sketchy though it is, resonates with what we know about Christianity elsewhere. Whatever their individual histories, places like Poundbury, St Albans and Llansadwrn provide glimpses of a vibrant, living Christianity in the west of Britain, one with its own peculiar quirks to be sure, but one that Christians from across the sea would, nonetheless, find familiar.

Western Britain's professional religious would have been similarly recognizable. By the fifth century the Church had developed an elaborate and highly articulated ecclesiastical hierarchy comprised of a myriad religious orders: deacons, priests and bishops (or secular clergy), who worked in the world; groups of monks, who lived communally under their abbots and their monastic rules; and hermits and holy women, who strove to spend their days as self-abnegating solitaries. We catch glimpses of all of these characters in western Britain.

Take, for example, Britain's bishops. We know little of substance about them, but it is clear, nonetheless, that the British Church, like the Church elsewhere, was ruled by them. Fourth- and early fifth-century accounts of important, empire-wide synods occasionally mention these men in passing. In 314 three British bishops travelled to a council called by the emperor Constantine himself. The Briton St Patrick, writing slightly more than a century later, complained that a coterie of British churchmen, presumably British bishops, had censured him. Thus we have evidence that at least some late Roman bishops survived the period of the fall; but we do not know who these men were or in what churches and territories their jurisdictions were anchored. In the lowlands of south-western Britain, former Roman towns like Caerwent and Weston-under-Penyard (*Ariconium*), although no longer towns, were centres of nascent royal power, and if these places had had bishops in the late fourth century they may well have had them in the fifth and sixth centuries. If so, episcopal spheres of influence may, in some places, have come to mirror those of emerging British kingdoms. There is also some evidence that Worcester, once a Roman small town, was home to another British bishop. Here, the church of St Helen's, lying just inside Worcester's Roman walls, sat, in later, better documented centuries, at the heart of a huge ecclesiastical territory, or *parochia*: indeed, at the end of the eleventh century it was serving as the mother church for a score of subordinate churches. The curiously far-flung reach of this little Worcester church may in fact mark the extent of an early British bishop's area of responsibility, a sphere of authority carved out a couple of centuries before the founding of Worcester's English episcopal see in *c.* 680, by British bishops whose episcopacy originated in the Roman world. Elsewhere, however, British bishops had become completely untethered from former Roman towns, and some apparently worked out of monasteries. There are hints, for example, that a bishop lived at Mynwyn, the precursor of the important monastery of St David's.

In spite of these extraordinary survivals, there were many places in Britain where bishops and their flocks did not survive. There is nothing, for example, to suggest that in the year 500 there were bishops in the ruined and deserted Roman towns of London or York, places we know to have had them before Roman Britain's collapse. Here, bishops and the communities they led disappeared alongside all the other trappings of *romanitas*. Moreover, there does not seem to have been a metropolitan bishop operating anywhere in western Britain, and this office looks to have been a casualty of the death of Romano-British provincial capitals further east, in particular Cirencester and York, which, judging from the pattern elsewhere in the western empire, may have been homes to metropolitans in the later fourth century. The long and the short of all of this is that although we are privy to few details about Britain's bishops after the fall it is clear that, while those in the eastern half of Britain vanished, others in western Britain survived; and their successors were still there at the end of the sixth century, in some cases leading communities of worshippers that had first come together in antiquity.

The monk Gildas's sixth-century jeremiad detailing the 'ruin of Britain', one of the only British texts to survive from this period, is much absorbed with the shortcomings of the secular clergy – those bishops, priests and deacons who lived in the world and interacted with the laity. Gildas disapproved of these men and denounced them for comporting themselves too much like sinning laymen. He excoriated them for their love of fine clothing and their toadying obsequiousness towards wicked kings. He drops horrified hints, as well, that many British priests, far from being celibate, were married. But, *pace* Gildas, these were hardly British sins, since similar charges could be levelled against churchmen across the crumbling western empire. In Gaul, for example, we know that bishops' wives were often powerful figures in their own right, and this may have been the case in Britain as well. The sixth-century Saturninus stone examined earlier in this chapter reads, 'here lies buried blessed ... Saturninus and his saintly wife. Peace be with [the two of] you'. Although Saturninus is given no title here, it has been argued that he was a bishop and his wife an *episcopa*, a common figure in contemporary Gaul. Here, then, is further evidence of the British Church's tandem development with Churches elsewhere in the former Roman empire. From Gildas's accountings of the alleged shortcomings of Britain's secular clergy, we can also draw up a list of the activities in which they were expected to engage: they should build churches; preach and celebrate the Eucharist; distribute alms; lead virtuous, even ascetic lives; sing the Psalms and have knowledge of the Bible. These would have been required of secular clergy in Italy, Spain and Gaul as well.

The driving force behind the British Church, though, at least from the sixth century on, was not the secular clergy, but rather monks, that is, celibates living communally under some sort of monastic rule. One of the sources of inspiration for the men who chose this path was the fourth-century Gallo-Roman saint Martin, whose life and deeds were well known in western Britain. By the mid-fifth century we can witness the founding of monastic communities in western Britain: St Illtud established a monastery at Llanillytd Fawr, in Glamorgan, and St Piran and St Cadoc founded monasteries soon thereafter. These men's examples were followed in the sixth century by dozens of others. Like founders elsewhere, British patrons established rural monasteries, and like their Continental counterparts, including St Martin, they did not turn their backs on the world, but rather engaged with it, preaching to lay people and committing their followers to the business of pastoral care. Thus, for example, the monk St Dyfrig and his successors, operating in Ergyng and Gwent, oversaw the building of dozens of churches for laypeople. By the seventh century, and possibly as early as the sixth, a dense network of churches (some sixty in all are mentioned in the early charters of the important monastery at Llandaff) were operating there. As a result, few people in the region, even those living in its most isolated valleys, resided more than a couple of hours' walk from a church. Many monasteries in this period were similarly involved in preaching and dispensing sacraments to those born in the faith. Other monks, however, probably worked as missionaries, proselytizing among people who were barely Christian, who had forgotten what little Christianity their ancestors had once had or who had never converted in the first place. Shadowy characters like St Congar of Cadbury Congresbury and St Kea of *Lantocai* (now Street) may have begun the churches later associated with their names as missionary stations and used them as bases from which to evangelize the pagan British peasantry of Somerset. Monks across the sea, including St Martin himself, engaged in similar activities to convert pagan peasants.

Abbots, under the supervision of bishops, ruled monks in Britain, as they did elsewhere in the former Roman world. And, as elsewhere, important local families often controlled monastic communities. For a number of years, the sixth-century British saint Samson lived in a monastery ruled by an abbot whose nephews had every expectation that they would lead the community in their turn. We can also see from St Samson's *vita* that there was a variety of monastic practices in sixth-century Britain – some more ascetic, some less – each offering a different kind of religious life. The monastery St Samson grew up in, so his biographer tells us, encouraged fasts and vigils, but the saint nonetheless yearned for a more rigorously ascetic life. He admired a holy man who lived on a nearby island, and longed to join him so that he could practise a more thoroughgoing asceticism. In spite of his obvious attraction to worldly renunciation, St Samson, the child of an elite family, had a good eye for horseflesh, and he travelled around the countryside in a chariot he had brought back from a pilgrimage to Ireland. We hear as well of monks participating in 'feasts of plenty and flowing bowls'. We know that monasteries had cellarers in charge of pots of honey, and that some monks imbibed until they were falling down drunk. Indeed, Samson's own beloved Abbot Piro was so inebriated that he stumbled into a pit and died of his injuries. But there were others who led lives of serious self-denial. Samson, for example, lived for a time in a cave. According to Bede, the most famous British monastery, Bangor-Is-Coed, had more than two thousand monks in the early seventh century, all of whom supported themselves by the labour of their own hands. Two thousand is, perhaps, better read as 'many' rather than a literal 'two thousand'; nonetheless, it is clear that there were thriving and austere monastic communities in the west when St Augustine made his landing in Kent in 597.

British monks and intellectuals of an ascetic bent, in turn, helped to pioneer the tradition of private penance and pushed the notion of *per-egrinatio*, the renunciation of one's homeland in the pursuit of heaven, a central ideology developed in early medieval Britain, and one that set the tone for much of monasticism and missionizing across Europe for the next few centuries. British churchmen were also active in Ireland; not only was the early Romano-British missionary Patrick working there, but later British churchmen went as well, and they seem to have taught the Irish their Latin.

Bound up with these ascetic impulses were late antique attitudes towards the body. Across the Roman world, the body, over the course of the third, fourth and fifth centuries, was becoming the locus of sin. By the end of antiquity, excesses of the body in the form of gluttony, homosexuality, sex outside marriage, even sex within marriage, had come to be seen as wicked, and they were actions thought to stand in the way of both personal and communal salvation. One popular remedy was for some members of the community to practise complete sexual abstinence and vegetarianism. In these years it also came to be felt that those who committed sins, in particular bodily sins, needed to make amends to God through penance. Churchmen in sixth-century Britain, from what little we know, were at the cutting edge of this new morality. Gildas, for example, condemned the priests of his own day for gluttony. The early penitential, that is, a list of sins and the penances assigned to each, associated with his name describes the diet of a penitent monk. He could eat as much bread as he liked and was allowed butter on Sundays. During the week he could eat dishes made with vegetables, fat, eggs and cheese, and he was given milk and whey or buttermilk to drink. These were hardly starvation rations, but the insistence on vegetarianism and moderation were very much in step with sixth-century religious dietary proscriptions found elsewhere in the former Roman empire. Gildas also condemned the secular clergy for their lust and their familiarity with strange women. According to the penitential traditionally attributed to Gildas, priests and deacons who had taken monastic vows, and who then had sex with either a man or a woman, were advised to do penance for three years, two more years than those making amends for bestiality. Sex with another person was a serious offence, indeed! The anonymous seventh-century Breton author of St Samson's *vita* suggests that these attitudes about the body were not limited to the likes of Gildas, but were held by other British holy men. Among the proofs of St Samson's holiness, for example, was his bodily asceticism: he ate neither flesh nor fowl, and no one ever saw him drunk. He was praised, moreover, for his ability to conquer his lust for both women *and* men.

In the year 600, then, people living in western Britain would have had no need for missionaries, mass conversions or large, open-air baptisms. This is interesting, given the yearning of Pope Gregory the Great (590–604) to convert the people of Britain. He seems to have believed that he was establishing a brand-new Church in Britain, rather than restoring the old Church of Roman Britain. But that Church, as we have seen, was alive and thriving among the British-speaking communities in the western half of Britain. By Gildas's day, moreover, the British kingdoms of Dumnonia, Dyfed and Gwynedd, among others, were up and running, and they were still there when Gregory's emissary Augustine (whom we now know as St Augustine of Canterbury) arrived. These were Christian kingdoms, polities ruled by Christian kings and peopled by men and women who were in no need of conversion. At the same time, a broad belt of territory, running from Shropshire, down through Worcestershire, Gloucestershire, western Wiltshire and Dorset, was culturally British in Gildas's day as well. In some places here, scatters of churches would have been fairly thick on the ground, and Christian practices were probably well established in lay communities. In the future, when the English-culture and -political zone moved westward into places like Dorset, Somerset and Worcestershire, English kings and churchmen would have little need to missionize or build ecclesiastical institutions from scratch.

CHRISTIANS AND PAGANS IN EASTERN BRITAIN

But that was the west of Britain. Things in the east were altogether different, because there was no long, slow slide to temper the transition from Roman to early medieval. The bulk of the native British population in places like East Anglia and Yorkshire did not have time to embrace Christianity before Rome's rapid demise, because most were *pagani*, that is, peasants, living in rural backwaters. In Gaul, people like these were made into Christians during the course of the fifth century, thanks to the hard work of urban bishops and Gallo-Roman aristocrats.

Without the survival in eastern Britain of either urban communities or Romanized (and therefore Christianized) elites, the Church in the eastern half of Britain did not endure.

In Kent, for example, where St Augustine and his missionary band began to preach in 597, we know that there had once been Christians. The Roman villa at Lullingstone, for example, had a house church. Its late Roman fresco of well-dressed, red-headed Christians caught in an attitude of prayer is a graphic reminder that many elite families in fourth-century Britain took to heart the new official religion of the empire. Archaeologists have also found the odd stray object in Kent marked with a Christian *chi rho*, so Christianity was not limited to the country houses of the great. But what of the descendants of Christians, whatever their ancestors' ranks, two centuries on? Eccles, a settlement not far from Rochester, bears a name taken from the Primitive Welsh *eglwys*, a word related to the Latin *ecclesia*, or 'church'. It is just possible that this name fossilizes the memory of a Christian community that persevered here after Rome's fall. If, however, there were still people in Eccles or elsewhere in Kent who thought of themselves as Christians at the turn of the seventh century, what they believed and how they practised their religion is difficult to say. Bede reports that Augustine, when he wished to meet with British churchmen, had to travel far to the west, indeed, all the way to the Somerset/Gloucestershire border, doubtless because this was where the closest British bishops could be found. This, in turn, implies that, whatever a recrudescent Christianity may have looked like, it had long been liberated from professional supervision, because the disruptions of the later fourth and fifth centuries had brought about the extinction of the Church hierarchy in this part of Britain.

Early in his mission to Kent, Augustine did come across a group of devotees to a long-dead man called Sixtus. Sixtus was apparently a local late Roman Christian, but his adherents were shaky both on his biography and on the finer points of the Christian religion. They did not know if Sixtus had met a martyr's end, they knew of no liturgy performed in his honour, and they could recount none of his miracles. Informal venerations like this, rooted in fourth-century practice, could have carried on for generations without a Church hierarchy or an orthodox understanding of Christian doctrine. Augustine himself found this Sixtus worrying, and in one of his letters he begged Pope Gregory to send relics of the 'real' Sixtus, a well-documented Roman bishop, so that the faux-saint's adherents could continue to petition their holy man but in actual fact venerate a proper Christian saint. The pope did dispatch the relics, but he ordered the Kentish shrine to be shut down. Gregory, a man ever keen on encouraging Augustine to incorporate pagan traditions into his missionary's repertoire, had an altogether different attitude towards potential Christian heretics. The story of Sixtus suggests that Christian practices may have survived as folk traditions long after the fall, but that the Church itself, with its hierarchy, its self-perpetuating priesthood and its careful teachings, did not. Perhaps in Kent, and elsewhere in the eastern half of Britain, there were people in the late sixth century like the present-day Bantu-speaking Lemba, a group living in southern Africa, who consider themselves Jewish, and have been shown by their DNA to have Jewish ancestors. In spite of their thousand-year separation from other Jews, they have cultivated the memory of their Jewishness and practise a kind of folk Judaism, one uncoupled from the Torah, from rabbis and from other, more formal structures of the religion. The Lemba, for example, keep kosher in their way – avoiding not only pork, but hippopotamus – and they perform male circumcision and female ritual bathing. But their traditional observances are only distant approximations of those of their long-dead ancestors. Was this true of Sixtus' adherents as well?

The fact of the matter is that most people living in eastern Britain at the time of Augustine's arrival would have been entirely innocent of the religion of Rome. Unfortunately for us, though, their religious beliefs and practices are as difficult to recover as those of the men and women who venerated Sixtus. Bede from time to time does describe pagan practices, but he was writing in the 730s, a full century after his kingdom's renunciation of the old ways. As a child-oblate, that is, a child given to a monastery at an early age to be trained for the religious life, Bede had been brought up by professed and professional Christians, and he had come of age in a household organized around the Christian calendar, the performance of Christian rituals and the production of Christian knowledge. Bede is therefore a singularly poor witness to things pagan; a man less likely than most to have encountered the traditional customs and celebrations that must have continued during the years of his boyhood in less rigorously orthodox households than his own. Certainly, first-hand information about paganism, gathered from ancient peasants or elderly thegns, is mostly missing from his history. But Bede was not an anthropologist nor was he an ecumenically minded professor of religious studies: he was an eighth-century monk, and this structured the way he gathered his information, formulated his questions and wrote his history. He was not interested in preserving the details of idol worship, only in the story of its dismantling.

His famous account of the meeting called by the Northumbrian king Edwin in 626/7 to determine whether Northumbria should become a Christian kingdom is a case in point. On first reading, Bede's account intimates that he knew quite a lot about pre-Christian religious practices and beliefs. One of the chief actors in Bede's drama is a man named Coifi, the *primus pontificum*, or 'chief priest', of the pagan Northumbrians, a man given two long soliloquies by Bede. Curiously, however, it is this pagan priest in Bede's account who first discerned the impotence of the old religion:

'Notice carefully, King, this [Christian] doctrine which is now being expounded to us. I frankly admit that, for my part, I have found that the religion which we have hitherto held has no virtue nor profit in it. None of your followers has devoted himself more earnestly than I have to the worship of our gods, but nevertheless there are many who receive greater benefits and greater honour from you than I do and are more successful in all their undertakings. If the gods had any power they would have helped me more readily, seeing that I have always served them with greater zeal. So it follows that if, on examination, these new doctrines which have now been explained to us are found to be better and more effectual, let us accept them at once without any delay ... For a long time now I have realized that our religion is worthless; for the more diligently I sought the truth in our cult, the less I found it ... I advise your Majesty that we should promptly abandon and commit to the flames the temples and the altars which we have held sacred without reaping any benefit.'

Bede ends the scene by telling us that,

When [Edwin] asked the high priest of their religion which of them should be first to profane the altars and the shrines of the idols, together with their precincts, Coifi answered, 'I will; for through the wisdom the true God has given me no one can more suitably destroy those things which I once foolishly worshipped, and so set an example to all.' And at once, casting aside his vain superstitions, he asked the king to provide him with arms and a stallion; and mounting it he set out to destroy the idols. Now a high priest of their religion was not allowed to carry arms or to ride except on a mare. So, girded with a sword, he took a spear in his hand and mounting the king's stallion he set off to where the idols were ... without any hesitation he profaned [the shrine] by casting the spear which he held into it; and greatly rejoicing in the knowledge of the worship of the true God, he ordered his companions to destroy and set fire to the shrine and all the enclosures ... The place where the idols once stood is still shown, not far from York ... it is called Goodmanham.

The temptation to construct a coherent picture of English paganism, lock, stock and doctrine, from this rhetorical masterpiece is great; to speculate, for example, on a hierarchy of pagan priests, based on Bede's description of Coifi as *primus pontificum*; to hold that English pagans were in the habit of worshipping idols in temples; to remark on the crude quid pro quo of paganism; to posit the existence of horse cults, spear totems and cross-dressing priests. And one might even be tempted to fill the great gaping holes in Bede's vignette with information culled from what is almost our only other written source on Germanic paganism, the Roman historian Tacitus' account of the religious practices of Continental barbarians in the first century CE, or Snorri Sturluson's thirteenth-century tales of Scandinavian gods. Given, however, that these authors were writing more than a thousand years apart, and that they had no knowledge whatsoever of early medieval Britain, this not only seems reckless, but pointless.

Interestingly, the picturesque details found in Bede's set piece are not supported with the author's standard rhetorical prop, that he had learned what he was reporting from particular, named witnesses, a device he employed again and again in his history to underscore the veracity of his claims. It is clear, moreover, from his depiction of the events of 626/7 that, aside from Coifi, Bede could not name a single royal councillor, nor could he detail the missionary Paulinus' activities at the Northumbrian court in the months proceeding the king's conversion. Indeed, Bede knew more about the pope's thoughts on the mission than those of Paulinus, because he had access to papal letters from the period, which constituted more concrete evidence than the vague and conflicting Northumbrian traditions on which he had to draw. A dispassionate reading of the description of this council, then, leaves one with the impression that Bede actually says little of substance about paganism, probably because he was innocent of its details.

Bede's vagueness on English paganism is present elsewhere in his writings. In his tract *On the Reckoning of Time*, for example, Bede tells us the names employed by English people 'in ancient times' to designate the months of the year, and in doing so he describes a cycle of festivals celebrated and sacrifices performed at key moments in the agricultural year. He begins his discussion saying that the New Year was called *modranect*, 'that is, Night of the Mothers . . . so I suspect, from the ceremonies which they performed while watching this night through'. Although the name 'Night of the Mothers' is evocative, it is difficult to know of what, and certainly, judging from Bede's hesitant 'so I suspect', he was himself not at all clear on the details of this holiday nor the reasons behind its observance.

Bede's ignorance of paganism is further compounded by his deliberate omissions. Had he chosen, Bede could have described practices and events in his own lifetime or the lifetimes of some of his informants that would have shed light on seventh-century paganism. He fails, for example, to mention barrow burial, something that continued to mark the landscape in his own day; nor does he describe the ritual structures present, at the time of conversion, at royal centres like Yeavering and Millfield; and he is thin on the details he gives of the pagan reactions that so often engulfed royal households after the deaths of their first Christian kings. He even resisted concocting vilifying set pieces revolving around the heathenism of the conversion-resistant kings of Mercia, the traditional enemies of his own Northumbrian people. His work, like all good works of history, has a central thesis and a grand narrative. His is the coming of God's new chosen people, the English, to Christianity. The cataloguing of heathen practices had no place in such a story.

PAGAN PRACTICES AND RITUALS

We can, however, learn much more about pagan practices by using the evidence of archaeology. Purpose-built sites, which acted as centres for ritual activity, appear, in the archaeological record of the later sixth and early seventh centuries. Elites, as we have seen, had begun to express

themselves monumentally during these decades, and one of the manifestations of this urge seems to have been some high-status households'
co-option, emendation and elaboration of ancient ritual centres such as
Slonk Hill and Yeavering, which we examined in Chapter 4. Indeed, the
'temple' at Goodmanham, desecrated in Bede's story of Coifi, may be
yet another such site. By *c.* 600, at newly refurbished centres like these,
elaborate, resource-squandering (and, therefore, archaeologically visible) ritual activities were taking place. Certainly, there is evidence, at
places like these, for the profligate killing of oxen, the placing of animal
heads on stakes and perhaps even human sacrifice. Highly visible ritual
sites like these, however, were very much a development of the last phase
of the pagan period and an expression of England's growing social
stratification. The co-option of ritual centres was one of the strategies
employed by newly minted elite families to overawe those around them
and to associate themselves with 'traditional' rites and holy places. But
elites must also, surely, have thrown resources at these sites to appease
or cajole the gods and spirits who controlled fate and the workings of
the natural world, so their investments were more than social strategy.

One of the implications of the late flourishing of sites like these, however, is that paganism, like Christianity, evolved as society evolved. It is
thus unreasonable to hold that people in the eastern half of Britain
c. 425 interacted with or understood their gods in the same way as they
did *c.* 625, or that the ritual practices sponsored by elite households in
this later period were perfect facsimiles of those undertaken by earlier
generations or by less organized, less resource-rich social groups. Places
where people made offerings to their gods *c.* 500, or sites held sacred
by poor families grubbing out livings in more marginal landscapes,
remain invisible to us. It is only the late form of paganism, and only its
most rarefied, extravagant expressions, that we can glimpse, however
fleetingly. It is also possible that, in the process of co-opting ancient
sites, people who were culturally English took up some of the beliefs,
deities and rituals long associated with such places, and that the 'Germanic paganism' encountered by the missionaries proselytizing among
the English incorporated vestiges of British or Romano-British religious
practices and beliefs. Finally, it is probably also the case that the new
monumentality of religion came about, in part, because English elites
were aping the building efforts of the ever enviable, sadly inimitable
Frankish elites, who were building churches at just this time, or

Scandinavian elites, who were constructing large mounds and elaborate ritual centres. As we have seen, English elites in this period were certainly copying Franks and Scandinavians in other ways. The building of mounds and emending of ritual sites by high-status English pagans may, in part, have been done to emulate the practices of foreign elites. Thus our clearest view of English paganism is that offered by sites that were both late and high-status; places where rites may well have been emended both by indigenous, British practices and by those that were imported, Scandinavian and Frankish.

Fortunately, many excavated cemeteries provide us with a range of evidence for more ubiquitous and long-standing ritual practices. Not everything, of course, associated with burial is dictated by belief. Flowers, for example, are not brought by modern mourners to the grave to appease God, nor to provide the dead with plants for their journeys to the afterworld. Similarly, some of the activity that surrounded death and burial in early England was social or personal. Nonetheless, some beliefs *were* expressed materially when the dead were consigned to their graves, and because of this traces still remain. Take, for example, the princely burials laid bare at Sutton Hoo. They reveal more than gaudy collections of grave goods: they provide glimpses of death rites – animal sacrifice, the dragging of ships by gangs of mourners from the river to the bluff, the stoking of pyres, the building of barrows. Excavations of other, more prosaic cemeteries, however, have taught us that it was not only great men who were treated to ritually complex funerals. More ordinary mortals, put in the ground at cemeteries like Spong Hill, in Norfolk, and Snape, in Suffolk, were also sometimes the beneficiaries of highly choreographed death rites. These people's graves suggest that extraordinary subtlety and variation were as much a part of their funerals as those of England's seventh-century kings.

The two broad categories of burial in fifth-, sixth- and seventh-century eastern Britain – cremation and inhumation – were governed by radically different sets of rituals and conventions, and both required those presiding over them to make a series of decisions about the dead. Cremators at both Snape and Spong Hill, for example, had to settle on how and where to burn the body. Should they build the pyre close to home and then carry what remained to the cemetery in a pot for burial, or should they, rather, cart the corpse to the cemetery and burn it in a landscape already dominated by the dead? Should they consign the cadaver alone to the flames, or cremate it with an animal? If they opted for the latter, should it be a companion, like a dog or a horse, placed dead, but whole, on the pyre; or should it be meat – dismembered pigs or cows, butchered cuts of mutton, whole lambs or suckling pigs? Or should it be an undomesticated beast like a fox, a roe deer or a beaver? Or should they leave the animals aside and instead drape the body with a bear skin? Who should attend the cremation itself – which might last ten hours or more – ritual specialists, family and friends or members of a much broader burial community? Should the ashes of the dead, once the fire had cooled, be gathered up and placed directly in the ground, or decanted into a ceramic pot? If a clay vessel was the choice, should its shoulders be decorated with specially chosen and highly symbolic stamped, moulded or scored designs, or would any old cooking pot do? Should purpose-made miniature shears, tweezers and razors be placed in the urn? Should trouble be taken to include in the urn melted brooches and beads along with bits of bone and ash? Should mourners erect a little mound or small post-built structure over the buried ashes?

Inhumators were faced with an altogether different set of choices. How large should they dig the grave and how deep? Should they align it with the rising sun or some nearby barrow? Should they lay the body directly in the ground, or line the grave with stones? Or should they place it in a coffin? A boat? On a bed? Should they wrap it in textiles or leather? Should they flex the corpse's legs or extend them? Should they place bits of charred wood or bracken in the grave? Pots of food or drink? Should personal possessions be included, such as weapons or brooches? Should the jewellery interred be heirlooms or everyday ware; best or broken? Should the grave be topped with a mound or marked by a post? Some of these choices would have been informed, perhaps even governed, by religious sensibilities and ritual requirements clear to mourners, if not to us. In any case, friends, family and perhaps even funerary specialists would have had to determine all of these things and more every time a person died.

That ritual stood behind burial is most obvious in a scatter of rare, anomalous inhumations. A handful of such burials contain more than the bodies of the much lamented dead: they include what may be the victims of ritual killings. One inhumation excavated at the cemetery at Welbeck Hill, in Lincolnshire, for example, was a double burial. Many people shared their graves in the early Middle Ages – mothers and their babies, for example, or members of a community who had been struck down at the same time by the same sickness. The burial at Welbeck Hill, however, requires some other explanation. Here, an old man was carefully positioned on his back in the grave. He was buried with a knife, a bucket and what must have been some kind of ceremonial spear, topped as it was with an unusable spearhead pierced and hung with bronze rings. The man's body, once laid out in the grave, was then covered with the corpse of a decapitated woman, her feet pointing towards his head. The circumstances behind this strange burial are unrecoverable, but its unsettling oddness seems the result of ritual behaviour. Similarly, at the cemetery at Bidford-on-Avon, in Warwickshire, a woman's bodyless head was buried with grave goods in a hole lined with limestone slabs. The burial of the head was done with the greatest of care, but what happened to the rest of the woman? Or again, two women at Nassington, in Northamptonshire, were each, alone of all the people interred there, accompanied in their graves by a broken knife, a silver finger ring and a child's skull. The headless woman at Welbeck Hill, the owner of the bodyless head at Bidford-on-Avon and the Nassington infants may have all died in their beds, but there is something unsettling, even hair-raising, about their burials. Some may be the result of punishment killings, and accusations of murder or witchcraft may stand behind them. But some of these second bodies probably functioned as grave goods. Anthropologists generally hold that human sacrifice is triggered not only by the desire to gratify powerful men, but to mollify the gods, and they note that across the planet such killings are almost always carried out by ritual specialists. These examples, then, smack of beliefs and practices aimed at the unseen world and officiated over by people whose special task it was to appease the gods.

Less sinister and much more commonplace burial practices also hint at systems of belief that were in operation not only in death, but in life. The women who were accorded grave goods in the sixth and seventh centuries were often laid to rest with mysterious collections of objects that were neither beautiful nor practical. Sometimes women wore these things in little bags around their necks: at other times, they carried them in bags hung on their belts. These bag collections have odd little jumbles of artefacts that to our eyes appear both curious and impractical. A typical one was recovered from a woman's grave at Purwell Farm, Cassington, in Oxfordshire. It contained a bronze strap-end that was at least a hundred years old when the woman was buried; two boar's teeth, one pierced; a fragment of glass and a collection of circular things: a bronze ring threaded with a loop of bronze wire; three discs, one bone, one iron and one lead; a disc-headed bronze rivet; an iron ring and a rolled-up length of iron wire. Many other bags contained the same assortment of ancient odds and ends – animal teeth, bits of glass and ringed objects – but they also often included cowrie shells, scavenged Roman coins, fossilized sea urchins and the knuckle-bones of sheep. These bags may have once held organic material as well: there are hints of seeds and herbs, bits of cloth and thread.

Objects like these seem, for the most part, to have been the preserve of women. Teeth are a case in point. All sorts of animal teeth were placed in women's graves. Pig teeth and boar tusks, horse teeth, dog or fox teeth, beaver teeth, even the teeth of oxen have been found. Very occasionally they are excavated in the graves of men and children as well, but they are much more typically recovered from the graves of adult women. It is reasonable to conclude that teeth were considered amuletic, that their wearing and burying had some shamanistic purpose and that they and their powers belonged to women. It also seems likely that the kinds of objects found in bag collections were thought to be apotropaic, and that women collected them to cure, protect, impart luck or control nature. Certainly, we know that the English, after the coming of Christianity, believed in the efficacy of such objects. Bede himself tells us that when plague arrived in late seventh-century Northumbria Christians attempted to ward it off with incantations and amulets.

Food also played some role in pagan funerary rituals. Most of the food one could imagine burying with the dead – grain or bread, leeks or porridge – has little chance of surviving centuries in the ground. Nonetheless, there is some evidence that food accompanied the dead in their graves. A pot-full of duck eggs, for example, was unearthed in the grave of a Suffolk child, and oysters still in their shells have sometimes been found in Kentish graves. On more than one occasion archaeologists have uncovered the remains of hazelnuts or crab apples in the bronze bowls found buried with people of rank. Pots, too, sometimes accompanied the dead, and some still contain the remnants of porridge or drink. Meat also turns up from time to time. At the cemetery excavated at Castledyke South, near Barton-on-Humber, for example, a number of people were buried with chickens or geese. One of the women interred in the Bronze Age barrow at Wigber Low had a side of beef on her lap, and one of the men buried at Sutton Hoo had lamb chops in his grave. And mourners who presided over the funeral of a child at Minster Lovell, in Oxfordshire, buried it with two cooked ox heads. Without texts to guide us, we can never know if this food was meant for use in the afterlife, was placed in the ground as a token of respect or was there to symbolize the bounty of a funeral feast. However we choose to read these offerings, though, what is being unmasked is activity driven, in some way, by beliefs about life, death and perhaps even the afterlife.

The animal remains found in human graves cannot, however, always be read as food offerings. Dogs of every age, size, shape and sex accompanied a similarly diverse group of humans in the ground: but even in the early Middle Ages Englishmen did not eat dogs. The bodies of these dogs are always whole, and their bones, unlike the bones of sheep or pigs, never bear the marks of butchery, so it looks as if they were put in the grave as bodies, rather than lumps of meat. Perhaps they were there to serve as or symbolize companions. Horses, too, occasionally accompany inhumed bodies. Almost three dozen horses (or, on two occasions, just their heads) have come to light in inhumation burials. Horses, unlike dogs, though, are found almost exclusively in the company of high-status, adult males. Sometimes these horses shared men's graves, but often they were buried on their own in pits dug nearby. At Snape a man was buried with an elaborate set of grave goods, including the head of an elderly pony, the bit still in its mouth. Horse heads may turn up in graves by themselves because of the daunting challenges presented by the digging of a hole big enough for a whole horse and the logistical problem of wrestling 500 kilograms of dead weight into the ground. But then again, the decapitation itself may have been a ritual act. At the cemetery at West Heslerton, in Yorkshire, for example, a whole mare was buried, but not before her head was removed. In any case, different animals seem to have been assigned different meanings in inhumation rites. Sometimes, as in the case of horses, they were there to mark high status, but at other times, as with dogs, they were not. But these animals may have also betokened adherence to a particular cult or represented not just grave goods, but bona fide blood sacrifice.

Cremators, on the other hand, used animals in their funerary rites in an altogether different manner. This is interesting indeed, given that inhumers and cremators often buried in the same cemeteries and may, in life, have shared the same hamlets and households. Of the 1,500 or so urned cremations uncovered at Spong Hill that survive well enough for study, something on the order of 650 include the cremated remains of animals. Of these, more than 250 contain the charred remains of horses – and not just bits and pieces of horse, but remains that lead us to believe that whole animals were killed at funerals and then dragged onto pyres. Something like 15 per cent of all cremations at Spong Hill were occasions on which horses were slaughtered, so the practice was ubiquitous. Women, moreover, more often shared their pyres with horses than did men. A whole range of other animals was burned on pyres as well – oxen, sheep and pigs were commonly represented by cuts of meat. Less often birds, wild animals, even fish were cremated with the human dead. The cremated remains of humans and animals are often intermingled in the same funerary urn, proof that humans, beasts and meat were burned on the same pyres. Sometimes, however, urns with mostly human remains share little graves with urns filled with mostly animal remains, pots known as 'animal accessory vessels'. In these cases, mourners went to some trouble after the conflagration to sort through and unmix as best they could what the flames had brought together. And in some cemeteries, like Spong Hill, the dead human's ashes were placed into a specially decorated urn, while the animal's ashes were placed in a plain domestic pot.

Cremators were more likely to include things like gaming pieces and sheep knuckles with their dead than were inhumators; and, although the age of the dead seems to have had some impact on determining the rituals surrounding death, cremators created fewer gendered burials than inhumators. What all this means is that contemporaries, sometimes contemporaries living not far from one another, were participating in wildly different funerary rites – one profligate in its use of wood and animals, the other more taken up with grave structures and personal adornments. That cremations and inhumations were taking place at the same time and in the same regions, indeed often in the same cemeteries, suggests that many people would have witnessed both rites, and that many, perhaps most, would have participated in both. This, in turn, suggests a broad range of ritual activities in the lives of individuals, a kind of heterodoxy of ritual practice and a large number of rites from which to choose. Beyond the variation, though, lay well-understood rules. Women were buried with cowrie shells, but men were not. Adults were often burned with companion animals, but children were more typically accompanied by joints of meat. Pyres, especially those stacked with animals, required careful building and tending and needed to reach a temperature of something like 850 °C. The special rules, the complex rituals and the tricky technology of cremation hint that ritual specialists may have been involved.

CONTINUITIES AFTER CONVERSION

When we consider the burial practices of the pagan period from the perspective of the altogether Christian tenth and eleventh centuries, their heathen aspects are thrown into high relief. The mortuary habits of later English Christians are best seen in the fully excavated cemetery at Raunds Furnells, in Northamptonshire. This graveyard grew up around a small tenth-century church. The graves uncovered at Raunds are quintessentially Christian, dug in a proper churchyard; many of the people interred here went into the ground with shrouds, but even corpses dressed in their clothes were stripped, before burial, of any personal or useful possessions like brooches or knives. Mourners at Raunds, moreover, placed no food in the ground: they lit no cremation pyres and offered up no animal sacrifices. The graves here were also carefully aligned, with every body's head pointed east in anticipation of the Second Coming. It is burials like these – inhumed, aligned, unaccompanied and limited to churchyards – that we have come to think of as 'properly' Christian and ones that we have been conditioned to expect of believers.

Still, when we take careful stock of the Raunds burials, we can see many of the same urges at work that had operated in the pagan period. Social difference, for example, continued to find expression in death. A special plot in Raunds churchyard was probably marked by a standing stone cross, and a couple of the people buried in it had been placed under elaborately carved grave slabs crafted by professional stonemasons. A handful of Raunds' 380 or so people rested in rare stone coffins, and an infant lay buried under the floor of the church itself, very near the altar. People in these specially marked graves may have also benefited from conspicuously expensive and socially restricted funerary rights. So, although archaeologists found no fine weapons or intricate brooches here, there were still special graves. Most of those buried at

Raunds, though – the peasants who tilled and threshed, milked and wove – were treated to less elaborately marked burials; not shabby, but plain, and most lay in graves that had been prepared with care. Many of the dead had stones placed around their heads or their necks were pillowed by them. Some even had their faces covered with large stone slabs, perhaps to protect them from the insult of an earth grave, or to provide some comfort in the ground. And although all the bodies in the cemetery were supine, the ways they lay on their backs varied: some, for example, had their arms at their sides, others had their hands clasped; some had their knees flexed, others their legs ramrod-straight. The disparate use of stones and postures are clues that it was the family, rather than the priest or sexton, who settled a corpse in its grave; otherwise, we would probably find greater uniformity. Most burials apparently took place within a day or two of death, but some bodies, judging from the tumble of their bones, had waited a few days before burial, either because people who died away from the village were carted home by their families for burial, or because no priest was on hand to officiate at the funeral in the first days after death. The bulk of the graves, including the fanciest ones, were dug south and east of the church, hinting that people deemed this the propitious spot; and babies were buried under the eaves on that side of the church, their graves given some protection from inclement weather. At the same time, a man terribly crippled by polio or tuberculosis lay at the northernmost reaches of the graveyard, and he, alone of all the people buried at Raunds, had a stone in his mouth. Centuries after the coming of Christianity there was still the drive to mark differences in social status and age, there was still a lack of uniformity and still hints of practices that skirted orthodoxy, all of which indicate that clerical control over burial was far from complete.

If this was the state of English burial almost a half a millennium after the coming of Christianity, what of the graves made during the infancy of the new religion? During the first 120 or so years of Christian England, say c. 600 to 720, burial rites and grave goods did undergo a sea change; indeed, they are so different that archaeologists often label them 'final-phase' to distinguish them from earlier, 'migration period' burials. The majority of people who died in this period were given no grave goods at all, or had only a knife at their waists. Cremations were now also very rare. Burials were often uniformly aligned, too, with the heads of most bodies in a cemetery pointing in the same direction. From what we have learned at Raunds, this constellation of practices, which we see here coalescing in the early seventh century, was going to have a very long run. But are these necessarily Christian habits? The temptation, of course, when looking at 'final-phase' graves is to remember that they were contemporary to England's conversion, and to attribute the novel rites which stand behind them to new beliefs. But correlation is not always the same as causation. Cremations, as we have seen, were already on the wane in the later sixth century; many communities abandoned the pyre habit long before their conversion to Christianity. Cemeteries were increasingly aligned in the pagan period as well; and the use of grave goods by fewer and fewer people was a trend decades old at the time Christian missionaries began working in England. So the habit of aligned, inhumed, unaccompanied burial predated conversion among many families and communities. At the same time, the grave-goods habit continued long after 597 among the great, including professional Christians, like the Northumbrian saint Cuthbert, whose body was not only adorned with a gold and garnet cross when first buried, but whose tomb was continually opened and augmented over the centuries with splendid new objects.

For those groups who continued to bury their fellows with grave goods during this 'final phase', the repertoire of objects changed dramatically. Although fewer individuals were now buried with objects, a handful of mourners continued to orchestrate very rich, indeed dazzling burials. So fewer people by the beginning of the seventh century, including people who were pagans, were treated to grave-goods burials. The repertoire of objects found in furnished 'final-phase' burials differs dramatically from those found a century earlier as well. Dead women no longer wore two or three outsized brooches and long strings of beads. Instead, they sported short, choker-like necklaces of small, monochrome beads and gold and silver pendants, which were sometimes enamelled or set with garnets. They hung girdle sets from their belts, which included everything from pendants made from beaver teeth to crystal balls, sieves, and bags, the mouths of which, at least in Kent, were sometimes supported by rings made from elephant ivory. Now clothes were often fastened with ornate pins or small cloisonné or garnet-set disc-brooches worn at the throat. The appearance of this jewellery in 'final-phase' graves is more likely to be the result of a change in women's fashions than of a transformation in ritual or belief. In particular, it seems that the peplos-style dress, which needed a fastener at each shoulder, had given way to sewn shifts. Elite men were now buried with small buckles at their waists, metal shoelace tags and knives with angled backs. But many other goods that had earlier accompanied high-status males in their graves – in particular spears and swords – had become rare. Beyond this, regional sets of grave goods and regional styles of dress were much less marked in 'final-phase' burials, with the new assemblages popular across the whole of the English culture zone.

Some 'final-phase' burials, however, do seem to have been affected by the new religious fashions of England after 597. The jewellery that accompanied women to their graves was sometimes decorated with Christian symbols. But whether people wearing objects decorated with crosses in their graves were Christian or simply enamoured of the latest Continental fashions we cannot say. Nonetheless, Christian symbols were incorporated into the designs of some of the most beautiful metal-work creations of the seventh century, and these objects were then buried with the dead. Take, for example, the mid-seventh-century Crundale buckle, an elaborate silver piece plated, in places, with thin sheets of gold. It was found in a rich Kentish grave, one that included yet another fancy buckle and a magnificent iron sword, the pommel of which had Style II animal ornamentation, a style of decoration reserved, as we have seen, for the most elevated objects. The Crundale buckle, like the sword it accompanied, was also decorated with a Style II beast. More interesting for our purposes, however, is the central decoration of the buckle: a long gold fish, fashioned in high relief and finished off with cabochon-set garnet eyes. The fish, of course, is a symbol of Christ. The buckle, moreover, like the great gold buckle found at Sutton Hoo, was fashioned with a hollow centre, a space perhaps meant to contain a Christian relic. A necklace dating to the second half of the seventh century, and found at Desborough in Northamptonshire, is also interesting. It is spectacularly beautiful and strung with biconical beads made from fine gold wire, little golden bullae pendants, and gold and cabochon garnet pendants, some round, some square and some triangular. Originally, a much larger oval garnet pendant hung at the centre of the neck-lace, but at some point its central position was lost and the necklace made asymmetrical with the addition of a gold cross. Someone had gone to some trouble, after the necklace was made, to restring the piece so that a cross would sit at its centre.

What are we to make of these Christian-looking grave goods? Just because both these pieces incorporate Christian symbols it does not necessarily follow that their owners were adherents of the new faith. They may, instead, have associated Christian symbols with high-class, Continental imports or 'modern' design. After all, many in the twenty-first century listen to American music and wear American-style sports shoes but are neither Americans nor lovers of the United States. By the same token, just because both kinds of object served as grave goods this does not mean that those with whom they were buried were pagans.

What did all of this have to do with the adoption of Christianity by the English? Perhaps the answer is 'not much'. Although English kings and churchmen, after conversion, forbade a mysterious (at least to us) constellation of activities that included not only divination and the carrying of amulets, but the eating of horse meat, dressing like stags and carving feet out of wood, no pronouncements were made which banned grave goods. Indeed, it seems that the conversion-period Church was quite uninterested in regulating burial – certainly the earliest English law codes promulgated by Christian kings and written by their churchmen have nothing to say about it. Cremation and animal sacrifice were not tolerated by the Church, but since both habits were on the wane by c. 600, neither required systematic legislative campaigns. There were also no texts written in the early Middle Ages which insisted on east–west burial, although cemeteries after the coming of Christianity were often aligned that way. But then again, many earlier, pagan cemeteries had already adopted such an alignment. Indeed, it may be that what we have come to think of as proper Christian burial, with no jewellery, no weapons and bodies lying supine with their heads pointing towards a notional Jerusalem, had been constructed out of older, ubiquitous late pagan-period practices.

We need to step back here, take stock and put together the disparate strands of what we know about ritual and burial practices, social stratification and the formation of kingdoms, because all these things come together in the seventh century when the English began converting to Christianity. By the year 600 steeply hierarchical societies were present across Britain, even in the English-culture zone, and some families there now controlled broad territories and were able to extract impressive tributes from large numbers of dependants. A handful of men in the

eastern half of Britain, moreover, were by this time not only calling
themselves kings, but a few were even the sons, brothers or nephews of
the kings who had ruled before them. Our lamentably limited texts
allow us to identify only thirteen English kingdoms and their dynasties
in the seventh century. In the north, there were two kingdoms: Bernicia
and Deira, which would eventually join together as the kingdom of
Northumbria. In a broad belt across the middle of modern-day England
lay the kingdoms of the East Angles, Lindsey and Mercia, and of the
Hwicce, the Magonsæte and the Middle Angles. To the south, there
were the kingdoms of Kent and the East Saxons, the South Saxons,
the West Saxons and the people of the Isle of Wight. There were doubtless other groups of English-speakers with kings in this century, but they
are not described in any surviving text, so their identities and histories
are lost to us. Many of these anonymous entities must have been quite
small, and, over the course of the seventh century, all would be co-opted,
conquered or cannibalized by those bigger, more competitive kingdoms
whose names and early histories were captured on parchment. In short,
kingdoms across the later sixth and seventh centuries were both coming
together and disappearing.

English kingdoms in this period, then, were not only numerous, but
were in a dizzying state of flux. Some peoples and kings, like those in
Kent, had come together as early as the mid-sixth century, but others,
like the West Saxons, only coalesced sometime in the seventh century.
The relative standing of each of England's most successful kingdoms
vis-à-vis the rest would also change dramatically. Bede informs us that,
around 600, King Æthelbert of Kent († 616) was England's most powerful monarch. Before he secured his dominant position, though, first a
king of the South Saxons and then a king of a people known as the
Gewisse (who would later come to form the core of the West Saxon
kingdom) had been the most successful of all English kings, and these
men, like Æthelbert after them, had been able to exercise a certain
amount of authority over other kings, as well as levy tribute and extract
military support from subordinate peoples and their kings. By the 620s the
power of Kent's king was on the wane, and first a king of the East Angles
and then Northumbria's king came to dominate. By the 640s Mercia
would be the most powerful English kingdom, and by the 680s the
kingdom of the West Saxons would come, for a time, to the fore. Bloody
contestation lay behind many of these ups and downs, and Bede's

account of the seventh century is littered with the corpses of assassinated and battle-dead kings. It is little wonder that the royal dynasties competing, colluding and fighting one another during this period were so willing to borrow, adopt and innovate as they strove to survive and thrive in an exceptionally cut-throat political environment.

Given the number of English dynasties in the seventh century and the many wars of expansion, it is hardly surprising that top families were intent on monumentalizing their power; indeed, it is clear that many saw their ambitious landscape interventions, their co-options of traditional cult sites and ritual landscapes, as well as their extravagant death rituals, as key means of convincing others of their rights to territory and resources. Successful high-status English families were also enamoured, as British elites had long been, with the Roman past, or what passed, in sixth- and seventh-century Britain, for the Roman present; that is, the wine-drinking, Christ-loving Franks just across the Channel, whose fashions many English strove to emulate and whose wine, jewellery and pottery they so eagerly sought, consumed and flaunted. It is hardly surprising that Christianity, which was, after all, the religion of Rome and the Franks, arriving as it did in a period of brutal political competition, would come to be used by kings as yet another way of getting ahead. Many an English king in this period, when first encountering foreign missionaries, must have considered conversion to Christianity as one more status-enhancing move, especially since the new religion came bundled with impressive writing and building technologies, and since one of the perks of becoming Christian was access to the expertise of foreign churchmen from more Roman parts of the world, who were willing and able to help convert-kings more efficiently administer their territories and more profitably manage their resources.

So, when Augustine and his fellow missionaries arrived in Kent in 597, declaring that they 'came from Rome', the Kentish king was probably open to these men's overtures, in part because he thought that conversion could help him triumph over competing dynasties. While conversion meant the end of some ritual practices embraced by royal households, nonetheless, because missionaries showed little inclination to impede the status-enhancing burial practices that were so central to kings' self-aggrandizing strategies, a change in religion did not interfere with one of the most basic means of political competition. As a matter of fact, Christianity, as we shall see, offered a series of novel mortuary practices which could be added to kings' repertoires of competitive burial display. At the same time the stone architecture that came with Christianity offered kings an impressive new medium for highly visible interventions in the landscape. Thus conversion would come to provide English kings with many new status-enhancing opportunities, which were essentially both more 'modern' and more 'Roman' versions of older methods of display.

It was not all smooth sailing, of course, and a number of royal courts initially resisted conversion or slid back into paganism after a year or a decade. But, as we shall see, so many important dynasties came to make the transition to Christianity in the first half of the seventh century that it appears that those which were initially reluctant to accept the new religion in the end had little choice but to become Christians themselves in order to stay in the game.

6

Missionaries and Converts: The Later Sixth to Early Eighth Century

In the later sixth and seventh centuries the English pagans we have examined, as well as the pagan Picts living far to the north, were heavily missionized, and the vast majority were made into Christians. One of the things our narrative accounts make clear about these developments is that kings were crucial in this transformation, because again and again we find that, once a king decided to convert, his people followed. The conversion of King Æthelbert of Kent and his people, the group initially targeted by the missionaries Pope Gregory the Great sent from Rome, turned out to be gratifyingly easy. The missionaries were doubtless aided in their work by the royal household's long-standing and intimate familiarity with Frankish Christians, including the king's own wife, Bertha. Within a couple of years, not only had the king and all the people of Kent been baptized, but Augustine, the head of the mission, was now archbishop of Canterbury, and he and his companions were settling into a newly built monastery and were busy overseeing the construction of several stone-built churches. In 604 yet another episcopal church and bishop were established in Kent, this time at Rochester. Churches and bishops were also spreading outside Kent. Sæberht († c. 616), the king of the neighbouring kingdom of the East Saxons, under pressure from Æthelbert – not only the most important man in the region, but Sæberht's uncle and his overlord – converted to Christianity along with his people, and he allowed the construction of yet another episcopal church, St Paul's, which was built in a corner of the deserted Roman city of London. The king of the East Angles, similarly subordinate to the king of Kent, also agreed to become a Christian. A generation on, when Æthelbert's Christian daughter was given in marriage to Edwin, the pagan king of Northumbria, she arrived at her husband's court with an Italian missionary by her side. As in Kent, the combination of

Christian wife and Roman missionary proved irresistible, and the Northumbrian king and his people soon agreed to baptism.

As effortless as the stories of some of these early conversions make England's transition from paganism to Christianity seem, our narrative sources also make it clear that a number of kings in the early days were far from exemplary Christians. Pope Gregory had been careful to advise his missionaries not to destroy pagan shrines, suggesting, instead, that they turn them into Christian places of worship. He also argued that traditional pagan rituals of cattle sacrifice should be transformed into Christian feasts. This is a humane approach to conversion, and it probably eased many early converts into Christianity. Nonetheless, this policy must have left new Christians confused about the differences between their traditional beliefs and practices and those promoted by the new religion. The most famous example of this is Rædwald, king of the East Angles, who converted to Christianity while visiting his overlord Æthelbert in Kent. When he returned home, however, he installed a Christian altar in his pagan shrine. He and others, although attracted to Christianity, wanted to adopt some components of the new religion, but to continue with traditional customs as well. The sons of the East Saxon king, Sæberht, for example, once their father died, refused baptism, and they endorsed their people's return to 'idol' worship. Nonetheless, they were quite happy to allow their father's old bishop to remain in the kingdom, as long as he provided them with the magical bread of the Christian Eucharist, which they were eager to eat. When the bishop refused, he was driven from the kingdom. Indeed, bishops and missionaries were expelled not only from this kingdom, but, after Æthelbert's death, from Kent as well. And when King Edwin died in battle in 633, Northumbria, too, abandoned Christianity for a time.

After a wave of setbacks and apostasies, however, in the 630s and 640s a pair of Northumbrian kings, Oswald and Oswiu, with the aid of a number of Irish monks and missionaries settled in Britain, turned their kingdom once again towards Christianity, and under their influence less powerful kings – like the kings of the West Saxons and the East Saxons – converted as well. In the 650s and 660s, the last of England's pagan kings, the kings of the Mercians, the South Saxons and the people of the Isle of Wight, converted. From this time on, neither kings nor their sons were tempted to return to paganism, and by the late seventh century all the peoples of Britain were Christian.

As clear as the basic narrative and chronology of the conversion are, the actual process of Christianization and the composition of the missionary groups who stood behind it are less well understood. At the same time, the religious beliefs and ritual practices of first-, second-, even third-generation Christians are also something of a puzzle. One of the objects of this chapter is to explore the processes of missionizing and conversion and to gain some sense of the look and feel of the Christianity which newly converted peoples came to embrace, not only in their first flush of enthusiasm, but five or twenty or fifty years after the missionaries first arrived. During the later seventh century both foreign missionaries and pious natives founded large numbers of religious communities, called *monasteria* in Latin and *mynstres* in English, and which modern historians call monasteries or minsters. Minsters would become central intellectual institutions and economic powerhouses in this period. We must get to grips with what life was like in communities like these and discover the ways these institutions came to shape the lives of the laity – not just kings and their familiars, but more ordinary people. To explore all of these issues, we shall look not only at textual evidence, but at material evidence as well.

MONKS MAKING CHRISTIANS

In the later sixth and seventh centuries monks from across Europe laboured to convert Britain's pagans. Each band of missionaries had its favourite saints and special liturgies, distinctive monastic observances and religious calendars, and each had its own set of cultural practices. The particularity of each group's Christianity, in turn, shaped the ways the different converts they made came both to internalize and to live their new religion. So this fact of multiple groups of missionaries had a profound impact on Britain's Christianization.

The best known of all the missionaries are the Italians, whose enterprise was launched by Pope Gregory the Great and lionized by the Venerable Bede. These men's religion was the Christianity of the late antique western Mediterranean, which meant that it had been tempered by towns and by the survival of Roman institutions. Although Rome and other Italian cities by this time were shadows of their former imperial selves, they were still vibrant places, with noisy markets, teeming industrial quarters and crowds of ninth- and tenth-generation Christians. Daily life for professional religious in places like these was founded on a money economy and written administration, and it invariably centred on an impressive late Roman church, a collection of wonder-working tombs and a staff of bureaucrats. Italian bishops ministered to the needs not only of townsmen, but of rustics living outside their cities' walls, and they spent much of their time administering complex pastoral-care and charity operations. In spite of – or perhaps because of – their worldly obligations, Italian bishops in this period found themselves increasingly drawn to monasticism, and by the late sixth century many, including Pope Gregory himself, were monks living in monasteries attached to their cathedrals. Gregory recruited Augustine and his fellow missionaries from his own monastery, and the ways these men lived their religion and imagined how it should look in eastern Britain were shaped in profound ways by their Roman upbringing.

Irish monks were also active in Britain, although they had not been sent by the pope, nor by Irish bishops, who were less central figures in Ireland than in places like Italy. Instead, they came because they subscribed to the notion that *peregrinatio*, or pilgrimage – for them, a lifelong exile away from family and Ireland – was a crucial component of ascetic life. These monks toiled not only among English-speaking pagans, but among the Picts of Scotland as well. Indeed, Irish monks had been preaching in northern Britain for a couple of generations by the time the Italians arrived: the most famous of the Irish missionary-monks, St Columba (521–97), founded his monastery on Iona, an island in the Inner Hebrides, in 563. He modelled his community – with its vallum-bound enclosure, its circular huts and its communal churches – on monastic settlements back home in Ireland. In the later sixth century Columban monks moved to establish a series of daughter houses back in Ireland as well as in Scotland, in both Irish-dominated Dál Riata and Pictish-dominated Pictland, and some of these religious foundations came to play starring roles in the evangelization of northern Britain. By the 580s a number of leading families in Pictland had been persuaded by these men, and at the time of Columba's death Iona and other Columban houses were staffed not only by monks who were culturally Irish but also by Picts: there was even a handful of English monks living in these communities, evidence that at least a few English-speakers converted to Christianity decades before Augustine's arrival.

A generation on, a handful of political refugees from pagan, English-speaking dynasties – men like Eanfrith (r. 633–4), a scion of the royal dynasty which ruled the northern kingdom of Bernicia – would become Christians during their exiles in Pictland; although, in Eanfrith's case, conversion proved short-lived. Other exiles, though, like the future Northumbrian kings Oswald (r. 634–42) and Oswiu (r. 642–70), fled to Irish Dál Riata, and they were not only baptized there, but remained committed Christians after their return home. By the 630s, Columban monks, as well as men coming directly from Ireland, with Oswald's and Oswiu's encouragement, were founding monasteries and evangelizing across the English-culture zone. In 635 one Iona monk, Aidan († 651), established a Columban-style monastery at Lindisfarne, an institution that would prove crucial in the conversion of both Northumbria and parts of the English midlands. Irishmen could also be found settling further south and east. One group, led by a man called Fursa, founded a monastery in East Anglia in the 630s with the support of two of the kingdom's newly minted Christian kings, probably at Burgh Castle, an abandoned Roman fort. The earliest graves in an inhumation cemetery within the fort are a series of unaccompanied burials aligned east–west. From radiocarbon dating, at least a few of these graves seem to be monastic burials from the seventh or early eighth century. Another Irishman, Dícuill, along with five or six companions, settled at Bosham, in Sussex, this time without any help from the local South Saxon king, who was pagan, and without much success among the locals. Yet another Irishman, Maelduibh, gave his name to Malmesbury, in Wiltshire, the site of an important early monastery. There were doubtless other Irish missionaries living and preaching among the English for whom no text-ual witnesses survive. The narrow, high-walled, stone church at Escomb, in County Durham, which dates to the late seventh or eighth century, is reminiscent of churches found in Ireland. Two sundials are built into the fabric of its walls, evidence that its inmates kept liturgical hours. Per-haps the monks who built at Escomb were Irish. A handful of early bishops working under English monarchs, moreover, bore Irish names, so Irish churchmen were familiar local figures when convert-kings began staffing their churches.

Besides Italians and Irishmen, two other groups of Christians were bumping up against the pagan English in the sixth and seventh cen-turies: the British and the Franks. Bede famously fulminates against the former because he believed that they had refused to introduce the English to Christianity; but it is likely, *pace* Bede, that many households in the increasingly English midlands had, in actual fact, been made into Christians not by foreign missionaries but by their British neighbours. Notably, a number of culturally British peoples who were coming under Mercian lordship in the first half of the seventh century, in particular the Hwicce, were Christian: at least some of the Hwicce's churches appear to predate the mid-seventh-century conversions in the region recorded by Bede. Two skeletons, for example, have been recovered from very near Worcester's cathedral. Both were aligned west–east and neither had any of the metalwork grave goods so beloved by English mourners. One, however, was wearing the remains of a garment embellished with a tablet-woven, gold-thread border, perhaps an ecclesiastical vestment. The radiocarbon dates of the two skeletons centre on the late sixth or seventh century (the one from 429–643; the other from 483–687), so it is almost certain that the earliest church at Worcester predates the English foundation of the see in *c.* 680. Similarly, three fifth- or sixth-century burials have been found underneath the church of St Mary de Lode, in Gloucester, which had originally been dug into the floor of a fifth-century timber structure built within the remains of what was probably a ruined Roman bath complex. A tenth- or eleventh-century stone church eventually came to replace it, and this second structure was built on the same site and followed the same alignment. This suggests that the building the stone church replaced had also served as a church. Both Worcester and Gloucester may, therefore, have had churches that originally served congregations of British Christians which had first come together in antiquity, and which had survived Roman Britain's collapse.

Late Roman Christianity also continued without interruption into the early medieval period among some communities in the West Country. This may be witnessed by the very large cemetery at Cannington, in Somerset, which once contained something on the order of 2,000 graves. People began burying at Cannington in late antiquity, and they were still at it half a millennium later, during the time when people in the region were coming to adopt the English language and English material culture. Throughout the cemetery's long history, from its foundation to its abandonment, the overwhelming majority of the dead were placed in the ground without grave goods and with their corpses aligned west–east. Even during the Roman period, moreover, the locals eschewed hobnail-boot- and decapitation-burials as well as Charon's obol. These facts do not prove that the people living around Roman Cannington were Christians, but they are suggestive. Elite British families residing in the neighbourhood, moreover, at least in the fifth and sixth centuries, were in contact with high-status Christian communities further west and may well have been serviced by British monastic communities in the region. So an argument can be made that many of the families who carried out burials at Cannington kept hold of their Christianity after Rome's fall and continued to practise certain late antique funerary rites. If this is indeed the case, these people could then have converted English-speaking newcomers filtering into the area, without the aid of Irish or Italian monks.

A final notable group of Christians in Britain were the Franks. Although Frankish churchmen had declined to evangelize among the English before Gregory the Great's Italian-led effort, Frankish Christians had, nonetheless, long been present in Kent. The most famous of these were a minor Frankish princess, Bertha, wife of the pagan-born Kentish king Æthelbert, and Bertha's bishop-companion Liudhard. Elite families in Kent at least three generations before Bertha's arrival, however, had been stuffing the graves of their dead relatives with a hotch-potch of Frankish consumer goods – everything from gold-and-garnet bird-brooches to wine bottles. Frankish traders (who were Christians) must therefore have been familiar figures in and around Kent. Some English skippers and traders in Kent probably also travelled back and forth across the Channel, and, after long dealings and close contacts with their more sophisticated Frankish trading partners, some may have converted to Christianity and, indeed, done so decades before their king. Augustine then brought more Franks to England: those initially accompanying his mission served as translators. As we move further into the seventh century we find English kings sometimes spending their exile in Francia, and later in the century it was not uncommon for religiously minded English women from royal households to travel there in search of monastic life or training. Some newly converted English kings also promoted Franks to bishoprics. So relations between royal English kindreds and individual Frankish churchmen were sometimes intimate. It is hard to establish an exact chronology for Frankish missionary activity in eastern Britain, but Augustine, in his letters to Pope Gregory, worried over the liturgical differences in Masses presided over by Roman and Frankish churchmen, perhaps because such anomalies had come to the fore when Franks began working in the English mission.

Despite their diverse origins, Christian missionaries in Britain had much in common. In the fourth and fifth centuries British Christians had helped convert the Irish, and as a result people in western Britain, Ireland and south-western Scotland (where many Irish had settled) cherished a number of the same saints, benefited from a shared literary tradition and helped pioneer an important set of pious practices, including private penance and pilgrimage. More recently people in Francia had fallen under the influence of a charismatic Irish monk called Columbanus (540–615), and he had introduced them to versions of Irish monasticism and piety, which many Franks came to embrace with enthusiasm. Indeed, a number of Franks working in England had either trained in Columbanus-influenced monasteries or had studied in Ireland itself. At the same time the home institutions of both Frankish and Italian missionaries were often splendid, stone-built establishments, with treasure-filled churches and crypts and comfortable dormitories with glass-covered windows. These men and the early generations of monks and nuns under their influence did their best to replicate this kind of monastic infrastructure in Britain. The different missionary groups operating in Britain, however, had come of age in Churches with varied liturgical practices and calendars, monastic regulations, strategies for salvation, even tonsures; and the various groups had diverse opinions about the obligations and rights of bishops and abbots and about what, exactly, constituted 'proper' monastic life. At times these differences led to tensions and disputes. Of equal importance is the fact that each group passed on its own particular traditions and practices to the individuals and communities it converted. So the Christianity taking root in Britain in the sixth, seventh and eighth centuries was far from monolithic, in part because of the different peoples involved in its evangelization.

CONVERTS MAKING CHRISTIANITY

Once established, Christianity's practice also varied considerably among laypeople, because gender, generation, worldly circumstance, level of contact with foreigners and proximity to royal power all affected the ways individuals came to understand and worship their new god. First and foremost, first-, second-, even third-generation converts carried on many of the traditional practices of their pagan ancestors. Indeed, our few written sources suggest that educated churchmen well into the eighth century encountered rituals which sat uncomfortably alongside their own notions of proper religion. The penitential ascribed to Theodore of Tarsus, a Greek who was sent by the pope in Rome to be archbishop of Canterbury (668–90), includes penalties for Christians who had confessed to eating food given out at pagan sacrifices, but the text goes on to counsel priests when assigning penance 'to consider the individual, of what age, or in what way brought up [and] what the circumstances were'. The same text also makes distinctions between people who made 'little offerings' to the old gods and those who did so 'truly to a great extent'. Here, we have intimations that thoughtful churchmen, even at the tail end of the seventh century, continued to make allowances for old people, confused first-generation Christians and members of households from the back of beyond, who thought of themselves as Christians, but who remained somewhat baffled by their new religion's requirements and proscriptions.

It is hardly surprising that distinct groups of laypeople understood in quite different ways both the demands of their new religion and the appropriateness of some of the practices of their grandparents. English society by this time, as we have seen, was sharply hierarchical. Most kings, for example, although illiterate, often found themselves in the company of ecclesiastics during these years, because missionaries and bishops often lived in their households. Because of this, kings and their intimates had ready access to vital information about Christian doctrine and practice. Indeed, quite a few members of high-status households, including a surprising number of kings, opted for the religious life in the seventh and early eighth centuries. A few, like the Northumbrian king Aldfrith (r. 685–705), even learned to read and write Latin. More ordinary households, though, had fewer opportunities to internalize learned versions of the new religion because their contact with missionaries, bishops and priests was more sporadic. It is telling, for example, that in the last decade of the seventh century the Kentish king Wihtræd (r. c. 690–725) issued laws mandating penalties for both free farmers and slaves who sacrificed to devils, but included no such fines for grander people, which suggests that while yokels might still continue to backslide

in this way, more prominent households would never dream of participating in such déclassé rites.

People living in modest households, then, would have remained
more heterodox in their understanding and practice of 'proper' religion
because they were often left after baptism to puzzle over Christian
dogma and ritual on their own. Bede admits as much in one of his
saints' lives, where he has a crowd of Northumbrian rustics complain
that, although Christian missionaries had put an end to their ancient
rituals and customs, 'how the new worship is to be undertaken, nobody
knows'. There were, however, efforts to educate and serve people like
these. In the late seventh century, for example, a nobleman granted
land at Breedon-on-the-Hill, in Leicestershire, to a group of monks
with the understanding that they would build a church and house a
priest there who could baptize and preach to people living in the area.
In spite of scores of such initiatives, though, 150 years after Augustine
had begun his mission, churchmen were still struggling to educate
lower-status laypeople, who lived at some distance from institutions
providing pastoral care, that is, basic services like preaching and other
religious education, baptism and penance. One Church council, the
Council of *Clofesho* (747), held 150 years after Augustine's arrival,
decreed that 'every year each bishop, going through his diocese, and
around it, and observing should not neglect to visit and should ass-
emble people of diverse condition and sex, at convenient places, and
should plainly teach, especially those who rarely hear the word of God'.
So, there must have been many places – even in the mid-eighth century –
without much preaching and many people in need of basic religious
instruction.

Although missionaries working in England, beginning with those
sent by Pope Gregory, often dealt with their confused lay charges with
remarkable sympathy, they were nonetheless unwilling to tolerate a
number of traditional practices, which laypeople apparently did not
know were proscribed. Archbishop Theodore, or a member of his circle,
for example, was horrified that English women, when attempting to
cure fevers, sometimes placed their daughters on rooftops or in ovens,
and he mandated long penances for the mothers who confessed to doing
this. It is impossible, given the terseness of the text, to know what
took place during one of these fever cures or why the churchman writing this penitential was so exercised by it. The language of the text is

frustratingly vague: was it the daughter who had the fever, or were others cured through this act? Were the ovens hot or cold? Did the girls and their mothers utter special incantations? Or was the problem here that child-bearing women rather than celibate men were acting as ritual specialists? Whatever the answers to these questions, the assignment of a stiff, multi-year penance, especially considering the same text's moderation when it came to 'little sacrifices to devils', suggests that something about this particular act crossed the line. The same text is also uncompromising against people who burned grain in the presence of corpses for 'the health of the living and the house'. Like the rituals surrounding fever cures, priestly attitudes towards this practice suggest that a firm line had been drawn by missionizing churchmen between harmless traditions, which they felt could be ignored or incorporated into Christian life, and bona fide heathenism, which demanded extirpation.

Higher-status individuals, although apparently less likely after conversion to sacrifice 'to devils' or put their daughters in ovens, carried on, nonetheless, with a number of traditional practices, the origins of which lay in paganism. Thus, although many more ordinary families had dispensed with grave-goods burial decades before the missionaries had arrived, a number of high-ranking households continued after conversion to pack the graves of some of their members with objects that must have given foreign missionaries pause. Sides of beef, whole geese, chicken eggs and bronze bowls full of crab apples continued to share grave space with high-status corpses, as did elaborate jewellery and weaponry. Indeed, many of the barrow burials we examined in Chapter 4 were contemporary with the first couple of generations of the Roman mission, and one of the striking things about a number of them is the mixed religious signals they telegraph. Weapons, food in the grave and barrows may strike us as pagan, but other objects placed with the dead in the first half of the seventh century – baptismal spoons, wooden cups decorated with crosses and splendid cross pendants – can be read as Christian. Perhaps these burials look the way they do, not because the dead themselves had been unsure of their own beliefs, but because the households overseeing their funerals were divided between enthusiastic Christian converts and determined pagan traditionalists. For example, in the case of the so-called 'Prittlewell Prince', whose grave has been excavated at Southend-on-Sea, in Essex, Christian retainers and kindred may have insisted upon laying gold-foil crosses on the dead man's corpse or sewing them onto his clothes, but his more conservative followers perhaps ensured that his grave was equipped with gaming pieces and dice. As we have seen, many impatient kings' sons during these years seem to have made decisions about their own religious affiliations in opposition to their fathers. A number apparently refused baptism, and many, after their fathers' deaths, returned their kingdoms to paganism. When an enthusiastic old Christian died and some of his surviving brothers, sons and nephews remained unconverted, funerals must have been tense arenas of ritual contestation.

Long after kingdoms had officially and finally committed themselves to Christianity – well into the first couple of decades of the eighth century – households headed by thoroughgoing Christians also continued to bury a few of their dead, especially their female dead, with lavish gold jewellery hung with Frankish-style Christian pendants. During this period living women from important families may have worn this kind of jewellery both to signal their kin group's wealth and to announce their family's new religious affiliation, in much the same way that some of their great-grandmothers had once worn gold bracteate pendants as a sign of their adherence to the cults of particular pagan deities. The jewellery of our dead Christian women, however, rather than being worn as part of their mortuary costumes, was now sometimes slipped into little bags or boxes and placed next to or on top of the dead women's corpses. There is no reason, therefore, not to see this jewellery as grave goods. Grave goods, as we have seen, had long shored up important families' social positions, and they continued to be used for the same reason generations after conversion.

For the first time, the women treated to grave-goods burials were also sporting little copper-alloy cylindrical containers on their belts known as 'workboxes'. About fifty have been found in Britain, and they are probably close relatives of similar objects excavated from Christian Francia and Spain. Indeed, a number of English examples are embellished with punched-dot decorations made in cross-shaped patterns. They probably had a magical or amuletic function, because a number have been found containing thread and bits of cloth, which may have been secondary relics. Given the late date of these 'workboxes' (they were in use from c. 675 to c. 720), the women suspending them from their belts were more likely to have been Christian than not. So high-status lay Christians must have found the use of these little containers and their contents perfectly orthodox. Nonetheless, they hark back to older amuletic and status customs.

A series of injunctions from the period, as a matter of fact, suggest that churchmen had begun to wage what would turn out to be a largely unsuccessful, centuries-long campaign against amulets. Again and again, English Church councils mandated that bishops preach against their use. Even at the turn of the ninth century the Northumbrian intellectual Alcuin (c. 735–804) was castigating Englishmen who were 'wearing amulets, thinking them something sacred. But it is better to imitate the example of the saints in the heart than to carry bones in little bags; to have Gospel teachings written in the mind rather than to wear them around the neck scribbled on scraps of parchment.' Clearly, Alcuin was complaining about baptized, catechized Christians, but he found these people's use of Christian talismans offensive. Not all card-carrying religious in Britain, though, would have agreed with Alcuin. One penned the following lines in an eighth-century prayerbook: 'I abjure thee, Satan, devil, elf, by the Living and the True God, and by the terrible Day of Judgement, that he may flee from a man who goes about with this writing with him, in the name of the Father, Son and Holy Ghost.'

English penitential and conciliar texts hint that churchmen also worried about activities taking place around traditional ritual sites, such as springs, wells, standing stones and groves. Provisions from English penitentials, probably dating from the eighth century, condemn the taking or discharging of vows on trees; and a tantalizing ash tree makes an appearance in a ninth-century description of the boundaries of a piece of property, where we are told that it was a tree 'which the ignorant call sacred'. St Columba, for his part, famously defanged a lethal well in the land of the Picts, which, his biographer tells us, 'foolish people worshipped as a god'. Even the English missionary St Boniface, working among Continental pagans in the mid-eighth century, felt the need to chastise people who worshipped saints in the 'wrong' places. In spite of these and similar condemnations, holy wells and yew trees in churchyards continue to this day to mark Britain's Christian landscape.

On a number of occasions we can witness professional religious and secular elites working hard to transform ancient ritual sites from pagan places into Christian ones. One remarkable remaking took place at Bardney, in Lincolnshire. There was probably an important settlement at Bardney controlled by the kings of Mercia, and the family founded a church there to serve as its mausoleum. But the new minster lay in a much older ritual landscape centred on a portion of the River Witham. Since the Bronze Age, people had been making monumental interventions into the landscape here. They had built a series of causeways and barrows along the river, and for several thousand years the locals had been throwing votive offerings – often weapons – into the waters near the ends of these causeways. As a matter of fact, these offerings continued from the Bronze Age, to the pre-Roman Iron Age, through the Roman period and on into the Middle Ages. So the foundation of this monastery (alongside an unusually large number of other churches along this stretch of river, almost all in close proximity to one of the causeways) may initially have been part of a campaign to Christianize an important pagan locale. Then again, the power of the Witham Valley may have encouraged the kings of Mercia to build a monastery at Bardney so that they could co-opt its magic.

One of Mercia's kings and his Northumbrian wife, Osthryth, a niece of the martyred king of Northumbria, Oswald, became special patrons of Bardney in the 680s or 690s. At that time, Osthryth translated part of her uncle's remains to the church (although not the king's arms and hands, which remained in the church of her father, King Oswiu, in Bamburgh, nor his head, which had been buried at the important minster at Lindisfarne). Bardney was the church which both she and her husband had chosen as their final resting place and, like many in the period, the two craved burial next to a saint. The Bardney monks, however, at least initially, proved hostile to the translation. According to Bede:

> They knew [Oswald] was a saint but, nevertheless, because he belonged to another kingdom and had once conquered them, they pursued him even when dead with their former hatred. So it came about that the relics remained outside all night with only a large tent erected over the carriage in which the bones rested. But a sign from heaven revealed to them how reverently the relics should be received by all the faithful . . . The bones were washed, laid in a shrine constructed for the purpose, and placed in the church with fitting honours, and in order that the royal saint might be perpetually remembered, they placed above the tomb his banner of gold and purple, pouring out the water in which the bones had been washed in the corner of the sanctuary. Ever afterwards the soil which had received that holy water had the power and saving grace of driving devils from the bodies of people possessed.

Perhaps with the washing of the king's bones, the powerful, pagan juju of the river was transformed and sanctified. Whatever the case, in spite of, or perhaps because of, its Christianization, the Witham Valley continued on as an important ritual place, and people not only came to venerate St Oswald but, as late as the fourteenth century, were still casting weapons and other metalwork into the river. Bardney's history, then, hints at the ways in which traditional rites and sites could both be absorbed into Christianity and co-opted by Christian kings.

What households of lower status than that of the king of Mercia were up to in terms of their own ritual practices is anyone's guess. There are hints, though, that more ordinary people, besides baptizing their children and at least occasionally participating in the Eucharist and penance, were gradually Christianizing the little habits of their daily lives, and in doing so were also making the religion their own. St Columba, for example, had taught local dairymen to make the sign of the cross before they milked their cows to keep devils from hiding in the bottom of their milk pails; and there was a tenacious tradition in Kemsing, in Kent, still practised on the eve of the Protestant Reformation, in which local farmers presented their seed-corn to the shrine of an otherwise unknown saint with an Old English name to protect it from mildew. And farm families in northern England were not nearly as interested in travelling to the official cult centres dedicated to St Oswald at Bamburgh or Lindisfarne to witness his relics' biblically inspired miracles, as they were in visiting the uncontrolled, open-air site of his martyrdom, a place where his head and arms had been displayed on stakes, or Heavensfield, where the king had put up a large cross before an important battle. It was at these places that farmers sought miraculous cures for their ailing livestock. So Christianity was becoming deeply enmeshed in farming practices during this period, which hints at the ways ordinary people were incorporating the new religion into their own lives.

Girls in ovens, workboxes, magical ash trees, holy kings, heads on stakes and the potent waters of holy wells and rivers suggest the continuation of older ways of thinking about the world, and they remind us that laypeople in Britain in the generations after their conversion transformed the Christianity of Italians, British, Irish and Franks into something quite different. Although elite households probably practised a version of Christianity more closely allied to the one lived by professional religious, some of their beliefs and practices diverge nonetheless; and the difference between the religion of the farmers and the monks must have been greater still. It is hardly surprising, then, that professional religious, with their book-learning, their rule-regulated communities and their *echt*-Christianity, sometimes found lay practices offensive.

SOCIAL STRUCTURES AND THE SPREAD OF CHRISTIANITY

Although people who were culturally English adopted Christianity in part because of the efforts of generations of missionaries drawn from across Europe, the social structures that governed life in Britain also helped facilitate the new religion's spread. The hardball politics of the later sixth and seventh centuries, a period when ambitious families fought to establish royal dynasties and to conquer the territories of neighbouring competitors, meant that many pagan princelings spent part of their youths in exile, often fleeing to the courts of Dál Riatan, Pictish or Frankish kings, who had been born Christians, or to neighbouring English kingdoms, which had come to Christianity more recently. Bede's history, as we have seen, is full of such exiles, and he often records these men's conversions during the course of their stay. Some exiles may have adopted Christianity out of gratitude towards their hosts and others because of a genuine turning of the heart. It may be, however, that some turned to Christ when they witnessed first-hand the power of kingship shored up by an imperial religion and buttressed by hard-working and literate celibates who were long-practised in the performance of powerful and mysterious ceremonies. Whatever their motives for conversion, the exiles and returns helped expose to Christianity many who were living in the most important pagan households.

The writings of Bede and other early hagiographers also make clear that kings themselves were crucially important in the dissemination of the new religion. First and foremost, a king, after consulting his advisers, apparently had the right to make decisions about his people's religion, his conversion often triggering weeks of mass baptisms, occasions during which aristocratic retainers, free farmers and slaves all presented themselves to missionaries so that they might be made into Christians. In Kent, for example, Bede tells us that King Æthelbert as well as others, believed and was baptized, being attracted by the pure life of the saints and by their most precious promises, whose truth they confirmed by performing many miracles. Every day more and more [of Æthelbert's people] began to flock to hear the Word, to forsake their heathen worship, and, through faith, to join the unity of Christ's holy Church.

Although Bede hastens to add that Æthelbert did not force any of his people to convert, he does say that the king loved believers more. Perhaps this does not constitute coercion, but the king's affection was a powerful motivator. Æthelbert, moreover, who was the overlord of lesser rulers, saw to it that the kings of the East Saxons and the East Angles also welcomed Augustine's mission. Something similar happened after the conversion of Northumbria's powerful kings, when we also find the lesser kings beholden to them welcoming missionaries into their own kingdoms.

After the initial mass conversion of a king and his people, Christianity spread and penetrated more deeply, at least among elite kin groups, because of the practice among well-connected families of sending their adolescent sons to serve in their kings' households. This practice tied the fortunes of leading families within a kingdom to the king and to one another, and it provided aristocratic boys with opportunities to establish their reputations as warriors and counsellors. So, as royal courts Christianized, sons from the kingdom's prominent families were exposed to the holy men, monks and bishops so often present at royal courts. It was during their service that the sons of the powerful in the seventh century heard regular preaching, participated in religious feasts and fasts and became attached to the saints favoured by their kings. Some time in their twenties or thirties, the king would give the most successful of these boys the resources they needed to set up their own households. And when well-rewarded retainers retired from the king's hall, the religious practices they instituted in their own households probably mirrored those they had learned while living with the king. Thus social emulation, so important in the spread of English material culture and language, now facilitated the dissemination of Christian practices into non-royal households. Beyond those inscrutable decisions of the heart, traditional political and social practices as well as aspirational behaviour encouraged noblemen to adopt the Christian teachings and ritual practices they had witnessed in their kings' households.

From such elite households, Christian practices then leaked out into the surrounding territories. Though contact at this level was less intimate, there were moments each year when a great man and his household arrived at a central place, their visits coinciding with the locals coming with their ox carts full of tribute. The greater and lesser men together would then spend some days airing disputes, settling legal cases and reaffirming bonds of loyalty and lordship. They may have even feasted together. At such times churchmen attached to lords' households would preach, especially if their stay coincided with an important feast or fast. Such exposure to high-status religious observances would have encouraged local families to adopt some of the ritual observances and religious practices of their lords.

Bishops in each of England's newly converted kingdoms played a central role as well, not only in spreading the Christian religion, but in ensuring its survival, for it was bishops who ordained clergy, consecrated churches and had charge of baptism. Strictly observant minster communities, like those extolled in Bede's *Ecclesiastical History*, also had social interactions with laypeople, which had a profound impact on lay Christianity. We know, for example, that at special moments in the liturgical year great crowds of laypeople came to Bede's own monastery of Jarrow, where they encountered preaching and the full wonder of the Mass in one of the monastery's own churches. During such feast days distinguished lay patrons and the relatives of monks, nuns and priests could deepen their religious commitment, and monastic preachers could educate them about their religious obligations. We also have a description of some of the observances that took place at Rogationtide, a festival that begins five Sundays after Easter. During these days laypeople sometimes joined churchmen in their liturgical processions, but they also helped shape this celebration into something more secular. Much to the horror of some religious, laymen along with some churchmen held horse races and feasts to mark the end of the holiday. It must have been difficult for people who had entered the religious life as adults to give up such things. For this reason, child-oblates were probably the easiest people to mould into 'proper' Christians. Unlike adult converts, they would have had few preconceived notions about religious practice and belief, and they could be made to spend their youth memorizing religious texts and liturgies. Often the only holy texts the parents of such oblates knew, at least in the early years, were the Lord's Prayer and the

Apostles' Creed, hardly comprehensive blueprints for Christian living, so the ideas of people who had come of age in lay households about what constituted a proper Christian celebration must have differed dramatically from those who had been raised by monks or nuns.

Some minsters also provided pastoral care to lower-status people. Many communities with monks and nuns, who mostly lived within the confines of their religious house, also had ordained clergy in their minsters whose job it was to deliver pastoral care. As a result, laypeople living near many minsters would have had easy access to preaching and baptizing. For those living further afield, some minsters' clerical staff travelled to small oratories built on their monasteries' lands or to well-known open-air meeting sites, where they would preach, minister to the sick and baptize. In the anonymous *Life of St Cuthbert* we are told of a shepherd living near *Osingadun*, which was probably the site of one of Lindisfarne's oratories. Although only a shepherd, this man is referred to as a *frater*, or 'brother', and his name was commemorated in a Mass. A number of monastic communities in the seventh and eighth centuries – both Irish-inspired and Roman-inspired – also set up networks of daughter houses, and these, too, delivered pastoral services to laity living further afield. Clearly, though, the closer one lived to a monastery, the better one's family was served. Such arrangements were, moreover, not unique to the eastern half of Britain: monastic communities in the British-language zone had long been involved in pastoral care, and many British communities housed not only contemplatives, but secular clergy, and were thus equipped to minister to the needs of laypeople.

Not all minsters, however, took an interest in ordinary Christians. Churchmen serving at a number of royal foundations may have been more intent on serving their kings' households and promoting their dynasties' holiest members as saints – a new status-enhancing move embraced by many royal families – than in providing pastoral care to local farmers. King Oswiu, for example, had a church within his stronghold at Bamburgh, where he brought his murdered brother Oswald's hands and arms, now venerated as holy relics, and this church may have served as his family's mortuary chapel. This was a private establishment, and its priests must have focused their attentions on the needs of the royal household and its special royal cult. There was a second church at Bamburgh about a half a kilometre from the fortress, and it was at this church that the famous holy man and bishop of Lindisfarne, Aidan, stayed when he came to Bamburgh. Aidan apparently developed this second church because the ecclesiastics at Oswiu's church did not feel themselves responsible for the spiritual well-being of people living in the surrounding countryside. One wonders if there were other royally sponsored communities whose personnel were not the least bit interested in teaching swineherds the Lord's Prayer or baptizing their babies.

Kings, as we have seen, were establishing religious communities during this period, but so, too, were nobles. Bede's beloved monastery of Monkwearmouth-Jarrow was founded by a Northumbrian nobleman, and under his leadership it developed into an intellectual and spiritual powerhouse. Founding families, though, even in Bede's monastic 'Golden Age', often ruled the houses they endowed for several generations, although this practice could diminish a community's monastic fervour. By the end of Bede's life, moreover, aristocrats were establishing houses kept even more firmly under their families' control; indeed, at times these noble benefactors may have acted as lay abbots, and their members sometimes kept wives. The deportment of inmates in these laxer communities would have been difficult to distinguish from lay households. Bede, for example, complained: 'It is rumoured abroad about certain bishops that they serve Christ in such a fashion that they have with them no men of any religion or continence, but rather those who are given to laughter, jests, tales, feasting and drunkenness ... and who daily feed the stomach with feasts more than the soul.' Bede and others worried about the ways in which secular values often undercut monks' distinctive ways of living, and they feared that monastic communities would succumb to the pleasures of the mead-hall. Bede hated these 'false' monasteries, as he called them, but one of their chief sins, as far as he was concerned, was not their fondness for feasting, but their lack of interest in pastoral care. In his commentary on a passage from Ezra ('And they appointed the priests in their orders and the Levites in their divisions to supervise the services of God in Jerusalem ...'), he pointedly wrote:

The order of devotion required that, after the building and dedication of the Lord's house, priests and Levites be straightaway ordained to serve in it: for there would be no point in having erected a splendid building if there were no priests inside to serve God. This should be impressed as often as possible on those who, though founding monasteries with brilliant workmanship, in no way appoint teachers in them to exhort the people to God's works but rather those who will serve their own pleasures and desires.

In places with minsters like these, whose founding families were primarily interested in bolstering their own positions in the world via impressive stone architecture and private cults, local people would have had little access to pastoral care.

There must have been thousands of common people in the later seventh and the eighth centuries who did not see a priest from one year to the next. And of course some of the priests ministering to such people were not up to the job. Indeed, Bede, late in life, despaired over uneducated priests who had to be taught the Apostles' Creed and the Lord's Prayer in English, and a Church council held a few years after his death urged priests who did not know Latin not only to memorize both the Creed and the Lord's Prayer in English, but to learn their meaning. This can only mean that there were priests in the eighth century working among the laity who did not know the essentials of the faith and who were as unclear on the fundamentals of the religion as many of their charges.

TWO CHRISTIAN COMMUNITIES

What was life like in and around England's new minster communities? First and foremost, these places were quite varied. Some early minsters were communities of nuns and priests headed by abbesses; others were houses of men living under a monastic rule and led by a bishop; still others were communities of priests, each living in his own house with his wife and children. Many regulated their lives with a rule, though none at this date followed the Benedictine Rule, as monks and nuns would come to do in the tenth century. Rather, early monks and nuns instituted 'mixed rules' to govern their communities, which had been cobbled together from an assortment of regulations used in a number of different religious households both in Britain and across the sea. Like secular high-status households, ecclesiastical households lived off the labour of others, and it is clear from a series of land grants, most dating to the final third of the seventh century, that kings and other wealthy patrons often granted their minster-foundations what must have been single 'multiple estates', estates with extensive territorial footprints and large labouring populations already habituated to the idea of giving over tribute to a high-status household. That secular rulers could afford such generosity reminds us how many resources the dozen or so seventh-century royal dynasties won in the three or four generations they spent conquering or co-opting smaller or less successful entities. In the later seventh century, when many were founding minsters, their astounding generosity to the Church suggests that they had territories to spare. Such endowments, of course, freed monastic inmates from having to labour for themselves, and they allowed monks, nuns and priests to live the same kinds of dignified, leisured lives as their high-status secular kinfolk. Bede's *Ecclesiastical History* and a series of saints' lives, along-side a handful of manuscripts, metalwork and stone sculptures produced at early minsters, allow us to reconstruct the extraordinary intellectual and artistic achievements of some of these communities, and enable us to view the religious dedication of many of their inmates.

The physical realities of daily life in such places, though, and the ways their inmates interacted with the local families who supported them, are less well documented. Fortunately, a number of minsters have been excavated, and their physical remains tell us much that is interesting, not only about religious life in this period, but about the relationship between lay and religious communities. The material evidence from two partially excavated communities – Hartlepool, in the kingdom of Northumbria, and Nazeingbury, in the kingdom of Essex – allows us to recover something of both the daily lives and lived Christianity of conversion-period ecclesiastics and of the laypeople who interacted with them.

Bede's history preserves some information about Hartlepool. From it, we know that the Irishman and Iona monk Aidan served as Lindisfarne's first bishop, and under his tutelage the English noblewoman Heiu founded a double-minster for men and women at Hartlepool around the year 640. Hartlepool sat on a peninsula separated from the rest of the Northumbrian coast by a strip of wetland, so for all practical purposes, and much like Aidan's own beloved monasteries of Iona and Lindisfarne, Hartlepool was an island minster. Indeed, the name Hartlepool means 'island of the hart'. Its siting thus reflects a close connection between this community and others in Britain founded by the missionizing Irish. But, like other minsters, Hartlepool's main buildings sat on high ground overlooking navigable waters, and this was a hallmark not only of monastic sites, but of high-status secular sites, providing those who controlled such places with impressively visible settlements and easy communications with more distant locales. So it would be a mistake to see Hartlepool's location as an attempt by its founders to ensure the community's isolation. Irish monks working across Britain were active in the world, and, although they often developed special island hermitages at some distance from their central operations, the communities they founded were sites of integration rather than seclusion. This certainly seems to have been the case with Hartlepool. Indeed, Bede tells us that many important men visited the monastery when it was headed by its most famous abbess, Hild (c. 614–80).

We know from excavations that Hartlepool's layout was also Irish-inspired. It was divided into bounded concentric zones, with workaday business taking place in the outermost areas of the site and ritual activities concentrated at its centre. Archaeologists working here have identified a male zone and a female zone, a craft-working zone, a high-status mortuary zone and a lower-status burial area. This is reminiscent of layouts found at early monasteries across northern Britain and Ireland, including the Irish Clonmacnoise, the Pictish Portmahomack and the early phases at British Whithorn. Hartlepool's inmates also seem to have lived in single-person cells, much as monks at Irish communities did, although the shape and style of these structures were not dictated by the Irish roundhouse tradition, but rather by the rectangular buildings found both in Britain, in the English-culture zone, and across the Channel in Flanders and northern Francia. These little buildings were timber, post-and-plank structures with drystone footings, and they may have had hipped roofs. On average, they measured only 4.1 metres by 2.3 metres, and thus were much smaller than domestic buildings found on contemporary secular sites, even low-status ones, so they would have been unsuitable for family groups. It is more likely, given their minuscule dimensions, that each one served as an individual cell. In spite of their small size, they were impressive little buildings. More timber was lavished on them than on many larger structures, and they were embellished in an extremely elaborate and unusual way. Some apparently had finely plastered interiors; decorative stonework elements running along their doorjambs; and exterior walls covered with thick plasterwork, some of which was made to look like blind-arcading, in order to give them the appearance of stone buildings. In other words, it seems that the people in charge of building Hartlepool aspired to stone buildings, even if they lacked the know-how or resources actually to undertake such work. Hartlepool's abbess Hild had learned the religious life from her sister – the mother of the king of the East Angles and a nun – who had trained at a Frankish monastery, so the desire for masonry buildings may have come from Francia via East Anglia. Still, Bede tells us that the Irish monk and bishop Aidan often came to Hartlepool to 'instruct' Abbess Hild, so influences on the monastery came from many directions.

Three different cemeteries have been partially excavated at Hartlepool. The first accommodated two different populations: the house's male priests and wealthy lay families. The lay graves were carefully edged with rings of pebbles. A number of children were also buried in this cemetery, but in a single zone, and their graves may have been focused on a shrine. The second cemetery, found at the greatest distance from Hartlepool's core and near a well called 'St Helen's Well', included men, women and children. These people, like so many others in County Durham (although unlike the high-status people in Hartlepool's first cemetery), buried their dead in stone-lined cists, a mortuary practice followed even before Rome's fall. These are probably the remains of local farm families labouring on Hartlepool's lands and at its headquarters, people who had been slower to abandon traditional British practices like cist burial than their social betters.

The third cemetery, located back in the monastery's central zone, was used principally for women, some of whose graves are marked with recumbent stones inscribed with crosses and bearing their names. Similar name-stones have been found at a handful of other Northumbrian minsters, but also, and interestingly, at Clonmacnoise, in Ireland, and they perhaps reflect pervasive links and contacts between Irish religious and the English inmates of this and other minsters throughout the north. Given the preponderance of women's skeletons and the name-stones in this cemetery, it looks as if it must have been the nuns' burial place, although a few men were buried here as well. Five of the markers have women's names, one has both a man's and a woman's name and one has only a man's. Many of Hartlepool's nuns would have lived in the world before they adopted the monastic life, and some were related to kings. It would be understandable if a few of the most important or dearest kinsmen of these women had been honoured with burial in this cemetery.

The name-stones, which were written in a variety of scripts that were also used in Northumbrian manuscripts, suggest that at least a few people at Hartlepool had an intimate familiarity with literacy and manuscript production. Bede mentions a man named Oftfa, who was a member of the community, and who, according to Bede, 'devoted himself to the reading and observance of the Scriptures'. So it sounds as if there might have been a school here as well.

No evidence for writing or intellectual endeavours survives from our second minster community, Nazeingbury. Indeed, almost everything we know about this place comes from the evidence gathered from the excavation of its cemetery. This establishment was not in Northumbria, but rather in Essex. The kingdom of the East Saxons, like a number of early kingdoms, had a start-stop history with Christianity: its king at the turn of the seventh century, a nephew of the king of Kent, had welcomed a missionary-bishop to London. His sons, one generation on, however, were less enthusiastic and moved the kingdom, upon their father's death, back towards paganism. By the 650s, though, a Christian was once again king in Essex, and he, like many mid-century kings, was interested in patronizing monks and minsters. Thus we find an East Saxon king giving the Irishman and Lindisfarne monk Cedd an abandoned Roman fort at Bradwell-on-Sea so that he could build a minster. At the turn of the eighth century another East Saxon king, in cooperation with a person who was, perhaps, one of his female relatives, founded a nunnery, this time at Nazeingbury. Our only textual witness for this second community is a late medieval description of two land grants, originally issued sometime between 693 and 709, which record gifts of land made by a king of Essex to a woman called *ffymme*. According to the charters, the king made this donation so that 'a house of God' might be built there. Given the terseness of these redactions, we are fortunate that archaeologists have not only located the cemetery of the establishment but have recovered some remarkable evidence from it, things that provide interesting insights into life and belief in England in the first generations after conversion.

More than 190 people were buried in Nazeingbury's cemetery over the course of the eighth and ninth centuries, about 120 of these between *c*. 700 and *c*. 800. This earliest group of dead was placed in graves carefully aligned with a small, rectangular timber building, which, given its location in the midst of a cemetery, probably served as the community's church or mortuary chapel: in Francia, where a number of East Anglian men and women went in the seventh century for their monastic training, mortuary chapels often sat at the centre of monastic cemeteries, and these buildings were often rectangular in shape.

Four of Nazeingbury's eighth-century graves were dug into the floor of the east end of this building, where an altar probably stood. The two earliest graves (one with a radiocarbon date of *c.* 660–720) contained the remains of women, each one at least 50 years of age when she died. Perhaps these two were the founders or earliest abbesses of the community; one may even be the *ffymme* of our charters. These women's burials were followed by two more interior burials: those of yet another woman and an extremely robust man who had died in his late thirties or early forties. We know from other, better documented, royal nunneries, that from the last quarter of the seventh century into the early eighth the widows and daughters of kings who had taken up the monastic life often acted as their families' religious specialists and as the promoters of dynastic cults, and that their churches served as sepulchres for themselves, their male relatives and for their family's sainted dead. The nuns at Nazeingbury may have been doing something similar. So one or more of the bodies buried within Nazeingbury's cemetery structure may have been venerated as saints: founders, patrons and early abbesses often were.

Sometime in the late eighth or early ninth century the community built a larger timber structure in the cemetery, probably another church, and the earlier building was taken down. In spite of these changes, people continued to bury close to the graves located in what had been the east end of the original structure. One man, whose grave was dug where the wall of the earlier church, 'Church One', had once stood, lay alongside the robust man. This second man had died around the age of 50. Archaeologists found a simple bone pin in his grave, probably a shroud pin, and this humble object and its context are evidence of a new, post-conversion, high-status burial rite. Although some people of means continued, as we have seen, to deposit valuable objects in the graves of their dead, including some that were embellished with Christian symbols, others were now opting for unclothed, unadorned burial at a prestigious Christian site, in particular in the cemetery of a monastic community or, better still, near the graves of a minster's very special dead. Indeed, the impression – not only from the excavation of Nazeingbury but those of other minster sites as well – is that one of the advantages of a minster burial was that the dead laid to rest in monastic cemeteries remained important members of religious households, and that their salvation continued to be of crucial concern to the community. We know from excavations that at the minsters of Wearmouth, Jarrow and Whitby religious inmates often passed through their houses' cemeteries, since those who wished to move from these communities' churches to their living quarters and workshops had to walk among the graves of the dead. Sometimes, moreover, as we have seen at Hartlepool, stone funerary monuments were erected on top of monastic graves, and some bore inscriptions which petitioned passers-by for prayers. English monasteries began as early as the late seventh century to memorialize their dead, keeping lists so that they could be commemorated in their liturgies. Because the bond between prayer-specialists and the dead was fostered in minster cemeteries, it is little wonder that burial in them was sought after by well-to-do, lay salvation-seekers, who believed that the prayers of the living could aid in the salvation of the dead. Archaeologists also excavated a Roman coin from Nazeingbury's shrouded man's grave. Perhaps it is residual, a coin lost in antiquity and present in the grave only by accident. Then again, someone may have deliberately included the coin in this grave because old habits die hard. Although grave goods are exceptionally rare in English monastic cemeteries, they are not unknown: three of the early burials excavated from the monastic cemetery at Wearmouth also included coins and a fourth contained a boar's tusk.

The grave of another Nazeingbury woman lay next to the man with the shroud pin, and thus close to the early 'Church One' burials. Given the date of her death, sometime after the building of the second church, and given the choice location of her grave, this woman was a Christian of some standing. However, she was placed in the ground with a horse-tooth pendant around her neck, a homely piece which she would have worn as an amulet rather than an adornment, but it is exactly the kind of object, as we have seen, that churchmen railed against. Given the context and the date of our two Nazeingbury graves, they cannot be read as evidence for recrudescent paganism, but they do suggest that conversion did not mean the death of magical thinking or the complete abandonment of the many little rituals people had learned while growing up, the practice of which, they must have felt, was entirely consistent with their Christian faith. Nor, as these graves show, did burial, even unaccompanied burial, cease with conversion to serve as a stage for the display of social status.

All the other people buried at Nazeingbury, though, were buried without grave goods and out of doors. The vast majority of skeletons excavated from the cemetery, so it turns out, belonged to adult women, a surprising number of whom had died after the age of 45. This suggests that many of the women laid to rest here had not been exposed to the hazards of pregnancy and childbirth. None, moreover, had the kinds of bone lesions found in people who have suffered from serious bouts of childhood illness or malnutrition. These women's teeth also show little wear, a sign that their diet was comprised of finely processed grain. Like the gifts of land to a grantee with a female name and the mortuary structure at the centre of the cemetery, these findings argue that Nazeingbury was a minster staffed largely by celibate, high-status women.

The bodies of most of the men, who made up a minority of the adults buried at Nazeingbury, tell a different story. Most had bones marked with the wear and strains of hard-working lives. Their teeth were also very worn, so they had eaten a different, rougher diet than the women. These men, along with a handful of hard-working women, whose bodies similarly exhibited signs of heavy labour and rough diet, probably served the nuns as servants, slaves, porters or reeves, and it would have been they, and not the ladies, who performed all the dreary tasks necessary for the day-to-day running of the Nazeingbury household, farming and tribute operations. Nevertheless, these people were afforded churchyard burials, so they must, in some sense, have been considered part of the community, and their graves conform to those of the religious women. So it seems that the nuns' slaves and servants adopted a complex of Christian mortuary practices. The labourers buried at Nazeingbury may have adopted other of the women's less archaeologically visible religious practices as well, such as fasting and keeping the Sabbath. We know that early kings issued laws mandating that laypeople observe both of these, but it is likely that the ordinary people who first adopted such practices served or lived near minster communities. Still, for most people, churchyard burials lay in the future, and it may have taken them longer to accept or practise additional religious obligations.

Archaeologists also recovered in Nazeingbury's cemetery the remains of a dozen children who died sometime in the eighth century. It is striking that three-quarters of them died when they were 5, 6 or 7 years old, the age at which child-oblates typically entered monasteries. Are these the remains of little girls who did not survive the transition from natal home to monastic household? Were the nuns at Nazeingbury alarmingly incompetent when it came to the caring of young children? Or perhaps these were invalids, brought to the nunnery by their parents, because they were deemed either unmarriageable or badly in need of a miracle. This is what their bones suggest: some had suffered from long-term illnesses, and all showed signs of serious childhood illness or anaemia. Something similar was going on at other early monastic sites. A number of very unhealthy early medieval children were discovered in one of the cemeteries attached to the monastery at Whithorn. One child buried there had survived a terrible accident and had never fully recovered from a crushed thigh. Many of the other Whithorn children had suffered from severe, long-term anaemia. Adomnán's *Life of St Columba* describes the way sick people were healed in and around Iona, some from St Columba's 'outstretched hand, some from being sprinkled with water he had blessed, others by the mere touching of the edge of his cloak, or from something such as salt or bread blessed by the saint and dipped in water'. Perhaps, like Iona, the communities at Nazeingbury and Whithorn had living saints or wonder-working shrines. The Whithorn children were buried, over a number of decades, in a single zone within the cemetery, and the funerary rituals marking their deaths may have been different from those of adults. Grown-ups there generally lay supine in their graves, but the children were found in a variety of positions, perhaps because people felt it appropriate, in ways they would not have thought for adults, to dispose of their bodies while still in rigor mortis. The body positions of the Nazeingbury children, on the other hand, were the same as those of adults in the cemetery, and they were interspersed among them, in a burial community in which men, women and children were integrated in death.

At Nazeingbury, sick children were not the only people in need of special care. A handful of men buried there, rather than looking like workers, look like lifelong invalids. The man whose grave contained the shroud pin and the Roman coin, for example, was very bow-legged, and he probably suffered from congenitally dislocated hips. In spite of his damaged legs, though, he had powerful shoulders, probably from a lifetime of moving about on crutches. Another Nazeingbury man was hydrocephalic and may well have been mentally impaired: he lived until his late twenties. A third man, who died in his mid-twenties, had Down's Syndrome. So it looks as if Nazeingbury was more than a community of celibate, aristocratic women, sickly children and hard-working, low-status helpers. It seems to have accommodated members of aristocratic kin groups who were unable to participate in the fighting, hunting, itin-erating and marrying so central to life in high-status, secular house-holds. Other monasteries may have provided a similar service. A tiny woman, dead by her mid-twenties and probably suffering from con-genital dwarfism, was buried at Jarrow, as was an elderly man terribly disfigured by Paget's disease; and in the cemetery attached to the mon-astery at Breedon-on-the-Hill, in Leicestershire, archaeologists have found a 9-year-old child with Down's Syndrome. Perhaps all of these people, too, were the special charges of religious communities.

One of the interesting things about both Hartlepool and Nazeing-bury is their hybridity and the close connections they must have had with other religious communities across Britain, Ireland and north-western Francia. This can only mean that monastic sites were chosen, not for their isolation, but because they allowed for easy intercourse with the surrounding world. This should remind us that the point of monasticism was as much about activity in the world as it was about contemplation and prayer. Another thing that comes through from an examination of these communities is what noble enterprises such places were, and how they were inhabited by people who may have been drawn to the eremitic life of the desert fathers, but who had been programmed by their natal families to broadcast their high social positions via archi-tecture and funerary display. It is also clear that laypeople – not just noble relatives, but workers and neighbouring farmers – interacted with members of these communities, and that social relations between very different lay groups both moderated life within minsters, and had a significant impact on the Christianity of the laypeople who came in contact with minster communities.

There are other things, though, to notice about our two monasteries. Unlike secular high-status sites, the controlling households of these places did not itinerate, but lived year round in a single place, something demanded by a monastic way of life. This, in turn, would have required minster communities dramatically to reorganize their supply oper-ations. Many minsters, as we have seen, when initially founded, were given rights over a tribute centre and all its bounty. Monastic inmates, however, probably needed to intervene more directly in the kinds of tribute they were owed, and they must have supervised their labour resources very carefully. If they did not, they would not be able to live off what was owed them. Indeed, it is likely that minster communities, instead of depending so heavily on tribute, had their slaves and most dependent labourers actually farm lands directly for them, and used what this land produced to help supply their communities year round. Minsters also sometimes required highly specialized production. Those that made manuscripts, for example, would have needed huge supplies of calfskin: one scholar has estimated that 400 hectares of pasture stand behind the vellum used in a single Gospel book. This, too, would have necessitated thoughtful management and direct intervention into the working lives of dependent farmers.

Thus, with the coming of monastic life, there were now two distinct types of high-status households, and perhaps double the number of high-status households than there had been before the coming of Christianity, so there were now many more people who needed to extract surpluses for their support. Both lay and ecclesiastical households, moreover, were interested in imports and luxury goods. Archaeological excavations have revealed that many early minster sites housed craftsmen and traders, and many were actively involved in trade. In this way, religious change led to profound economic transformation, which would be a contributing factor to the rebirth of urban communities in the eastern half of Britain.

The Rebirth of Trading Communities: The Seventh to Mid-Ninth Century

Within a generation or two of 400 all the towns of Roman Britain had ceased to function as towns. As we have seen, craftsmen and traders drifted away, and local authorities ceased to function. Over the course of the next 200 years Britain's former small towns collapsed and decayed, and most had all but disappeared by 600. The former public towns, though, were a different matter. They had died as well, but with their massive defences, monumental stone buildings and grand port facilities, Roman Britain's cities continued to haunt the landscape; and, rather than reverting to pastureland or scrub, they changed into fantastically ruinous sites, marked by scores of tumbledown buildings and acres of rubble. Thick blankets of dark earth (the product of the grasses, brush and trees that colonized, died and decomposed in moribund towns alongside the wood, wattle and thatch of their abandoned buildings) gradually came to cover the wreckage, and creeping marshland slowly undermined whole, crumbling neighbourhoods. A poignant late Anglo-Saxon poem describes one such place:

> Wondrously ornate is the stone of this wall, shattered by fate
> the precincts of the city have crumbled
> and the work of giants is rotting away.
> There are tumbled roofs, towers in ruins ...
> An earthy grasp holds its lordly builders,
> [who are] decayed and gone [in] the cruel grip of the ground,
> while a hundred generations of humanity have passed away ...
> [Once] there were bright city buildings,
> many bathhouses, a wealth of lofty gables.
> [There was] much clamour of the multitude,
> many a mead-hall filled with human revelry,

until mighty fate changed that . . .
The site is fallen into ruin, reduced to heaps . . .
[Thus, these] stone courts are collapsing . . .
The place has fallen into ruins and is reduced to heaps . . .
[But it was once] a fitting thing, the city . . .

(*The Ruin*, trans. S. J. Bradley)

In the late sixth and early seventh centuries sites like these would have been familiar to anyone travelling the still-used Roman roads or rowing down the rivers that had once watered and linked the towns. The collapsed carapaces of Britain's once vibrant urban communities – places like Verulamium, Canterbury and London – continued to effect a certain pull, since even in their ruinous states they remained the most visible relics both of Rome's glory and its collapse.

A WORLD WITHOUT TOWNS

A few of Britain's kings, beguiled by *romanitas* and skilled at appropriating other people's pasts, established themselves within the wreckage of such places, finding odd corners inside the cities' tumbling walls where some still-standing monument might serve as a backdrop for their own circumscribed glory. Here, the powerful sometimes maintained halls, which they visited from time to time to entertain local allies, collect tribute and, once they had converted to Christianity, establish their bishops. Such appropriations, however, do not allow us to claim that there was continuity of urban life in Britain after Rome's fall, or, indeed, that urban life was revived in Britain by these men's occasional presence.

We can see that this is the case when we think about the archaeological remains of post-Roman Verulamium. Verulamium was a once-important Roman public town located in territory controlled, well into the seventh century, by British elites. From painstaking excavations we know that in the couple of generations following Roman Britain's collapse, individuals or groups with the ability to marshal the labour of others oversaw the construction of corn-dryers, bread ovens and a barn within the dying town, as well as a Roman-style water pipe. The people who stood behind these activities did not undertake them, though, to maintain public services, the way late Roman administrators would have done; nor had they acted because grain was still being processed for and sold at the town's market or because grand families continued to have running water in their houses. Instead, this activity looks like a private undertaking, the efforts of a powerful family which periodically came to Verulamium to worship at the town's wonder-working shrine, and perhaps even to bury its dead near the holy corpse of St Alban. Such visits, because of the collapse of any kind of market economy, would, out of necessity, have been coordinated with the locals' giving over of tribute. These renders, in turn, required that the controlling household's agents had the means to dry, process and store grain as well as the ability to water livestock driven in by local tribute-payers until butchers could do their work. What archaeological evidence there is, then, suggests that Verulamium, rather than limping along as an attenuated urban place, had evolved into a ruralized tribute centre, one that took advantage of mouldering infrastructure, recyclable building materials and a great late Roman shrine. Whatever Verulamium was in the post-Roman period, though, it was not a city.

A few English households similarly established themselves in ruined towns. For example, by the time Augustine arrived in Kent in 597, King Æthelbert clearly had rights to *Durovernum Cantiacorum*, because it was within his power to give the missionary land both inside and outside Canterbury's still-standing Roman walls. Prior to 597, moreover, Æthelbert himself may have taken advantage of these rights. Although archaeologists have yet to locate an early hall in Canterbury, they have uncovered more than three dozen sunken-featured buildings (or SFBs as they are called) clustered around the back of the ruinous Roman amphitheatre. A couple of these structures date to *c.* 450, but they seem to have gone out of use before others were built in the mid-sixth century. SFBs were multi-purpose structures, used to house a variety of craft activities and workers. More important for our purposes, though, SFBs had their floors suspended over earthen cellars, which means that they could provide dry storage for grain, and because of this they would have been a central feature of any tribute centre. Some of Canterbury's SFBs, moreover, were demolished and then rebuilt in an organized fashion, suggesting a single, controlling figure. A couple of other finds in this area – shards from a fancy pot, traces of gold working, the fragments of a shield mount – also hint at the presence of a great personage.

Taken together, this evidence suggests that by the late sixth century an important person had an establishment within Canterbury's walls. Evidence provided by Bede makes it likely that this man was the king of Kent. From Bede's history, we know that the king's household spent a fair amount of time in the neighbourhood, because for some fifteen years prior to Augustine's arrival Æthelbert had had a Frankish, Christian wife who was in the habit of worshipping at the church of St Martin, half a kilometre east of the city walls. She apparently established St Martin's in a dilapidated Roman building, which she had had shored up and remodelled to look like a Frankish church. Indeed, St Martin's, which still stands, may be the first masonry building after the fall to be rebuilt and reoccupied at the behest of an English ruler. Since building with brick and stone were lost arts in England, masons from Francia must have been brought in, and no one would have gone to all this trouble unless they planned to put the church to regular use. The kings of Kent doubtless had residences at the major tribute centres of Milton Regis, Faversham, Eastry and Sturry as well, but none of these places were a pleasant morning's stroll from St Martin's, the way a hall lying in the shadow of the amphitheatre would have been. When Æthelbert, moreover, extended hospitality in Canterbury to Augustine, his forty followers and their assorted Frankish helpers, he had to feed them all, day in, day out, for months at a time. Only at a well-established tribute centre could he have provided such extravagant hospitality.

In spite of what was probably a royal presence in Canterbury, most of the former walled town remained deserted. The entire western half of the city had reverted to water meadow, and the north-eastern quarter, which the king in time would grant to Augustine, was uninhabited. We know this because when archaeologists excavated a section of the cathedral that Augustine himself built they found that its foundations sat atop a thick layer of dark earth which had been forming on the site since the mid-fifth century. The building, moreover, was not aligned with the Roman street grid, probably because that was no longer in evidence. Only a few ruined buildings remained, which the cathedral's first masons mined to build their church.

Augustine and his followers spent much of their time and energy in the first years of their mission constructing churches inside Canterbury's walls and just outside its east gate. They dedicated these buildings to the same saints as the churches near their own home monastery of St Andrew's, in Rome. Canterbury's new cathedral, for example, like Rome's Lateran, was dedicated to Christ. Another of Canterbury's early intramural churches shared the exceptionally rare dedication of 'the Four Crowned Martyrs' with a Roman church very near St Andrew's. Canterbury's extramural monastery, now called St Augustine's, but originally dedicated to SS Peter and Paul, honoured the same two saints who had extramural basilicas just outside Rome. And just as St Peter's in Rome was built to house the bodies of dead popes, so, too, was Canterbury's SS Peter and Paul meant to act as a mortuary church for England's archbishops. Yet another of the mission's early Canterbury churches was probably dedicated to St Pancras, a martyr beheaded in early fourth-century Rome, once again reflecting the dedication of a church near St Andrew's. Imported Frankish or Italian stonemasons built these churches, and their work must have required considerable outlays of the mission's resources. This campaign was either a wildly optimistic act undertaken by missionaries intent on recreating holy Rome brick by brick, or the work of a group of homesick Italians engaged in the doomed and depressing enterprise of simulating the city they loved in the squalid shell of a former Roman provincial town. Whatever their intention, their efforts, like those of the king of Kent, meant that there was once again life in Canterbury. Still, in this initial phase, recolonization did not make Canterbury any more of a city than Verulamium. Both post-Roman re-establishments are more reminiscent of the palace/ritual complex found at Yeavering than they are of Roman-style urbanism, except that, rather than building within rural landscapes freighted with meaning, those active in Canterbury and Verulamium chose evocative, ruined townscapes.

There was not, then, continuity of urban life in late sixth-century Britain, nor were towns instantly reconstituted with the coming of Christianity. Yet, even with the absence of towns, an extraordinary range of luxury goods moved into and around Britain. In Kent, for example, on the eve of the Roman mission, high-status graves were filled with exotica. Many of the foreign imports came from the Rhineland and Francia, but some things hailed from more distant shores. The raw glass, for example, employed by northern craftsmen to fashion the beautiful beads English women strung between their brooches, came all the way from Egypt. The elephant-ivory rings used to make the bags some women hung on their belts were gathered in Ethiopia; the garnets and amber prized by English craftsmen originated in India and the

Baltic. British elites in western Britain also had access to exotic goods during this period, although they, too, resided in territories without towns. Royal and monastic households in south-western Scotland, for example, fostered relations with foreign traders. In the mid-sixth century merchants from western France were bringing quantities of fine black tableware and glass, dyestuffs, salt and wine to Dunadd and Whithorn.

In Britain's English-culture zone, some foreign goods may have arrived in the packs of circular migrators who journeyed between their old communities on the Continent and their new ones, distributing goods available on either side of the Channel to allies, relations or lords. Given the ubiquity of such frippery, though, professional traders must have also been involved. By the late sixth century they would have hauled boatloads of merchandise across the Channel to exchange with the agents of Englishmen who had become the masters of surplus. Both the foreigners and the agents would have been important figures in an England dominated by families that were simultaneously socially anxious and flush with resources. Indeed, the graves of a few of these middlemen may have actually come to light in Kent and the Upper Thames Valley. Here, archaeologists have excavated a number of burials dating between the mid-sixth and the seventh centuries, which include the kind of scale-and-weight sets used in bullion transactions along the edges of the Frankish world. The small size of these scales suggests that they were used in transactions that required the weighing out of precious gold, and, as it turns out, the sets of weights that sometimes accompanied scales in English burials were calibrated for one of two gold currencies – Byzantine or Frankish *tremisses* – so the users of these scales may have been traders who needed to calculate the equivalents of Byzantine or Frankish gold coins during the course of their dealings, or the English agents who stood on the other side of the bargaining, men commissioned to swap their lords' surpluses for imported goods or precious metal. Other evidence also points towards bullion transactions and foreign merchants. Throughout the sixth century a substantial number of coins from the Continent arrived in Britain. A hoard (now lost) of something like ten Frankish coins which dates to *c.* 530, was discovered in Surrey at Kingston upon Thames in the nineteenth century. A late sixth-century lead Byzantine port-tax seal has also been recovered from Putney. The coins and the seal hint at foreign merchants, foreign merchandise and Englishmen with things worth trading.

English craftsmen and their wares also travelled before towns existed. The remains of their artistry – offcuts of metal, chunks of glass, little waste beads of lead and mercury – are found on high-status sites throughout Britain. Itinerant craftsmen during this townless phase also produced more quotidian objects. A number of cremation urns, for example, have been identified as the handiwork of single groups of potters, because they bear decorations made with the same sets of antler-stamp dies. One such set of pots, crafted by the so-called Sancton/Baston potters, has been identified in cremation cemeteries from the East Riding of Yorkshire all the way to southern Lincolnshire. Although a single band of craftsmen decorating their wares with the same set of stamps made these pots, the clay they used differed from cemetery to cemetery. This suggests that the pot-makers ranged widely, making urns and firing them in makeshift kilns for a week or two, then moving on. The long and the short of all this is that exotic goods and craft items, as well as traders and craftsmen, could and did circulate in the absence of towns.

As we have seen, moreover, by the end of the sixth century it was common for local farm families and aristocratic households to congregate around high-status sites during tribute time. For a few days each year or season, the masters of these places, travelling in the company of their special friends and dearest kinfolk, would take up residence and work to reaffirm old friendships, assert rights to the fruits of local people's labour and settle disputes. This would have been an ideal time for itinerant craftsmen and traders to come and do business. The intensification of social differentiation over the course of the sixth century, then, alongside the formation of territories and kingdoms, and the linked development of systems of tribute, all converged to encourage, perhaps even necessitate, trade in the townless sixth century.

In spite of all this extra-urban activity, however, bona fide towns, after an absence of a century and a half, did begin to develop around the year 600. Four such places have been made famous through archaeological excavation: London, at a site just west of Roman *Londinium* (sometimes called *Lundenwic* in the literature), Southampton (often called *Hamwic*), Ipswich and York. Over the course of the seventh century these settlements evolved into real towns, places with substantial year-round populations engaged primarily in craft and trade activities rather than agriculture. Archaeologists and historians sometimes refer to places like these as *wics* or *emporia*, and they were developing in this period not only in southern and eastern Britain, but across the whole of the northern world in Scandinavia and the Baltic, up and down both sides of the Channel and the North Sea and along the banks of the Rhine and Meuse rivers. Each *wic* developed in its own way and under a unique set of circumstances, which means that some, in the end, were more closely tied to royal power, others more engaged in international trade networks and still others grew to be places of specialized craft production. Nonetheless, all shared certain characteristics and formed a loose economic network, with individuals, goods and ideas travelling between them.

IPSWICH AND ENGLAND'S OTHER EARLY TOWNS

Let us examine, in some detail, the beginnings of Ipswich, one of these new urban communities. Sometime around 600, traders and craftsmen began doing business on a patch of unoccupied heathland on the banks of the River Gipping, in Suffolk. These people could have congregated in the ruins of the former Roman small town of *Combretovium*, 18 kilometres upstream, but instead they chose a sheltered spot near the head of the Orwell estuary, at a ford on the north bank of the river. In Ipswich's earliest years local farmers and tribute-takers may have gathered at the site periodically, some making the trek with wagons or pack animals, others arriving in dugout canoes, in hopes of swapping surplus foodstuffs or household crafts for items they could not produce on their own. The arrival of foreign traders a couple of times a year could have precipitated or formalized such gatherings. These men would have come in larger, plank-built ships with cargoes of French wine, glass bowls and fancy textiles, the kinds of status-enhancing novelties that wealthy locals craved. It is more difficult to fathom what the people of southern Suffolk had to offer in return. Perhaps victorious war bands herded their unlucky captives to the riverside when Frisian slavers came ashore: we know from Bede that Mercians were doing just that in London. Or timber, desperately scarce along the Frisian coast, may have figured in some exchanges, especially since merchants' livelihoods depended on their wooden ships. Whatever they had to trade, it looks as if the ad hoc and episodic overseas exchanges began to be organized and formalized, and that somewhere around the year 600 Ipswich developed into a year-round settlement. By the early ninth century Ipswich would sprawl across some 50 hectares, but for most of the seventh century it was a much smaller place, covering something of the order of 6 hectares. Still, by the standards of the day, it was a substantial agglomeration, larger than contemporary high-status sites like Brandon, in Suffolk, or Yeavering, in Northumberland. Ipswich, moreover, would not have needed much infrastructure to handle considerable trade. Piers, warehouses and shops were unnecessary, since all merchants had to do was drag their ships ashore and conduct business out of the holds of their boats.

Ipswich's early inhabitants buried their dead, the way most rural people did, in cemeteries laid out just beyond their settlement's edge. One of their cemeteries lies at the heart of the modern-day city at Buttermarket. The graves here, like those in contemporary rural cemeteries, betray something of the social composition of early Ipswich. Women and children were found among the dead, so we know that Ipswich was more than a seasonal encampment of traders and craftsmen. From Buttermarket's graves we also know that early Ipswich was no craftsmen's collective. Like other seventh-century places, this was a ranked community, and its members marked differences in social status, age and gender in their death rituals. Most of the dead had few or no grave goods, but a handful were awarded imported glass palm cups, impressive jewellery and weapons. One of Buttermarket's most elaborate burials, for example, which dates to the middle decades of the seventh century, is of a man kitted out with grave goods and dress accessories that we would expect to find in a Rhineland cemetery. It seems that he was a foreigner, buried by people who had accompanied him from home and who knew just the sort of things to put in a high-status Rhineland grave. A little Frankish 'black ware' from the Rhineland, which dates to Ipswich's earliest years, has also been recovered, as has a hand-built Frisian cooking pot, that is, a kind of vessel not for trade but for everyday use, and an object, therefore, which suggests that some living in Ipswich had come from across the sea and furnished their houses with possessions they had brought from home. It also looks as if, from the very beginning, some people living in and around Ipswich either had close relations with people in eastern Kent, or were themselves from Kent. A few people burying at a nearby contemporary cemetery at Hadleigh Road, across the river from Ipswich, were placing Kentish brooches and glass in the ground. At Boss Hall, another cemetery close by, a woman who died around 700 was buried with a stunning Kentish brooch and a collection of Kentish-style pendants. English traders from places besides Kent were also probably active at Ipswich. A number of the women in the Hadleigh Road cemetery had square-headed brooches and amber beads, things rare in the corner of south-eastern Suffolk where Ipswich lies, but common further north and in inland communities around present-day Bury St Edmunds. So in Ipswich's first three generations one of the most distinctive things about it is the number of people of means living in the neighbourhood who were probably born somewhere else.

Archaeologists have found analogous evidence at other of England's early trading communities. Excavations at both Southampton and London have produced a handful of people buried in alien costumes as well as artefacts suggesting that at least a few foreigners were setting up house there. In Southampton, not only have archaeologists uncovered workaday foreign pottery, but they have come across the remains of a rabbit dinner, an animal (and a dish) unknown to the English until the Norman Conquest. There is also an admittedly problematic document from the archives of Saint-Denis, in Paris, which claims that two brothers with Frankish names bequeathed land to that monastery in *Lundenwic*; this may be more evidence for well-established enclaves of foreign traders in early London. In any case, it looks as if small groups of well-to-do foreigners lived and died in England's earliest trading communities.

The presence of Frankish, Frisian and Kentish traders, permanent or otherwise, in Ipswich, Southampton and London is also disclosed by the remains of objects crafted elsewhere. A huge number of shards of imported pottery have been recovered from Ipswich, as they have from England's other early towns. Some of these ceramics may have arrived as trade goods in their own right, but the bulk probably came as containers for wine, salt or dye. Potters in the Rhineland and Frisia fashioned the majority of Ipswich's imported pottery, although a few pots can also be assigned to northern France. These ceramics not only tell us something about goods trafficked in Ipswich's first generations, but hint at the diverse origins of Ipswich's alien merchants: it may well be that groups of Frankish and Frisian traders from the bustling entrepôts of Dorestad, in the Netherlands, and Quentovic, near Calais, competed with Kentish traders for East Anglian goods and business. So not just outsiders but a variety of outsiders (including people from Kent) seem to have been an essential element in all of England's early trading communities. Indeed, it seems that different groups of outsiders – and the competition that probably existed between them – were a driving force behind the rebirth of towns in this part of the world.

Although international trade was what Ipswich's prosperity was founded upon, local-born craftsmen and their families probably comprised the majority of the town's permanent population, and most of what they made was neither exotic nor aimed at the consumers of foreign exotica catered to by the foreigners. From their rubbish, we know that Ipswich craftsmen plied a variety of trades: iron-smithing, loom-weight making, antler-working, cobbling, weaving. Many of the goods they produced ended up in the hands of fellow Ipswich craftsmen, who spent their days making other useful things, or resident merchants too busy or too rich to fashion combs or shoes for themselves. Thus craft workers provided the goods and services needed by traders and other town dwellers, and their market was very much self-generated. Some Ipswich craftsmen may have traded their wares to local farmers, but the range of goods early Ipswichmen produced was no greater and the execution, by and large, no better than the objects crafted on many of the period's rural sites.

It also seems that those who lived in Ipswich in its first generations engaged in farming. Field boundaries have been found just 200 metres east of the first settlement, suggesting that in the early years many craftsmen walked to their fields each day as well as laboured at their workbenches. In the seventh century the line between urban and rural could be tentative, with sites in the countryside producing crafts and townsfolk raising some of their own food. Except for a greater emphasis on craft working, a slightly larger population, some foreign residents and better access to exotic goods, seventh-century Ipswich would have had much in common with larger rural settlements, especially those in which powerful families or religious communities had their halls, because sites like these often had craftsmen of their own, as well as access to foreign goods.

In its earliest years Ipswich was also probably a poly-focal settlement, as, indeed, were a number of similarly dated trading communities across the Channel; and this may be yet another defining characteristic of

England's earliest towns. The fact that Ipswich was poly-focal, and probably began as a series of discrete market areas, suggests that it operated under the aegis of more than one indigenous group or household. Three cemeteries, moreover, have been excavated in and around Ipswich, and there was probably a fourth somewhere in the neighbourhood of modern Ipswich's Elm Street, each corresponding to a distinct burial community in early Ipswich. Each group was burying at least a few of their dead with weapons and with glass and metalwork from Francia and/or Kent, and one person at Hadleigh Road was also laid to rest with a hanging bowl from western Britain. Members of each of these burial communities had access to objects brought into Ipswich by foreigners, perhaps because they had some stake or authority within the settlement itself. But what there is no sign of at Ipswich during this period is a single dominating power.

This picture of seventh-century Ipswich is broadly commensurate with that emerging for Southampton and London. In these places, too, we have evidence from the early seventh century on for poly-focal settlements built on stretches of riverbank and ringed by multiple cemeteries which contained a few people who might be foreigners, and others who had access to foreign goods; for small, year-round populations comprised of men, women and children; for enclaves of wealthy foreign traders from a variety of places, including Kent; and for unusually good access to foreign commodities.

In the years around 720, Ipswich, London, Southampton and probably York expanded rapidly. A key piece of evidence for Ipswich's dramatic growth is found at the Buttermarket cemetery. At this time, the people of Ipswich ceased to bury their dead at Buttermarket, and the cemetery was redeveloped with little thought for the dead. When archaeologists excavated the site they recovered numerous small silver coins, known as *sceattas*, minted between the years 710 and 760. It seems that sometime in the early eighth century the Buttermarket cemetery, because of the pressures of a rapidly expanding population, was transformed from a burial place to a market site, becoming an area where bargains were struck and coins changed hands. By the mid-eighth century the area was further developed. Metalled roads now crisscrossed over the tops of the forgotten graves, and people built houses and workshops for themselves along the roads' frontages. From this time on there is evidence of a growing intensity in craft production across the settlement and of an increasing dependence on rural suppliers for food and raw materials. Similar rapid growth, witnessed by the redevelopments of seventh-century cemetery sites, also took place in Southampton and London. The obliteration of these communities' one-time peripheral cemeteries points to the rapid expansion, in the first half of the eighth century, of urban populations, trade and the economy itself. Indeed, in the decades following 720 these towns grew to their greatest size, each one covering between 40 and 60 hectares. As near as we can tell, the population of all three towns doubled or tripled during this period, with Ipswich and Southampton home to perhaps 2,000–3,000, and London to somewhere between 5,000 and 10,000. To put these figures another way, London may have had as many as 2,000 workshops by the early eighth century and Ipswich something of the order of 500 or 600.

From the early eighth century on potters came to be the most organized and productive group of workers in Ipswich, and they began to turn out pots on a massive scale. Archaeologists have found a small industrial enclave, about 300 metres north-east of the earliest settlement, in an area with easy access to water and a quarry of London clay. Pottery-making here dates to *c.* 720, but production expanded dramatically in the second half of the eighth century, only ceasing sometime after *c.* 850. Indeed, Ipswich's pottery production must have fuelled its eighth- and early ninth-century boom. Elsewhere in England, potters built pots by hand and then fired them in bonfires. At Ipswich, ceramic workers coil-built pots, finished them on slow wheels or turntables, and then fired them in bona fide kilns. Not only did their techniques lend themselves to industrial-scale production, but Ipswich potters produced pitchers, a popular and utilitarian object made nowhere else in England. The pots made by the thousand in Ipswich were unlovely things, but this did not stand in the way of their wide appeal.

Ipswich pottery went further afield than anything else the town produced. Ipswich potters furnished almost everyone living in the kingdom of East Anglia with pots: Ipswich ware was ubiquitous in grand and humble places alike. The profligate spread of these pots tells us that all sorts of people, living in all kinds of settlements, had economic links to Ipswich, because, without such connections, Ipswich ware could never have penetrated the East Anglian hinterland so thoroughly. Ipswich pots also travelled beyond the borders of the kingdom, and can be found as far south as Kent and as far north as Yorkshire, although, outside East

Anglia, Ipswich ware was limited to high-status settlements or to other trading sites. From 750 to 850, for example, Ipswich potters produced most of London's pottery; indeed, it was so ubiquitous that most Londoners seem to have used it. Its regular use in far-off towns and grand estate centres must have come about because agents working for wealthy Kentish or Yorkshire tribute-takers, including monks, nuns and merchants from London and York, all did regular and direct business in Ipswich and brought back its pottery alongside other, less archaeologically visible goods. Ipswich pots spread rapidly in the generation following 720, and coin loss in the town became more common during this period as well, doubtless because coin use increased. This, then, is probably the time when thoroughgoing trade networks came to link towns like Ipswich to their hinterlands and towns with towns, and it is in this period that the four great trading communities really came into their own.

Ipswich, Southampton, York and London were all more recognizably urban in the mid-eighth century than they had been in the mid-seventh, but they were still different from towns of a later period. For one thing, the rhythms of urban life were more affected by seasonal changes than they would be later. Ipswich's population, for example, would have mushroomed each year in the months of good weather. It was then that captains involved in the trans-Channel trade beached their boats on the town's foreshore. Both the traders and the rowers aboard their ships needed accommodation and supplies during the days or weeks it took them to transact their business. So, too, did the agents of monastic and aristocratic households. Those purchasing large consignments of Continental wine, for example, would have had to marshal carters or coastal captains and their crews, and these men and their animals, too, would need food, fodder, wood for their cooking fires and places to sleep. It was during these busy summer months that urban craftsmen – shoemakers, potters, bone-workers – would have found the highest demand for their wares. Once the weather turned, and seaworthy ships ceased to travel, other seasonal patterns would have come to the fore. It was in the late autumn, when farmers culled their herds for winter, that the livestock given over as tribute and used by lords to feed their urban dependants, was most likely to have been driven into town. Tanners would have been at their busiest during these months, and lumber and firewood brokers would have occupied themselves selecting trees to cut and season in anticipation of the next summer's trade. The dramatic annual rise and fall of Ipswich's population and the seasonality of some of its pursuits are just two of the ways Britain's early towns and their economies differed from what would come later.

These communities also developed more haphazardly than later towns, in part because of this seasonality. It is clear, for example, that people engaged in particular occupations were not as rigidly organized into neighbourhoods as later craftsmen would be, and it is also true that some households practised more than one craft. This may be because people like tanners and bone-workers needed off-season occupation in the cattle-shy months of late winter and early spring. At the same time, though, what authorities there were in the towns must have been less proficient at governing than they would be after a couple of hundred years' practice. Town officials in later periods, for example, worked hard, for safety's sake, to regulate the most noxious and dangerous trades, and they made sure that groups like tanners and fire-using potters were confined to single-craft neighbourhoods or located away from a city's heart. But many neighbourhoods in eighth-century towns housed a jumble of occupations, and one of the consequences of this habit was frequent and devastating fires. Individual houses and sometimes whole neighbourhoods also burned during this period because town-dwellers habitually built their hearths too near walls or dangerously close to low-hanging eaves, which suggests that there was little policing of construction. There was some tentative zoning, however. Ipswich's bone-workers and potters congregated on the outskirts of the town, in a quarter where clay and water were close at hand; and the coin finds from Buttermarket point towards a commercial district. At Southampton, too, we find a concentration of bone-workers on the town's edge, and people with better access to foreign goods congregating in an area along the riverfront: perhaps this was a little district of traders' establishments or elite residences. And, in London, horn-workers' shops could be found sensibly near butchers' yards. In all these cases, the exigencies of individual professions – and, therefore, individual agency – rather than administrative fiat, seem to stand behind whatever early zoning there was, but it is possible that some was the result of a powerful guiding hand. Market areas, for example, were increasingly mandated by kings and their reeves in order to facilitate the collection of tolls and policing of sales.

Other evidence also suggests that powerful figures were coming to exert influence in the towns. The building and upkeep of town river-fronts and roads sometimes required massive amounts of raw material and labour organized across households and neighbourhoods. In London, for example, someone in the 670s or 680s oversaw the felling of large numbers of oak trees and the gathering of large amounts of brush-wood and rubble, for the building of a major embankment along the Thames foreshore. This was communal infrastructure rather than a single household's improvement, and the project must have been headed by a person with enough authority to marshal considerable outlays of labour, timber and stone. A couple of London's early roads suggest something similar. One, running from the Strand to the old Roman road now marked by Oxford Street, was laid out in the seventh century. It and its associated drainage ditch were carefully built and maintained, and the road was given a durable, compact-gravel surface, which was then kept free of rubbish and potholes for decades. The engineering and upkeep of this thoroughfare stands in stark contrast to the state of the alleyways meandering off it. These secondary paths were rarely cleared of refuse, and they were habitually strewn with household rubbish, industrial waste, even rotting animal carcasses. It seems, then, that there was a controlling power in London by the late seventh century, capable of organizing major infrastructure projects and some maintenance, but there was no one with enough authority to insist that these high stand-ards be met throughout the town. The squalid, garbage-strewn alleys and vacant lots, the dearth of safety regulations, the hit-or-miss zoning, the dangerously designed buildings and the potholed trackways were not, however, peculiar to England: contemporary Italian towns, in spite of their long, uninterrupted history as urban places, were dogged by similar hazards.

There are other reasons, besides the occasional 'public works' project, to suspect that powerful lords – either lay or ecclesiastical or both – were involved in towns in some central way. One is an argument based on animal bones. The people of Ipswich, so the remains of their dinners tell us, ate a fairly restricted range of animals. The bones them-selves show that most of the meat eaten by Ipswich's residents was driven into town on the hoof (although it looks as if pig-headed and unherdable swine arrived in town dead, butchered and cured). The majority of these animals were arthritic oxen, who had worked long seasons pulling ploughs or carts, and elderly, castrated rams, who had served out their years as wool-producers. Given their age, it is likely that these animals were brought to town by tribute-takers, who had, for their part, received them as food renders: it is only natural, after all, that farmers who owed cattle or sheep as tribute would give over spent animals when they could. These tough old beasts hardly made ideal eating, and this, in turn, suggests that most townspeople, at least in seventh-century Ipswich, were not buying the meat that ended up in their dinner pots. Indeed, one suspects that if townspeople had purchased food on the open market, those who could afford it would have sought out tasty young animals or bargained with country boys for venison and game birds. The eating of tired old animals, in turn, suggests that great lords gave over some of the animals they had received from their rural dependants each year to their urban dependants, who, in return, were obliged to perform craft or trade services for their benefactors. Still, meat resources broadened over time. In London, for example, it seems that there were new possibilities in the eighth century for purchasing more succulent cuts of meat on special occasions, because more things were being sold in town markets and because some townsmen had more economic independence and were leading more comfortable lives thanks to the wealth they had accrued from manufacturing and trade.

These animal bones must be kept in mind when we attempt to characterize the economies of England's new towns. In many ways, towns and their craftsmen appear to be an integral part of the same redistributive system that was operating in the countryside, as entangled in in-kind renders and obligations to their lords as farmers in rural hamlets. In the seventh century, especially, the market was much less in evidence, and obligations and reciprocity seem to have been driving forces in town economies. Not all towns, though, were equally entangled in these obligations, and relations between rural tribute-takers and townsmen changed over time. Southampton's animal bones, for example, hint that townsmen depended almost entirely on meat renders even in the eighth century, which leads us to believe that they continued to be beholden to whatever West Saxon elites fed them. In London, on the other hand, an important shift from provisioning to markets helped transform urban dinners and urban lives over the course of the seventh and eighth centuries.

THE NEW NON-TOWNS

Just because 'real' towns had come at last does not mean that they were the only type of trade or craft-making settlement developing in the period. Other site types, not quite rural, not quite urban, and some never year-round, came into being as well and were, like the towns themselves, central to the new economy. Many of these places, moreover, carried on for centuries and could have come to dominate the economy, although, in the end, none did.

Droitwich, in Worcestershire, was one such place. Salt-rich brine springs are ubiquitous around Droitwich, and in the second half of the sixth century salt makers at Droitwich built ten hearths from stones which they probably salvaged from an abandoned Roman villa 3 kilometres away. Each of these hearths was about 2 metres long and sheltered behind a wattle fence. At the salt hearths, men built fires and set large lead pots over them to evaporate the brine. Forty litres' boiling created something on the order of 13 kilograms of salt, so clearly they would have given over much of the salt they made as tribute or exchanged it for other things. The successful operation of the ten Droitwich hearths in the waning years of the sixth century required a complex set of exchanges and supporting activities. First and foremost, the saltmen needed a large and steady supply of wood to fuel their fires. Lead, too, had to be procured, and it is likely that one group of specialists mined it and that another fashioned it into pans. Potters, some living as much as 20 kilometres away, had to dig clay, shape pots and fire them, and then cart them to Droitwich, where salt makers lowered them into brine wells to collect the salt-rich waters or used them to store and ship the salt. Local farmers needed to raise extra pack animals for salt traders and for reeves, whose lords would have sent them periodically to fetch the salt. Other farmers needed to supply livestock, mostly cattle and sheep, to feed the saltmen and their families. We can see the dim outlines of a region with a whole series of specialist or semi-specialist producers, cooperating, coordinating and exchanging, but nonetheless remaining scattered across a rural landscape rather than gathering themselves into a single settlement. These developments are especially interesting when we think about their chronology. They happened across the period when control of the region around Droitwich moved from British-speaking to

English-speaking elites, and Droitwich's history helps to remind us that crucial economic transformations occurred independent from, even in spite of, high politics. By the eighth century Droitwich was generally known as *Saltwich*, that is, 'salt town'. By this time some kind of communal organization, probably overseen by the king of Mercia, is visible: as at London, people in Droitwich built an ambitious river revetment and brushwood trackway that required coordination, cooperation and resource gathering across households.

Droitwich could not have been unique: there are hints of other specialist production sites for iron, tin and lead; and they probably followed the pattern of Droitwich more closely than they did Ipswich or London, in that Droitwich was less town-like than either of these other places, specializing as it did in the manufacturing of a single product, depending for many of its needs on craftsmen living elsewhere, and little involved in foreign trade.

Yet another important settlement type developing in this period was the seasonal marketplace and manufacturing site. The best understood of these is *Sandtun*, a settlement established, in the very late seventh or early eighth century, on the shifting, wind-blown dunes near West Hythe, in Kent, on a sheltered inlet that looks towards France. People came to *Sandtun* each year in the good weather, but left in autumn about the time the herring began to run. The soil here was too poor for cereal cultivation, so the people spending summers at *Sandtun* had to get their supplies from farmers raising and processing grain elsewhere. Some of *Sandtun*'s summer residents fished, others busied themselves with the hard work of salt making, and still others were involved in trade. Some of the merchant ships making their way up and down the coast of Suffolk, Essex and Kent stopped along the way at *Sandtun* to trade Ipswich's distinctive ceramics, shards of which are found in great quantities at the site. Continental goods reached *Sandtun* as well, evidenced by impressive amounts of Continental pottery. So either Frankish traders came to *Sandtun* with boatloads of goods or some of *Sandtun*'s summer residents made overseas journeys themselves. Perhaps the minster communities at Lyminge and Canterbury (communities we know had rights in a later period over the site and some of its salt) controlled *Sandtun* in this early period and had their reeves meet with Frankish traders on the sand dunes to exchange local salt for French wine. Middlemen at *Sandtun* may have supplied exotic goods to the trading community of

Fordwich, just outside the walls of Canterbury, and they doubtless played a key role in turning the region's surplus of hides, salt, cloth and unfree humans into silver. Similar seasonal communities probably dotted Kent's – and England's – southern and eastern coasts and estuaries. Although the families who came to *Sandtun* to fish, to trade or to make salt did so for only part of each year, they came year in, year out, generation after generation, until sometime in the 850s or 860s. At this point the settlement failed, as so many coastal places did, victims of viking raids and the economic dislocations that followed in their wake.

Other sites developing during the late sixth, seventh and eighth centuries may have operated, not only as seasonal markets or fairs, but as semi-permanent sites of high-status craft-working. In the same decades that Ipswich developed into a permanent, prosperous and bustling community, two other settlements were founded less than 10 kilometres away, one at Barham and the other at Coddenham. Both places have produced remarkable collections of metalwork, some English, some Frankish and some even from western Britain. Many of the metal artefacts collected at Coddenham are broken-up pieces of finely made gold jewellery, and, taken together, they look like goldsmiths' scrap. This implies that high-status metal-working, of a kind not actually undertaken in Ipswich, was taking place here. But it is also clear that some people at Coddenham were in the habit of scavenging old Roman sites for scrap metal and were fashioning more quotidian objects with it – base-metal clothes fasteners, belt-stiffeners and the like – which suggests that smiths here catered to two quite different clienteles and markets. Coins were also found on the site. Two were gold, one from London and the other from Kent, and they date to 660 and 670 respectively; twenty-three others were silver, and minted in Kent, London, East Anglia and Frisia between c. 675 and 700. It looks as if either traders with goods from Francia, Frisia, Kent, London and western Britain regularly did business at Coddenham, or traders from Ipswich with coins they had got from their dealings there were regulars at the site. One of the gold coins, moreover, was cut, a sure sign of commercial coin use; and metal detectorists have also recovered a folding balance there, which would have been used to weigh precious metal during exchanges. At nearby Barham, a quantity of English, Frisian and Frankish coins and metalwork, as well as metalwork from western Britain, has also been recovered, and, judging from the date range of the many coins,

Barham was a place of regular and persistent commercial activity from the mid-seventh century to the mid-eighth.

Both Coddenham and Barham have also produced evidence for the presence of controlling local elites. A seventh/eighth-century cemetery on the ridge above Coddenham boasts among its many graves two chamber burials. One contained the body of a woman wearing fancy, Frankish-style shoes, who had been laid to rest on an elaborate, iron-framed bed. She was placed in the ground with a gold pendant made from a Frankish coin dated to the 630s. A second coin in her grave, a silver *sceat*, dates to the late seventh century. The second chamber burial contained the body of a man who was also wearing Frankish-style shoes and who shared his grave with a Frankish copper-alloy bowl, a wooden bucket, a spear, a seax and a shield. This man's weapons are especially interesting, because both the shield and the spear were apparently decorative rather than functional. This man was not so much an East Anglian warrior as a man dressed to impress. Archaeologists have also excavated a large wooden hall nearby, more than 10 metres in length. A cemetery has also been found near Barham, and some of its dead, too, were provided with an impressive array of fancy, imported grave goods. Taken together, these finds suggest that a couple of households near the developing trading site at Ipswich encouraged, founded or controlled a couple of market and craft sites that were economically related in some way to Ipswich.

Perhaps other elite households in Ipswich's hinterlands were also encouraging local farmers, tribute-takers and craftsmen to gather near their halls and were welcoming traders from Ipswich, Kent, Frisia and Francia. Because these sites were operating during the same period that Ipswich was moving towards urbanism, they may have acted as important nodes in the economic system developing in this period, which drew the foreign goods available at Ipswich further inland, and simultaneously siphoned off wealth from the countryside and funnelled it back towards the market at Ipswich. Similar sites were almost certainly developing around London, if the profusion of -*wic* place names found up and down the River Thames is anything to go by, and the same thing was clearly happening around the Southampton waters as well. Many farmers living near Ipswich must have also taken advantage of their proximity to the towns or the smaller markets popping up in their shadows to exchange some of their own surpluses for high-quality quernstones or Ipswich ware. By the early eighth century these things would be ubiquitous on quite humble sites in East Anglia, so people living in these places must have had dealings with traders in Ipswich or some of its linked inland markets.

So it seems that large, permanent enclaves of foreign traders in places like Ipswich, London and Southampton stimulated economic activity in the surrounding hinterlands, and that important and ambitious households in their shadows were helping to transform the economy of England by overseeing their own seasonal trading and manufacturing sites further inland, so that they, too, could get their hands on foreign exotica, profit from trade and improve their standing in the world. These places, in turn, encouraged local lords and farmers to exchange their surpluses and even, increasingly, to produce for the market.

From the seventh century on, moreover, many different kinds of household – royal, monastic, aristocratic – were coming to demand ever more specialized production from the people living within their territories, with the needs of places like Ipswich, Southampton or London in mind. Indeed, rural settlement patterns began to shift during the seventh and eighth centuries, in part so that elites might rationalize the tribute due them to fulfil the needs of the towns and townsmen, so that they might exchange what they did not need for luxury goods and coin. We know that important lay and ecclesiastical households must have had agents dealing directly with urban traders by at least the middle of the eighth century, since finds from the period's high-status sites show these places were well integrated into both regional and international exchange networks. The only way this could have happened is if those who controlled high-status sites had regular dealings with traders and provisioners in the towns.

TOWNS AND NEW-STYLE KINGS

Historians and archaeologists used to attribute the rebirth of towns in eastern Britain to kings, and some even went so far as to argue that kings created these places so that they might guarantee their own access to status-enhancing goods, or, indeed, ensure that they had a monopoly over them. We now know, however, that, although English kings would eventually come to regulate these places, they were not their founders.

Instead, it seems that all sorts of individuals and households had a hand in their creation – Frisian slavers arriving in hopes of swapping Continental luxury goods for a little human flesh; tribute-takers with great herds of cattle and a thirst for French wine; farmers with a couple of piglets and a dugout canoe; families willing to risk giving up full-time farming for full-time pot-making; reeves who could organize carters to move bulky goods from a town's foreshore to rural halls. It was the coming together of all of these types at the moment when kings and other lords were gaining control over more surpluses than their households could ever use and when members of elite families were beginning to experiment with monastic living. All these groups and individuals came to embrace commerce in the seventh and eighth centuries, because it allowed them to turn sheep or wheat into luxury goods, silver coins and even town-made pottery.

Although it is clear that kings were not the founders of England's early towns, it is nonetheless certain that the fates of towns and kings were inextricably linked, because, although kings had not made towns, towns by the later seventh and the eighth centuries were beginning to remake England's most formidable kings. To understand how this happened, we need to return to those kings who had come, by the middle of the seventh century, to rule England's largest and most successful agglomerations of peoples and territories. By this time, men like the kings of Northumbria, East Anglia, Kent, Sussex and Wessex all ruled relatively large and prosperous kingdoms, but all found themselves in increasingly dangerous competition with the same formidable foe: Mercia.

Mercia's rulers, like all successful seventh-century kings, had a gift for violence. When we first catch sight of a Mercian king, around the year 600, he is lording it over a small territory centred on the middle stretches of the River Trent. By the middle decades of the seventh century, however, Mercian kings and their fighting men had broadened their dominion ruthlessly and dramatically, especially during the reign of the kingdom's last pagan leader, Penda († 655), a ferociously capable warrior king. Although Penda was often the victor in his military encounters against neighbours and competitors, he did not always drive a kingdom's defeated ruler out, but instead sometimes allowed him to remain as king, as long as he submitted to Mercia, rendered tribute and promised to join in at least some of its wars. Just how often Penda was able to transform enemies and potential rivals into subordinates is hinted at in Bede's depiction of the men who joined Penda's war band on its last, fatal campaign. The historian tells us that thirty members of Penda's army were 'royal leaders'. These individuals were apparently kings or kinglets who, at some point, had submitted to Mercia and were now going to war against its enemies. British kings sometimes accompanied Penda's host as well, so these men and their peoples, too, must have provided Mercia with annual tributes and warriors.

Here, then, we see the development of a kind of hegemonic kingship, one that cut across regions and ethnic communities. Penda held sway over an assemblage of territories and their English- and British-speaking peoples, not as an integrated whole, and certainly not as a 'king of England'. Rather, he had authority over a jumble of tribute-rendering, warrior-providing entities. Similar hegemonic kingships are in evidence in Northumbria, where we find the kings acting as overlords to groups of Picts and northern British peoples, as well as to the Scots of Argyll. And in the eighth century the great Pictish king Onuist (r. 729–61) would subordinate all the kings of northern Britain to himself. Such rule-by-agglomeration, common throughout Britain and Ireland in the seventh and eighth centuries, was highly unstable, and it was quite common for subordinate peoples and kingdoms either to be hived off by rival hegemonic kings or to wiggle free whenever they could. Our evidence hints, though, that Penda, in the latter part of his reign, moved to stabilize what must have been an inherently unwieldy operation by bundling some subordinate peoples and territories into new kingdoms, which he then gave out to his sons and other trusted kinsmen, and which they, in turn, ruled as subordinate kings. In this way, Penda placed carefully chosen intervening rulers between himself and the dozens of native elites and local strongmen over whom he held some authority. This innovation helped him manage the face-to-face, personal relationships so critical to hegemonic kings and their high-status subordinates. Even if important local lords living, say, in the newly constituted kingdom of the Middle Angles never laid eyes on the great man himself, they would nonetheless have feasted with his son, who had been made their king; and these men would have understood that the local surrogate of the Mercian king could wreak vengeance on them if they plotted against his interests. What Penda did not do, however, was integrate all of the peoples and territories subordinate to him into a single kingdom. The thing that made Penda the envy of great men throughout Britain was not the fact that he was sole ruler of a large kingdom, but that he had *imperium* over dozens of kings and peoples.

The prodigious wealth hegemonic kings like Penda could reap from wars waged with the help of their polyglot, loosely organized war bands was brought home, in the summer of 2009, by the discovery, in Staffordshire, of an extraordinary cache of early medieval war-loot – more than 5 kilograms of finely wrought gold objects and more than a kilogram of silver metalwork. One long band of gold found in the hoard – probably once attached to a shield, a sword hilt or a sword belt – is inscribed, in imperfect Latin, with a stunningly bloodthirsty biblical paraphrase: 'Rise up, O Lord, and may thy enemies be scattered and those who hate thee be driven from thy face.' Judging from the execution of its letters, this piece was made in the eighth century. The hoard, however, also contained dozens of objects crafted in the later sixth and seventh centuries. Like the inscribed piece, most of the hoard's treasures had been stripped from military equipment, although the blades to which a large number of them had once been attached are nowhere to be found. It seems that it was the custom, after battle, for victors to remove the precious-metal decorations found on the weapons, shields and helmets of vanquished enemies. Perhaps the stripped gear was then handed out to the king's followers as gifts. This hoard, however, seems to have been a self-consciously curated store of battlefield spoils – a cache of the most precious adornments looted from defeated warriors' gear, preserved and augmented by its owners for five or six generations. Given the splendour of these treasures, their broad date range and their burial in the Mercian heartland, they probably belonged to the Mercian kings. Because these spoils had been gathered and retained for generations, rather than melted down and transformed into splendid new objects, the collection may have had a ritual function. One can well imagine how this treasure might have been displayed on important occasions, and how the stories of individual pieces could be recounted to strengthen the bonds between the disparate peoples who made up 'greater Mercia', and between Mercians and those allies and tributaries with whom they sometimes made common cause. Such retellings would have underscored the shared histories and triumphs of what were, in reality, quite distinct peoples and affinities.

Clearly, given the evidence of the Staffordshire hoard, warfare could bring victors immense wealth, but it was also an activity in which hegemons, out of necessity, had to participate. The more Penda took from other peoples, the more he could give to his followers; and the more he could give to followers, the more followers he had, and thus the more he could take from other peoples. Still, warfare was hard, risky and sometimes fatal. The glittering loot victors gathered, moreover, had its limitations, and it did not translate directly into something that better enabled kings to administer what they had won with the blades of their swords. Yet for a century and a half after Penda's death Mercian kings continued to make war and extended their *imperium*, and by the mid-eighth century they controlled most of the lands and peoples found between the Humber and the Thames and between the modern-day border of Wales and the western edges of the Fens. At times they even subjugated some of the largest and most successful English kingdoms, places like Kent and East Anglia. So, while in Penda's day the limitations of treasure were hardly noticeable, over the course of the late seventh, eighth and the early ninth centuries, warfare, plunder and submissions would grow to be insufficient for kings' needs. It is fortunate for Mercia that it was ruled, for over a century, by three long-lived and talented kings – King Æthelbald (r. 716–57), King Offa (r. 757–96) and King Ceonwulf (r. 796–821). And it was fortunate, as well, that urban communities were developing rapidly in just these years, because under these three kings, although warfare and violence would continue on as mainstays of Mercian power, the new possibilities opened up by towns came to be exploited by these men, and, in the process, kingship was transformed.

One of the problems confronting all three of Mercia's great kings was how to benefit from the enormous tributes given to them each year by subordinate peoples. Some of this tribute, according to Bede, came in the form of 'royal treasures and gifts', but the bulk must have comprised agricultural surpluses – herds of cattle especially, but also perhaps bales of wool, hams, beer, hawks and honey – in short, the kinds of things every lord received from local farm families, except on a much grander scale. Because of the nature of this tribute, Mercian kings would have commanded an extraordinary supply of foodstuffs and livestock, much more than they and their allies could ever use. Most of these riches, moreover, could not be stockpiled for more than a few years, without spoiling or dying on the hoof. So what Mercian kings needed to do on a very grand scale was something that many surplus-collecting lords in this period were beginning to do: exchange the tribute their households did not need, either for status-enhancing goods or, better yet, for silver coin, which transformed foodstuffs, fodder and livestock into a longer-lived, more easily transportable, more flexible form of wealth. Mercia's kings needed access to markets, to traders, to foreign merchants and to coin. In short, they needed towns; and yet the Mercian heartland, which lay west of the more commercialized southern and eastern coastal zones of Britain, had no great entrepôt of its own.

It is hardly surprising, then, that we find that even before Æthelbald fought his way to the throne Mercia's landlocked kings laboured and connived to gain control and keep hold of London. And although London would, on occasion, fall under the authority of some competing dynasty, for most of the late seventh, eighth and early ninth centuries Mercian kings were its masters. London not only provided Mercian kings with a large and thriving market in which to exchange their tribute, but gave them access to an international market where they could sell the large amounts of salt now being produced annually at Droitwich, a settlement in which they were increasingly involved as manufacturers, regulators and toll-takers. There is also some evidence that lead, wool and slaves were being taken from the Mercian heartland and exchanged in London, and there were doubtless many other Mercian products – leather, grain, livestock – which were finding buyers along the foreshore of the Thames.

London, however, functioned as more than an outlet for Mercian surpluses. It was an astonishingly productive generator of wealth for Mercian royal coffers, not because it helped Mercian kings win wars or extract tributes from neighbours, but rather because it was through the running of London that the Mercian kings were learning to govern; once they took hold of London, they gained control of its market sites, and these market sites came with toll-collecting operations. It was these London tolls that must have made Mercia's kings the wealthiest men in Britain.

Mercian kings were hardly the inventors of controlled market sites and toll-collecting in London, and by the time King Æthelbald began profiting from London tolls they had been in operation for a couple of generations. Indeed, it is likely that English kings in the south and east of Britain, who lived in a commercializing landscape, and who had been missionized relatively early in the seventh century, were first tutored about tolls by foreign missionaries and foreign merchants, who were increasingly present in this period, and who were eager to explain to English rulers just how kingship was practised in more politically and economically developed parts of the world. In the early days the merchants and the ecclesiastics together probably encouraged kings to involve themselves directly in trade and trading sites. Frisian and Frankish merchants wishing to conduct business in England, for example, may have urged kings to intervene in trade in order to guarantee the safety of their goods. Traders, by explaining to English kings how business was done elsewhere, would have introduced them to the notion that they could profit from trade, since kings across the Christian world were given a cut of commercial transactions in return for a guarantee of security. Not only would foreign merchants have been used to this regime at home, but it is likely that tolls were less costly than the losses incurred at dangerously unregulated market sites, where foreign merchants would have found themselves at the mercy of local shakedown operations and brigands. Churchmen may have similarly taught their royal charges about tolls, because these men, too, knew at first hand how those who supervised trade in cities like Dorestad, Tours, Rome and Antioch grew rich from tolls, and because their own communities had need of safe trading sites.

By the last third of the seventh century it is clear that English kings, whoever their teachers, had internalized these lessons, and that they were moving to implement them. One of toll-collecting's many advantages was that it required little infrastructure or administrative support; all that was needed was a market site with a controlled entrance, a toll collector and perhaps a small group of armed enforcers. In spite of the low overheads of these toll-operations, they were enormously profitable. The tolls imposed on goods offered for sale by foreign merchants in England were probably 10 per cent of the value of the goods, a standard levy in the early Middle Ages throughout the Frankish, Byzantine and Arab worlds. Because the charge of 'a tenth' was ubiquitous, this amount would have seemed 'natural' to the Italian, Frankish and Greek churchmen now advising the Christian kings of England, as well as to the Frisian and Frankish merchants doing business with them. Some of the tolls kings came to collect in this period were paid in coin, but others would have come to the king in the form of pre-emption, that is, some fraction of a foreign trader's choicest merchandise was given over as the price of doing business at a controlled trading site.

English kings had certainly grasped the potential of tolls by the 660s. A text dated to this period describes the ways in which kings of Kent were now insisting that Kentish men buying goods in London had to make their trades in front of a couple of trustworthy witnesses or the king's resident reeve in London, a man who was labelled both a '*wic*-reeve' and a 'toll collector'. One suspects from the titles used of this official that he was not only responsible for keeping the peace and guaranteeing sales within London (that is, the *wic*), but that he was collecting a toll on the king's behalf in return for this service.

Tolls like this were essentially free money for an already powerful king, whose bidding people did, and they became a source of near unimaginable riches, the kind of wealth made possible by governing rather than fighting. In Mercian London, with its hundreds of workshops, its crowd of foreign traders and the large amounts of Thames Valley surplus being exchanged in its markets, the king of Mercia's toll collectors must have gathered warehouses full of goods and sacks of silver for their king each year, riches that would have dwarfed the glittering war-loot recovered in the Staffordshire hoard.

It is also likely that, under King Æthelbald, Mercian kings began minting their own silver coins. Æthelbald would have been interested in producing coins because they allowed some of the tributes he was collecting, both from his own estates and from subordinate peoples and kingdoms, to be turned into coins, which he could then use to pay for churches, churchmen and written administration, and to exchange with foreign traders. Although the *sceattas* struck during Æthelbald's reign never bore the king's name, the way later coins would do, this coinage was probably regulated by him. No such uncertainty, however, surrounds the coinage of Æthelbald's successor, King Offa. Not only did King Offa effectively control coinage, but, under his direction, his name and sometimes his face came to embellish a new flatter, thinner coin – the penny – a denomination which helped bring English currency in line with the silver coinage of the Franks. A study of the dies that produced Offa's pennies suggests that millions of coins were struck for him during his long reign. These coins were not made within the Mercian heartland itself, but rather in the southern and eastern coastal regions, where trading communities were thick on the ground, where foreign merchants were exchanging foreign silver for English goods, and where King Offa, as the dominating force south of the Humber, was able to take control of the mechanisms by which foreign coins entering the kingdom were turned into English pennies. It seems that the king's moneyers were producing coins not only in London and Canterbury, but somewhere in East Anglia as well. The weight of Offa's coins changed dramatically over time, and his minters, towards the end of his reign, were moving to match their weights to Frankish currency. Those who turned foreign currency into English pennies took a small percentage of the precious metal in return for reminting, something Offa apparently insisted upon. Whether it was the king who received this silver, or minters, who doubtless had to buy the right to make coins from the king, the Mercian masters of the bulk of England's eighth-century mints had found yet another extraordinary source of income, and one, like tolls, that required little infrastructure or administration. In a very real sense towns domesticated England's warrior kings, because they provided those who understood their potential with far greater riches than warfare ever could. Indeed, towns were one of the evolving institutions of this period that must have come to convince kings that governing was more profitable than plundering; that taxing and toll-taking were surer and more lucrative than war.

8

Norse and Natives: The Late Eighth
to Late Ninth Century

In the middle of the eighth century, before they had got into the habit of
raiding wealthy communities in Christian Europe, most Norse people
made their living as farmers. In Denmark, where a number of early
medieval settlements have been excavated, we know that hamlets at the
dawn of the Viking Age often comprised clusters of six or seven farmsteads. Each establishment, fenced off from its neighbours, would have
had a half dozen buildings or more. Some would have served as smithies
or pottery-making sheds, and others may have housed low-status workers. Each household also had a single longhouse, often, in this early
period, divided in two by a solid wall, with a central hearth on one side
for its human inhabitants and stalls on the other for the over-wintering
of cattle. The few settlements excavated in Sweden hint that communities here tended to be smaller, with two or three farms to a hamlet,
rather than six or seven. Settlements in Norway are more elusive still,
but one, a place thriving in the ninth and tenth centuries at Ytre Moa,
in Sogn, was an isolated farmstead. The buildings here were very small,
and made from wood-panelled stone and turf walls, an entirely different building technique from that used further south. Thus Scandinavia
shows a considerable diversity in settlement size, building techniques
and farm layouts. Those who lived in Denmark and Sweden generally
grew more cereal crops and had larger and more productive farms than
the people who lived along Norway's mountainous coast, but even families in northern Scandinavia cultivated barley, oats and rye. Ancient
pollen recovered by archaeologists reveals that most people in the region
also raised flax, hemp and woad for weaving and dyeing, and cabbage,
onions and beans for the pot. Wherever they farmed, though, Norse
peoples spent much of their time worrying over their livestock. Typically, farmers raised cattle and horses both for traction and for meat;

and they milked, sheared and ate their goats and sheep. In many places, because of the emphasis on animal husbandry, shielings, or upland pastures, lay at the heart of the annual cycle of farm life. At the beginning of summer households would drive their animals to distant, high-country pastures, and some of their members would follow, spending the warm months watching over herds and milking and making cheese, which could be eaten during the long months of winter.

Perhaps more than people elsewhere in north-west Europe, the Norse also fished, hunted and trapped. This was especially true in areas where the growing of grain was a particularly thankless task. Indeed, archaeologists have discovered hundreds of pits in Norway – dug between the Neolithic period and the end of the Viking Age – strung out along the migratory routes of reindeer and moose, and used to trap unlucky beasts who strayed or were driven into them. In some parts of Sweden and Norway, farmers also extracted soapstone and carved it into loom weights and cooking pots; or they cut slate and sandstone which they then fashioned into whetstones or grindstones. These items were essential for the running of every household, but extras could be made and traded, as could surplus walrus-skin ropes or reindeer hides, and their makers could exchange these things for necessaries or status items that they were unable to produce on their own. In short, the evidence from the period's settlement archaeology points both to broad self-sufficiency and impressive versatility, virtues that developed out of the harsh realities of Scandinavian weather, soil and scarcity of arable land.

Many Norse people also had another, special skill: boat building. A boat for fishing, sealing or getting down the coast was a necessity in Scandinavia, not a luxury. Fortunately, Scandinavia had an abundance of raw materials needed for boat making. Most farmers, for example, had easy access to hardwood timber as well as local supplies of bog iron, which many, judging from the ubiquitous finds from farmstead smithies, knew how to smelt and fashion into wood-working tools, nails, washers and rivets. The need for boats and the availability of boat-making materials meant that many coastal farmers built their own; and by the middle of the eighth century some had begun crafting astonishingly sophisticated, seaworthy vessels. They had very strong hulls, which could take a beating in the North Atlantic, but they also had shallow draughts, making them as swift and sure in rivers as they were in deep ocean waters. Scandinavian boats were also easy to beach, and they could be dragged overland to get from one river to the next or to avoid rapids and waterfalls. They were oared for speed and manoeuvrability, and by the mid-eighth century they had masts and single sails as well, a technology adopted from Frisian and Frankish traders who had been trawling the Baltic Sea in recent decades in search of walrus ivory, fur and amber, because these things fetched good prices from Frankish and English elites.

The interest of Christian traders in the raw materials circulating around the Baltic helped to transform life in the region. Their inadvertent introduction of sail technology made it possible for relatively modest men to involve themselves for the first time in sea voyaging, since they no longer needed to muster rowing crews of thirty or more, but could now man their boats with four or five sailors. This allowed them to sail to local, informal beach markets, a kind of trading site increasingly common along the Scandinavian coasts in the late seventh and the eighth century. The quickening of trade with Christian Europe changed the region and its people in other ways. The eighth century witnessed the emergence of a large number of seasonal and a few year-round craft and trading communities within Scandinavia. At settlements like these, well-to-do farmers could exchange their surpluses for Carolingian wine or fancy silver jewellery, possessions they could flaunt, give away or bury with their dead relatives. It was also in such trading centres that many Norse-speakers would have got their first glimpses of the luxuries available in Christian Europe.

As commercial activity quickened, and as Scandinavia came to sit at the centre of an intricate web of exchange networks that stretched across the Baltic, a number of entrepreneurial individuals within Scandinavia moved to take advantage of the new economic possibilities. Some, for example, managed to supplement their livelihoods by collecting tribute from peoples to the north and east, peoples whose languages, material culture and way of life were different from their own. By 750 or so Norse entrepreneurs had established a trading centre at Staraja Ladoga, in Russia, where furs were apparently gathered by Norse chieftains from Finnish-, Saami- and Slavic-speaking tributaries, and then traded to Frisian or Frankish merchants. One such tribute-taker, a Norwegian named Ottar, visited King Alfred's court in the late ninth century. While there, he described how he gathered tribute from the Saami each year, explaining to the king that it came in the form of the skins of [reindeer] herds, bird feathers and whale-bone and in ship's ropes which are made from the hides of whales and seals. Each one pays according to his rank. The noblest must pay fifteen marten skins, five whales and one bear skin, and ten measures of feathers, and a bear- or an otter-skin coat, and two ship's ropes, both to be sixty ells long, one made of whale's hide and the other of seal's [skin].

Chieftains like Ottar became wealthy from the trade, and they were exposed to silver-rich, luxury-hungry merchants and kings whenever they ventured south or west of their own lands.

Others in Scandinavia over the course of the seventh, eighth and ninth centuries worked hard to produce goods for local markets. At Naes in Zealand, for example, archaeologists have excavated a settlement that was thriving in the eighth and ninth centuries. They have found the remains, not only of a couple of prosperous longhouses, but of dozens of weaving sheds and more than fifty carefully engineered, wicker-lined wells. These wells had been purpose-built for flax processing, and it looks as if the settlement was a major centre of linen-cloth production. The site was manufacturing much more linen than its inhabitants could ever use, so those occupying the site's longhouses must have profited from its trade.

Archaeologists have excavated another, even grander site in West Zealand, on the shores of Lake Tissø. To the north of the main site lay a hall, occupied in the sixth and seventh centuries, which appears to have been the residence of a great man, but there were also signs of market and craft activities. Some time in the second half of the seventh century the settlement shifted south. At this point a huge longhouse was built which was then rebuilt on a number of occasions until the early eleventh century. Almost a hundred weapons have been found near this site, along with spurs, bits and the bones of hunting-dogs and larger-than-average horses. It was also around the longhouse that archaeologists excavated almost all the site's imported artefacts. The spike of insular and Frankish metalwork, dating to the eighth and ninth centuries, may signal trade links; but it could equally represent evidence of raiding. The ninth- and tenth-century Arab coins found there similarly suggest that those who came here were hooked into the great web of exchange networks connecting the Middle East to the Baltic. Clearly this was a high-status complex, and its proprietor had access to the riches of the world. But, unlike most of the period's grandest sites, little evidence has been found here for agricultural production. Instead, to the north and south of the longhouse lay zones thick with workshops, probably several hundred at the settlement's height. There are also the remains of booths, which traders would have occupied seasonally and from which they transacted their business. Many weights for the measuring of silver were found in these zones, as well as cut coins, both of which indicate trade.

Archaeologists have also uncovered a special enclosure here, which they have interpreted as a cult site and believe was related in some way to the numerous weapons deposited during the period as votive offerings in the nearby lake. They may have been gifts for the god Tyr: Tissø, in any case, means 'Tyr's Lake'. The whole site, with its dearth of run-of-the-mill agricultural buildings and permanent, low-status housing, looks seasonal. It seems that people spent a few months here each year and organized their comings and goings around some recurrent market, perhaps held in conjunction with a great religious festival, the way we know that the fair at Uppsala (a fair known as the *Distingen*, or 'the Thing [or meeting] of the goddess Díser') was held on the first new moon after midwinter. The site at Lake Tissø was very much affected by changes beyond Scandinavia. It testifies to the presence of elite households in Scandinavia with the resources to build lavish accommodations for themselves and to patronize, perhaps even co-opt, an important cult site and a profitable market and manufacturing centre. One of the site's excavators has gone so far as to argue that by the ninth or tenth century the place had the look and feel of a Scandinavian version of a Frankish palace, complete with luxury accommodation, a centre for worship (albeit a pagan one) and an area set aside for commercial activity.

Some of Scandinavia's seasonal trading places – Ribe and Hedeby, in Denmark, and Birka, in Sweden – grew rapidly into bona fide, year-round settlements under the watchful eyes of local kings and chieftains, who were consolidating their positions in part through their control of such sites. These were men who sought to monopolize the manufacturing and trade of luxury goods within their territories, and who hoped to mimic their more economically savvy Frankish and English neighbours and collect tolls and taxes on foreign trade. It is, moreover, clear from the morphology of places like Ribe, Hedeby and Birka that powerful individuals stood behind them. They were laid out in organized fashion, with grids of streets, carefully marked property boundaries, and what must have been communally funded, constructed and maintained public boardwalks. As early as the eighth century, then, it seems that a handful of far-sighted men understood the promise of such communities, and that they had begun to move aggressively to found, patronize, regulate or usurp them.

Contacts with Christian Europe were also transforming the political culture of Scandinavia, particularly in Denmark, parts of which abutted the Frankish empire of Charlemagne (r. 768–814). Here, local leaders were becoming Carolingianized. One, a Dane named Godfred, attacked the Abrodites, a client people of the Carolingians, and forced them to pay him tribute. During the same campaign, he razed a Carolingian-controlled trading community at a place called *Reric*, which is probably located under present-day Gross Strömendorf. He kidnapped the merchants living there and transferred them to Hedeby, in his own territory. He apparently moved them there because he hoped to profit from tolls on their trade, just as Frankish and English kings did, and he wanted easy access to the luxury goods produced in Christian Europe. This Godfred is an interesting man. We know from the Frankish Royal Annals that he had cavalry at his disposal. He understood the value of merchants and tolls, and he was able to carry out his very clever plan of moving an entire, up-and-running trading community to his own territory. Not only did he transplant this community, but he ordered a giant earthwork built around it to protect it from the Franks, so he was a man who could undertake public works and mobilize teams of labour to carry them out. In some ways, he was very much a sub-Carolingian figure. He could fight on horseback like a Frank; he collected tribute like a Frank; he oversaw trading communities like a Frank; he undertook ambitious public works projects like a Frank. And he called himself king, like a Frank. He learned how to act like a Frank from the Franks themselves, because the Danes and the Franks, thanks to Frankish imperialism, were now neighbours, and there was no longer a buffer zone between the two peoples. So Godfred had watched and learned and copied the ways of the Franks' great king Charlemagne, and he was now successfully beating them at their own game. But, as a Norseman, he had one thing that the Franks did not have: a fleet. In 810 he led 200 ships against Frisia, defeated the forces the Frisians mustered to fight off the attack and gathered tribute from them. This was an outrage, because the Frisians were supposed to pay tribute to the Franks, not the Danes. Charlemagne was furious. He gathered a large army to fight against Godfred, but before he had the opportunity to do so Godfred was killed by one of his own followers. While he lived, however, this upstart had successfully challenged Frankish power. After his death Godfred's kingdom collapsed. Yet many of Godfred's men had acquired an appetite for status and wealth. Since they could no longer gain riches by following the now-dead Godfred, they would have to do it on their own. So why not join with a boatload or two of friends and raid the Frankish coastline or attack a Frisian trading community? Why not loot a monastery in Britain or Ireland?

In any case, there is evidence that by the later eighth century Norse society was socially stratified, that some were involved in distant and profitable exchange networks and that many were familiar with the riches of Christian Europe. At the same time, less fancy folks, in particular Scandinavian free farmers, were extraordinarily versatile: they were good stockmen and hunters, keen traders and the masters of homely crafts. During the months when farming duties were less onerous or after local fairs had finished, Norsemen could take to the seas. They could sail to markets like Ribe, on the west coast of Jutland, or Birka, in Sweden, with furs, whetstones, even eiderdown; or they could shake down Frisian merchants in the Baltic or raid Frankish settlements. Or they could sail west, in search of promising new lands, places where they could establish themselves, their families and their flocks or escape from local elites, newly consolidating their power at the expense of others in their neighbourhoods. Each of these activities held out the possibility of a bright, new future.

RETHINKING CATASTROPHE FROM THE MARGINS

One of the earliest recorded raids in Britain by vikings (the name used to describe Scandinavians when they acted as pirates or invaders) took place at the tail end of the eighth century. Three ships, so we are told, hailing from Hörthaland in Norway, arrived along the south coast of England in 789 at a place called Portland, in Dorset. *Port* is the Old English word for 'market', so Portland was probably the site of a market, perhaps a seasonal beach market, held under the aegis of the king. The king's reeve, mistaking the strangers for merchants, asked them to accompany him to the king's hall, doubtless to take a cut of their wares for his lord, a commonplace practice, as we have seen, at regulated market sites. The ships' crews, however, either because they did not understand the proceedings or because they were up to no good, murdered the reeve and his helpers. With sorry, if slightly inaccurate hindsight (given that these men were from Norway), the chronicler laments, 'those were the first ships of Danish men which came to the land of the English'. By the 790s Norse pirates were raiding northern Britain's coastal monasteries. These attacks were given extensive treatment by ecclesiastical writers, who were shocked that pagans had desecrated some of the holiest sites in Europe, and who worried that God had sent this fearful scourge because of the sins of His people. Irish monasteries were falling prey to viking attacks in the 790s as well, and after the turn of the ninth century religious communities far to the south, like the coastal monasteries of Kent, were acquiring refuges in more protected, inland places, so that they had safe havens during the raiding season.

As terrible as these early hit-and-run raids were, and as devastating as their consequences were for the monks slaughtered at their altars or the farm girls kidnapped and then sold into slavery, things got decidedly worse. By the mid-ninth century growing numbers of Norsemen were engaged in such operations, and they became more ambitious in their goals. Indeed, many turned from get-rich-quick plundering operations to sustained, multi-year campaigns organized around the twin goals of territorial acquisition and political conquest. In 865 the *micel here*, or 'Great Army', arrived in England, and its operations were both long-term and devastating. Within a year its men captured York and eliminated not one, but two rival factions of the Northumbrian royal house and installed a puppet king to do their bidding. Two years later they killed the king of East Anglia. The kingdoms of Wessex and Mercia managed to hold out longer, and both fought against the Danes with a fair amount of success. At times, though, they found it prudent to buy the army off, rather than engage it. In the end, Mercian and West Saxon successes proved ephemeral, and over the course of the next five years the great marauding army gained control of Mercia and installed yet another quisling king. Then, in 878, with a surprise attack at Christmastime, they drove England's last standing monarch, King Alfred of Wessex, into the marshes of Somerset. In eleven terrible years – between

867 and 878 – England's five great kingdoms were brought to their knees by the men of the *micel here*.

Of course, as every British schoolchild should know, our story does not end in the winter of 878. King Alfred, in the end, fought his way back from his swampy retreat and won a surprising and surprisingly decisive victory against the Danes. Although there would be a half century of hard fighting ahead, Alfred, his son and daughter Edward the Elder (r. 899–924) and Æthelflæd 'lady of the Mercians' († 918), and his grandson Athelstan (r. 924–39) eventually drove viking rulers out of England and pacified the Norsemen who were settled there. More importantly, their dynasty came to rule a kingdom that encompassed the whole of Britain's English-culture zone. And they came, moreover, to rule not as hegemonic kings of Wessex, the way Mercia's kings had once ruled, but as kings of the *Angelcynn*, that is, as kings of the whole of the 'English folk'. The extraordinary story of Alfred and his heirs has, over the course of the last millennium, become the story of all of Britain, and it often serves, in the popular imagination, as a kind of proxy for the experiences of all the peoples of Britain. The trouble, however, with making this story stand for all the rest is that it has led to a flattening out and homogenizing of experience. Neither the story of the West Saxon kings nor the seeming inevitability of their triumph comes close to capturing the dramatically different experiences of people whose lives were transformed because of Norse raiding, campaigning and settlement. Britain was a wildly diverse place in the later eighth and the ninth centuries, even its English-speaking regions. Geography, wealth and proximity to power all determined, in crucial ways, the number of Norsemen particular native groups had to confront, as did local politics. But, even in those areas where vikings rarely ventured, the period was transformative.

For many of Britain's kings and nobles, the eighth and ninth centuries were simultaneously times of terrible danger and great opportunity. The art of successful hegemony, mastered by Mercia's rulers before the ruinous Norse raids of the ninth century had begun, was something to which kings across Britain still aspired, but the politics of the period were so confounded by Norse interlopers that only a handful of dynasties – the kings of Wessex, the extended ruling family of the Welsh kingdom of Gwynedd and the macAlpin dynasty in Scotland – managed, in the end, to yoke together impressive, if somewhat friable polities. By the second half of the tenth century Wessex had absorbed the once independent kingdoms of East Anglia, Kent, Mercia and Northumbria; and Gwynedd, by the same time, could claim lordship over much of Wales west of Offa's Dike (the earthwork King Offa had had built across a long stretch of the Welsh Marches). Both kingdoms had done more than simply survive viking incursions; they had adroitly taken advantage of the harm viking raiders and armies had inflicted on other dynasties and kingdoms. And although these new-model polities came apart periodically along old, political boundaries, especially during child minorities and succession disputes, single families nonetheless managed to carry on or reassert these extended kingships generation after generation.

When we look back on the ninth century, knowing how the story ends, such outcomes seem inevitable. But the truth of the matter is that things could have turned out differently. If one more English dynasty had survived the *micel here*, the West Saxon kings' heroic, unifying campaigns against the vikings might have played out as destructive wars waged between competing kingdoms, with invaders playing off both sides against the middle. Or if Picts had kept Norse immigrants from settling in northern Scotland, they may have forestalled the Norse takeover of Shetland and Orkney, events that could, in turn, have hampered Norse access to the Irish Sea. To remind ourselves of the contingency of history, of its surprising outcomes and the unpredictable consequences of historical events, it is instructive to think about Britain in these years not from the perspective of the eventual winners, but from the viewpoint of kingdoms and peoples who would, in the end, lose. So let us see how this period looks, not from Alfred's court settled comfortably at Winchester nor in the texts produced by members of his household, but rather from the material evidence surviving from the small, landlocked Welsh kingdom of Brycheiniog, from the venerable (and vulnerable) Mercian monastery of Repton, and from the Pictish settlements of Orkney.

THE DEATH OF A WELSH KINGDOM

From at least the eighth century the kings of Brycheiniog had controlled territory centred on Llangorse near Brecon, and not only had they patronized an important monastic community there, but its church probably served as the family's sepulchre. In the late ninth century

Brycheiniog's king, Elisedd ap Tewdwr, expended considerable resources to develop royal interests at Llangorse. In 889, or soon thereafter, it seems that the king began to build an extraordinary new residence *in* Llangorse Lake, the largest lake in south Wales. We have unusually precise dates for the site's beginnings, because the oak timbers used in its construction were felled in the five summers between 889 and 893. The new royal settlement took the form of a crannóg, an artificial island cannily constructed from boulders, scrub and oak-planked and post-and-wattle revetments. It sat about 40 metres from shore and was probably joined to land by a long raised walkway. When finished, the man-made island served as a platform for domestic buildings, the most important of which would have been a great timber residence.

The decision to build a crannóg at Llangorse is at once impressive and improbable, at least in the context of Wales, where, so far as we know, there were no others. Many great men in contemporary Ireland, however, resided in crannógs; indeed, the remains of some 1,200 have been identified there. Because of their ubiquity in Ireland, it seems likely that Elisedd was intimately familiar with that place and its elites, and that he had come to believe that possession of a crannóg of his own would bolster his standing in Wales. Crannógs, however, are tricky to build, and their construction demands special skills and know-how. This suggests that the king had to bring at least a few workers over from Ireland to realize his dream.

Why would a late ninth-century Welsh king have gone to all this trouble? According to later genealogies, the kings of Brycheiniog traced their ancestry back to Ireland, so it is possible that Elisedd commissioned the crannóg to underscore his Irish ancestry, perhaps in an attempt to construct a unique identity for his family and his people and set them apart from competing groups both within Brycheiniog and outside its borders. The successful completion of such an elaborate and idiosyncratic site, built in part with the sweat of labour-owing locals, was also a way for the king to demonstrate his ability to extract dues from his subjects, and was, thus, a concrete display of his power. Indeed, those who did the dirty work during the crannóg's construction had to row or raft out more than 13 metric tonnes of stone.

This undertaking was also about making an impression on aristocratic subordinates and equals. The creation of a crannóg was an extravagant act, but there are hints that once it was finished it became the site of lavish living. The most remarkable witness to this is a fragment of textile, a sodden, charred, waterlogged mess when archaeologists first recovered it. It was probably once the sleeve of a woman's dress. It dates from the late ninth or early tenth century and is made from finely woven linen which was then embroidered in minute stitches with two different kinds of imported silk thread. The skilful execution of both the cloth and its embellishments suggests that it was made in a workshop by professional artisans. Although it is clearly an insular production, artisans copied its designs – long-necked birds nestled in vine scrolls and fierce little three-legged lions with upright tails – from the figured silks of Central Asia and Byzantium. A delicately enamelled, multi-coloured hinge was also recovered from the site, all that remains of a house-shaped reliquary. Such shrines have also been found on Irish crannógs, and this one, too, is of Irish workmanship. The remains of an Irish-type pseudo-penannular brooch has also been recovered from Llangorse, yet another sign that those living there were working hard to underscore connections to Ireland. Poets as well as artisans may have been patronized at Llangorse crannóg. Some literary scholars have argued that it was here that the famous Llywarch Hen poems were composed. This cycle of stories includes many about Brychan, Brycheiniog's eponymous founder. Although its tales are set in the distant past, the world they recount, a world plagued by foreign raiders and internecine wars, could just as easily be late ninth-century Wales. A small copper-alloy boss has also been found there, possibly a book mount, further evidence of literacy at Llangorse. Archaeologists have also recovered part of a cast copper-alloy drinking horn alongside a mountain of domestic animal bones, as well as those of red deer and wild boar, the remains of hunting, feasting and food renders. Finally, and interestingly, archaeologists have found the bones of wasp-waisted, greyhound-like hunting-dogs and a corgi-sized lapdog. Here, then, in a small, soon-to-be-forgotten Welsh kingdom, is evidence of grandiosity; of a labour-squandering, foreign-style royal residence, an art-encrusted Christianity, women dressed in stunning textiles and a sophisticated court culture. Such high living was a time-honoured strategy, long adopted by great men seeking to enhance their reputations.

The last decades of the ninth century were also, of course, troubled times, and a determinedly inaccessible settlement like a crannóg must have had its more practical charms. From 852 until about 919, vikings, some from Dublin, others from East Anglia, periodically raided north Wales, especially Anglesey. Occasionally, though, they struck closer to home: they over-wintered in Dyfed in 878, and they were raiding in Brycheiniog and Gwent in 896. They returned to Wales again in 903, 914 and 918. Indeed, it may be no coincidence that Llangorse crannóg was built around the same time as a combined force of Welsh and English warriors successfully fought against the vikings at the battle of Buttington (near Welshpool, Montgomery).

The kings of Brycheiniog also had to worry about more familiar enemies. The crannóg may have been built in part as insurance against those determined hegemons, the sons of Rhodri the Great, king of Gwynedd (r. 844–78). Rhodri had availed himself of the opportunities opened up by the chaos spawned by viking raids. He made a career of picking off less fortunate Welsh kingdoms and incorporating them into greater Gwynedd. By 872 he was in control of all of north Wales. As a result, Gwynedd had become a more serious threat to Brycheiniog than its traditional adversary, Mercia. Although the English did periodically lay waste to Welsh lands during these years, Elisedd nonetheless found it to his advantage to make peace with the English, in order to keep Gwynedd at bay. In 881, after one of the now-dead Rhodri's sons allied himself with the vikings settled in York, Elisedd and Alfred the Great became allies, although Elisedd was very much the junior partner in the relationship. Other Welsh kings, including the kings of Dyfed, Glywys-ing and Gwent did the same. Eventually, though, Rhodri's sons aban-doned their viking friends, and they, too, made common cause with Alfred. It is not entirely clear how this new friendship affected Alfred's earlier, but less powerful, Welsh allies in Brycheiniog, but it is clear that their neighbours in Glywysing and Ystrad Tywi were abandoned. What-ever the case, in spite of agreements, submissions and joint military operations, permanent friendship between the English and the men of south Wales remained elusive. By 916 Elisedd's son Tewdwr's relations with his English neighbours had so soured that they held him respon-sible in some way for the murder of a Mercian abbot. Three days after the killing, Alfred the Great's daughter, Æthelflæd 'lady of the Mercians', ordered her men to attack Llangorse, and, according to the Anglo-Saxon Chronicle, they 'destroyed' it (whatever that might mean) and captured the king's wife and thirty-three of her companions.

Although we know from excavations that the crannóg was destroyed by fire, we cannot say if it was burned in Æthelflæd's raid. We do know that c. 925 the king settled a lawsuit at Llangorse monastery, so the royal household may have continued to reside in the neighbourhood. After 934, though, we lose sight of the kingdom and its king. Brycheiniog may have carried on for a decade or two more as an independent state, or it may have been overrun by Rhodri the Great's grandson Hywel Dda (r. c. 920–50). Whatever the case, the genealogies of the dynasty end with Elisedd's grandson. So in spite of all of the efforts of the kings of Brycheiniog, their crannóg was short-lived, and the kingdom did not survive. It disappeared in the Viking Age, not because it was destroyed by viking invaders, but rather because it fell victim to Welsh and English competitors who were better able to profit from the chaos of these years.

So, from a couple of sentences of text, but, more importantly, from the mountain of material evidence uncovered during Llangorse's excavation we can perceive the dim outlines of a strategy developed in dangerous times, one that was at once optimistically forward looking and fearfully insecure; one in which the king did what he could to differentiate himself from his subjects and impress neighbouring aggressors. Here was a man who would make alliances with traditional enemies if that is what the circumstances required, but who could shift his friendships as the situation demanded. Difficult times required compelling, sometimes extravagant, innovation; and the willingness of Brycheiniog's rulers to see opportunities in novel approaches speaks of individuals who did not know that their kingdom's days were numbered. It also suggests that Alfred the Great was not the only innovator in ninth-century Britain. Brycheiniog, too, had an extraordinary king, who was as interesting and inventive as Alfred the Great, and yet the Welsh king and his strategies are simply not part of the story. The kingdom and its king have disappeared from our histories, not for lack of evidence, but because the evidence detailing their history is material, rather than textual, and, because of this, historians have simply ignored it.

A WINTER IN MERCIA

In spite of its impressive name, the *micel here* which arrived in England in 865 was no unified force. It had begun as scores of semi-autonomous boat crews, drawn from different social groups and regions. Under special circumstances, large fleets like this one would divide for a time. In the winter of 861, for example, when a viking fleet found itself in France at the mouth of the River Seine, it 'split up according to their brotherhoods into groups allocated to various ports, from the sea coast right up to Paris'. These groups could and did operate under the leadership of a handful of 'kings', often with stunning success, but up close in their winter camps the individuals who made up this great, marauding force must at times have been struck by the strangeness of some of their companions, because they were a motley bunch with a variety of social and cultural practices, unlike each individual boat's crew, which was made up of a small coterie of friends and kinsmen from back home.

Take the men of the *micel here* who spent 873–4 at Repton, in Derbyshire. The Anglo-Saxon Chronicle reports that

> the army went from Lindsey to Repton and took up winter quarters there, and drove King Burgræd [of Mercia] across the sea . . . And they conquered all that land . . . And he went to Rome and settled there . . . And in the same year they gave the kingdom of the Mercians to be held by Ceolwulf, a foolish king's thegn; and he swore oaths to them and gave hostages, that it should be ready for them on whatever day they wished to have it, and he would be ready, himself and all who would follow him, at the enemy's service . . .

It was no accident that the army chose Repton as its winter camp. Repton was home to one of Mercia's most venerable religious communities, a double minster founded eight or nine generations earlier by a scion of the Mercian royal house. It was also here, at the very end of the seventh century, that one of England's most renowned holy men, St Guthlac, himself a kinsman of Mercian kings, learned the ways of monasticism after he had converted to the religious life. It may have also been at Repton that the monk Felix penned the *Life of St Guthlac*, a *vita* promoting Guthlac's cult. If so, the community possessed a fine library and an excellent school. The church at Repton, moreover, had long served as the burial site for Mercia's kings. Included among its distinguished dead were the great king Æthelbald, murdered in 757 by his own bodyguard; King Wiglaf, who died in 840; and Wiglaf's doomed grandson Wigstan (or Wystan), who was assassinated by dynastic rivals in 849. An elaborate royal crypt under the chancel of the church, probably built specially for King Æthelbald, would have housed the royal bodies by the time the vikings came. Another stone building, this one two-celled, lay 60 metres west of the church. It had been up and running since the seventh century and had probably served as the royal mausoleum before the construction of the crypt. It was still standing, although in some disrepair, when the viking army arrived.

Over the centuries, the minster at Repton had benefited mightily from both royal patronage and the pilgrimage trade. The murdered Wigstan had become the focus of a saint's cult, one popular enough to require the enlarging of the stairways to the crypt so that a crush of pilgrims might be accommodated. The pretensions of the new and improved structure were great: its barley-sugar columns mimicked those that pilgrims could see at St Peter's, in Rome. Between its pilgrims and its royal benefactors, Repton grew wealthy. Its church had coloured-glass windows and a lead roof, and its cemetery contained magnificently carved stone crosses and grave covers. It would have been well endowed with estates, too, its lands carefully organized in such a way that the farm families living on them could provide the community with most of what it needed each year in foodstuffs, fodder, building materials and labour. Repton in 873 was an important place, a rich place, a well-provisioned place. With its dead kings and saints, its well-heeled inmates and its history, it was also a ritually and politically significant place. The vikings' co-option of the site must, therefore, be viewed as a political act, one meant to impress upon the people in this part of Mercia that new men had come to possess ancient power. The taking of Repton was also fuelled by pragmatism, because the viking army could feed itself by parasitizing the minster's ancient structures of provisioning.

The army arrived in the autumn of 873. It was an army intimately familiar with victory, having conquered the kingdom of Northumbria in 867 and the kingdom of East Anglia in 869. Mercia's king and his wife, as the vikings settled in, fled to Italy, where they would die as exiles. And, as we have seen in the quotation from the Anglo-Saxon Chronicle, some deal was struck between the army and Ceolwulf, who, despite the Chronicle's dismissive description of him as a 'foolish king's thegn', was probably a member of Mercia's ruling dynasty and a man who continued to rule in Mercia until c. 879.

During their months at Repton the vikings wrecked the place. By the time they left, the church had suffered serious damage to its windows, roof and upper walls. The ancient, stand-alone mortuary chapel had been ruined and part of the cemetery dug up. The library and archives may have been destroyed as well; and, although the church was restored in the first half of the tenth century, its ancient monastic community had been disbanded.

The first grand act of vandalism took place when the vikings threw up a ditched, D-shaped enclosure, one that incorporated the church itself into its defensive line. After the enclosure was finished, it looks as if the north and south doors of the church's nave served as a fortified entrance into the precinct. At both the top and the bottom of the 'D', the ditch terminated at the cliffed banks of the River Trent, and this provided the monastery's occupiers with both the protection of the river and access to their longships. As they dug the ditch, they cut through the church's ancient cemetery; Repton's excavators have found bits of human bone and coffin fittings there, much disturbed. So during their initial occupation, the army did violence to the church, its churchyard and to its Christian dead.

Other outrages soon followed. Of course, the vikings needed to put their own dead in the ground. The remains of two have been found just north and east of the church, the first of a long series of corpses buried in this area: isotopic analysis of their teeth tells us they were probably from Denmark. The most dramatic of the two burials was that of a man who had died horribly, perhaps in a skirmish fought for Repton itself. A sword or a spear had been driven through his eye and deep into his skull. After he had fallen to the ground he had received another weapon's blow to his leg, one that nearly severed his hip joint and probably emasculated him. Both of these wounds were unsurvivable. Nonetheless, his spine shows further signs of sharp trauma, not on the outside, but the *inside*, evidence that he had been disembowelled. After his grisly death, this man received an elaborate interment next to the church, in an area never before used for burial. He was placed in the ground with a silver Thor's hammer hung around his neck and was accompanied by a sword in its scabbard and two knives. The wing of a jackdaw was placed in his grave as well, and before it was sealed a boar's tusk was wedged between his thighs, perhaps to serve as a proxy for his missing penis. Another, younger man was buried in a grave dug next to his, and the ground above the two was then paved over with a rectangular patch of stone, made up, in part, from a smashed, standing-stone cross. With its weapons, its jackdaw (perhaps a symbol of Odin), its Thor's hammer and the boar's tusk, this burial is decidedly un-Christian. Indeed, Christians would have viewed such a burial, as well as the strange rituals that doubtless accompanied it, as sacrilege, even if they had not taken place within an arm's length of the church's chancel. Other burials followed. Not far away, a man in his late twenties or early thirties was buried with a gold ring and a handful of pennies dating to the mid-870s. An analysis of his tooth enamel suggests that he came, not from Denmark, but from south-eastern Sweden, and this serves to remind us that, although many in the *micel here* were Danes, not all were.

An even grander burial was placed in what had probably been the old mausoleum, the stand-alone structure west of the church. After the *micel here* had constructed its camp this building lay outside the D-shaped enclosure. The principal burial here was that of another man, one whose body and strange grave were badly disturbed in the late seventeenth century. As far as we can tell, though, he was placed in a stone coffin or cist after the walls of the building were slighted, and he may have been accompanied by the weapons, coins (all belonging to the first half of the 870s) and other grave goods found during the structure's modern re-excavation. Around his body, arranged in neat stacks by type, were the bones of at least 264 people. These were disarticulated bones, rather than corpses or skeletons, when people laid them around the dead man, and therefore they had long been in the ground. Although the vast majority belonged to adults, and over 80 per cent to men, there were women among the dead. The radiocarbon dates secured from a sample of the bones suggest that some belonged to people who had lived in the late seventh or early eighth century and others to those alive during the ninth century. Some of these bones, therefore, may be those of Mercia's kings. But others probably came from the graves that were disturbed when the ditch was dug across the cemetery, so are probably the remains of the monks and nuns of the early double minster and local worthies whom the community had favoured with churchyard burials. After the bones of the long-dead Mercians were arranged around the newly dead viking, the shortened walls of the structure were roofed, and a barrow was built on top of it. Then, at the south-west corner of the mound, mourners dug another grave, this one containing the bodies of four children. One, somewhere between 8 and 12 years of age, lay supine in the grave. The other three, two of whom were between the ages of 8 and 11 and one who was about 17, were crouched on their sides, and had been placed on top of the bottom child. They were accompanied in their grave by a sheep's jaw. This is all that remains of some unfathomable ritual act. One cannot help but wonder whose children they were, and one cannot help but fear that their last hours were terrifying.

Four kilometres down the road on open heathland, another cemetery – this one in Heath Wood, near Ingleby – was founded. This place, too, had burial mounds, nearly sixty in all. But here the dead were not being inhumed, but cremated, and animals were being sacrificed to the flames. Again, horrified Christian locals would have been shocked at the sight of horses, sheep, dogs and human carcasses heaped on pyres, disgusted by the smell of burning hair and flesh.

Two quite distinct audiences must have witnessed these dramatic funerals – the members of the *micel here* itself and English people still residing in the neighbourhood. The latter must have still been there. After all, Ceolwulf, 'the foolish king's thegn', and his entourage would have had periodic contact with the leaders of the army. Reeves employed by the religious community probably continued to gather dues owed to the monastery to feed its terrifying new proprietors. Local peasant families, moreover, unlike their former king, did not have the wherewithal for a dignified exile in Rome, and had no option but to stay at home and milk their cows. They doubtless continued to provide food levies. How else could an army settled in a single place for so many months survive? For all of these people, the desecration of Repton's church and cemetery, alongside the wildly aberrant pagan funerals held both in the shadow of the church and at Heath Wood, would have been a terrible abomination. It must have seemed like the beginning of the End Times, an event all good Christians knew would come.

The other audience for the funerals would have been members of the army itself. Judging from the over-the-top burials at both Repton and Heath Wood, these were difficult months for the men of the *micel here*. Many had been campaigning by this time for eight long years, and some must have grown tired of the life. Tensions, too, may have been intensifying between factions within the army. Certainly, the extraordinary inhumations near the church and the sixty cremations at Heath Wood hint that survivors felt the need to assert the importance of their dead friends and kinsmen in particularly dramatic ways. There must have been competition, too, not only between those burying at Repton and those burning at Heath Wood, but among the Heath Wood cremators themselves, who were busily destroying wealth every time someone died. One also wonders if they were trying to make some point to the locals. Who, after all, was actually moving all the sand, earth and stone that went into making the barrows? Was it members of the army itself, or were nearby Christian farmers being forced to labour on them? What better way to make clear who was now in charge? Newfangled traditions, either freshly invented, as happened at Repton, or ramped up, as they were at the cremation cemetery at Heath Wood, suggest insecurity and competition.

By the autumn of 874, the *micel here* had left Repton; when it did, it split in two. Half followed one of their leaders back to Northumbria, and within two years the men were taking land and settling down there. The other half left for East Anglia, to establish bases from which to make war, once again, on Alfred the Great. Some of the men, though, must have stayed on at Repton, or filtered back. A hogback stone-carved monument, often used by Norse converts in England to mark the graves of their dead, was found in Repton's churchyard; and a woman, who died a generation after the events of 873/4, was buried in the cemetery with grave goods. In the generations that followed, a number of people chose to bury their dead around the mound over the old mausoleum, but grave goods and other anomalies – the things that marked these folks as Norse incomers or even second-generation colonizers – gradually disappeared, as the sons and grandsons of the *micel here*'s soldiers Christianized, assimilated and became English.

ORKNEY AND THE MAKING OF A COLONIAL SOCIETY

It seems reasonable to postulate that in the years before the vikings began wreaking havoc on treasure-rich monastic communities like Lindisfarne and Iona, Norse explorers and traders were already nosing around Orkney, familiarizing themselves with its headlands, currents and Pictish inhabitants. Orkney and Shetland together form an archipelago of some 170 islands which lie a couple of days' sail from Norway, and, because they are strung out from north to south in a chain more than 200 kilometres in length, Norsemen sailing west would have had a hard time missing them. It was this leg of the journey, though, that was most hazardous, because it required sailors to travel out of sight of land and denied them the comfort of beaching their boats after a long day at sea, requiring them instead to spend a nerve-racking night adrift in their open, undecked ships. After Orkney, though, the journey grew less difficult, because from this point on, sailors could travel all the way to Ireland in sight of land. Thus, Orkney provided Scandinavians with what must have been both a necessary and a relief-filled stopping-place. Once there, sailors could make course corrections, rest a bit and take on water and food. Or they could wait for favourable winds, other ships and decent weather before embarking on the next leg of their voyages. It seems likely, therefore, that people from Norway came to know Orkney in the early days of their westward explorations, and that individual Norse captains and their crews would, out of necessity, have cultivated friendships and trading relations there. Some may have even over-wintered in the Northern Isles in the early days, if they left their return home too late in the season.

Even after Norse seafarers turned to piracy, some of Orkney's inhabitants may well have continued to cultivate friendships with Scandinavian visitors, since it was in everyone's interest that Orkney remain a neutral port-of-call: after all, if vikings laid waste to the place, neither Orcadians nor Norse sailors would have ready access to provisions. The late ninth-century *vita* of the Irishman St Findan supports this picture of coexistence and cooperation. It describes how Norse slavers operating in Ireland in the 840s were in the habit of making a stopover in Orkney on their way home, where they 'disembarked, recuperated, travelled here and there over the islands and waited for a fair wind'. Findan, who was captured in Ireland, made a dramatic escape from his captors during one of these stopovers, and a couple of locals, who must have been Pictish Christians, took him to an Irish-trained bishop still living on the islands, a man with whom he spent the next two years, 'enjoying the many benefits of his kindness and generosity'. The saint eventually left Orkney, not because he and his Christian host were driven out, but because Findan longed to see Rome. St Findan's sojourn in Orkney suggests that a full two generations after Norse pirates had taken to the seas, and at a time when the author of the *vita* described Orkney as 'lying next to the land of the Picts' (in other words, as a place no longer under Pictish political control), some natives were still living there in peace.

There are reasons, then, for thinking that at least some Picts and Norsemen cooperated in the opening years of the Viking Age, and that Pictish families, institutions and settlements persisted into the ninth century. By *c.* 825, though, the nature of viking activity across the British Isles and Ireland changed. Between this time and *c.* 850 viking warriors managed to make sustained and organized assaults against Ireland, and they were doing so primarily from bases in northern Scotland. In short, about the same time as Findan's stay considerable numbers of Norsemen must have been establishing themselves in the Northern Isles, in spite of the fact that there were still Picts there. And over the next hundred years the Pictish language, Pictish names for places and Pictish material culture would not only be supplanted by Norse replacements, but erased, and Orkney would become little Norway. Unlike Orkney's earlier inhabitants, mid-tenth-century Orcadians lived in Norse-style longhouses and stabled their livestock in Norse-style byres. They ground their grain with Norse-style horizontal mills, depended for their livelihoods on Norse-style boats and ate a Norse-style diet that was high in fish. They used traditional Norse soapstone vessels rather than indigenous ceramic pots and built their houses, in part, from timber rather than stone, even though both soapstone and wood had to be imported. In short, people living in Orkney within a hundred years of Findan's sojourn had come to be archaeologically indistinguishable from Norse people living elsewhere in the North Atlantic. This wholesale importation of Norse culture was, moreover, more thoroughgoing in the Northern Isles than anywhere else in Britain. Because of this, it could be argued (in much the same way that people used to argue about the Romano-British populations of eastern England) that Norse incomers put every last Pict in Orkney to the sword.

Still, there is the *Life of St Findan*, with its Christians and its Picts. There is also the work of geneticists, which indicates that, although many Norwegians did indeed settle in Orkney, considerable numbers of Picts remained. The mitochondrial DNA of modern Orcadians shows that about a third of today's Orcadians' female ancestors originated in Scandinavia, which is certainly a large number, though the other two-thirds can be traced back to the region's indigenous population. The islanders' Y-chromosomes show that their male ancestry is an admixture of Celtic and Norwegian genes, but with the indigenous making a larger genetic contribution than the Norwegian. Doubtless, this genetic legacy is the result of scores of singular, life-changing events (to say nothing of the movement of people *after* the Viking Age). Sometimes male raiders must have rowed ashore and ended up taking local girls as slaves, concubines or wives. At other times, so the genetic evidence makes clear, whole families moved from Norway, including Norse women and girls with their telltale tortoise brooches and pinafore dresses. Once again, we are reminded that migration and assimilation are processes rather than events, not only stretching across generations, but playing themselves out differently at their beginning than towards their end.

Other evidence also supports a picture of Pictish survival and acculturation, albeit in the face of high levels of migration. Many of Orkney's Norse settlements sit aside or astride Pictish ones. This is the case for ninth-century Pool, on the island of Sanday. Here, a Pictish circular drystone building which lay at the heart of the pre-Norse settlement continued in use in the ninth and tenth centuries. Eventually, the people living at Pool remodelled the structure and incorporated it into a Norse-style, bow-shaped hall. During the generations in which the people of Pool inhabited and maintained this building, they also carried on making and using Pictish-style pottery and bone pins. At the same time, though, they were preparing their food in soapstone vessels, and some combed their hair and picked nits with a particular type of antler comb: these objects came from Norway. This mixing, for a time, of native and Norse objects and building styles at Pool cannot tell us if Norse people settling at Pool had married into native families or if they had enslaved them. Nonetheless, the site's artefacts suggest that not all the people living here in the year 1000 – no matter what their language or their cooking pots – could, in reality, trace their ancestors back to Norway.

Orkney burials from this period also reveal interesting things about the nature and intensity of Norse settlement, and about the ways it changed over time. One of the most dramatic of the period's burials, the Scar boat burial, contained a clinker-built ship from Norway which mourners had chosen as the burial chamber for three people: a child about the age of 10, a man around 30 and a woman perhaps in her seventies. The man had the large hands of a lifelong rower, and the woman had sat cross-legged for much of her life: both were apparently people of means. Those who oversaw their funeral placed a broken, or 'killed', sword in a specially made sheath beside the man, as well as a quiverful of arrows, a comb, a set of whalebone gaming pieces and probably a shield. The old woman wore a beautiful brooch, a kind worn by high-status women in the far north of Norway, and she was given a comb, sewing and weaving equipment and a carved whalebone plaque used for pressing linen. Almost everything in the burial, including the boat, was from Scandinavia, and much of what can be dated – the brooch, the whalebone plaque, the combs – was made in the ninth century. So, at first glance, the Scar boat burial looks like the burial of early Norse settlers, who arrived in or around the same time as St Findan. The skeletons' radiocarbon dates, however, tell a different story: the three had died in the tenth or eleventh centuries, long after the first generations of settlement. Whoever buried these people chose to provide them with very fine, but very old, grave goods, perhaps self-consciously Norse at that. The whalebone plaque and the boat were also ritually charged objects, and they hint that a solemn pagan ceremony may have preceded the closing of the triple grave, in spite of evidence that many of Orkney's Norse settlers around this time were becoming Christians.

The Scar burial is particularly interesting in the context of other burials, because the earliest Norse graves uncovered in the Scottish Isles look much less stereotypically pagan and Norse than the later Scar burial. For example, archaeologists have excavated seven skeletons from a small family cemetery at Cnip, on the Isle of Lewis. The earliest of the Norse-style burials at Cnip had few grave goods. Both a 6-year-old child and an infant went to their graves wearing simple necklaces, a Norse rather than a Pictish practice. Only one Cnip burial, however, that of an adult woman, had elaborate grave goods: a pair of tortoise brooches, a glass-bead necklace, a ringed pin, a belt with an elaborate matching buckle and strap-end, a knife, a whetstone, a needle case, a sickle and an antler comb. Although these are the classic grave goods of a high-status Norse woman, and some of these objects had, indeed, originally come from Scandinavia, the strontium isotopes in the woman's tooth enamel tell us that she had spent her early childhood on Lewis. Furthermore, radiocarbon dates suggest that she was buried a couple of generations *after* those in the cemetery who had few or no grave goods. The strontium isotopes in the teeth of the other Cnip skeletons tell us that not only this woman, but another of the adults and all three of the children had been born in the neighbourhood. The two remaining adults, however, had not spent their childhood on Lewis. One, a man, was probably from the Inner Hebrides or Northern Ireland, and the remaining woman, a person who died a generation or two before the woman with the fancy grave goods, had grown up in England, either in the South Downs, or, perhaps more likely, in the Yorkshire Wolds. So the most Norse of the Cnip 'vikings' was not only born late, but she was born on Lewis, and two of the cemetery's early 'vikings' were very probably an Irishman and an English girl. It seems, therefore, that people in the Hebrides and Orkney, whatever their genetic origins, felt the need to underscore their Norseness, not so much during their initial settlement as some hundred years after it had begun.

It turns out that the most elaborate 'viking' burials in Orkney date to the century between 850 and 950, and that most of these probably fall in the latter half of this period. This, in turn, suggests that the need for Norse survivors to impress and display or to signal their Norse identity, at least in their death rituals, was less pressing in Orkney in the first half century after their arrival than it came to be after the Norse earldom of Orkney was established sometime around 850. This may be because there was little need to direct profligate funeral displays at native Picts in the early years, either because potential Pictish competitors had been driven out, or because they were cooperating with their new neighbours. Indeed, the burial evidence suggests that it was only after a substantial number of Norse households had established themselves and only after Norse culture had come to dominate Orkney that survivors deemed competitive funerary display necessary; and it is likely that by this date the choreographers of such obsequies were directing their performances at competing households or cliques which also identified themselves as Norse.

The next period, the century between the 930s and the 1030s, is when some two dozen viking hoards were hidden away in northern Scotland, including the largest treasure cache ever found there – the 8 kilograms of silver swag buried in Skaill, on Orkney. This hoard included neck rings, brooches, hack-silver and coins from around the Irish Sea, although one coin had been minted in far-off Baghdad. Large hoards like this one probably belonged to big men, who used their stores of treasure to maintain gangs of followers. Like the burials, the evidence of the hoards argues that it was only during a later period that multiple, competing factions operated in Orkney, and that their chiefs' aspirations were often paid for by their seasonal pirating activities. According to the twelfth-century *Orkneyinga Saga*, one such man, a chieftain named

Svein, had grown rich from both Orkney's good farmland and its central position at the heart of the vast Norse North Atlantic world:

> This is how Svein used to live. Winter he would spend at home on Gairsay where he entertained some eighty men at his own expense. His drinking hall was so big there was nothing in Orkney to compare with it. In the spring he had more than enough to occupy him, with a great deal to sow, which he saw to carefully himself. Then, when that job was done, he would go off plundering in the Hebrides and in Ireland on what he called his 'spring trip', then back home just after midsummer, where he stayed until the cornfields had been reaped and the grain was safely in. After that he went off raiding again until the first month of winter was ended. This he used to call his 'autumn trip'.

If only we knew what language the grandparents of Svein's eighty men had spoken or the kinds of pins the ancestors of the people who reaped his grain had worn!

At the Norse-period settlement at Westness, on Orkney, it looks as if rye and flax were being grown for the first time. Rye had long been grown in southern Norway, and Norse settlers may have introduced it here. Flax was introduced in some places in Orkney during the late Pictish period, but at others it was not cultivated until the coming of the Norse, so this crop, too, may have been brought to Westness by the Norse. Flax cultivation and the processes that go into making it into linen are complex. Indeed, across Orkney, it looks as if flax came to be widely cultivated after the coming of Norse settlers, more barley and oats came to be grown, and there was an intensification of dairying as well. In short, many agricultural regimens established during the late Pictish period intensified after the coming of the Norse. The Norse did not completely reorganize farms, flocks or fields, but people were eating differently there after the Norse had begun to settle. The Picts buried at Westness before the Viking Age, although they lived on an island 10 kilometres in length, ate very little that came from the sea, and they did not feed their livestock seaweed. The Viking Age skeletons recovered from the cemetery, though, belonged to people who ate much more fish. Orientation towards the sea and towards flax cultivation would have transformed the lives of Picts and half-Picts. Occupations, rhythms of work, cuisine, styles of dress were all dramatically transformed. These people now built byres for their cattle, and imported wood for the floors and benches of their houses, as well as for their boats. But indigenous skill and know-how would have transformed the lives of colonizing Norse, too. Traditional Norse-style halls could not be built from wood alone in near-treeless Orkney, but instead came to be constructed for the most part from dry stone and turf, and local knowledge of this building material would have aided in the transformation. Orkney was also better cereal country than Norway, and the Norse in Orkney became more dependent on cereal cultivation than their relatives back home.

So there are hints that Picts and part-Picts persisted in Orkney, but that over the course of the ninth and tenth centuries they came to swap their material culture, their language and their ways of dress, and in doing this became indistinguishable, at least archaeologically, from the newcomers, be they neighbours, masters or relatives. In Ireland, where contemporary texts survive, we know that by *c.* 850 Irish-speakers who hailed from Norse colonial enclaves within Ireland came to be called the *Gall-Ghaoidheal*. An interpolator of an early set of annals described them thus: '[these] Gaels and foster-children of the vikings ... were people who had forsaken their baptism, and they were called vikings because they behaved like vikings and had been fostered by them.' Were similar transformations taking place among Orkney's Picts?

Perhaps the Picts' almost complete swapping of cultures is explained, in the end, by the fact that although the people of Orkney, before the coming of the Norse, had long been connected by language, politics and culture to mainland Picts, some living on the islands may have long hankered for autonomy. According to a late seventh-century notice in the *Annals of Ulster*, Orkney was 'destroyed' in some kind of punitive expedition by the Pictish high king Bridei son of Bili, which suggests that there were periodic tensions between mainland and island Picts. By the middle of the ninth century the Pictish kingdom on the mainland had failed, and the Scot Kenneth macAlpin had co-opted it. At this point Orkney Picts may have preferred to make common cause with Norse-speakers rather than Gaelic-speakers.

Orkney during this period, of course, was not the only place Norse colonists chose to settle. Across the North Atlantic – in Shetland, the Hebrides, the Faroe Islands, Iceland and Greenland – people who thought of themselves as Norse (be they genetically Scandinavian, or Irish or Pict) lived in remarkably similar houses, ground their grain with very particular kinds of millstones, favoured jet and lignite arm-rings and certain kinds of ring pins, and made little hexagonal bronze bells. These things were subtly different from similar articles made in Scandinavia, and they were widely used by the Norse colonial peoples of the North Atlantic. Even Norse personal names not found in Scandinavia were borne by men across the Norse North Atlantic, from Orkney, to the Hebrides, to Iceland, to the Isle of Man. Thus over the course of the Viking Age the people of Orkney became uncoupled from other communities of Picts, as well as Scots and Northumbrians, peoples with whom they had long had relations. Now, their affinities were not just with Scandinavia, but more particularly with other North Atlantic Norse. This was a major cultural realignment.

Our three disparate narratives are joined by nothing but chronology. All three provide glimpses of the diverse realities faced by natives and newcomers in the ninth and tenth centuries, quite different from those of Alfred the Great and his friends. None of them tells the same tale. What they do, instead, is point to the dramatic remaking during the Viking Age of societies across Britain, and they hint at the transformations of individuals, communities and whole peoples. Small kingdoms disappeared and came to be absorbed into larger, newer entities. Viking warriors not only looted and pillaged, but worried in their winter camps, and many eventually settled down and became Englishmen. In other places, natives threw in their lot with Norse newcomers and came to be Norse themselves. Indeed, so diverse were the experiences of people living through these years that no master narrative, no matter how compelling, does justice to the lives of those who experienced them.

9

New Towns: The Ninth
to Eleventh Century

Even though eighth-century England was home to a number of important year-round trading communities, seasonal markets and production sites, it was not a very urban place, certainly not as urban as Roman Britain had been. In the ninth century, though, England, as un-urban as it was, began to *de*-urbanize, as commerce, trading communities and peace fell victim first to the occasional viking raider and then to the vikings' great marauding armies. Indeed, some of England's most town-like places – including the once-booming settlement of *Lundenwic*, just upriver from the site of Roman *Londinium* (and located where the Strand is today) – experienced near-terminal economic decline. Other places in the ninth century – like the seasonal trading settlement we examined in Chapter 7 at *Sandtun* – fared even worse and were abandoned. Perhaps most alarming of all, York, the premier commercial centre in Northumbria, was not only captured by vikings in 867, but would remain under their control for most of the next eighty-seven years. These were dramatic and terrible setbacks for the families who had long made their livings by trading and craft-working; for the lay and secular elites, who had got into the habit of demanding tributes with an eye towards the market; and for kings who had grown rich on tolls. Yet, improbably, given the dire state of urban and quasi-urban settlements *c.* 850, a mere two hundred years later there would be more than a hundred thriving towns in England, with something like a tenth of the kingdom's population living in them. Towns by the middle of the eleventh century, moreover, not only served as centres of population, production, commerce and demand, but had become a crucial component of the English state. What accounts for this remarkable resurgence of urban life and for the growing importance of these communities? Who should be credited with their origins? And who profited from this development?

Knowing what we now know, it is not surprising to find that kings and vikings together serve as a partial answer to these questions, and their combined activities form the backdrop against which the revival of urban life took place. Among all English kings, Alfred the Great (r. 871–99) especially deserves credit. With the help of his children Edward the Elder and Æthelflæd 'lady of the Mercians' and his Mercian son-in-law, Æthelred (r. c. 883–911), he established a network of fortified settlements known as *burhs* (a cognate of our word 'borough') to defend English territory and people against viking attacks. The resources he used to fortify and defend these places were provided by landholders, each of whose share of the burden was assessed in accordance with the number of hides of land he held. Although Alfred instituted both this network of fortified settlements and the systematic burdening of landholders for its support, he invented neither. Instead, he was borrowing freely from the administrative and military innovations pioneered by the kings of Mercia, especially kings Æthelbald and Offa, who had insisted that landholders share the burden of the kingdom's defence and therefore required them to help fortify sites important to the Mercian kings. The first of Alfred's *burhs* were in his own kingdom of Wessex; but by the late ninth century the king and his helpers had begun to found them in the part of Mercia that was still under English control, and a number of these were extensions of the fortifications instituted in the eighth century by Mercian kings. After Alfred's death, as his son, daughter and grandson King Athelstan wrested the east midlands and the north of England from viking political control, they further extended this network of fortified places. Alfred and his successors also placed mints in *burhs* and demanded that they serve as regulated market sites. Rectilinear street plans were laid out in some of them as well, and this provided organized grids of streets on which craftsmen and traders could settle.

On the flipside of these developments stood the vikings. One of the economic consequences of their looting and pillaging was that huge amounts of silver were released into the economy which before their arrival had been hoarded in royal and ecclesiastical treasuries. But vikings, aside from stealing silver and providing Alfred with a reason for founding *burhs*, also had a more positive hand in England's urbanization. A number of the Norse, before settling in Britain, had travelled the extraordinary trade routes pioneered by Scandinavians and which gave Baltic traders access, via the Russian river-ways, to the markets of Byzantium and the Arab world. People like these, as they settled into trading sites in the British Isles, began bringing in bolts of silk, spices and other luxury goods and selling them to elite families – both natives and immigrants from Scandinavia – who had silver to spare. Some Norsemen living and trading in Britain were also the proud owners of newer, larger North Sea cargo vessels, which were crucial for the expansion of the economy, because they enabled tenth-century traders to haul much more than had been possible in the eighth century. Finally, many less well-travelled and less well-off Norse immigrants took to town life. As they settled down in England, they transformed some of the settlements they had co-opted – places like Lincoln, Stamford and Thetford – into bustling manufacturing sites, becoming full-time shoemakers, potters and smiths.

The history of towns in this period is most often thought about against this historical background, and, because of this, towns themselves are more often treated as institutions – centres of royal power and administration, or as bulwarks against the Danes – than as communities. As a result the role of kings and vikings in their development is well understood. Other groups and individuals, though, were centrally involved in the resurgence and flourishing of urban life. In order to determine who these people were, and what roles they played, we are going to look at the long histories of just two towns – Worcester and London – not only to isolate the commonalities in their histories and investigate the ways kings and vikings participated in their making, but to understand how their local and particular histories, both during the Viking Age and before, and the many individuals who ended up living in them also contributed to making them the towns they came to be.

A BISHOP'S TOWN

Worcester was a real bishop's town; indeed, the place had been dominated by its bishops since the late seventh century. In its pre-Christian incarnation, though, Worcester had been a Roman small town, its people specializing in the dirty and unglamorous work of iron-smelting, iron-working and large-scale cattle-rearing. Like most small towns, Roman Worcester was not a very grand place, but it did have an oval circuit of earthwork defences, perhaps originally the defences of an Iron Age fort, which enclosed an area of some 10.5 hectares. It is the survival of these defences after Roman Britain's fall that explains Worcester's re-emergence as a central place in the early Middle Ages. Around 680, when Archbishop Theodore established an episcopal see for the kingdom of the Hwicce, its new church, dedicated to St Peter, was built inside Worcester's still standing walls. Such juxtapositions were common in the seventh century, and, across lowland Britain, ecclesiastical communities could be found settling in the corners of ruined cities or abandoned forts, not only because such places provided them with ready-made enclosures and a source of quarried stone, but because associations with Roman sites, however ramshackle, conferred prestige.

Although Worcester at the time of its see's foundation was no longer urban, it was probably already home to a British religious community living just inside the defences and staffing the church of St Helen's, an establishment that continued, long after the inception of the episcopal community, to act as the mother church for a large territory. By the end of the eighth century St Helen's and St Peter's had probably been joined by two other churches – St Margaret's and St Alban's – so Worcester, before the coming of the vikings, was an overwhelmingly ecclesiastical place. Its population during these years was also more substantial than most contemporary settlements, since each of Worcester's churches was home to a community of clergy (and, perhaps, their families), and since most members of ecclesiastical households, unlike their high-status lay counterparts, stayed put rather than itinerated between tribute centres. Members of Worcester's ecclesiastical communities, therefore, needed food, firewood and shelter year-round, which crews of resident low-status workers had to organize, store and prepare. Worcester's professional religious and their labourers also required storage buildings, animal pens and housing, so the footprint of this settlement would have been substantial.

It is impossible to say how Worcester's different churches and the men who staffed them interacted, but it is clear that the bishop was the most important figure both within the settlement and in the surrounding countryside, where he came to accumulate vast tracts of land. His rights to receive some of the bounty produced by the people who farmed them ensured that his community not only lived in comfort, but that it had cash. We know, for example, that the bishop occasionally commuted in-kind renders owed to him by local farm families (which according to two texts dating from the late eighth and mid-ninth centuries included ale, mead, grain, bread, livestock, hams, cheese and candles) to money payments. At other times, he may have sold the surplus renders accumulating in his storehouses. The bishop also controlled some of Droitwich's astonishingly productive saltworks 11 kilometres up the road, and he must have sold the salt not needed by his community. One indication of this is that in the late ninth century Ealdorman Æthelred reserved wagon and pack-animal tolls levied on salt traders in Worcester for the king, which suggests that these men were already in the habit of attending a market here, probably because the settlement was a convenient place to load salt onto boats beached on the Severn's foreshore for transport downriver and to the coast. Two *sceattas* lost in the early eighth century testify to coin use in the settlement as well: one was found just outside the Roman defences' northern gate and the other between the river and the main Roman road leading into the compound from the north, hinting that land running along the Severn and hard by the entrance of the walled compound sometimes served as marketplaces. Outside another early medieval minster, this one at Barking, in Essex, the remains of luxury goods have been found – things like glass fragments from drinking vessels, gold thread from elaborate textiles and pottery from Ipswich – as well as evidence for trade and craft production, including coins and waste from glass-making. Both the location of these finds and the artefacts themselves suggest that a small, riverside commercial and craft-working zone had developed at Barking by the early eighth century. We know that the bishop of Worcester in the mid-ninth century was in possession of goods like those found at Barking: at one point, for example, he gave three drinking vessels, presumably of glass, to a Mercian king in return for a confirmation of his rights to land. So perhaps a zone similar to the one uncovered at Barking could be found along the Severn. Worcester's bishop also had commercial interests in far-off London. By the eighth century, he had two ships there, which thanks to the Mercian king Æthelbald's generosity, had immunity from tolls; and in the ninth century he gained both commercial privileges and property in London. These advantages provided the Worcester community with access to all the enticing wares foreign merchants were hauling into London. So there are hints that the bishop's household across the eighth and ninth centuries involved itself in trade, and used ships, surpluses and coins to acquire exotic items similar to the ones excavated along Barking's riverfront.

In the late 890s this settlement – an ancient, enclosed, high-status site with a permanent population of professional religious and their helpers, and a place with at least periodic contact with traders and craftsmen – went through a profound transformation. It is at this time that the Mercian ealdorman Æthelred, son-in-law and ally of Alfred the Great, established a *burh* at Worcester as part of the larger campaign in which he and his West Saxon in-laws sought to extend the network of West Saxon fortifications into English Mercia. The choice of Worcester is hardly surprising: dozens of older sites – which include everything from minsters, to early trading settlements, to Iron Age hillforts, to royal vills, to unpopulated places with still-standing Roman defences – were remodelled, fortified (or refortified) and stitched together into a system designed to provide local people with a refuge from the vikings as well as protected and regulated trading places.

Æthelred had the bishop's full cooperation as he transformed what had essentially been a private ecclesiastical settlement into a much more public place. As a first step, the ealdorman promised the bishop half of any profits generated by the remodelled *burh* from market tolls and judicial fines. The contemporary text describing this arrangement asserts that the ealdorman, in granting the bishop half these dues, had made a generous, indeed salvation-worthy gift; but Worcester's episcopal *familia* may have seen things differently. After all, before Worcester became a *burh* the bishop had been its unchallenged master. Within a couple of years, moreover, the bishop found himself leasing the ealdorman's family a prime block of Worcester's riverfront in a newly laid out district between the *burh*'s major thoroughfare and the Severn, perhaps the site of its pre-*burh* river market. So the bishop's willingness, in essence, to allow the ealdorman to take 50 per cent of the *burh*'s revenues along with some of its choicest landholdings shows us what a terrible threat he deemed the vikings to be. Indeed, his bargain is one of many made during this period which illustrate the ways in which ancient and relatively independent communities, both lay and ecclesiastical, came to surrender resources and autonomy to kings or other strongmen in exchange for the promise of security. There is also, as we shall see, evidence that other important lay lords were given property within the *burh*. Again, such intrusions, in more peaceful times, might have been resisted, but during these years of emergency the bishop must have appreciated the presence of arms-bearing secular lords in town when viking armies were on the prowl.

The walls Æthelred used for his new *burh*'s defences were, for the most part, Worcester's still-standing Roman walls, but the north end of the ancient defences, although left standing, was superseded by a new earth-and-timber extension enclosing a further 7 hectares of former pastureland. Even after its enlargement, though, Worcester was quite a small place compared to many other *burhs*, and, because its episcopal household and other religious communities already took up so much space within the original Roman enclosure, the settlement must have continued in the early tenth century, in spite of the presence of the ealdorman and other, more local, secular lords, to have an overwhelmingly ecclesiastical character.

In the eastern half of the area newly enclosed by defences, Æthelred or his helpers laid out a regular grid of streets. Eight large urban lots, or *hagae*, were established along the modern-day High Street, four on either side, each encompassing about a third of a hectare. Ninth-century Worcester's large *hagae* have parallels at other *burhs*, and, as elsewhere, they probably served as urban manors for the most important landowners in the region. Giving important laymen a stake in the *burh* made it more likely that they would work hard to build, maintain and defend it. Still, secular stakeholders in the early days probably only resided in town periodically, when attending the bishop or participating in a meeting of the shire court, so Worcester's population, as long as these large *hagae* were intact, would have remained relatively sparse. Over the course of the tenth century, though, it became standard for tenants who leased rural estates from the bishop to receive *hagae* in Worcester as part of their agreements; so either more *hagae* were laid out, or some of the large original properties were divided.

The High Street during this period became the *burh*'s major thoroughfare, and the street itself probably served as a marketplace, in the way such streets often did in *burhs*. This was a sensible arrangement in the late ninth and early tenth centuries when *burh* populations were small enough for a wide street to provide adequate space for a market, and when a lack of suburbs meant there was plenty of empty land outside the walls to accommodate larger, seasonal markets such as cattle markets. Thus, as the *burh* developed commercially, regional lords not only acquired accommodations in the town, but also came to have a local market outlet for the surplus produced on their estates.

In spite of the changes wrought by Æthelred's extension of the walls and the laying out of a handful of streets and *hagae*, it took at least two generations for Worcester to develop into a 'real' town, with a relatively large and diverse population of craftsmen and traders living cheek-by-jowl along crowded streets. As important as the bishop and the ealdorman were in the foundation of the *burh*, it was the decisions of hundreds of more ordinary families to immigrate to the settlement and scores of local lords to take advantage of its markets that fashioned Worcester into a genuinely urban place. Worcester's increasingly urban character by the middle of the tenth century is witnessed by the rise of a suburb called Sidbury, an enclave of craftworkers that grew up outside the walls along the main road leading south from town. Suburbs like this could be found in many tenth- and eleventh-century towns, and, like Sidbury, they usually developed along major approach roads, which were often themselves the sites of extramural markets. Another sign of Worcester's increasingly urban character is that proprietors of some of the large *hagae* along High Street had begun, by the mid-tenth century, to subdivide them, and over the course of the next couple of generations they would subdivide them again and again. Indeed, by the mid-eleventh century these once large parcels had been converted into a jumble of small, irregularly shaped tenancies rented to traders and craftsmen, probably because their owners had discovered what an easy source of cash such rental properties could be. We know, for example, that just after the Norman Conquest Worcester's notoriously wicked sheriff, Urse d'Abetot, held twenty-five houses in Worcester's marketplace, and that they provided him with annual rents totalling 1,200 silver pennies. Their prime location may have made them especially lucrative, but Urse was also the kind of man who exploited his tenants. Elsewhere in town, rents seem to have hovered around 13 pennies a year, a nice cash supplement for the rural landholders lucky enough to control a *haga* or two. Thus, it looks as if the character of Worcester evolved over time, as it moved from a more or less ecclesiastical enclosure to a place where many of the bishop's most important tenants came when attending borough or shire courts or visiting the bishop, and who perhaps were beginning to bring the surplus from their estates to a market there, and finally into a much more crowded place with streets full of craftsmen and

traders, some living outside the walls and all of them paying rents to
their landlords.

Only limited evidence survives to tell us what trades the people living
along Worcester's streets and in its suburbs practised. There were certainly iron-workers and tool-sharpeners in town as well as people making iron ploughshares, and there were tanners, too. Other townspeople
were manufacturing lime, a substance used by both tanners and stonemasons. The source of Worcester's lime is interesting, given the town's
ancient origins: lime-makers were burning the limestone remains of
ruined Roman buildings in and around the settlement. Doubtless, people
living in Worcester produced other goods. There may, for example, have
been wool- or cloth-workers, although archaeologists have not found
tools related to large-scale textile production in their excavations. Still,
evidence for the kind of upright treadle looms ubiquitous in urban
weavers' workshops in the twelfth century has been recovered from
nearby pre-Conquest Gloucester. The people of Worcester, moreover, ate
more mutton than people living in England's northern towns, perhaps
because entrepreneurial lords were pasturing large herds of sheep in the
surrounding countryside. So there is some evidence for an increase in
the period's and the region's wool and cloth production, and it would
not be surprising if some of Worcester's traders and craftsmen made
their living weaving, dyeing or selling cloth.

The people of Worcester, however, did not live on sheep alone: judging from the heaps of bones excavated in the town, many kept pigs,
geese and chickens in their back gardens. From a couple of the town's
excavated cesspits we also know that people here ate apples, perhaps
even pears, and this may mean that smallholders or lords in the surrounding countryside had planted orchards and were growing fruit
specially for the town market. Similar market gardening was apparently developing around many other towns in the eleventh century,
and local farmers could have also been growing industrial crops like
flax and hemp for Worcester's rope- and sack-makers. As Worcester's
population grew over the course of the later tenth and eleventh centuries, open spaces and large *hagae* within the town filled with residents,
and so food markets selling meat, cereals and other staples would
have grown in size and importance. As the market for these staples
expanded, the amount of pasture and ploughlands needed to supply the
town increased dramatically, drawing ever more rural producers into

urban markets, and providing them with coins which they could use to pay their rents and taxes or spend on goods made by Worcester's craftsmen.

Worcester's townspeople traded not only among themselves and with people living in the town's hinterland, but with producers from other regions. The bulk of their pottery was relatively local, fashioned by men running kilns in the Cotswolds, but they occasionally got hold of storage jars and cooking pots from further north or east. Worcester craftsmen sharpened iron implements with whetstones made from Pennine sandstone, and they used grinding stones from Shropshire. Still, there are few signs of foreign merchants or merchandise here. A church in Worcester dedicated to St Gudwal, a Breton saint whose relics belonged to a monastery in Ghent, is an exotic rarity for this landlocked little town, but its dedication is more likely to have been inspired by the private devotion of one of Worcester's most famous bishops, St Dunstan, who had spent time as an exile in Ghent, than to be the work of a group of homesick Flemish merchants. Indeed, the outsiders doing business in Worcester were probably by and large from nearby regional trading and manufacturing centres like Gloucester and Droitwich; some may have even been from Wales. Other English towns in this period, though, did considerable business with foreigners. People in the somewhat larger town of Oxford, for example, had access to a wide range of pottery from northern France, Belgium and the Rhineland, as well as whetstones from Norway, none of which were available in Worcester. The difference in access may well be because Oxford lay on the Thames upriver from London, while Worcester sat on the less commercially developed Severn.

The ecclesiastical character of Worcester also evolved during this period. At some point in the tenth century the northern and eastern edges of the episcopal precinct were redeveloped. This probably happened in the 960s, when one of England's great monastic reformers, St Oswald, set out to transform Worcester's episcopal household into a community of Benedictine monks. At this time the northernmost portion of the Roman defences, made redundant by Æthelred's late ninth-century extension, were knocked down, and a new boundary was established closer to the church. At the same time the High Street, which after the foundation of the *burh* had probably run both the length of the newly enclosed area and through the cathedral close, now stopped before the monastic precinct. In this way casual, secular traffic no longer moved through the minster close. At Winchester, a similar closing-off had taken place when the three reformed monastic communities were fenced off by walls or hedges so that they 'might serve God more peacefully, removed from the bustle of the citizens . . .'. The redevelopment of Worcester's monastic close not only had the virtue of separating Oswald's reformed monks from the wicked influence of townsmen, but it opened up to commerce a section of land once taken up by the episcopal precinct, and a whole new neighbourhood was laid out, doubtless to the profit of the bishop. So this ambitious redevelopment looks to have been driven both by reformed monastic zeal and by urban speculation.

Worcester's cathedral had long had a monopoly on burials, and the two episcopal churches, the old St Peter's and the newer St Mary's, built in the tenth century by the reforming Bishop Oswald, had a cemetery laid out between them. What little of the cemetery has been excavated suggests a heavily used burial ground with a telltale jumble of intercut graves. But even in Worcester's pre-urban phase there is evidence that important local families sought burial in the shadow of the cathedral, and that they chose to erect memorials to their dead in its cemetery.

Over the course of the tenth and eleventh centuries a number of churches, none with cemeteries of their own, were founded in and around Worcester, a sign, along with the town's increasing number of cesspits, of its burgeoning population. The church of All Saints, for example, probably began as a gate church. After the Norman Conquest an extramural cattle market took place in front of the church, and this may have been the case before the Conquest, too. Sidbury, the suburban development outside the south gate of the town, came, in this period, to have two churches. All in all, by the late eleventh century there were something on the order of ten churches in Worcester. The quite humble majority residing in town were well served by a host of small churches, and, because of them, townspeople may have begun to develop highly local neighbourhood identities based on their worship-communities, in the way we know town-dwellers did in later centuries. Townspeople in Worcester also seem to have been forming a town identity and a sense of communal entitlement; indeed, they were organized enough and self-conscious enough in 1041 to carry out a tax revolt against King Harthacnut († 1042) and to defend themselves against the king's very tough household troops, not only surviving a bloody and determined onslaught, but winning, in the end, the right to return to their homes without penalty.

By 1086, the year of the Domesday survey, Worcester had something on the order of 2,000 residents, and its saintly bishop Wulfstan had not only increased the number of monks in his community from twelve to fifty, but had recently broken ground for a massive new cathedral. Although this church would dominate the city skyline until the twentieth century, the town could no longer be described as an ecclesiastical enclave, the way it could three centuries earlier. Many town families remained tenants of the bishop or his monks, but they now had altogether different relationships with him than the eighth-century slaves and servants of Worcester's earlier minster communities had had. And the urban tenements, found not only in densely packed streets in the heart of the walled city but in districts beyond Worcester's 890s fortifications, are evidence that the town's ecclesiastical character was much diluted, and that the families of craftsmen and traders at this point far outnumbered their ecclesiastical betters. By this time, the king and the local earl were receiving more money from judicial fees than the bishop, a sign that secular powers, over the course of the tenth and eleventh centuries, had gained considerable authority within the community at the bishop's expense. The town's prosperity, moreover, was fuelled less by the needs of its episcopal household than by an increasingly productive countryside, gradually transformed by nucleation and agricultural intensification, and by a landed elite who were hungry for markets, cash and consumer goods.

Worcester in the late tenth and eleventh centuries was thus part of a wider, busier, more productive world than it had been in the eighth century, and the prosperity it generated was shared, at least in some small way, not only by its churchmen and local landholders, but by its lime-workers and ironsmiths, something that certainly had not been the case in 800. Indeed, some townsmen must have been prosperous enough to worry about the safety of their profits, their tools and their inventories, because archaeologists have found a number of eleventh-century keys and padlocks in their excavations of the town. In short, Worcester had moved from being a Hwiccan bishopric, to a central place in the larger Mercian kingdom, to a town in the kingdom of England. Still, in spite of its transformations, at the end of the eleventh century Worcester's economic connections remained mostly local.

THE BIG CITY REBORN

Worcester is representative of many of the period's small regional towns. But how did more cosmopolitan towns develop in this period? London's history can help us answer this question. London's traders and craftsmen in the seventh, eighth and early ninth centuries could be found, as we saw in Chapter 7, on the Strand, a couple of kilometres upstream from the walled and mostly deserted (except for the religious community surrounding the bishop of London) site of Roman *Londinium*. The Strand settlement had, over the course of the seventh and eighth centuries, become the largest and most important mercantile community in the British Isles. Unfortunately, in the ninth century its success made it an irresistible target for enterprising vikings. They first attacked in 842, and they struck again nine years later. By the mid-860s, the Thames Valley, the south-east coast of England and East Anglia were all focuses of sustained viking campaigns, a state of affairs that would prove ruinous for many traders and craftsmen trying to conduct their business along the Strand. In 871 normal commercial life in London must have been near-impossible, because the *micel here*, after staying some months upriver at Reading, occupied London and spent the winter there. The Mercian king, in whose territory London lay, probably paid the vikings to leave. We know that the bishop of Worcester had to scramble to raise money 'because of the very pressing affliction and the immense tribute of the barbarians in that same year when the pagans stayed in London'. A handful of impressively large hoards of mostly Mercian pennies, hidden away *c.* 871, have been unearthed in and around London, and they probably represent the hard-earned capital of money-flush Londoners who buried their silver before fleeing – or attempting to flee – the pagan army. Yet another large hoard, this one secreted *c.* 872, was discovered 11 kilometres south of London, in Croydon, and it contained more than local, English pennies. Indeed, with its coins from Francia, Baghdad and a variety of recently fallen English kingdoms, and with its little collection of ingots and hack-silver, it bears all the signs of Danish swag. Together, both the English hoards and the viking one point to economic disruptions and people on the move. Other evidence similarly signals profound dislocations around London. A number of settlements in London's hinterland, for example, were stripped of their livestock and workers during these years, and others were temporarily abandoned. As a matter of fact, the vikings occupied London on and off, as they did nearby Fulham and Benfleet, and it may have even been without a bishop for a time in the 870s or 880s. All in all, these must have been dismaying decades for people born into families who had long made their living along London's Strand.

In actual fact, London had been in crisis decades before the first viking campaign against it. The Strand settlement suffered from a series of devastating accidental fires in the years on either side of 800, yet there are few signs of rebuilding in the early ninth-century town, hinting at economic difficulties and population decline. London was a centre of international trade, and so the troubles of the wider world – which by the early decades of the ninth century included disruptive viking attacks on many of London's minster-based customers and Continental trading-community partners, as well as political instability within the great Frankish king Charlemagne's former empire – brought about a precipitous commercial decline across much of north-west Europe and affected London years before townsmen actually confronted vikings in the flesh. Beyond this, it is clear that vikings operating along the Kentish coast had grown from nuisances into genuine threats as early as the first quarter of the ninth century. By the late 880s London's difficulties were acute, and, according to his biographer Asser, King Alfred moved to 'restore' London and 'make it habitable again', which apparently involved requiring the few people still living along the vulnerable, and by this time mostly deserted, Strand to move inside the walls of Roman *Londinium*. He then entrusted the city and its defences to Ealdorman Æthelred.

In spite of Asser's assertion that Alfred was responsible for the walled city's refoundation, it seems that some individuals had already moved inside the Roman defences, particularly in an area close by the River Thames at present-day Queenhithe. People in the late ninth century came to call this area 'Æthelred's Hythe' in honour of Ealdorman Æthelred, but it is clear that they had been using the site before Alfred's 'restoration'.

The remains of two women constitute our earliest and most perplexing evidence for this. One of the women had been placed in a grave dug along the high-tide line at the river's edge: given her burial's isolation and its peculiar location, we should consider it anomalous. The second woman, whose skull had been smashed in by a terrible blow, had either been murdered or executed. After her death those who had charge of her body placed a layer of bark on the banks of the river, followed by a layer of reeds and then the corpse itself. They then covered the dead woman's face, genitals and knees with moss and blanketed her corpse with yet another layer of bark. When they had finished, they staked the body and its wrappings to the foreshore and probably built a gravel mound over the grave, creating an unsettling landmark for all those who paddled down the river. Radiocarbon dates taken from the bark place this woman's death sometime between 670 and 880, in other words in the years preceding Alfred's 'restoration'. Other, more commonplace activities, though, also took place here. Two Northumbrian coins have been found, and they suggest that traders were doing business along this section of the Thames foreshore as early as the 840s, the decade in which these coins were minted.

Elsewhere within the walls of the Roman city, there are also hints that people had moved in before the date of the official 'restoration'. Around the middle of the century texts were coming to refer to London as *Lundenburh* rather than *Lundenwic*, suggesting that by this point things were happening within the Roman walls. The bishop of Worcester was also granted a property and commercial rights in 857 'not far from the west gates', a turn of phrase which intimates that his establishment lay just inside the Roman walls, rather than in the old Strand settlement a couple of kilometres outside the defences. Royal moneyers were also probably working within the walls before 889. King Alfred issued a series of pennies in London, first in cooperation with the Mercian king and then, after much of Mercia fell to the vikings, in his name alone. Some of these latter coins are embellished with a monogram of the word 'London' on their backs, and these were probably struck eight or nine years before the 'restoration'. In *c.* 880, however, it is hard to imagine moneyers operating in the dangerously exposed ghost-town that was now the Strand, especially since viking raiders were so often present on the Thames.

Still, once Æthelred took charge of London, he moved quickly to transform the area around Æthelred's Hythe. Two documents detailing grants of land in this area, the first dated 889 and the second *c.* 899, together preserve details of two abutting *hagae*. In the first, Æthelred and King Alfred awarded the bishop of Worcester property at

Hwætmunde stane, which the charter goes on to describe as an 'old stone building', probably the still-standing remains of the Roman baths at Huggin Hill, and a place where the bishop was allowed to hold a market free from tolls. The two men granted the other *haga* to the arch-bishop of Canterbury. Both bishops, by the time of the second grant, were allowed to moor ships off their *hagae*; nonetheless, the king was to have tolls from all the goods exchanged at the market held along the river's edge. Ealdorman Æthelred, the bishop of Worcester and the arch-bishop of Canterbury were all Mercians, and all were firm allies of Alfred the Great. The ealdorman and the bishop of Worcester, moreover, were working together at just this time on the transformation of Worces-ter into a *burh*. It is interesting to see them all cooperating here with the common aim of re-establishing economic stability and settlement within London's Roman walls.

It is also interesting that Æthelred chose to encourage the develop-ment of this particular stretch of river, especially given the site's long history. The Roman past was much more present in London in the ninth century than it was in Worcester, because London, as the most impor-tant city in Roman Britain, had once had scores of monumental build-ings. In the late ninth century their ruins at times presented serious impediments to resettlement. London's riverfront, for example, was a tangle of rotting Roman piers and quays, and its looming, late Roman riverside wall denied access to those approaching it from the Thames. One of the reasons Æthelred may have concentrated his efforts on the area around Æthelred's Hythe (and, indeed, one of the reasons why it may have been a site of activity in earlier years) is that this particular patch of riverbank was relatively unencumbered by ruined Roman revetments, since most had been dismantled here in the late Roman period. A gate may have also pierced the riverside wall nearby, and this would have provided access from the new settlement within the walls to the beach market.

Over the course of the late ninth and the tenth centuries the two bishops developed their *hagae* as commercial sites. Their initial inter-ventions, judging from the dendrochronological date obtained from one of the timbers excavated here, took place *c*. 890. It seems, then, that soon after the initial grants the bishops oversaw the building of a modest infrastructure to provide better facilities for the beach market. Archae-ologists have found the remains of trestles used to support gangplanks as well as mooring posts and a mat of timber, which perhaps served as a resting place for modestly sized beached boats. Not only was the trading shore improved with an eye towards commerce, but it seems that merchants, some from across the sea, did business there. Archaeologists have recovered three rare, London-struck Alfred the Great halfpennies along the water's edge, and they have found Frankish brooches and a Norse-inspired strap-end, all dating to the late ninth century.

A century on, these initial improvements were swept away by a series of more ambitious quays. Large amounts of wood were used in their construction, much of it recycled. Its builders had salvaged some of it from a mid-tenth-century Frisian coastal tramp, and other timbers came from a broken-up, Norse-style, clinker-built ship, all of which hints at the array of foreigners active at the new London site. More remarkable still are the remains of a magnificent, mid-tenth-century, three-storey aisled hall. Before it was taken down and its oak recycled, it was either a fancy wooden church or a high-status domestic building. Some of the techniques used in its construction were the same as those employed by shipwrights, and it tells us something interesting about the people who were commissioned to build high-status buildings in port towns like London. Before its dismantling, the building must have stood nearby, given that various still-pegged joints held together when segments of the building were moved to the foreshore. The bishop of Worcester or the archbishop of Canterbury, whose *hagae* abutted the quay, was the most likely owner of the building. In the eleventh century these revetments were replaced yet again, this time by an even more ambitious series of embankments comprised of dumps of twigs, branches and firewood-grade timber, held in place by strakes and posts. This embankment, according to dendrochronological dates, was first built *c.* 1021 and then repaired and extended *c.* 1045.

The improvements made along the shore around Æthelred's Hythe make an interesting contrast to the Roman timber quay. In the first century CE, Roman engineers built their quay from timber taken from 200- and 300-year-old oaks. The earliest medieval riverside works, on the other hand, were cobbled together from wood coming from much younger trees, and, as we have seen, from a good deal of salvaged timber as well. In an age without saws, and at a time when all boards were hewn with axes, it is little wonder that people salvaged whatever timber they could. The carpentry techniques used to build the first medieval waterfront were, moreover, quite basic, especially compared to those employed by Roman dockworkers. So the early medieval riverside, unlike its Roman predecessor, was hardly a marvel of engineering or requisitioning, but it does represent a quick-and-dirty improvement in a world with little engineering know-how, few resources, less ruthlessly organized slave labour and a much smaller state. Each iteration of the early medieval waterfront project was, moreover, built out of everything from coppiced round wood, which had grown for something of the order of ten years, to oak trees from twenty to ninety years of age. And each instalment, much like the Roman quay, lasted about thirty years. Thus, much of the wood needed to maintain and rebuild the Thames embankment during the tenth and eleventh centuries would regenerate in time for its periodic refurbishments, something that cannot be said for the magnificent, centuries-old trees used by first-century Roman builders. The early medieval waterfront was therefore sustainable in a way that its first-century predecessor was not. The early medieval waterfront, in contrast to the Roman quay, was a patchwork of different individual property owners' efforts, rather than a single, state-sponsored project, and it speaks to the hard work, ambitions and initiative of wealthy individuals in the late ninth, tenth and eleventh centuries, who were coming to play a starring role in the rebirth of English towns.

The pair of *hagae*, laid out at the height of the viking wars as part of King Alfred's initial effort to revive and protect London, had clearly been a roaring success. The siting of Æthelred's Hythe towards the western edge of the Roman city was particularly well chosen for people wishing to accommodate boats and traders coming from the heart of England *down* the River Thames, and it suggests that, at its initial refounding, the new London, although a place where a few foreigners continued to do business, was primarily an English, rather than an international, trading centre. This idea is supported by the pottery excavated from tenth-century London, the overwhelming majority of which came from the Thames Valley. But levels of international trade picked up, especially around the turn of the millennium. From this time on London minters regularly struck something like a quarter of all the pennies in circulation in England at any one time. Foreign traders were funnelling huge amounts of foreign silver currency into the port, and it was this foreign silver that was melted down and made into English pennies.

In the generation or two before the Norman Conquest people in

London were also beginning to put up timber-cellared buildings, which suggests that they needed more storage space for their booming businesses. What might account in part for the new volume of trade is that merchants around the North Sea were beginning to use larger ships, and, as more of them came to London, the area around their favourite destination of Billingsgate developed rapidly. Although this spot had been a focus of activity in the late ninth or early tenth century, perhaps because there had been hopes in the early days of rebuilding London's Roman bridge, this area did not take off the way the riverfront in the western part of the city had. But by c. 1000, because Billingsgate's landings lay in the eastern half of the city, the area was considerably more convenient for international shippers coming *up* the Thames, especially after London's bridge was finally rebuilt. Indeed, from a text detailing tolls owed to the king around the turn of the millennium we know that merchants from Normandy, France, Flanders, Ponthieu and the lands along the Meuse and the Rhine were paying their dues to the king's reeve at Billingsgate for expensive bulk products like timber, fish, whale blubber, wine and vinegar; and for lightweight luxuries such as gloves, fine linen, silk and pepper. Interestingly, archaeologists have recovered a number of objects from Billingsgate that look like Anglo-Saxon pennies (and were, indeed, struck with official coin dies) but are made from lead rather than silver. It appears that royal officials gave these lead pieces to merchants after they had paid their landing and customs fees, and merchants, in turn, could then show them to other officials as proof of payment when exiting port or as they moved with their merchandise through controlled gates or markets.

The area inside the Roman defences was very large, and it took a century or more from the time of King Alfred's 'restoration' for London not only to develop its entire riverfront, but to grow into its walls. In the late ninth and early tenth centuries it was the riverside markets and an inland marketplace along Cheapside that were the places with populations. But London expanded rapidly from around 1000 in everything from population, to density of buildings, to number of streets, churches and cesspits. By the early eleventh century, for example, Fresh Wharf's riverfront property had been divided into at least four smaller *hagae*, something reminiscent of the fragmentation of Worcester's larger properties. The area around Æthelred's Hythe had similarly been subdivided, each new plot with buildings constructed using a variety of different techniques and architectural styles, perhaps reflecting the skills and building customs of the city's English and foreign-born population.

By the eleventh century, undeveloped intramural areas at some distance from the riverfront and lying to the north of Cheapside were also beginning to urbanize. Around this time, for example, a neighbourhood began to develop close to the site of the Roman amphitheatre and where, in the twelfth century, the London Guildhall would be built. This part of London – south of the Roman wall, but north of the area laid out and developed in the late ninth and the early tenth centuries – was apparently initially divided, much as Worcester had been, into a number of large *hagae* attached to the rural manors of important men. Three street names in the area preserve the memory of these arrangements. One is called Aldermanbury, after the 'ealdorman's enclosure', another *Staeninghaga*, or the '*haga* of the people belonging to the manor of Staines', and a third Basinghall Street, from 'the *haga* attached to Basingstoke'. Elsewhere in London (and not only at Æthelred's Hythe) we can find hints of similar large *hagae*. Around the year 1000, for example, a wealthy man, in atonement for the killing of his own mother, gave the monks of Ely land in London, which came to be called *Abboteshai*, or 'the abbot's *haga*'.

We know that people had begun living just south of the old amphitheatre site in the late tenth or the early eleventh century, because archaeologists have found their rubbish. Some of the neighbourhood residents were throwing away fancy scabbard chapes, carefully embroidered shoes and old horse harnesses after they had worn them out. And from the remains of their dinners we know that at least some people in the neighbourhood ate venison, crane or herring on special occasions and served these culinary wonders on imported ceramic dishes. Clearly, at least a few of the people depositing garbage here were well-to-do, although the remains found in the rubbish pit of some of the things we think of as high status – such as figs and grapes – may have been more readily available in London than elsewhere, and, therefore, less special here than they would have been on rural sites. Some people in the neighbourhood also wore (and eventually threw away) lovely copper-alloy brooches. Others, though, used lead and tin jewellery, and perhaps this second group was not as prosperous as the people throwing away fancier personal adornments. We know that this base-metal frippery was made in London itself, because a hoard of similar pewter pieces, probably a craftsman's inventory, was discovered in Cheapside in the nineteenth century. Closer to the centre of town, archaeologists have also found the waste from a ring-maker's workshop. This man did not have the wherewithal for a lathe, so he made his little rings by hand from cheap materials like slate and bone. These were very modest pieces of jewellery, and they suggest that even poorer members of London society could afford small acts of personal vanity.

There was also considerable debris from fine metal-working in the amphitheatre rubbish, so some neighbourhood residents must have been metal-workers. Although the houses of the people who were throwing things out have not been found, the remains of a couple of their livestock pens and sheds have been excavated. All in all, these are the kind of outbuildings one would expect to find along the semi-rural edges of an expanding city. The people living here, in contrast to Londoners who lived in more crowded neighbourhoods closer to the river, kept and bred a fair number of animals, not just the standard backyard collections of town chickens and pigs, but cattle, horses, sheep and goats, many of which they stall-fed and stabled during the winter months. Householders were raising some of these pigs and chickens for their own tables and keeping cows and sheep for milk. But given the number of young horses present on the site, it may be that a few people living here were breaking and training horses for a living. We also know from a contemporary text describing tolls in London that there were people travelling to a market near the river at Billingsgate and supplying traders with pigs and hampers of hens and eggs, and that women were hawking butter and cheese there, so it is possible that some of the households in the amphitheatre neighbourhood were producing food not only for themselves, but for city markets. However they were using their animals, women here would have got out of bed to the crowing of roosters to milk their families' cows and sheep, and householders, whatever their main occupation, would have spent part of each week mucking out animal pens and barns and keeping an eye on the wattle fences around their houses to ensure that livestock was either kept in or kept out. As a matter of fact, from the astonishing amounts of wattle used both in this area and elsewhere in the city, we know that large numbers of people in London's hinterland were busy pollarding and harvesting young trees for the London market, and that they must have sometimes carted their newly cut wattle rods and strakes into this very neighbourhood.

A few families living near the amphitheatre site buried their dead in a little cemetery next to the local church of St Lawrence, which, although rebuilt in stone soon after the Norman Conquest, was probably a timber building in the early eleventh century. A number of men, women and children laid to rest in the cemetery had been placed in pegged wooden boxes, carefully constructed from planks made from seventy- or eighty-year-old oaks. Perhaps the coffin maker, given his special skills, also made boxes and other wooden items for the living. A number of St Lawrence's dead also had hazel or willow branches in their graves, objects that may have been placed with them to symbolize the Resurrection or to invoke Psalm 23 ('For although I walk in the midst of the shadow of death, I will fear no evil, since you are with me; your rod and your staff console me'). The practice itself, though, never mind its Christian symbolism and context, originated in Scandinavia. Indeed, half the graves excavated at an eleventh-century cemetery in Lund included just such rods. This burial rite, in turn, suggests that London was not just a place where foreigners lived, but a community developing an interesting and cosmopolitan culture all its own out of the many traditions brought there by people coming not only from the English countryside, but from Scandinavia, France, Germany and elsewhere.

In spite of the well-made coffins at St Lawrence's and the obvious prosperity of some of the people who attended Mass there, the view from the graveyard was insalubrious. Mucky cattle pens and the local tip stood within view; and, judging from the kinds of insects living in the nearby mounds of refuse, the cemetery was damp, foul smelling and home to great clouds of disease-carrying flies.

OTHER TOWNS AND TRADING SITES

As we have seen, there were dramatic differences in the size of London's and Worcester's populations, their connections to the wider world and the extent and economic activities of their hinterlands. Both London and Worcester were also singular places, with their own particular histories, trades and residents. Nonetheless, early medieval London and Worcester also shared similar histories and chronologies. The look and layout of both places, for example, even in the tenth and eleventh centuries, were determined, in part, by their former Roman selves; and long before either became *burhs* they had been important places, and some of their early residents had collected and consumed surpluses and involved themselves in exchange. For both towns, King Alfred's interventions marked an important new beginning, and, for both, decisions made in the 880s and 890s affected the ways they developed in the first half of the tenth century. At both Worcester and London, moreover, full-blown urbanism was not a reality until the middle of the tenth century, and it was really only in the eleventh century that their economies took off. Both Worcester and London also grew and prospered because kings placed mints within their walls and because they insisted that people come to market there. Yet, even after London and Worcester became *burhs*, it is also clear that the king was not the only actor. Secular and ecclesiastical elites committed large amounts of energy and resources to the development of these places. At the same time, by the mid-tenth century landholders across England were producing considerable surpluses and using towns to exchange what they raised on their estates for manufactured goods and for cash, and these activities go a long way, as we shall see in the next two chapters, towards explaining England's urban boom.

The commonalities shared by London and Worcester were also shared by many other English towns, regardless of their size or location. Indeed, towns with similar trajectories could be found in regions hardly touched by vikings as well as in places heavily settled by them. This is certainly true for the 'five boroughs' of the east midlands. After the men who fought in the *micel here* (including some of the men who had wintered at Repton) conquered territory here and 'shared out the land', they divided the region into five discrete territories, each with a fortified centre (hence the name 'five boroughs') thrown up on a navigable river and near an important road. Each of these places, though – Derby, Leicester, Lincoln, Nottingham and Stamford – had been home to an important religious community or had acted as an estate centre before the coming of the vikings. After West Saxon kings and their helpers reconquered the region all came to be incorporated into the same network of *burhs* as Worcester and London, and all five, by *c.* 950, were beginning to develop into bona fide towns. In short, these communities and the people who lived within them had similar histories to the towns and townsmen in areas never settled by vikings.

Lincoln was the largest of the five boroughs. Like London and

Worcester, it had been founded by the Romans, and the fact that it had served as a late Roman administrative capital meant that when the vikings arrived it still had impressive fortifications and sat at the hub of a well-developed road system. Naturally, this ancient infrastructure had an impact on Lincoln's urban development during the tenth and eleventh centuries. Like London and Worcester, the area within Lincoln's walls, in the beginning, was mostly empty, and at the tail end of the ninth century it was home to no more than a few hundred people. Yet by the Norman Conquest Lincoln had a population of somewhere between 6,000 and 10,000, roughly the same as it had been in 350. So, in spite of its Danelaw locale and one-time history as a viking stronghold, Lincoln developed across the centuries in similar ways to London and Worcester.

Like the other two towns, Lincoln by c. 1000 was also connected to the wider world through networks of exchange and trade, although the scope and scale of its connections were closer to London's than Worcester's. Lincolnshire craftsmen procured grinding stones from the Pennines, jet from north Yorkshire and hones from Kent and Gloucestershire. Its people used pottery made in Thetford, Grimston, St Neots, Ipswich, Stamford and Torksey, as well as the occasional vessel from York and Winchester. Like some Londoners, there were also people in Lincoln who had impressive international contacts. Walrus ivory and amber from Scandinavia and beyond were available in town, as was a little pottery from the Baltic, ceramics and quernstones from the Rhineland and glazed wares from France and the Low Countries. There was even a little silk from Baghdad or Byzantium and a handful of vessels from far-off Syria and China.

As at Worcester and London, the towns of the five boroughs had thriving food markets, and it is clear that well-to-do people in towns across England were avid in their pursuit of the same kinds of high-status foodstuffs as could be found on the dinner tables of important rural landholders. Pheasants were occasionally eaten in Lincoln, and evidence for a peacock dinner has been recovered at Thetford. The cod, herring and haddock eaten there would have had to have been hauled from the coast, nearly 50 kilometres away. By the second half of the eleventh century the well-to-do in Lincoln were even eating veal and lamb, so there must have been people living in the hinterlands of Danelaw towns, just as there were around London and Worcester, who were now earning their living by provisioning townspeople. As at Worcester and London, there were clearly high-status households in Danelaw towns – doubtless headed by merchants, important rural land-holders and professional religious – who not only could afford to eat well, but now had sufficient leisure time to hunt with goshawks and sparrowhawks, because the remains of these birds have been recovered from many northern and eastern towns.

Towns other than London and Worcester were also producing increasing amounts of goods during this period in increasingly organized ways. There is evidence from Lincoln, for example, that new, more efficient looms were being used in textile production, and that spindle whorls manufactured in the town, rather than being handmade from clay, were now being made from stone on lathes, which suggests that crafts-men working there were producing higher quality textile equipment more efficiently. Towns besides London were also producing low-quality frip-pery. In York, for example, there is evidence that not-very-well-made lead brooches and pendants were being churned out, decorated with clumsily executed animals and pseudo-runes. These objects were imitations of more carefully made silver pieces that wealthy people would have worn. So it looks as if low-status residents in many English towns were able, in the eleventh century, to acquire little luxuries for themselves, their wives and perhaps even their sweethearts.

Many towns in England besides Worcester and London also experi-enced rapid suburban expansions. Again, this is something we find in Lincoln. One of Lincoln's earliest suburbs, *Butwerk*, lay just east of the lower city's defences. In the tenth century the people living here made large amounts of pottery, a fire-using industry wisely located outside the centre of town. *Butwerk*, like some of Worcester's suburbs, also served as an extramural market site, the memory of which is preserved in a local Old Norse place name, *Bagerholmegate*, which means 'the water meadow of the hawkers'. Wigford was another of Lincoln's early sub-urbs. It was comprised of a long street's worth of houses, which ran south from the lower town. It was apparently a prosperous mercantile quarter, and its churches' cemeteries were festooned with elaborately carved stone grave slabs, suggesting one-upmanship and competition between local churchgoers. These people's embracing of competitive Christian burial is interesting, given that some of the purchasers of these monuments must have been members of immigrant families who had only recently converted to Christianity. In later tenth- and eleventh-century Lincoln, though, it is clear that townspeople were as enthusiastic in their church building as people in London and Worcester, and by the end of the eleventh century there were something like thirty Lincoln churches.

Given the influx of Scandinavian settlers, the ethnic composition, not just of Lincoln, but of other Danelaw towns, may have been quite different from towns further south or west, but this diversity is surprisingly difficult to substantiate. For example, many of Lincoln's moneyers – Geirfinnr, Steinbitr, Ubeinn, Kolgrimr, Sumarlithi, Dreng – bore unmistakably Norse names. But naming is a complicated business, and the children of Scandinavian immigrants sometimes bore English names while Norse names were given to babies whose grandparents were English. Indeed, in resolutely un-Scandinavian Worcester, one of the town's moneyers, just before the Norman Conquest, was named Vikingr. Similarly, after York fell into the hands of viking rulers, people making and wearing metalwork in town sometimes had objects embellished with Scandinavian-inspired designs. Yet a close examination of this material suggests that these objects were actually made in England, and look quite different from similar pieces crafted in Scandinavia. Indeed, they were heavily influenced by artistic styles originating both in pre-viking York and in contemporary southern England. So a taste for these objects was hardly a straightforward declaration of Scandinavian identity. Or again, town-dwellers in the eastern Danelaw ate more goose than people living in towns further south and west, and this may reflect the culinary tastes of immigrants. Then again, goose may have been popular simply because the fenlands were rich in geese, and enterprising people in eastern towns' hinterlands had learned that wild birds brought a good price in urban food markets. Still, there are a few subtle but more convincing signs of difference between town-dwellers of English and Norse ancestry in Danelaw towns. One is found in the shoes made by York's leather-workers. Ostensibly identical-looking shoes made in York from the late ninth century on were actually fashioned in two distinct ways and used two quite different sets of sewing techniques. Neither technique produced a different or more handsome shoe, and neither led to a cheaper or a better-made product. So the remains of York's shoes may represent the work of two distinctive groups of shoemakers, each with its own quite different craft traditions. Perhaps the people using one set of techniques were immigrant craftsmen and their children, and those using the other were native-born shoemakers and their heirs.

Thus towns across England, whatever the ethnic composition of their population or region in which they lay, had much in common. At the same time, though, each had an individual history which made it more than simply a generic town: instead, each was a distinctive community, different from all the other towns in England. Each urban community's particularity may have given rise to home pride and communal identities, something clearly present in our written sources by the twelfth century.

Although towns grew and prospered across much of England during the tenth and eleventh centuries, none, with the exception of Chester, developed in the north-west of England or in Wales and Scotland. Still, goods were manufactured and exchanged in these townless regions; and seasonal trading sites grew and developed there, which facilitated trade across the whole of the Irish Sea zone. One such site is Llanbedrgoch, in Anglesey. It had been an important high-status settlement in the pre-viking period. Artefacts excavated from the site suggest that, in the generations before the vikings began raiding, it had served as the centre of a 'multiple estate', and that the people who controlled it had connections, either through trade or gift exchange, to a wider world: the metalwork jewellery worn by the people living here, for example, was influenced by both Irish and Northumbrian artistic traditions. In the late ninth and tenth centuries, though, the settlement was dramatically enlarged and elaborated. A road was built within the site; stone-footed buildings were constructed and a stone wall now marked the perimeter of an enclosure of about a hectare. So ambitious were these changes that the excavator of the site believes that they may represent the work of the Welsh king Rhodri the Great or his sons. Some of the people living at Llanbedrgoch during this second phase continued to make their living from cereal farming, but others in the settlement were now devoting considerable amounts of time to trade and craft production, in particular metal-working. They were using hack-silver and scales in their commercial transactions, so they were participating in the same bullion economy as other people around the Irish Sea and Scandinavia. The designs being used on the metalwork made at the site were also heavily influenced by Scandinavian motifs. Between the hack-silver and the metalwork it seems likely that Scandinavians were living and working here, or at the very least the people living here had Norse tastes or Norse customers. It is clear that exchange was taking place, but, given the size and heft of the enclosure, it may also be that this was a regulated trading site, and that the person to whom it belonged was collecting tolls.

Other sites, like one near Meols, on the Wirral peninsula, have also disgorged impressive amounts of Viking Age metalwork. As at Llanbedrgoch, the remains of merchant balance sets were found at Meols; and it looks as if this was the site of a market. The things traded here show Norse influences, but they were nonetheless hybrid pieces; and the kinds of dress accessories found in Wessex and English Mercia were also traded here. The site at Meols, however, looks less like a regulated trading space than Llanbedrgoch, and it may have been a less legitimate sort of place, run by Norse people settling in the area, who were operating a car-boot-sale kind of market, a toll-less alternative to the royally controlled and heavily regulated market not far away at the English *burh* of Chester.

The kings and vikings with whom we began this chapter played starring roles in the revival of towns and town life in the later ninth, tenth and eleventh centuries. So, too, did English bishops, craftsmen and traders. But vitally important transformations in landholding, farming, settlement and lordship were also taking place in the vast rural seas surrounding every *burh*, and these developments were crucial to the success and growth of towns, because they led to increasing surpluses, the very things that fed town markets and put food on townspeople's tables. Some of the changes happening in the countryside were economic and some cultural, and some were the unintended consequences of West Saxon policies designed to fight vikings, reconquer territory and rule a growing kingdom. It is to all these changes that we now turn.

10

Kings and Surpluses: The Ninth to Eleventh Century

Alfred the Great and the viking leader Guthrum, whom Alfred had defeated, drew up a treaty sometime in the early 880s which included an agreed-upon boundary between the lands under English and viking political control. The Danes were to have free rein in the lands north and east of Watling Street, a region which came to be called the Danelaw, and Alfred was to rule the peoples and territories south and west of that line. Thus Alfred not only had authority over Wessex, the kingdom long ruled by the men of his family, but was now overlord of southern Mercia and Kent as well, defunct polities which only a couple of generations earlier had been led by competing dynasties. For much of the rest of his reign, Alfred laboured to secure his newly enlarged kingdom, not only protecting it from viking marauders and settlers, but keeping it safe from English competitors, including even some of his own relatives.

Fortunately for his dynasty and for the men and women living in West Saxon-controlled territory, not only was Alfred a skilled ruler, but so, too, were a long line of his descendants. When Alfred died in 899, his son, Edward the Elder, became king; and Edward, in turn, was succeeded by his sons – Athelstan, Edmund (r. 939–46) and Eadred (r. 946–55). And, after a short hiatus, Eadred was succeeded by King Edmund's son Edgar the Peaceable (r. 959–75). All these men, building on the foundations laid by Alfred and cooperating with important secular lords and churchmen, including influential Mercians, transformed viking-bedevilled southern England into a much larger and more secure kingdom, which by King Edgar's death in 975 would be one of the best-administered and wealthiest states in Europe. Following in the footsteps of Alfred the Great, his son and grandsons ruled the ever-expanding collection of peoples and lands under them not as tribute-gathering hegemons, but as kings of a single people, all subject to the same duties and burdens.

Crucial for the triumph of the West Saxon dynasty was its ability to raise the resources necessary to wage a series of decades-long wars of expansion. By the end of 920, Alfred's son, Edward the Elder, was king of a kingdom with a northern boundary that ran not along Watling Street, but rather the southern banks of the River Humber. And over the course of the next thirty years the dynasty would extend its authority even further; indeed, the kingdom would eventually run from the tip of Cornwall all the way to Yorkshire and beyond. There were, needless to say, defeats and setbacks as well as victories. In the decades before 920, Norwegians, both from Norway and from Hiberno-Norse settlements in Ireland, began raiding and colonizing along the north-west coast of England. By 919 one of their leaders had gained control of Northumbria, and he went on to establish a kingdom across the Irish Sea, centred on Dublin and York. The Norsemen who ruled this kingdom for more than thirty years were not, so it transpired, the natural allies of the descendants of the men of the *micel here*, who had not only settled in the Danelaw a generation earlier, but had raised families there and were beginning to convert to Christianity. These people were coming to prefer the rule of English kings to Hiberno-Norse ones, and many, in the end, threw in their lot with the West Saxons. Only in the late 920s did King Athelstan manage to wrest temporary control of York away from the Hiberno-Norse, but until 954 the town passed back and forth between West Saxon kings and Norsemen. From the second half of the 950s, though, the house of Wessex finally gained control of York and its hinterlands for good. From this time on, members of the West Saxon dynasty truly ruled as kings of England and all the English, a group so broadly defined during this period that it comfortably included the descendants of vikings.

The achievements of the West Saxon dynasty are extraordinary; indeed, they are so extraordinary that it is necessary to ask how exactly King Alfred and his heirs were able to accomplish all that they did. A partial explanation lies in those *burhs* we examined in the last chapter. This is because *burhs* not only were a crucially important component of the West Saxon kings' strategy to defeat the vikings, but became the centres from which royal power was exercised, and places to which subjects came to render much of what they owed their king. Beyond this, as dozens of *burhs*, over the course of the tenth and eleventh centuries, evolved into full-blown towns, they both facilitated the spread of coin use and helped to create new wealth, developments that Alfred's heirs then harnessed and used to their own advantage.

As we have seen, Alfred, in order to protect his kingdom from viking interlopers, constructed fortresses across Wessex. When he did this he was not innovating but rather building on the work of earlier Mercian kings, who had established the all-important principle that landholders had an obligation to help defend their kingdom by supplying the king with the resources he required to build and maintain bridges and fortifications, and by providing the fighting men he needed if he was to field armies and defend his strongholds. These obligations of 'wall-work', 'bridge-work' and *fyrd-* (that is, military) service', often called the 'common burdens' by historians, came, during this period, to be levied on every hide of taxable land held by royal charter. In England, we first catch sight of the common burdens in individual land grants made by the Mercian king Æthelbald in the late 740s, but Æthelbald and his successor Offa worked to transform these particular impositions into generalized obligations shared by all landholders. Material evidence for eighth-century Mercian kings' success in imposing 'wall-work' is present both in Offa's Dike and at the Mercian royal centres of Hereford, Tamworth and Winchcombe, where archaeologists have uncovered fortifications dating to the eighth century. By the end of his reign King Offa was imposing the common burdens on lands held by minsters in Kent, and by the 840s West Saxon kings were also burdening landholders in their kingdom with these exact same duties. The imminent threat of viking attack explains both the widespread imposition of these obligations, and the willingness of most landholders to concede to them. The century-long war waged by Alfred and his descendants allowed for both the extension and the routinization of government, and many landholders during the long years of emergency became habituated to military levies. At the same time, English kings and their helpers grew increasingly adept at governing. West Saxon kings, during the years of perpetual crisis, were able to demand an unusually large number of resources from their subjects in the form of manual labour, money and military service, which churchmen and lay landholders, given the ugly alternative of viking conquest, were generally willing to concede. Vikings, so it turned out, made excellent common enemies, especially because, as pagans, they were easy to demonize.

As we have seen, Alfred, his children and his Mercian son-in-law Æthelred used the resources made available by the common burdens to fortify numerous sites across Wessex and English Mercia, and by the early tenth century more than thirty *burhs* were in place. Although some of these sites used older Roman or Mercian fortifications as part of their defences, the network of *burhs*, as it stood in the early tenth century, was extremely impressive and is proof that West Saxon kings were able to persuade others to help them defend the territories they ruled against a common enemy. The high costs of defence were accepted not only by landholders in Wessex and English Mercia; as Alfred's descendants began conquering lands north and east of Watling Street, the peoples of the Danelaw came to shoulder exactly the same obligations. By 921 Æthelflæd and Edward the Elder had clawed back all the lands which had fallen to the Danes south of the Humber, and, as they did, they incorporated a series of new *burhs* into their defensive system, including the five boroughs, giving West Saxon kings a foothold in places where they had never before had any lands or authority. Thus, as a result of their *burhs*, members of the West Saxon dynasty had dozens of central places across the kingdom from which they could govern. These places turned out to function better as sites of royal authority than kings' tribute centres had done in earlier generations, not only because they were fortified, but because many had grids of streets, marketplaces and growing populations. People in the hinterlands of many *burhs* during this period were coming to take advantage of the markets held in them, in order to sell surplus and buy manufactured goods and luxuries. The market function of these places came to be so important that a number of *burhs* established at the height of the emergency which were difficult for local people to travel to were abandoned in the early tenth century, and nearby sites more conducive to trade came to take their places. So, for both those governing and those being governed, *burhs* were coming to be convenient meeting places.

Burhs, though, were not the only institution facilitating the rapid development of royal administration and power. The administrative unit of the shire was another all-important structure used by kings during this period to extend their reach into the localities. The West Saxon kingdom itself had long been subdivided into shires. Originally, each West Saxon shire probably centred on an important royal tribute centre. In earlier centuries, moreover, when Wessex was first expanding, some of the ancient kingdoms it absorbed – places like Sussex and Surrey – were made into shires as well, as they came to be integrated into the kingdom. Each shire was headed by an ealdorman, who was both an important royal official and a nobleman, and a man who helped the king exploit and rule the shire under his authority. Over the course of the tenth century both 'English' Mercia and the newly conquered territories north and east of Watling Street were shired as well, and all came to be supervised by ealdormen. Some of the northern shires were constructed out of older, indigenous administrative divisions, but other shires were new creations. Whether West Saxon or Mercian, in southern England or the Danelaw, by the tenth century a *burh* lay at the heart of each shire, and all the landholding men of the shire were organized to build, maintain and defend their *burh*.

Over the course of the tenth and eleventh centuries *burhs* also developed into places where people in the surrounding countryside came to resolve their most important legal disputes at periodic courts held by the king's representatives. *Burhs*, which by the mid-tenth century were within a day's walk of most of the kingdom's population, made it possible for English kings to rule localities in ways that their predecessors in the eighth century could not. It became standard for great meetings of the most important landholders in each shire to be held twice a year, and these meetings would be presided over by the local bishop and the ealdorman, who together acted as the king's representatives. At these shire courts, lawsuits were heard and royal directives, such as the announcement of laws, levies or notices of important appointments, were publicized. By the eleventh century the king had come to rely more and more on a shire-reeve, or sheriff, to look after his local interests, and it was this official who became the king's chief representative in each shire.

By the mid-tenth century we also have evidence that the shires, as a matter of course, were further divided into smaller administrative units, known as hundreds in the south of England and as wapentakes in the north. The idea of the hundred, like that of the shire, probably originated in Wessex; and, like the shire, it too came to be imposed on regions newly incorporated into the kingdom. In principle, each hundred was made up of 100 hides, and ideally each contained an important royal estate, a minster church, a marketplace and a site where criminals could be put to death. In many places, though, hundreds had either more or less than 100 hides, and there were also hundreds without royal estates or minster churches. The hundred itself was nonetheless ubiquitous. Like the shire, the hundred had a court, but its court met much more frequently than the shire court – every four weeks – and it is likely that it was at the hundred court that most people in the kingdom had direct contact with the English state. Hundred courts were especially charged with dealing with issues having to do with theft and breach of the peace.

The shires and their associated hundreds were crucial institutions, which helped the state not only to keep the peace, but to collect the common burdens. The king, to take but one example, would have expected the twelve hundreds which constituted Worcestershire (each conveniently made up of 100 hides), to provide him with 240 fighting men to defend the *burh* at Worcester, if he ordered a levy of one fighting man for every five hides of land, as we know was the custom by 1066. Similarly, taxes could also be collected on each hundred's 100 hides; so, again in Worcestershire, if the king were to levy a tax of two shillings on every hide, each of Worcestershire's hundreds would be expected to collect 2,400 pennies for the king and give them over to his sheriff. Thus, within the administrative framework made up of *burhs*, shires and hundreds, extraordinary resources were not only demanded by the king, but collected by him as well.

Because so many *burhs* developed into towns, kings were also able to gain considerable control over the economy. Kings in the tenth century worked hard to regulate commercial activity, insisting that certain kinds of commercial transactions take place in towns in front of royal reeves. This not only limited the opportunities for thieves, but also ensured that the king got his tolls. Much effort during this period was also spent on improving England's coinage. From King Athelstan's reign onwards, coins were minted in *burhs* and nowhere else, something which had not been the case in earlier centuries.

The remarkable English coinage of the tenth and eleventh centuries owes something to the innovations of King Offa, who had insisted that foreign moneys be remade into English pennies, and that all the coins minted in England should be marked with his name. These were ideas carried on by Alfred's heirs. By the early tenth century coinage was firmly under royal control, although there was considerable diversity in the coins produced in the various regions within the kingdom, and it looks as if the supervision of coin-making during this period was delegated to royal officials working under the king. Around 973, though, King Edgar overhauled both the look of England's coins and the system whereby they were produced. From this time on, moneyers, working in some sixty mints, each one located in a *burh*, were producing very large numbers of highly uniform coins, struck with centrally produced dies. Each coin, after Edgar's reforms, not only bore the king's name and his portrait on its front, but on its back it had the name of the *burh* in which it was produced and the name of the moneyer who had made it. In this way, the king could monitor the quality of the coinage. And, of course, the more reliable the quality of the kingdom's pennies, the more willing people were to use them.

From the time of Edgar's reforms, in surprisingly short cycles – initially about every six years, but from 1036 onwards every three years – all the coins circulating within the kingdom were recalled and reminted into new coins. When people brought their old coins to their local town mint at recoining time, perhaps as much as 15 per cent of their value was taken as a fee for the service. But after each reminting the weight of each coin would decline a little, and hence the people who brought in their coins, in spite of the steep surcharge for reminting, would have got the same number of coins back. Eventually, a new series of coins would be created, the weight standard would be restored, and the whole cycle would begin over again. This shows a sophisticated understanding of money, and hints at fiscal policies developed by royal administrators, which allowed kings, through periodic recoinages, to cream silver off the top of the economy.

Kings, of course, were interested in overseeing a uniform and trustworthy currency, in order to put silver into their own coffers. But they also wanted to encourage people to use coins, because people with coins are easier to tax. Coin-owning landholders were going to become especially important to kings when the vikings resumed their raiding in the late tenth and the early eleventh centuries. Very large coin payments during this period – in some years millions of pennies – were handed over to the vikings in exchange for their promise to leave the kingdom, and tens of thousands of English coins dating to this period have been recovered from Scandinavian hoards. The English state in the early eleventh century, moreover, began to levy a tax based on the hide which was known as the *heregeld*. The state used its revenues to pay for mercenaries and mercenary fleets, which were now employed both to fight off foreign invaders and to enforce the collection of taxes. The better the coinage and the more readily available it was, the easier and more trustworthy people found monetary transactions to be, the more likely people would exchange their surplus for coins, and the easier it would be for the king to collect his *heregeld*.

A widely available coinage in which people had confidence, and which was highly standardized and controlled by the state, had beneficial economic effects. At the same time, safe, regulated markets were held not only in the *burhs*, but at well-known sites within each hundred. All these things led to economic development, and encouraged lords, who needed silver to pay their taxes, to produce ever more for the market.

REMAKING THE LANDSCAPE, CREATING A SURPLUS

The vikings, the West Saxon conquest of the Danelaw, the institution of the common burdens, the founding of *burhs* and their metamorphosis into towns and the precocious currency reform of English kings are all part of a single, important story, which was unfolding at exactly the same time as a second, equally extraordinary set of developments was taking place in the rural hinterlands surrounding every *burh*. It was during this period that settlement patterns, farming practices and the means whereby landholders extracted surpluses from their landholdings were all changing rapidly and dramatically. The chronological relationship between these two sets of events and any relationship of cause and effect which might have existed between them are difficult to establish. Nonetheless, these two seemingly quite disparate tales together came to remake England.

Although the two tales are linked in some fashion, their relationship is not a simple one. A number of excavations in Yorkshire, for example, have revealed a landscape in flux in the later ninth and tenth centuries. A settlement site at Wharram Percy, for example, was occupied both before the coming of the vikings and during the initial period of Scandinavian settlement. And yet a new, planned village known to archaeologists as the 'South Manor' was laid out near the earlier settlement sometime in the tenth century. Or again, people had long lived in a settlement near West Heslerton, but they moved, or the settlement shifted,

sometime in the later ninth century, and by the tenth century the settlement had shifted yet again, and was now located where the village of
West Heslerton can be found today. Something similar was also taking
place at Cottam, where an older settlement shifted to a new site sometime in the late ninth or early tenth century, and then shifted yet again a
generation or two later. Thus in Alfred's, Edward the Elder's and Athelstan's reigns here and elsewhere in the Danelaw there is evidence for the
profound shifting of settlement sites, and also, as we shall see, for a
whole series of important new agricultural practices and technologies.
It is tempting, knowing, as we do, that vikings were settling in, that
kingdoms were rising and falling and that Wessex was expanding, to
use these events to explain the transformations taking place in the Yorkshire countryside. But this would be a mistake. Such changes were not
limited to the Danelaw, but could be found across much of lowland
Britain; indeed, in some places these transformations date well before
the Viking Age, and in others to a period when vikings were no longer
a threat. So how can we characterize these changes? Who was responsible for them? And who, in the end, profited from them?

As we have seen, in the seventh and eighth centuries, kings, great
secular lords and wealthy religious communities in England, Wales and
southern Scotland often controlled territories encompassing thousands
of hectares of fields, woodlands and moors. Although they rarely
exploited their holdings directly, they did develop estate centres where
their agricultural dependants, most of whom lived on farmsteads and in
hamlets scattered throughout their lands, delivered the tributes they
owed them. Since in the early days much of what was given over to the
masters of such territories was consumed by their own households,
rather than sold on the market, and since most of these renders were
perishable, there was little point in demanding more. So Britain's lords
were often powerful, but distant, or so it must have seemed to many
farmers. This was certainly not a world in which peasant tenants living
in villages spent their days labouring in common fields that covered the
greater part of their lords' carefully managed estates. Nonetheless, some
settlements in this early period had relatively large populations. The
sites of important religious communities such as Llancarfan and Caerwent, in Wales, or Barking and Worcester, in England, were home to
dozens of year-round ecclesiastical residents, craftsmen, slaves and servants, as well as occasional groups of pilgrims and lay patrons. Minster

sites like these would have been among the most populous places in Britain, but even the largest of them in the seventh and eighth centuries would not have housed more than a few hundred souls.

Sometime in the eighth or ninth century territories like these began to come apart, particularly in lowland Britain. Around this time, a number of kings and religious communities began to feel obliged to divide some of their outsized, tribute-rendering territories into a number of more modest holdings of five or ten hides, which they would either give outright or lease to their most important secular followers. This practice quickened over the course of the tenth and eleventh centuries, and by the eve of the Norman Conquest thousands of English thegns (landholders in some ways similar to the gentry of the later Middle Ages) had come to possess their own small estates. These holdings were much more compact than earlier territories, and they commanded many fewer resources. The people behind their creation were apparently aware of this, because they often took special care, when dividing up older territories, to make each new estate a viable agricultural entity. Again and again we find older territories split into a number of long, thin, five-hide estates, each of which had a share of riverbank, some woodland and some access to nearby trackways or roads. It must have been a momentous occasion when thegns first received such a holding, because the new estates were often named after them. In this way and during this period, large numbers of English place names were coined: we find, for example, a Wiltshire thegn called Alfred holding Alverstone, or 'Alfred's estate', and the Leicestershire thegn Osbeorn holding Osbaston, or 'Osbeorn's estate'. By the time the Domesday commissioners set out in 1086 to survey the wealth of England for their master William the Conqueror, thousands of such small, prosperous manors had come to take the place of earlier 'multiple estates', and they were presided over, not by some great and distant lord, who visited the neighbourhood only at tribute time, but by country gentlemen whose entire fortunes were bound up in five or ten hides of land. So these new-style landholders were going to have to manage their relatively limited resources directly and aggressively if they hoped to live like lords.

By the later twelfth century large parts of Britain – in a central zone running from the coasts of Dorset and Hampshire all the way north through the midlands and into Yorkshire, County Durham and Northumberland, and then along the east coast of Scotland – had relatively large, nucleated villages, many with a dignified hall for its lord (who controlled the lion's share of the communally ploughed fields), and between ten and sixty peasant households, each of which held something on the order of 6 or 12 hectares of land, and all owing considerable labour services and rents to their lords. Just a hundred years earlier, the Domesday commissioners still found scores of old-style 'multiple estates', most in the hands of the king or the Church, as well as thousands of small farmers yet to be enmeshed in village life and communal, common-field ploughing, especially in the West Country and in East Anglia. So even towards the end of the eleventh century, many people's labour remained relatively unencumbered by the demands of their lords; indeed, a few continued to render tributes of honey, wheat and cattle, the way their great-great-grandparents had. Still, the move in many parts of lowland Britain was towards these new-style estates, settlements and labour practices.

What kind of work had to be undertaken to allow for the move from large territories to small estates? To support more lords, it was necessary to bring more land under the plough, and the land itself had to be exploited more intensively. How was this done? Who stood behind these changes, and who in the end were the winners and losers? As is so often the case, our texts are mostly silent on the details of this revolution, but material remains survive which help us answer these questions. One of the places we can study some of the processes behind such revampings is at Shapwick, in Somerset. People living in the neighbourhood around Shapwick had long been part of some larger territory, but sometime, probably in the tenth century, their scatter of hamlets and farmsteads gave way to a single, more populous village. During this transformation, traditional settlement sites surrounding the present-day village were reorganized: hamlets and farmsteads were abandoned, and two new common fields were laid out where the former settlements and fields had once sat. As the landscape around Shapwick was remade, farmers moved into a single village site located at Shapwick itself. This settlement was not only new, but planned, a lord or his reeve having laid out sixteen unequal village plots between two parallel roads. Each was designated for one of the displaced families, the larger ones presumably for the households of higher-status farmers, the smaller ones for low-status workers and slaves. We know that all of them eventually resettled in the village, because each plot in Shapwick was occupied by the late tenth or eleventh century.

Although we can see the results of the laying out of a new, planned village and common fields at Shapwick, it is harder to determine the work that went into making new small estates like this one economically and agriculturally viable. Fortunately, we can discern some of the steps behind such reorganizations from excavations carried out in and around Yarnton, in Oxfordshire. Sometime in the late eighth century the people living at Yarnton came to farm more intensively than their ancestors had. We know from the remains of insects found near Yarnton in land running along the River Thames that over the course of this period fewer dung beetles – creatures who live off the manure of cattle and horses – resided there than in past centuries, and that this low-lying land now supported the kinds of insects found in meadow habitats. This, in turn, tells us that the people of Yarnton during this period had undertaken the hard work of transforming a piece of the Thames floodplain from pastureland into hay meadow. This was no easy task, because it required them to rethink how they were going to feed their livestock, since now, from February until early June (when they could finally mow their hay), livestock could no longer graze along the riverbank. Fencing was critical in this process, something emphasized in an early law code which mandated that:

> If ceorls have a common meadow or other shared land to fence and some
> have fenced their portion and some have not [and the cattle get in] and eat
> up their common crops or their grass, then those who are responsible for
> the opening shall go and pay compensation for the damage which has been
> done to the others.

All this rethinking and fencing were apparently worth the trouble, since the new hay meadow would have produced dramatically more fodder than the previous agricultural regimen and enabled Yarnton's farmers to over-winter larger numbers of cattle.

More cattle meant more traction for ploughing and carting and more manure for fertilizing fields; and at some point these new resources enabled the people of Yarnton to extend their arable land dramatically. Seeds found within the settlement, which must have been brought there with cereal crops at harvest time, show that plough-tolerant weeds survived while their more delicate cousins did not. The seeds of clay-loving plants were also present in the settlement for the first time. This, in turn, suggests that farmers had come to extend their cereal fields into the heavy claylands nearby, soils that had not been tilled in this neighbourhood since the fall of Rome. The ploughs employed to cultivate these clays were probably 'heavy ploughs' with mouldboards and asymmetrical coulters, since the simple breaking-ploughs of the early Middle Ages were not up to the job of cutting through heavy clay, mixing in manure with the soil and creating the deep furrows necessary for the successful cultivation of these fertile, but waterlogged, soils. But these ploughs were transformative even in lighter soils, because they turned them over completely, and so kept weeds from choking cultivated fields. This kind of plough is probably described in one of the many riddles, little entertainments, written in Old English by eleventh-century monks:

> I keep my snout to the ground; I burrow
> deep into the earth, and churn it as I go,
> guided by the grey foe of the forest
> and by my lord, my stooping owner
> who steps behind me; he drives me
> over the field, supports and pushes me,
> broadcasts in my wake. Brought from the wood,
> borne on a wagon, then skilfully bound,
> I travel onward; I have many scars.
> There's green on one flank wherever I go,
> on the other my tracks – black, unmistakable.
> A sharp weapon, rammed through my spine,
> hangs beneath me; another, on my head,
> firm and pointing forward, falls on one side
> so I can tear the earth with my teeth
> if my lord, behind me, serves me rightly.

Ploughs like this were pulled through the heavy clays by very large plough-teams, employing as many as eight oxen and measuring as much as 12 metres in length. These teams were very hard to turn, so the men who intended to plough with them usually laid out their new fields in very long strips, so that ploughmen would not have to turn their teams more than once a day.

Both the larger fields and the clayland soils required more livestock for ploughing and manuring, and these extra animals had to be fed. Unfortunately, arable land was often extended at the expense of pasture, so there was now considerably less grazing land. One of the ways out of this bind was to raise hay, which brings us back to Yarnton's hay meadow. But new crop-rotation practices, too, were critical for solving this dilemma. Each village household came to have rights to a certain portion of the ploughlands scattered across the new common fields. One of the village's fields would lie fallow each year, both to rest the soil and to provide the community's livestock with pasture, but, since each household's strips were distributed throughout the common fields, each one would always have some land under cultivation. With a two- or three-field system of crop rotation, plough animals could graze both on the year's fallow field and on the stubble left in productive fields after they had been harvested.

What led the people of Yarnton to institute the changes they did? It is possible that the great man to whom the people of Yarnton had traditionally given over their tribute had transferred rights over them to the nearby minster at Eynsham; if so, Yarnton's farmers would now have had to produce for an elite household permanently settled only a few kilometres away, rather than a peripatetic lord who only occasionally resided in the neighbourhood. If this is indeed what happened, it could have meant that Yarnton's new masters insisted that the people farming there give over more specialized renders or larger tributes. This could explain why the people at Yarnton worked hard to produce more grain from the ninth century onwards, as evidenced not only by the new fields they were laying out, but by their building of a new granary. It may also account for why they had apparently begun to raise more ducks, geese and chickens, as witnessed by the new fowl-house they built. Then again, it may have been the people of Yarnton themselves who were behind these moves, since the dating of our evidence suggests that these changes were taking place before the period when 'multiple estates' were breaking apart in the region.

As people remade the countryside, agricultural regimes were revolutionized. Farmers living in these transformed landscapes were now producing more grain and livestock than their ancestors had, and they were cultivating a greater variety of crops. This is certainly true at Yarnton, where more free-threshing wheat and oats were being grown than in past centuries, and a more diverse set of plants was being cultivated, including flax and hemp. People were harvesting grapes and plums, too, so it is possible that they were managing vineyards and orchards, things that had disappeared from Britain with Rome's fall. The plant and pollen remains recovered at another site, this one at Market Lavington, in

Wiltshire, also reveal a noticeable increase in cereal-plant pollens, which points to agricultural intensification. Evidence gathered at Market Lavington argues, as well, that heathland vegetation was retreating in the face of expanding arable fields and hay meadows, and that a variety of soils, including heavy clays, were now being cultivated. Although this intensification began at Market Lavington as early as the late seventh century, it increased fairly dramatically around the year 900. Indeed, from the early tenth century onwards, it looks as if farmers at Market Lavington were cultivating a host of new crops, including rye, hemp, flax, opium poppies and grapes. As at Yarnton, however, we cannot say who was directing this activity. Was it some lord interested in maximizing the productivity of his one and only five-hide estate, or were the first steps taken, rather, by farmers, who understood that more oxen, more manure and more fodder could transform their lives?

Whoever the individuals were who first initiated new farming practices, there are signs, as we move into the tenth century, that lords were beginning to monopolize them, because they were becoming increasingly interested in producing surpluses for the market in order to obtain cash. So, for example, in the tenth century we can see the monks of Glastonbury embarking on a carefully planned campaign during which they created planned, nucleated villages and laid out new field systems on some of their Somerset estates. But all sorts of landholders, not just the wealthy monks of Glastonbury, were coming to manage their lands more profitably. To give but one example, on the eve of the Norman Conquest a middling Devonshire thegn named Hecca the Sheriff was becoming quite a prosperous man. He seems to have been cagily accumulating holdings which, although they had neither impressive thegnly compounds nor large working populations, had very low tax assessments and substantial amounts of pastureland. Hecca was probably snapping up these properties in order to run large flocks of sheep on them, because by this time there was a good market for wool. So strategies adopted quite independently by local communities in the eighth century to farm in new ways and produce greater surpluses may have become the preserve of lords by the tenth or eleventh century.

The kinds of changes we have just examined had a dramatic impact on settlement sites. As we have seen, the new ploughs required large teams of oxen to cut through clay soils. This led many households with the wherewithal to keep only one or two oxen to club together and plough with their neighbours so that they could extend their fields into the claylands. Cooperative ploughers must have often found it easier to harness their jointly owned teams when everyone supplying animals lived in close proximity, and this may have encouraged people to leave their traditional hamlets and isolated farmsteads and move into larger villages. But the clay soils themselves may have also drawn farmers into villages. This is because many clays are impossible to work when wet. Spring ploughing is especially difficult, and there are often fewer than seven days when soils like these can be ploughed. Living next to the people whose oxen helped make up their plough-teams allowed farmers to maximize their ploughing time. Hay meadows also pulled people into villages. Farmers who had worked together to create hay meadows needed to mobilize substantial numbers of people in short order when it was time to cut the hay, because haying, like spring ploughing, is not just labour intensive, but can take place each year on only a handful of days. Thus large plough-teams, clay soils and the extension of hay meadows pulled many people away from scattered hamlets and farmsteads and drew them into larger villages which sat at the centres of their new cooperatively farmed lands.

NEW-STYLE LANDLORDS

Lords in many places by the tenth century probably stood behind the creation of village communities, and there is evidence that large numbers of them were encouraging, tempting, cajoling or forcing rural workers to move from traditional, scattered settlement sites into new-style villages. As thegns settled onto their five- or ten-hide estates, many of them established planned villages like the one at Shapwick. When they did, they expected low-status workers and slaves to move there as well. This is doubtless because many lords understood that it would be easier to control the labour of people who lived within view of their own halls and just down the road from their estate managers. But lords may have also provided the capital needed to lay out and exploit new fields: if so, they would have been in a good position to extract concessions from higher-status but resource-strapped farmers, whom they could not compel to move. Lords may also have enticed the families of free farmers to settle in their new villages by providing amenities that most farmers could not afford to build for themselves. Thousands of lords, for example, oversaw the building of mills in the tenth and eleventh centuries, and these must have acted as powerful magnets for resettlement, because they freed the labour of farmwomen and slave girls for other tasks, such as the potentially cash-generating activities of spinning and weaving. Lords in these centuries, as we shall see in Chapter 12, also founded village churches, which often had priests and cemeteries. This, too, may have encouraged families to leave their ancestral farmsteads. Indeed, village communities with churches and mills were being founded, not just in Britain, but all across north-west Europe during this period, in part, one suspects, because lords and farmers alike were coming to feel that village life was proper life. An eleventh-century English tract on estate management describes the way good lords provided people living in their village and working on their estates with a harvest feast after corn reaping and a drinking feast after ploughing, celebrations that would come to feel natural, even traditional, soon after families had settled into village life. So the twin phenomena of nucleation and resettlement were widespread, and they were probably driven by some combination of lordly intervention, changing agricultural practices and the shifting social and cultural preferences of rural workers.

At Yarnton and Market Lavington we are confronted with a chronology which suggests that agricultural intensification and crop diversification began taking root before great territories were broken apart, but that both quickened in the tenth and eleventh centuries, probably encouraged by the proprietors of new, small-scale estates. Nonetheless, since intensification began before the splitting apart of great estates, other forces besides the breaking apart of 'multiple estates' must have stood, at least at the beginning, behind these developments. One such force was probably the new opportunities available for those with goods to trade, in the decades when places like London, Ipswich and Southampton were beginning to boom. When Alfred's *burhs* came to be fully fledged towns the advantages of growing for the market would have become clear to most lords in possession of estates in their hinterlands; and at this point they may have come to co-opt these changes systematically.

Landlords during these centuries, however, were not always successful in settling their workers into planned villages. At West Cotton, in Northamptonshire, for example, an ambitious proprietor laid out a new village sometime in the tenth century. In it he built a dignified compound for himself and his family alongside a mill; and he also laid out a series of more or less equal plots separated by earthworks on which local workers were to settle. Apparently, however, fewer farmers could be persuaded to move to the thegn's village than he had hoped, because a number of these plots remained unoccupied.

Rights to an increasing share of rural workers' labour was critical for the success of England's emerging country gentlemen, and many thegns during this period worked hard to strengthen their grip on the labour of others. An eleventh-century tract on estate management, for example, tells us about the obligations of the *gebur*, a low-status labourer who spent most of his time working on his lord's demesne (the land exploited directly for the lord's own benefit), and a person now probably housed with his family on a crowded little lane in the shadow of the lord's own residence. The *gebur*

> must perform week-work for two days each week of the year ... and for three days from the feast of the Purification to Easter ... And from when the ploughing is first done until Martinmas, he must plough one acre each week [for his lord], and he himself must present the seed to the lord's barn ... When death befalls him, let the lord take charge of whatever he leaves.

And in a little dialogue written to teach boy-monks Latin, known as Ælfric's *Colloquy*, the ploughman, when describing his work laments:

> Oh, I work very hard. I go out at daybreak driving the oxen to the field, and yoke them to the plough. Because I fear my lord, there is no winter so severe that I dare hide at home. Each day I must yoke the oxen and fasten the ploughshare to the plough. Then I must plough a full acre or more every day ... I have a lad driving the oxen with a goad, who is now hoarse because of the cold and from shouting.

The inescapable thrust of these two texts is that reeves were extracting heavy labour services from their lords' agricultural workers.

Stories preserved in a number of eleventh-century saints' lives describe the growing social gulf between landowners and their workers, and they detail the intensity with which landholders were now pursuing both profit and leisure. One story in the *Life of St Kenelm* preserves the following story:

> At that time the priest in Pailton, as was the custom, directed that the feast of St Kenelm should be celebrated by a break from work. When the lady who presided over that village heard this, as she reclined at dinner on that very feast-

day, she refuted it with arrogant pride, hurled impatient words at the saint, and commanded with haughty contempt that no work should be interrupted, 'Just because of Kenelm,' she said, 'I don't know why we should lose a day's profit.'

In a different *vita*, this one of the eleventh-century bishop of Worcester St Wulfstan, we read of a thegn who passed his summer days, not sweating in the fields the way his peasants must have been, but rather sitting in the shade of a nut tree next to the church, where he sat 'dicing, drinking and amusing himself with other games'. The intimacy of these accounts shows lords in close and unflattering focus, the way they would have been seen by the people who farmed their lands, since lords and rural workers now so often resided in the same villages.

Many farmers residing in new, planned villages and ploughing in their common fields began, over the course of a few generations, to drift downwards both socially and economically. In the tenth and eleventh centuries many relatively high-status rural workers came to live beside bonded tenants; and reeves, so contemporary estate-management texts tell us, expended considerable effort in subjecting these people to similar kinds of onerous labour services as those shouldered by lower-status families. At the same time, there is some evidence that people without much land were now having to hire themselves out for wages. Because of these changes, large numbers of rural workers were coming to look not so much like the farmers of the earlier Middle Ages as like medieval peasants.

HINTS OF CHANGE IN WALES AND SCOTLAND

Hints of transformations like those just described for England can also be found in Wales, but it is more difficult to generalize from the evidence here, because there is considerably less of it. Still, the scope and scale of both the landscape's and lordship's remaking in Wales seem to have been both later and slower. There is certainly considerable evidence for the same kind of fragmentation of 'multiple estates' in Wales as was taking place in England. After the late eighth century, for example, gifts of land to monasteries were modest in comparison to earlier grants – measuring in the tens of hectares rather than the hundreds – and these later parcels may represent holdings carved out from larger and older territories. It also seems that some multiple estates were being broken into their component *trefi* or *villae*, as they are called in the charters, and alienated to form single-settlement landholdings typically comprised of about 50 hectares. Sometimes these smaller holdings were named after their new proprietors, just as they were in England, with appellations like *Tref Iri* or *Villa Conuc*. Many people, however, even in the eleventh century, continued to give over renders of food, and, in places where this still happened, people had less time, less ability or less interest in producing surpluses to sell on the market. Similarly in Scotland, there is some evidence to suggest that between *c.* 750 and *c.* 950 larger territories were fragmenting into units which were much the same size as those now found in England and Wales. The people holding these districts, moreover, may have begun to build their own, proprietary churches, something that was also happening in England.

By the eleventh century a few Welsh landholders were also engaging in the same novel farming practices as landlords in England. The religious community at Llancarfan, for example, although it continued to collect renders of food and clothing from outlying workers and lands, had people known as *hortolani*, or 'gardeners', labouring in their demesne fields. These *hortolani* may have led lives similar to some of the low-status agricultural workers in England, who were finding themselves spending most of their time working on their lords' demesne. There is also pollen evidence in Wales from the ninth century on which hints that in some places woodland was being cleared and cereal fields extended. The pollen evidence also points towards the beginnings of a diversification of crops in Wales, and it may suggest that fibre crops were now more commonly cultivated. The turn of the millennium also witnessed the beginnings of a system of upland pastures, something like the shielings we found in Scandinavia, and they must have increased the size of Welsh landholders' flocks. But there is nothing to suggest that Welsh lords during this period had systematically taken hold of the labour of agricultural workers settled on their estates, the way lords in England had done; and there is no evidence for the widespread laying out of planned villages and common fields.

Because no towns developed in Wales or Scotland during this period, and because there was no money economy, landholders in Wales and Scotland would have had to work harder to exchange estate-grown surpluses for other things. This made their situation quite different from that in which large numbers of English landholders, who lived within a couple of hours' cart-ride from a town, found themselves. One of the results is that both English kings and English landlords, because of their easy access to markets for the surpluses grown on their estates, came to be considerably richer by the eleventh century than elites elsewhere in Britain. As we have seen, moreover, the needs of the English state and its ability to convince landholders that they were obliged to pay the king a money tax based on the number of hides they held, combined with landholders' own desire to live well on their small estates. This latter desire led many to seek town markets, where they could trade the surpluses of their estates for silver coins and little luxuries.

11

Selling Surplus and Buying Status: The Tenth and Eleventh Centuries

Landholders' elevated social status came to be expressed in new ways across Britain in the tenth and eleventh centuries, as new-style farming practices and lordship took hold, and as town economies began to boom. English landholders thrived within this monetizing and commercializing economy, and the general impression one gets is that they were growing steadily richer. These were the people who, by the mid-tenth century, stood on the winning side of the transformations in landscape and lordship, and who began, during this period, to pioneer new forms of genteel life. Social differentiation and conspicuous consumption were, of course, hoary traditions by the year 1000, and privileged families had long lived well. Nonetheless, lords in this later period came to expend their resources and underscore their elevated status in new ways, both because they had different sources of wealth from their ancestors, and because there were now different kinds of status-enhancing commodities available to them. Indeed, lords' access to traders and craftsmen living in local towns came together with their new-found ability to raise cash, and transformed their lives. Nowhere in the British Isles is this more true than in England; elsewhere in Britain, because towns and currency were more slow to develop, the newfangled forms of social display, although beginning to take hold, did so in much more muted fashion.

ENGLISH ELITES AND TOWNS

Now that both regulated markets and traders could be found in England's many towns, it is hardly surprising that landowning families were coming to hold property in them. Thegns eagerly sought markets where they could exchange for cash the wool and corn produced on their estates. In part, after the institution of the *heregeld*, they needed money in order to pay the silver pennies they owed the king in tax for each of their hides of land. Because of this obligation, English landlords were required to organize their estates in such a way that cash was one of the things they produced, so they needed to manage their affairs in ways that took advantage of markets, merchants and money. In short, they needed to cultivate and maintain connections to the towns near their holdings. Thegns, however, involved themselves in towns not only for their taxes' sake, but because they wanted to purchase items there that were unavailable to their rural workers, and which they increasingly used to mark their own elevated social status.

Much of what we know about the connections between landowners and towns comes from William the Conqueror's great survey, Domesday Book. In this extraordinary document we find that all kinds of rural landholders had managed, by the year 1086, to gain rights over both urban property and urban people. English earls, for example, who, in the eleventh century, were members of the wealthiest and most politically significant families in the kingdom, were very active in towns. Domesday Book records the Godwinesons – England's premier family in the 1040s, 1050s and 1060s – holding property in thirty-seven towns across the length and breadth of the kingdom, which suggests that town holdings were crucial to the running of their landed empire. Because of their duties as earls, the men of the family had official responsibilities in the towns of their earldoms, and this probably helped them to consolidate their hold on towns and townsmen. Still, Earl Harold, the most successful member of the family, and a man who would become king of England in 1066, had interests not only in the towns of his earldoms, but in towns like Droitwich, Lincoln and York, where he had never acted as earl. Similarly, several dozen of England's most influential thegns – men important enough to attend the king's court – also had rights over townsmen and property in a number of towns. One important Derbyshire thegn, a man called Siward Barn, had interests in towns as far apart as Gloucester, Lincoln, Warwick and Winchcombe; and another, Ulf Fenisc, whose estates centred on Lincolnshire and Yorkshire, was an important player not only in the town of Lincoln, but in Huntingdon and Wallingford as well. Even very modest landholders, who possessed little more than five hides of land, often held at least one property in their local county town; indeed, Domesday Book preserves the names of hundreds of middling landholders who did.

Landholders also spent considerable energy during this period cultivating personal, affective relationships with townspeople. In the Norfolk town of Thetford, for example, forty-one townsmen made themselves men of Robert fitzWimarc, an important royal official and kinsman of the king, who also happened to be one of the wealthiest people in England. Thetford's craftsmen and merchants must have felt that Robert's connections and privileged position at court might aid them in their dealings with the king's local representative and help them procure satisfactory judgements in town courts. The lordship exercised by people like Robert not only enabled them to build considerable followings in towns, but often entitled them to money forfeitures arising from breaches of the peace within their townsmen's houses and also, perhaps, fines from offences committed by the townsmen themselves. Such fines could be extremely profitable: one eleventh-century bishop, for example, received 300 pennies each year for pleas pertaining to his possessions in the little town of Wallingford.

Relationships and property in towns also helped rural landholders sell or exchange surpluses from their estates. Several thegns are recorded as holding the right either to take tolls or to be exempt from them, as well as to hold a court where sales could be vouched as legal. This suggests that some thegns were actually overseeing their own market sites in towns. Thegns' men in towns sometimes also paid them rents in-kind, which provided them with important necessities, such as iron and salt, or status-enhancing food like herring or salmon. Indeed, we find a number of thegns receiving just these commodities from their urban dependants as in-kind rents. But, for the most part, entanglements with townsmen and control over urban property provided rural landholders with cash, not only from rents, but from money-making ventures like town mills, fisheries and wharfs, which we know many were coming to control. A number of landholders also developed town property in order to increase the amount of cash in their coffers: as we saw in our examination of Worcester, the proprietors of large urban manors sometimes developed these properties into less glamorous, but more profitable, tenements for craftsmen and traders, probably because lords were hungry for the cash rents such developments could bring. The most dramatic example of this recorded in Domesday Book is the work of a thegn in the town of Lincoln: just after the Norman Conquest, we find him building thirty-six houses and two churches in a Lincoln suburb.

England's landholding elite not only developed their urban holdings and retinues, but did so aggressively. The Godwinesons, for example, worked hard to procure urban tenements. The family had been especially successful in the towns of Sussex, Surrey, Middlesex and Kent, where many of their estates lay. They controlled the majority of urban tenements in Chichester, a town whose hinterland was dominated by the estates of the family and their men. The Godwinesons and their men also held something like half of all property in Lewes and the whole of Steyning, including 118 properties which they had appropriated from an abbey. Romney was a town, according to Domesday Book, of some 150 *hagae*, and should have belonged to the archbishop of Canterbury; but by the early 1050s, Earl Harold's father, Earl Godwine, had managed to wrest twenty-one *hagae* away from the archbishop and another fifty were held from him by a family client. Clearly, Godwine was an important man in town. Earl Godwine had also seized 225 townsmen in Hythe from the archbishop. Harold Godwineson was in possession of a large amount of land in London, which he had taken away from the monastery of St Peter's, in Ghent. It was located in Billingsgate, which sat just across the river from Southwark, a London suburb dominated by the family. Earl Harold also held Lambeth, that is, the 'the landing place where the lambs are offloaded', across the river from London. So it is clear that the family moved firmly, sometimes even illegally, to acquire significant stakes in the towns of the south-east.

Thegns also pursued urban property. We can catch them buying, leasing, inheriting and stealing it in Domesday Book. Indeed, some of these men's holdings had very complicated histories. Rights to seven townsmen in Droitwich, for example, along with a salt-working establishment, passed rapidly from one holder to another in the mid-eleventh century. In the 1040s a local thegn named Wulfgeat had given them to the monastery at Evesham when he placed 'his grant upon the altar when his son Ælfgeat became a monk there'. The abbot, in turn, leased this property to his uncle, who died 'in Harold's war against the Norwegians', at which point it reverted to the Church. In less than twenty years the rights to these townsmen and the saltpan had been given away, leased and repossessed. So we can see the easy transfer of town property and the ways in which it could be used by lords to endow churches, to solidify friendships and probably to raise cash.

A handful of rural landholders held so much property and so many rights and men in particular towns that they must have been *the* dominant forces within them, in much the same way that the Godwinesons would have been in Chichester or Steyning. During Edward the Confessor's reign (1042–66), for example, one thegn held at least eighty-six plots of land in Canterbury, an impressive share of this ancient ecclesiastical city. Another thegn, who was the dominant force in the town of Wallingford, also held forty-two houses in Oxford, along with another eight plots of land, thirty acres of meadow, a mill and the benefice of one of Oxford's churches. A wealthy Englishwoman is recorded with thirty-two houses in Northampton; and a man with the unfortunate name Eadmær 'the terrible' held fifty-two townsmen in Berkhamsted, in Hertfordshire, which must have constituted the bulk of this small town's traders and craftsmen. These and other thegns held sufficient property in particular towns to dominate them or to compete with bishops, earls and other royal officials for the hearts, minds and dues of their inhabitants.

Rural landholders, who were busy at just this time building churches on their rural estates, were also building them in towns, some of them even in stone, an indication not only of their piety, but of their determination to mark their presence in towns with monumental architecture. A number of London's churches, for example, bore the names of their gentlemen founders. St Nicholas Acon, founded sometime between *c.* 1050, when St Nicholas was first venerated in England, and 1084, when a man named Godwine and his wife donated the church to a monastery, preserves the Norse name Haakon, doubtless this church's founder. All Hallows Gracechurch on Lombard Street was granted to the archbishopric of Canterbury by a man named Beorhtmær of Gracechurch. St Dionis Backchurch takes its name from Godwine Bac, who gave the church to Canterbury when he became a monk. Vestiges of a few of these pre-Conquest London churches survive to this day. The earliest church of St Bride's, for example, was apparently a single-cell stone structure, put up in a new suburban development sometime in the eleventh century. It and other early London churches were probably founded only a couple of decades before the Norman Conquest, evidence both of the prosperity of their landholding builders and of these people's desire permanently to inscribe their presence on the urban landscape.

Thus by the middle of the eleventh century English landholders both great and small held rights and property in the towns, and the wealthiest among them did so as a matter of course. These men granted, purchased, leased or stole urban tenements, and they developed them. Their interests in towns provided them with market outlets for the surpluses raised on their estates, and they produced cash. But landholders were not just offloading grain and wool in towns or getting their hands on important, basic commodities such as ironwork, salt or pottery there: they were also buying lovely or tasty things. It was these purchased luxuries that came to serve as the new status-markers of the age, and they signalled high status as obviously and effectively as weapon-burials once had.

NEW-STYLE CONSUMPTION

Everywhere we look in the decades on either side of the millennium, we see well-to-do landholders spending their resources in particular and visible ways. They were spurred on in this period to display and consume by both optimism and anxiety: optimism because of the growing opportunities for them to buy more comfortable lives; anxiety because of the fear that less distinguished people might do the same. This pair of emotions is perfectly reflected in two typical late tenth- and early eleventh-century kinds of texts: those on estate management and those which carefully articulated the attributes required of members of various ranks of society. When read together, they suggested ways that lords could improve their own abilities to consume and, at the same time, keep others in their places. Not only were landholders in this period embracing high-end consumption, but status consumption was both broadening and accelerating, as the things necessary for genteel life were first acquired and flaunted by members of the greatest families in the land, and then pursued by larger numbers of more middling landholders. There are four particularly visible sites of conspicuous consumption in the later tenth and eleventh centuries – the dinner table, the clothed body, thegnly compounds and pious benefactions. In order to see how the new status symbols operated, we shall look at each of these in turn. But we also want to examine things like high-status food and clothing because they allow us to uncover something of the lived experience of well-to-do people in this period, something that our more traditional textual sources rarely allow us to do.

Nothing reveals the life of landholders in the tenth and eleventh centuries better than the food they consumed. Food serves as an extremely effective social marker because whole classes of comestibles were increasingly available to those with cash, workers and leisure, but only to them. Eating was also an activity in which conspicuous display and generosity intersected: great men's high living and hospitality allowed them to demonstrate their elevated social positions both to the friends with whom they dined and to their own peasants, who often, in this period, lived nearby, and would have been envious witnesses to their conspicuous eating practices.

From the animal bones found on the period's high-status sites, we know quite a lot both about what landholding families ate, and how their diet differed from that of their social inferiors. The most important difference was that well-to-do landholders, unlike the people who ploughed their fields, ate what they hunted. Red deer and roe deer were enthusiastically pursued and eaten on many thegnly establishments, but the bones of these animals are almost never excavated from low-status rural sites. Part of venison's charm may have been that deer hunting was such an extravagantly inefficient way of putting food on the table, a time-consuming diversion that required not only leisure, but the setting aside of scarce woodland resources to ensure a good supply of game. Thegns who wished to feast on venison also needed hunting-dogs. Archaeologists sometimes find small bells on the period's high-status sites, which may well have hung from these animals' collars; similar bells can be seen on the dogs embroidered onto the Bayeux Tapestry. Even thegns with only a few hides of land employed dog-keepers if they could, which suggests that modest landholders did whatever it took to hunt, because this activity was a defining pastime of high-status people. One very modest thegn, for example, who makes an appearance in an eleventh-century saint's life, had his hunting-dogs cared for by a deaf-mute; others, so we learn from a tract on estate management, made each of their free but low-status workers feed and care for one of their hounds.

Landowners in the period also enjoyed falconry. The bones of stunning arrays of game birds have been recovered from the sites of many thegns' residences. Remains of more than a dozen different species of wildfowl, for example, were found in the rubbish generated by a wealthy household living at Portchester, in Hampshire. Especially large numbers of curlew were discovered there. These birds are the classic prey of trained raptors. Wild birds also take centre stage in contemporary descriptions of dining. Each week between Michaelmas and Lent, for example, a pampered community of priests living at Waltham Holy Cross, in Essex, dined on blackbirds, plovers, partridges and pheasants.

Leisure time, the joys of the chase and roasted plovers were pleasures reserved for high-status people, and they would have been outside the experience of ploughmen, who no longer feasted with their lords the way cowherds had done in Cædmon's day. Still, grand dinner- and hunting-parties were hardly eleventh-century innovations: great men had long used food and the sports related to its pursuit to accentuate social differences. The high-status household living at Flixborough, in Lincolnshire, in the eighth century had controlled a large, tribute-producing territory, and, although some of the food and dining equipment found there – like porpoises and glass drinking cups – had been bought or traded for, much of what its members dined on had been either caught in the hunt or given over by subordinates as tribute. They hunted and feasted on roe deer and crane, grouse and wild ducks, but also ate large quantities of mature cattle, which had been rendered to them as tribute. In contrast, in the eleventh century not only were landholders eating venison and game birds, but fewer of their meals consisted of spent ploughing animals, like those that had once been eaten by the masters of Flixborough. The differences in the kind of beef served at the finest tables in the eighth century and the eleventh may, in part, be explained by different tastes and cooking practices, but it is also likely that the broad economic transformation we have examined provided later households – in spite of the fact that most lords now controlled much less land than eighth-century tribute-takers had – with an ability to procure younger, more tender animals for their dinners, because they now managed their holdings more directly, intensively and efficiently, and because of the development of the market. Indeed, there is evidence from the middle of the eleventh century onwards to suggest that a few people living on high-status sites may have been buying some of their meat from town butchers. The animal bones recovered from Flixborough's latest occupation date to the late tenth century, and they may shed some light on the chronology of changing elite diets. At this time the people in charge of Flixborough were probably eating quantities of mature beef because the transformations brought about by urbanization, agricultural intensification and an increasingly monetized economy had yet to take hold in this corner of Lincolnshire. Had mid-eleventh-century rubbish been found at Flixborough, we may well have seen younger animals making an appearance at its master's table.

Marine species, in particular porpoise and herring, were another important component of the high-status diet in the eleventh century, and they required considerable resources to procure. It is not surprising that porpoise was sought out by wealthy landholders, given that it had been considered a luxury food as early as the eighth century, and that it was still deemed a delicacy in the thirteenth. Herring, though, which was the cheapest fish by far in the later Middle Ages, is a surprise. The herring industry was becoming organized from about the year 1000, yet herring fishermen, herring renders and herring bones are closely associated in the eleventh century with the most powerful men and institutions of the realm – prominent courtiers, powerful thegns and the most important monks and bishops – and these men received thousands, sometimes tens of thousands of herring each year from their fishing fleets. Herring, it seems, was special food, served only at the finest tables.

Well-to-do landholders were also eating freshwater fish. Hundreds of manors had fisheries by the time of the Domesday survey, and they were valuable manorial appurtenances. Like the thousands of mills and churches cropping up in the period, they must have been built by thegns for their own benefit. Fish stews, that is, artificial storage ponds, used as 'living larders', although rare until the twelfth and thirteenth centuries, were being built by lords before the Norman Conquest, presumably so that they might stock their own tables. Like marine fish, freshwater fish required relatively large investments from lords if they wished to ensure the provisioning of their households. Monks seem to have been especially eager to make such investment, because of the Benedictine Rule's proscriptions of meat eating. But we should not mistake monks' eating of fish as a class-neutral dietary practice. Monks could have adopted the beloved eleventh-century saint St Wulfstan's preferred diet of leeks, boiled cabbage and bread as a way of adhering to monastic dietary proscriptions, or, indeed, they could have eaten like the men and women who laboured on their estates; but they continued, with their fish dinners, to eat like the noblemen most of them were. Conversely, noble families probably came to eat more fish during this period because they wanted to eat like monks, at least during the major fasts of the Christian calendar. Behind fish on the table lay considerable outlays of capital for those who caught fish with their own fleets, raised them in their own stews and fisheries or bought them with money. Such a monasticizing dietary practice, then, was not only conspicuously pious, but also expensive, and thus an excellent way of demonstrating high status.

The landowning elite was not only eating better cuts of meat and an ever expanding group of animals: its members, in the eleventh century, were eating more elegant dishes in a more elegant manner. Sauces, spices, white bread, a choice of dishes at every meal, cooks, even serving boys were all part of English high-status dining by the eve of the Norman Conquest, and what all these things represent is not just food, but cuisine, a development that anthropologists often take as a sign of growing social stratification. We can also hear the grumblings of peasants in eleventh-century saints' lives as they complained about their lords' eating practices: they were scandalized that thegns reclined as they dined while peasants sweated in their fields; and annoyed that thegns could be found gorging themselves while petitioning workers stood waiting for their attention. It may have been the quantity of food, as much as the quality, that irked the peasants. Certainly Normans after the Conquest were impressed by the number of meals eaten by great men before 1066. Others were in awe of the size of English portions: when a Norman knight, held captive after the Conquest by the rebel Hereweard the Wake, was finally released, all he could talk about was the vast quantities of food his captors ate!

At the same time as particular foods and dining habits were coming to be associated with genteel life, some townsmen were also coming to have the wherewithal to buy themselves more dignified dinners. It seems that fish, for example, could be bought in towns for cash in the eleventh century, and that the fishing industry was beginning to commercialize. Indeed, the fisherman appearing in Ælfric's *Colloquy* tells us that he could have sold many more fish than he was able to catch each day, which suggests that people who were not rich enough to keep their own fishing fleets or build their own fisheries or stews were eagerly buying fish on the market. Indeed, townsmen settled around the not very elegant neighbourhood of Flaxengate, in Lincoln, began in the eleventh century to eat more fish, and they were consuming game birds, too, although they were eating ducks rather than the more impressive swans and grey herons consumed by the very rich. Although the wealthiest Lincolnshire craftsmen and traders may not have been able to put crane on the table, they were eating some wild birds and fish, and, thus, beginning to eat like thegns. A few people feasting in towns, however, did manage to eat as extravagantly as the greatest households in the realm. The remains of one excavated Thetford dinner, for example, include peacock; and some people in the cosmopolitan London neighbourhood near the site of the Roman amphitheatre, which we examined in Chapter 9, were dining on venison, crane and herring. Given the urban location of this latter site, diners could not have been catching these animals themselves, but must have been purchasing them in the city's food markets. The ability of London, Lincoln and Thetford townsmen alike to dine like their social betters may have caused a certain amount of unhappiness among thegns. Indeed, there are hints in this period of attempts to restrict the consumption of particular kinds of food to people of the highest rank. An eleventh-century description of the renders given over to the proprietor of an estate at Tidenham, in Gloucestershire, suggests as much with its insistence that 'every rare fish which is of value – sturgeon or porpoise, herring or sea fish' belonged to the lord, as if the eating of these exotic creatures was the preserve of the privileged few.

One of the things that made game and fish such effective vehicles for displaying status was that they were limited to those who had time on their hands to catch them, rights to the labour of others to haul them or a mountain of pennies with which to purchase them, and this restricted their consumption to a tiny minority. Certainly neither slaves nor free farmers would ever have the means of procuring such delicacies for their own tables. But other kinds of food, besides meat and fish, could also be bought with money. Around the turn of the millennium, the king singled out Rouennais merchants trading in London, and who were dealing not only in porpoises but in wine, for special privileges, doubtless because he wanted to ensure the supply of these items for his own table. Other lords would also have been pursuing food on the market, in particular wheat for bread and wine for their tables. The attraction of these items of food and drink was not simply that they were delicious, but that they were special, and rather than being manor-grown, and rather than being what local ploughmen or swineherds ate, they were purchased with silver, and this made them prized.

Special clothing, like food, was also extravagantly consumed in the later tenth and eleventh centuries, and, like food, its pursuit by landholders allows us interesting glimpses into their lives. So elaborate was some landholders' dress by the turn of the millennium that churchmen actually began to preach against it. One sermonizer, for example, felt it necessary to exhort his listeners that 'we must be adorned with good and proper deeds, not with gold and lavish silk clothing, if we wish to be at the right hand of the Lord Saviour Christ'. The same man also asked his audience two rhetorical questions and then gave them an unsettling answer: 'Where will [a dead man's] frivolous garments be? Where will the ornaments and expensive attire be with which he once clothed his body? . . . Where you once saw luxury textiles embellished with gold, you now see a bit of dust and the remnants of worms.' Homiletic fulminations did little, however, to dampen wealthy laypeople's enthusiasm for finery. English manuscript illustrations of the period allow us to see something of what the critics saw. They show great men dressed in short tunics with flared skirts, edged around their cuffs, collars and hems with broad bands of fancy textiles, probably patterned silks. The elaborate borders on these clothes seem to have been stitched onto garments fashioned from linen or wool, something that would have minimized the use of expensive trim and maximized its effects. But bordered garments were rich men's attire, and the peasants depicted labouring in the period's illustrated calendars never wear them.

The most precious fabrics used in tenth- and eleventh-century clothing were the silks produced in Byzantium. The most spectacular of these were made in imperial workshops for the Byzantine emperor himself. As a result of their limited and highly regulated production, the only people who had access to these breathtakingly beautiful textiles were the beneficiaries of imperial largesse. Few English people, including even the king, were in a position to receive diplomatic gifts from the Byzantine emperor. It seems likely, therefore, that the finest silks in England would have been those acquired by English kings who had themselves received them as hand-me-downs from popes or German emperors, who were relatively frequent beneficiaries of Constantinople's gifts.

Although special silks woven in imperial ateliers would have rarely been seen on the backs of Englishmen, more pedestrian pieces were widely available by the time of the Norman Conquest; indeed, almost a quarter of all textiles recovered from the excavation of 16-22 Coppergate, in York, are silk. This lesser-quality silk was ubiquitous, in part because by the tenth century the production of medium- and low-grade Byzantine silk was many times greater than it had been a century earlier, and the manufacturing and sale of these lower-quality fabrics were not controlled by the Byzantine state. As a result, by *c.* 1000 it was easy for English pilgrims travelling to Rome and the Holy Land to purchase silk. But English people, by this time, could also buy silk from merchants within England itself. The long-distance trader in Ælfric's *Colloquy* is portrayed as supplying the wealthy with 'purple cloth and silks, precious jewels and gold, [and] unusual clothes ...'. Silk, moreover, has been excavated in London, Lincoln and York, so it was clearly available in the kingdom's major international trading centres. Merchants were even hawking silk in less important towns. Indeed, the monks of Ely managed to procure an embroidered silk chasuble from a Thetford town-dweller. And, interestingly, textile finds from York suggest that bolts of lower-quality silk were being brought into the kingdom and then tailored into articles of clothing by local craftsmen. So it is likely that many thegnly families may have bought their best outfits in towns for cash.

Acquisition of the most spectacular textiles and clothing, as we have seen, would have been limited to those who received diplomatic gifts. But from the mid-tenth century the ability to get hold of luxury textiles was trickling down the social hierarchy. The most elaborate secular clothing was apparently first adopted by the king in the mid-tenth century, as he attempted to follow fashions current at the German and Byzantine courts. But by the mid-eleventh century some of these ostensibly royal fashions had been co-opted by powerful courtiers. Long silk robes, first adopted by King Edgar the Peaceable, were also being worn by earls on the eve of the Norman Conquest. But it was not just the earls who were dressing in this manner. A Northumbrian thegn travelling in Rome was mistaken by Italian bandits for an earl because of the splendour of his attire. And, although the very top strata of society doubtless continued to be the only people who could get their hands on all-silk robes, many townswomen, if the textile evidence from Dublin is anything to go by, were wearing silk scarves and using silk thread when they hemmed garments or made fancy braids. Silk ribbons and bags have been found in York, London, Lincoln and Winchester, and they were probably ubiquitous there.

In the late tenth and eleventh centuries gold-embroidered clothes were also being worn by a variety of prosperous people. They had probably been rare in the tenth century. A thick gold trim was dramatically painted onto Edgar the Peaceable's cloak in an illustrated land grant made to a monastery at Winchester in 966, and, indeed, when Ely Abbey inventoried its valuable textiles, it recorded that the silk cloak King Edgar had given that community was so thickly embroidered with precious-metal thread that it looked like a chain-mail hauberk. Archaeologists, too, have uncovered small amounts of gold braid and gold-thread embroidery from ninth- and tenth-century secular garments. In the eleventh century, though, the number of examples increases dramatically. In part, this is probably because gold debased with copper and silver, as well as silver gilt itself, was beginning to be used to make gold thread. This made it much less expensive and must have put it, for the first time, within the reach of prosperous thegns. All of this suggests that there was a growing market for exotic threads and textiles as well as luxury clothing, and that across the tenth and eleventh centuries there was an ever-widening circle of people who could afford them.

The wearing of elaborate clothing, like fish eating, was a practice shared by laypeople and churchmen alike. We have, for example, the annual clothing allotments for two groups of well-heeled, eleventh-century ecclesiastics, the canons of Waltham Holy Cross and the monks of Glastonbury Abbey. The Waltham priests were each given the staggeringly generous clothing allowance of 480 pennies per annum, that is, nearly 700 grams of silver. A text from Glastonbury Abbey from the same century is more specific about what clothes monks at that institution were to receive each year. Each, so we are told, was to have 'two cowls, two frocks, two shirts of a cloth woven from wool and flax, two pairs of breeches, four pairs of stockings and a new pelisse . . . shoes for the daytime and in winter for the night and two bed covers. And they should also have ten pairs of slippers . . .' The emphasis here was on high-quality cloth rather than fancy silk. Nonetheless, the clothes that monks at Glastonbury were wearing were far from peasants' rags.

Besides fancy clothing, people of substance would have had chests full of tapestries, bedclothes and bed-hangings, and many gave their favourite ecclesiastical institutions elaborately embellished copes, altar cloths and drapery. Earl Harold presented his foundation at Waltham Holy Cross with great quantities of stunning vestments and hangings. The most ostentatious of his textile gifts was a chasuble ornamented with 26 marks' worth of gold. Vestments like this are all-pervasive in the written sources of the eleventh century. They often comprised the most valuable objects within religious communities' treasuries, and they were regularly given in the eleventh century by the open-handed rich.

Thus, landholders were putting expensive food on their tables, exotic clothing on their backs and beautiful textiles in the treasuries of their favourite churches. They were also spending freely during this period on their domestic quarters, which brings us back to the period's new, small-scale estates, which, as we have already seen, were coming to be a standard feature of England's new, more nucleated settlements. Of course, it was possible to distinguish high-status sites from farming hamlets even in the seventh and eighth centuries, but these earlier sites were quite different from those that came to be built in the tenth and especially eleventh centuries. By the early eleventh century we have a clear articulation of what a thegn's country estate should look like, because a text known as *Gebyncðo* describes the kinds of structures it should include: a kitchen, a church, a bell-cote and a gated enclosure surrounding the lord's domestic court. A more detailed set of buildings can be inferred from another eleventh-century text, which includes several long lists of implements that a reeve would need in order to manage his lord's estate. The tools in the text are organized by the buildings in which they were stored. It first describes those tools kept in the kitchen, then in the dairy, the granary, the buttery, the pantry, the cattle barn and finally in the bake-house and brew-house. Thus, we can begin to see the constellation of structures that were coming to make up a thegnly *setl*, buildings that would continue to be ubiquitous on seigneurial farmsteads even in the late twelfth century.

Establishments like these have been discovered in places as far apart as Hampshire, Oxfordshire, Northamptonshire and Lincolnshire, and their excavation allows us to see how such sites developed across the ninth, tenth and eleventh centuries. Archaeologists working at Faccombe Netherton, in Hampshire, for example, uncovered two fairly substantial buildings that constituted a lord's hall, which were constructed some time between 850 and 925. These first buildings, however, were not enclosed by a boundary ditch the way later buildings on the site were. Sometime c. 940–980 the original buildings were replaced with six new structures and a church. The compound was rebuilt yet again in the very late tenth or early eleventh century. At this point, the proprietor erected a large manorial hall alongside a private chamber, doubtless the living quarters of the landholder and his family. A separate kitchen was also built, as well as a latrine. These buildings, along with the church and churchyard and about half a hectare of land, were enclosed by a substantial earthen bank and ditch, not to make the site defensible, but rather to make it a more impressive feature in the landscape. The combination of a more public hall, where people could be entertained and manorial courts could be held, and the detached private quarters, built as living accommodation for the lord's family, is found not only at Faccombe Netherton, but at Goltho, in Lincolnshire, Cheddar, in Somerset, and Raunds Furnells and West Cotton, in Northamptonshire; and this 'hall-and-chamber' arrangement continued to be found on manorial sites well into the twelfth and thirteenth centuries.

Not only was a whole constellation of buildings now expected at a thegn's *setl*, but when landowners planned such sites it looks as if they organized their suites of buildings in ways that they deemed particularly dignified. In some places, the different structures were situated around central courtyards. Perhaps more commonly, though, thegns built them in 'long ranges', that is, as single rows of buildings. This long range of buildings would have presented a striking façade to people approaching them from afar. Many of these compounds, moreover, had fancy entryways leading through their impressively banked and ditched enclosures, which were themselves further enhanced by posts and auxiliary ditches. Some of these sites even had gatehouses – all in all, an imposing group of buildings and enclosures.

The upgrading of thegnly residences was going on at breakneck pace in the eleventh century, and they represent massive expenditures of labour and resources. But the lives lived in these compounds were not simply about the exploitation of peasant labour or the squandering of prime timber and stone: they were about cash. One of the clear differences between ninth- and early tenth-century thegnly establishments and those of the late tenth and eleventh centuries is that the latter appear to have been much less involved in craft activity – jewellery-making, potting, bone-working and the like – and yet later sites are often littered with manufactured goods. These things were now purchased with money from urban craftsmen or merchants.

Many thegnly establishments, as we have seen at Faccombe Netherton, included churches among their many buildings, and in the eleventh century churches were becoming a common component of lordly compounds, especially in the east and north of England. It is unsurprising, therefore, to find that churches were also becoming focuses of conspicuous consumption. Thegns who were founding or refurbishing proprietary churches were following in the footsteps of the most powerful lords in England, who were not only putting up churches on their own estates to provide pastoral services for rural workers, but also endowing more rarefied communities of secular priests; and they sometimes provided them with funds for huge churches. The transepts of the church at Stow in Lincolnshire, for example, which date to the eleventh century and were built with the aid of the earl of Mercia and his wife, are 26 metres in length, and the arches of the central crossing are 10 metres tall. This must have made it one of the largest buildings in the British Isles. It is a testament both to the earl's piety and to his family's wealth. The size of the church built by Harold Godwineson at Waltham Holy Cross is more difficult to establish. Fortunately, we know more about the ways Harold chose to embellish its interior. He provided the church's main altar with three large Gospel books bound in gold covers and five other books bound in covers decorated with silver gilt. The large number of beautiful books at Waltham hints that Harold was a connoisseur of deluxe manuscripts, an expensive pastime, since elaborately illustrated and bound codices could be considerably more expensive than working estates. They were an important and conspicuous form of pious giving in the eleventh century, not just for Harold and other earls, but for thegns, who sometimes gave them to favoured religious communities. Harold lavished large amounts of precious-metal artwork upon Waltham as well – vessels for the altar (silver for regular services, and gold for feast days), gold and silver reliquaries and candlesticks, all of which, so a chronicle written at the house assures us, 'the work of wonderfully skilled craftsmen'. Among the precious objects Harold gave are two of an interesting and apparently popular class of religious benefaction among the very rich during this period. The first was a collection of gold and silver crosses. We have evidence from half a dozen religious communities for groups of life-sized crosses cluttering the interiors of churches by the eleventh century. We know that they were not only given by Harold, but by a number of other earls and prelates. Another extraordinary gift bestowed by Harold upon Waltham was a collection of life-size statues of the twelve apostles and two lions, all covered in gold. The life-size crosses and figures of saints were apparently one of the great forms of benefaction in the eleventh century, and they are described in churches across England during this period. They must have been wildly expensive, and their commissioning seems to have been de rigueur for habitués of the royal court. Such objects were rare before the mid-tenth century and seem to constitute a novel form of conspicuous giving.

The amount of precious-metal artwork at Waltham alone, in the form of figures, crosses, church plate and vestments, was staggering. We know that when William the Conqueror's son, William Rufus, stripped Waltham of many of its treasures, they were valued at over £6,000, an extraordinary sum. When pondering the resources squandered on Waltham, one is reminded of Sutton Hoo's Mound One burial. In a very real sense, Waltham Holy Cross was the eleventh century's moral equivalent of the earlier burial, and Harold poured resources into the church, in which he planned to be buried, for many of the same status-enhancing reasons. We know less about what thegns were giving churches, but we sometimes catch sight of them commissioning crosses, books and luxury vestments for their favourite religious establishments; so, many seem to have been giving as conspicuously and expensively as they could.

In the end, there are dozens of examples of high-end aristocratic consumption new to this period. The tenth and eleventh centuries saw the fairly widespread adoption of window glass in secular buildings, and the eleventh century saw the advent of meticulously made shoes embellished with bands of silk-thread embroidery and the importation of figs and peacocks. All these bear witness to the new and remarkable ability of members of the landed classes to extract wealth from the countryside in order to trade it for money, and then to deploy it on a kind of life impossible to imagine four or five generations earlier or a few rungs down the social ladder.

LIVING IT UP IN WALES

Since no towns developed in tenth- and eleventh-century Wales, perhaps Welsh monasteries – made prosperous because of the monks' careful management of their resources and a growing insistence that their dependants give them more of their labour and crops – were becoming important consumers of Wales' growing surpluses and its new, specialist crops, both of which are hinted at by the pollen evidence. Some monastic sites were acquiring monumental stone sculptures during this period as well, so either monastic communities themselves or their most generous patrons must have had considerable resources to be able to pay for them. These same communities may have been consuming other, less archaeologically visible surpluses as well – barrels of honey, well-woven habits, lavish entertainment and the like. Seasonal trading sites were also developing in Wales during the tenth and eleventh centuries, and they are evidence that some people in Wales had surpluses to trade and others had craft-goods to hawk. Archaeologists have investigated one such site at Llanbedrgoch, in Anglesey. In the eighth and ninth centuries the site had probably served as the centre of an important Welsh lord's estate, and towards the end of this period it came to be defended by an impressive circuit of stone walls, either because the site's proprietor wanted to live in a site that looked like an Irish ring fort, or because he felt the need to protect the settlement from raiders. By the late ninth or early tenth century considerable amounts of Scandinavian-influenced, Irish Sea-style metalwork were present at Llanbedrgoch, some made by craftsmen working on the site, and some probably brought by traders beaching their boats at the nearby bay. Scandinavian-style weights and hack-silver have also been recovered at Llanbedrgoch, so the people here were trading within the vast, coinless economic zone of the viking world. It is impossible to know whether the site at Llanbedrgoch was headed by a Welsh king or lord or by some Scandinavian interloper; but whatever the case, craftsmen working within the settlement made a variety of metalwork objects, such as fashionable ring pins and belt buckles, which must have tempted the local Welsh families with surpluses to exchange. At the same time, the people living and working on the site, whether Welsh or Norse, needed food and raw materials, which farmers in Anglesey may have given them in return for manufactured goods.

There is also interesting evidence recovered from a Cornish farming hamlet at Mawgan Porth, which may give some clues to what was happening on low-status rural sites in Wales. Although Cornwall had been absorbed by this time into the kingdom of the English, its people continued to have more in common with the Welsh than the English. From its excavation, we know that the people of Mawgan Porth spent most of their time engaged in subsistence farming and shellfish gathering, but a silver penny, struck not far away in Lydford, in Devonshire, was found on the site, so the people here must have sold at least a penny's worth of surplus now and then. The stone they made their querns from had been quarried 20 or 30 kilometres away, so some kind of trade stood behind its acquisition. And among considerable amounts of handmade, local pottery a single fancy pitcher was found on the site, and it, too, must have been purchased or traded for. The money economy, exchange and agricultural practices that created surpluses, therefore, were all impinging on the people of Mawgan Porth, perhaps at the insistence of a lord.

Food also conferred status in Wales during this period, and feasting was an important high-status activity. Monastic households in Wales had cooks, butchers, bakers and officers who oversaw their kitchens and bakeries, and this may have been the case in important secular households as well. There are also hints that Welsh lords, like their English counterparts, ate special food. According to his eleventh-century Welsh *vita*, when St Cadog was a boy he rejected the more sumptuous foods of his father's household in favour of bread and water. We also hear about loaves of wheat bread in the *vita*, although Cadog, because of his piety, sometimes ate oats. At the same time, it is clear that fishing rights and weirs were developed, exchanged and fought over by Welsh landlords. Hawking rights, like fishing rights, were given in charters, and we can catch glimpses of aristocratic retinues hawking, and kings catching ducks with the help of their favourite birds of prey. And the people living at the royal crannóg at Llangorse, whom we studied in some detail in Chapter 8, judging from the remains of the hunting-dogs and red deer found there, to say nothing of roe deer and wild boar, must have hunted and feasted. They were also catching geese, ducks and the occasional swan. Welsh noblemen evidently participated in some of the same social practices related to food as the neighbouring English, and Welsh and English lords shared similar tastes for venison, freshwater fish and game birds. Nonetheless, there is no indication that Welsh elites ate much food that had not been raised by their dependants or which they had not caught themselves. Certainly, there is no sign that they ate herring, and we know that they typically drank mead or beer, rather than imported wine.

In Wales, high-status dress is also more difficult to track than it is in England. Welsh kings and noblemen did wear luxury apparel, as the astonishing fragment of textile recovered from Llangorse crannóg attests. There are a few textual witnesses to elaborate costumes. According to his eleventh-century biographer, St Cadog, in spite of his royal birth, despised 'the pomp of royal apparel', and he wore meaner clothes when he went to church. Perhaps he was objecting to the same cloth-of-gold clothes that one king stripped off and gave Cadog when seeking his forgiveness. One man, moreover, speaking in a tenth-century text, admonishes his servants not only to mind his gold and silver while he is away, but to 'stay behind and guard my clothes', so clearly exotic apparel was both present in Wales and highly prized. Indeed, in one transaction, a queen's cloak, a piece of red linen and a fancy outfit were traded for land. The giving of purple mantles, moreover, is a common poetic trope in the Welsh poetry of this period. Fine clothing, then, was available in Wales, but it is impossible to determine how far its wearing had descended down the social ladder. It seems unlikely, given Wales' dearth of towns, that local landowners were buying silk-embellished clothes locally, the way they sometimes were in England. Very fancy articles of clothing appear to have been objects of patronage and gift exchange as much as they operated as a form of social display.

Although Welsh churches, like English ones, were given Gospel books, bell shrines, crosiers and reliquaries by their lay patrons, church treasuries were much barer in Wales than in England. There are few descriptions of gold and silver ecclesiastical paraphernalia in the period: St David's shrine, stolen in the late eleventh century, for example, was gold and silver, and St Cadog's similarly purloined reliquary was gilded. Nonetheless, the only Welsh ecclesiastical metalwork to survive from the ninth, tenth and eleventh centuries is a group of seven handbells made from iron and copper alloy. At the same time, there are less than a dozen extant early medieval Welsh manuscripts, and only three are illuminated. Contemporary notices of lay donations of precious objects are also few and far between. Still, not only did craftsmen in Wales in the eleventh century produce a number of monumental stone crosses, but someone had to commission and pay for them. Welsh kings and lesser lords were also enthusiastic participants in an expensive and conspicuously pious practice: they employed what wealth they had on extravagant almsgiving. The eleventh-century *Life of Cadog* pointedly describes the saint's feeding of hundreds of paupers and widows at Easter, and the common refrain in the obituaries written in the famous Welsh chronicle *Brut y Tywysogyon*, is the high praise for dead men who had been 'generous towards the poor and merciful towards pilgrims and orphans and widows'. Gerald of Wales, describing Welsh open-handedness in the twelfth century, tells us that 'In Wales no one begs ... for the Welsh generosity and hospitality are the greatest of all virtues. They very much enjoy welcoming others to their homes. When you travel there is no question of your asking for accommodation or of their offering it: you just march into a house and hand over your weapons to the person in charge.' Largesse to the poor, to pilgrims and to strangers was costly in the early Middle Ages, and its practice was as conspicuous as the bestowing of precious objects. Given the constraints imposed on Welsh lords by Wales' lack of towns and its dearth of silver, it is little surprise that almsgiving was such a dominant feature of Welsh high-status piety.

MONEY, STATUS AND POLITICS

By the eleventh century, it is clear that extraordinary wealth was being wrung from the English countryside and put into the purses of the kingdom's landholding elites. According to Domesday Book, the God-winesons were holding land which was, in one way or another, producing about £8,400 per annum. This sum is perhaps better expressed not in pounds – a term of account in the eleventh century – but rather in the only coin of the realm, the silver penny: 2,016,000 pennies in all. Had the Godwinesons been able to collect all that was due to them in money in a single year, their two-million-and-some pennies would have added up to 2.75 tonnes of silver. Of course, large aristocratic households would have fed and clothed hundreds of people, and they would have eaten their way across scores of estates as they itinerated across the kingdom – but they would not have consumed the equivalent of 2 million pennies' worth each year. The family would also have had to expend vast sums on gifts and feasts to cultivate or maintain friendships, alliances and solidarities – but again, not 2 million pennies' worth. Family members, moreover, had been in possession of their outsized holdings for more than a generation, and so the surplus cash from their estates must have added up over the decades. Although no other family in the kingdom was anywhere near as rich, nonetheless, thegns who held estates valued on the order of £40 per annum would have had total incomes of almost 13 kilograms of silver each year; and if they were able to realize even a tenth of this in cash, they would have had for-tunes. Even a thegn with a single five-hide manor could have realized almost half a kilogram of silver in profit each year, which he could then use to purchase stone for a church, special shoes or herring.

As we have seen, behind some of the food, the textiles, the building and the pious gifts stood money-consumption. Not all these things, of course, would have been purchased, since gift-giving was still an impor-tant social activity, but some would, and this is a crucially important development, one with profound social implications. It seems that particular uses of money and a particular kind of engagement with the increasingly commercialized economy were now both prerequisite for genteel life and socially restricted. For most people living in eleventh-century England, money was less a means of exchange than a form of tribute. It was one commodity among many that every household needed to produce in order to meet its obligations, no matter how hum-ble or how mighty. Its rendering at a few well-defined moments each year was a requirement, like dues in-kind or labour services. At Eardis-land, in Herefordshire, for example, Domesday Book records that the reeve 'had the custom ... that when his lady came to the manor, he would present her with eighteen *ora* of pence [i.e. 360 pennies], so that she would be in good spirits'. Here, as elsewhere, pennies helped to structure social relations between individuals and their superiors, between tenants and their lords, between people and the state. The people farming at Eardisland must have acquired the pennies they needed each year for their lady by selling surplus or hiring out their own labour. For the vast majority living in England, the value of the penny, though, was too high to buy much of anything at all, and they would have only used pennies for special occasions like this. In 1130, for example, we know that a penny could buy a quarter of a sheep's carcass, so in the year 1000 it was not a coin that low-status workers could readily spend. Ordinary people must have depended on barter when they traded, and limited their money transactions to annual or semi-annual interactions with their lords, their priests or with local royal officials. But for thegns and earls – and indeed for townsmen – money was coming to act as a common medium for commodity exchange. By the eleventh century landlords had piles of pennies from their peasants, their mills, their churches, their urban tenants, their cash crops and their renters, and they seem to have been using them to buy all the necessary accoutrements of genteel life. It seems that one of the great gulfs between those who prospered in the eleventh century and just about everyone else was created by the ability of the former to participate in the commercializing economy regularly, as consumers.

The exchange of high-status goods did in some cases remain embedded in social relations, but more and more the physical manifestations of gentility could be pursued in the marketplace; and, increasingly, access to the period's new status-symbols was a function of how much coin one had, rather than whom one knew. As one churchman wrote, in some despair, 'he who has pennies or silver can get anything he pleases.' The same churchman had harsh words for wealthy, but ignoble swells: 'It is one thing for someone to be rich if his ancestors have bequeathed possessions to him; it is another if someone becomes rich through greed. The latter's greed is accursed before God.' Still, because the commercial use of money was socially restricted, it allowed the period's elite to maintain a fairly close monopoly on high-status goods. This monopoly must have been imperfect, given a contemporary churchman's snide remark that a *ceorl* with a gold-plated sword but without five hides of land was still a *ceorl*. Reeves and merchants, prosperous freemen and sheep farmers were 'thriving to thegnhood' in the period because they, too, had access to cash. But for the vast majority who laboured in the fields, the barriers erected by this two-tiered use of money must have been nearly insurmountable. By the end of our period there was a gaping chasm between low-status tenants on village crofts, who used the odd penny to pay rents or taxes, and the proprietors of thegnly halls, who spent scores of coins in their pursuit of the good life.

The story of the tenth and eleventh centuries, as told in the last three chapters, is the story of extraordinary and unprecedented prosperity, especially for those 4,000 or 5,000 households lucky enough to be the proprietors of England's increasingly ubiquitous small-scale estates, which were slowly but inexorably coming to transform not only the landscape but social structures and cultural practices as well. Thus, the history of this period is very much about increasing wealth and about the ways in which landowners, living in an era of steady population growth and agricultural innovation, were coming to monopolize much of the period's increasing production for themselves. The ability of these people, in the end, to harness the kingdom's increasingly productive landscape and labour practices for their own well-being, and the ways in which they pioneered novel forms of elite life, were at the expense of their agricultural dependants, who, during these same years, were coming to find more and more of the fruits of their labour disappearing into the coffers of their landlords. Well-to-do landholders, though, were not the only people thriving in these years. The state, too, grew during this period, because English kings and their helpers were able to revolutionize the way coins were made, reminted and controlled, and they were increasingly skilled at collecting ever larger amounts of tolls and taxes. This story of an expanding economy, a prosperous middling elite, an increasing surplus, booming towns and a strengthening state is crucially important, because this world was going to have a very long run. Indeed, the myriad prosperous towns, the thousands of country gentlemen, the open fields and common ploughing regimes, the large dependent peasantry, the impressive reach of the English state, even the locations and names of many present-day English villages, not only developed in this period, but would continue to sit at the heart of culture, society and the economy for the rest of the Middle Ages.

The story told in the last three chapters is clearly inscribed both in the English landscape and in the material remains recovered from the period. Still, this tale is sometimes lost in our more traditional, text-driven histories. This is because high politics consumed men writing in the late tenth and eleventh centuries, and naturally modern historians have come to share the concerns of our writers of texts. In these kinds of histories, high politics drive the narrative, because politics, rather than peasants or porpoises, were on the minds of the contemporaries who chronicled the period. And because the decades after the death of Edgar the Peaceable in 975 were a period of intense political competition and disruption, the broad and crucially important cultural and economic shifts that we have spent so much of our time examining, and which so clearly affected everyone living in the period – be they king or slave, high-status woman or low-status worker – are often pushed aside in order to make room for a narrative of trying times.

What were the troubles complicating the lives of politically prominent people in this period? One problem that dogged the English political classes from the death of Edgar the Peaceable all the way to the Norman Conquest was the royal succession. In 975 factions coalesced around each of the dead King Edgar's two young sons, and one of the boys, Edward the Martyr, was murdered, an inauspicious beginning to the reign of the surviving son, Æthelred 'the Unready' (r. 978–1013 and 1014–16). Æthelred's reign was an unhappy one, in large part because, soon after his accession, Swein Forkbeard, son and heir to and deposer of the Danish king Harold Bluetooth, with the help of a fearsome group of professional viking warriors known as the *Jomsvikings*, began raiding England. By the mid-990s the English state was having to raise huge amounts of tax – known as the danegeld – in order to bribe the vikings to go home. Swein, unfortunately for King Æthelred's reputation, eventually ceased his annual shakedown operations and moved, instead, to a sustained campaign designed to make Swein himself king of England. Indeed, in 1013 Swein won the kingdom for himself. Although Swein died within a year of seizing the English throne, his son Cnut (r. 1016–35), after a short, bloody hiatus, became king. Many people in England must have found the idea of a viking king distasteful, especially the men who were fast friends and firm allies of the old dynasty. Some of their discomfort was justified, because Cnut's accession was marked by an ugly purge, during which a number of members of England's leading families were mutilated or assassinated. As the dust settled, a handful of new families rose to prominence, some English, some Danish, including the Sussex thegn Earl Godwine and his brood of half-English, half-Danish children. In spite of its bloody beginnings, Cnut's reign was a long and successful one; but upon his death there was yet another succession dispute; and each of his two sons, Harold and Harthacnut, had a short reign and died without heirs. Æthelred the Unready's son Edward the Confessor (r. 1042–66), long exiled in Normandy, was brought back home to rule, but as the years of his reign wore on it became clear that he, too, would die childless, knowledge that created instability throughout the second half of his reign. Unsurprisingly, upon his death, in January 1066, there was yet another disputed succession. Earl Godwine's son, Earl Harold, became king, but William, duke of Normandy, and Harold Hardrada, king of Norway, each believed himself to have a better claim, and within ten months both Harolds lay dead, and the duke of Normandy was king of England.

This brief political narrative makes the century before the Norman Conquest seem like little more than an unhappy period of political murder, invasion and court intrigue; and no doubt many thegns, during these years, worried in their halls as the news of defeats and political murders, and as the demands for ever more tax money to pay off the Danes, came to their attention. Yet life went on, and these men, their families and their peasants carried on transforming the landscape, building halls and mills, eating porpoise and selling their surpluses in England's hundred or so rapidly expanding towns. Although the dismaying politics and high taxes of the period must have sometimes discouraged landholders, for most of these years individual opportunity and economic optimism were in the air. Indeed, somewhat ironically, the mountains of coins recovered from Scandinavia, which date to Æthelred's and Cnut's reigns, are themselves proof of the jaw-dropping prosperity of England in these years. The demands for silver levied on landholders, collected by the king and then handed over to vikings in 991, 994, 1002, 1007, 1012 and 1018 were enormous. A new tax, called the *heregeld*, which was assessed on the hide, was collected as well in many years between 1012 and 1051, and its proceeds were used to hire mercenary fleets, mostly from Scandinavia, which in turn were used to prop up the Anglo-Danish regime and enforce the payment of taxes within England itself. So these levies and taxes funnelled huge amounts of English silver into Scandinavia. Exact sums are difficult to determine. Chroniclers living through this period report very large sums of money paid to the Danes. In 1018 alone they were purportedly given £82,500 – that is, more than 19 million silver pennies. Such figures may well be bitter exaggerations, but, whatever the real sums, payments must have been immense, given that thousands of coins bearing King Æthelred's and King Cnut's names have been recovered from Scandinavian hoards.

In spite of the large size of these gelds, highly technical arguments made by numismatists persuasively make the case that more English coins ended up crossing the North Sea in this period than can be accounted for by danegeld and *heregeld* alone, and that a substantial fraction of the tens of millions of English pennies exported during this period found their way to Scandinavia because of trade. Indeed, many more coins from the mints of London and the towns in the eastern Danelaw have been found in Scandinavia than should be the case if these pennies came as danegeld or *heregeld* alone, because the burdens for these taxes were borne equally by landholders across the kingdom, and not only by people living in the hinterlands of England's eastern towns. This in turn suggests that trade between Scandinavian entrepôts and York, Lincoln and London was brisk. And however these coins ended up in Scandinavia, in order for the English to be able to send millions of pennies across the North Sea, year in and year out, they needed access to a large and continuous supply of silver. The silver they needed was not being mined in Britain itself, so it had to come from elsewhere. It is most likely that England's huge and seemingly endless stock of silver was being replenished by the coins shipped in by Continental traders, particularly German ones, because German mines, during just this period, were disgorging vast amounts of precious metal. All of this suggests that production, surplus and trade were taking place at an extraordinary rate during these years, in spite of political disputes and marauding viking armies. English landholders were not only selling enough surpluses to pay their taxes, but conspicuously spending in the way their elevated social status now demanded.

So, with or without political disruptions, England in the century before the Norman Conquest was a place where towns and money really mattered, and where careful management of estates, rather than deft swordplay, was the best guarantee of the good life. Indeed, the implementation of new farming practices, the developing of urban property and the collecting of ever more rents, services and fees from peasants were *the* means by which wealthy people were able, not only to flaunt and exaggerate their social position, but to solidify and improve it. Landholders, during this period, fought when they had to, and hundreds of them died in Æthelred the Unready's and Harold Godwineson's wars. But the truth of the matter is that these men were no match for the professional household troops that kings of this period were coming to prefer, and who were available, like so many of the period's desirable commodities, for cash. Thegns were successful because they were gentlemen farmers, not because they were warrior aristocrats. At the same time, the efficiency with which English landholders were able to wring silver out of their estates, and the efficiency, in turn, with which the state was able to wring silver out of landholders, made the English formidable adversaries for their neighbours. In the following centuries, England's wealth would come to fuel its territorial ambitions across the whole of the British Isles and Ireland.

12

Clerics, Monks and the Laity:
The Ninth, Tenth and
Eleventh Centuries

By the early ninth century, communities of professional religious across Britain were in crisis, and the rich monastic life detailed by Bede was disappearing. These troubles are reflected materially in a variety of ways, the most obvious of which is the cataclysmic decline in book production, in terms of both the number of manuscripts made and the quality of the Latin, the handwriting and the decoration used to embellish them. Deluxe metalwork and high-quality stone sculpture, also produced in quantity by craftsmen labouring at eighth-century monasteries in England, Scotland and Wales, were now disappearing as well. More alarming still is the fact that copies of texts known to have been in Northumbrian libraries in Bede's day had vanished from England by the tenth century. By this time many of the minsters once staffed by a combination of monks, nuns and clerics (the latter are also called secular priests) were now the exclusive preserves of clerics alone.

It is clear that the vikings stand behind some of monasticism's troubles and transformations. In areas where their raids were relentless and their settlement most disruptive, ecclesiastical institutions sometimes collapsed. This seems to have been the case with the Pictish monastery at Portmahomack, on the Tarbat peninsula in north-east Scotland. After some terrible incident, when part of the monastery and its workshops were burned and its elegantly carved stone monuments were smashed, production of monumental stone sculptures and vellum ceased, and the centuries-old cemetery went out of use. Although people continued to live at the site, after this event it ceased to serve as home to a major religious community, and became, rather, a secular farmstead. Given the fact that the monastery lay, in the ninth century, on the frontline of Norse expansion (never mind the remains of three men found there who had sustained terrible injuries from sword blows), vikings are the most likely explanation for the demise of this once vibrant monastery.

Bishoprics that had been around for centuries also ceased to function across the east and north of Britain at more or less the same time as the Norse began settling in. Even those communities which were able to reconstitute themselves after short hiatuses were unable to sustain the kind of intellectual, liturgical and communal life practised in Bede's day. Some kind of religious community, for example, was re-established at Repton after the site's terrible year of viking misrule. Once a double minster led by an abbess, it was now, in its later incarnation, a mother church staffed by a small community of secular priests, whose main mission was to provide pastoral care to people living in the area. The community was still apparently in possession of its most precious relics, but there is no sign that its ancient library or school survived. St Cuthbert's old community at Lindisfarne also transformed itself dramatically during this period. Not only did its members flee their long-time home at Lindisfarne with Cuthbert's body, but they 'wandered' for more than a century before settling down at Durham. During their travels they evolved into a group which, although still headed by a bishop, was made up mostly of married clerics who lived in their own houses and whose legitimacy and considerable power grew out of their position as hereditary protectors and controllers of Cuthbert's wonder-working remains.

Viking depredations, however, were not monasticism's sole source of woe. St Cuthbert's community is a case in point. It settled for a time at Chester-le-Street, in County Durham, on land provided by a viking king of York, a fact which should remind us that it was possible for religious communities not only to survive in Scandinavian-controlled parts of Britain, but sometimes even to thrive. It is also clear that pagan interlopers were not the only people inflicting harm on religious communities; noble English Christians were also annexing monasteries or their property during this period, and, although groups of priests both in the Danelaw and in 'English' England continued to live beside their ancient churches and lead some form of organized religious life, generally by c. 900 the bulk of their ancient endowments had fallen under lay control. As a result, they had fewer resources and much less independence. There are indications that Wales' ancient monasteries were also losing parts of their endowments at exactly the same time, and that congregations of priests were taking over what had, in earlier centuries, been better endowed communities of monks. By the eleventh century we find that the ancient and wealthy Welsh monastery at Llandough – in the seventh century a large community of monks ruled by an abbot – had evolved into a small, not very important, not very well-endowed community of secular priests. In short, the decline in artistic production with which we began this chapter and which we can chart across the whole of Britain can, in part, be explained by the fact that religious communities' endowments from the eighth century onwards were in precipitous decline, and because of this they no longer had the resources to fund metal, stone and vellum masterpieces or to feed scholars and contemplatives.

Christian kings and lords during this period sometimes moved against the powers and possessions of religious communities because of greed; but they also did so out of political expediency. East Anglia's bishop and his household, for example, disappeared sometime in the late ninth century, during the Norse incursions; the bishopric was not, however, reconstituted. Instead, the whole region seems to have been placed under the jurisdiction of the bishop of London, and it is hard not to suspect that the West Saxon kings, to whom London's bishops were beholden, had encouraged this, as they strove to establish control over ecclesiastical institutions which just a few years earlier had been allied to other English dynasties, now – fortunately for the kings of Wessex – defunct. It would have been against West Saxon interests, as well, if East Anglia's new Danish masters could appoint and control bishops; better, apparently, for the tens of thousands of Christians in the area to have no resident bishop at all.

During these same years large blocks of land once controlled by early monasteries could be found in the hands of the West Saxon kings, but, when the viking threat abated, rather than restoring lost endowments they gave them out as rewards to loyal lay followers, or they kept the lands themselves, integrating them into their own royal holdings. This apparently happened at Cheddar, in Somerset. Cheddar, by the early tenth century, was the site of both an ancient, and once richly endowed, minster and a royal hall. By this time the church and the king's hall, which both sat inside the monastic enclosure, were only about 250 metres apart. The minster had the choicer location, so it probably predates the king's hall, which seems to have been shoehorned into the site. Within a couple of generations of the king building his hall within

Cheddar's monastic enclosure the royal estate seems to have further encroached upon the minster, because by the time of the Domesday survey in 1086, the king controlled almost everything that had once belonged to the minster, save the church itself and a couple of hides of land. There is considerable evidence to suggest that this was a typical scenario in the years in which West Saxon kings rationalized their estates and consolidated their power.

So at the dawn of the tenth century there were still many religious communities in Britain, but their landed endowments were much diminished, and they were no longer staffed by contemplatives and scholars. Life at these places probably included some kind of shared liturgy, but the work of their members was now primarily pastoral, and their churches first and foremost acted as the heads of mother parishes. Men living in such communities, unlike ecclesiastical inmates in earlier centuries, tended not to hold all their churches' property in common, but rather to divide up their various dues and renders among themselves. And, unlike earlier communities, many priests no longer lived as celibates, but had come to believe, as one eleventh-century churchman wrote, that 'it is right that a priest love a decent woman as a bedmate.' Wives and children meant that some communities of priests no longer dined in communal refectories or slept in communal dormitories. So although religious communities carried on in the generations before, during and after the viking crisis, their economic underpinnings had diminished, and their habits of living had come to mirror more closely those found in secular households.

REFORMED MONASTICISM AND ANCIENT RELIGIOUS COMMUNITIES

In England, in the middle of the tenth century, there was both a major revival of monastic life and a revolutionary reimagining of how that life should be lived. A number of the West Saxon kings, including Alfred the Great, had embraced monastic reform, because they believed that 'good' monks pleased God, and God's favour in a time of war and reconquest was critical for their own success. There are hints that, as early as the 930s, King Athelstan knew and was impressed by monks trained at reformed Benedictine houses across the Channel; but it was really only with King Edgar the Peaceable that a new-style Benedictine ideology became *the* ideology of the West Saxon royal court and the driving force behind programmatic, centrally directed change in organized religious life. At the heart of the new monasticism lay the sixth-century Rule of St Benedict as it had come to be understood at the eighth- and ninth-century Frankish royal courts of Charlemagne and Louis the Pious, and as it came to be practised in monasteries across the Channel, especially in Ghent and at Fleury. The particular interpretation of the Rule adopted by England's tenth-century reformers was ideologically charged, and its adherents propounded the notion not only that Benedict's Rule provided a vastly superior guide for those wishing to live a religious life, but that the reformers' own reading of the Rule was its only reading. Furthermore, the reform's staunchest proponents believed that the religious communities that ordered their lives, not on the Benedictine Rule, but rather on traditions that had evolved in England over the past three centuries, were lax, even sinful.

Pragmatic considerations also lay behind King Edgar's enthusiasm for reform. As West Saxon kings brought the Danelaw, bit by bit, back under English control, they came to appreciate that well-endowed religious houses beholden to their dynasty, and which practised similar styles of religious life and were ruled by abbots and bishops committed to a unified kingdom, could help stitch together what had only a few generations earlier been a collection of sometimes hostile kingdoms. Such houses under their loyal heads would act as West Saxon bulwarks in recently conquered territory. They would also institute a variety of uniformities across England – in religious practice and architecture, as well as in the meeting of local assemblies and law courts which were held near them, and which were becoming crucial to the smooth functioning of the state. Reformed abbots and bishops could also aid kings in the running of the state, and they would be in the position not only to advise their royal masters, but to help them raise armies and build strongholds, not just in Wessex, but in Mercia, Kent and East Anglia as well.

The group of monks who persuaded West Saxon kings that the new-style monasticism was both part of God's plan and in the kingdom's best interest worked hard for decades to implement their vision. The movement was led, for the most part, by men who were both monks and bishops. One of the most important of the first generation of reformers was St Dunstan (*c.* 909–88), archbishop of Canterbury, and a man deeply affected by the changes in monastic life and culture taking place across the Channel. He was a monk committed to the refounding and reforming of individual monastic communities, in hopes of bringing about a spiritual renewal in England. Two fellow monk-bishops, St Oswald († 992), bishop of Worcester and archbishop of York, and St Æthelwold († 984), bishop of Winchester, moulded Dunstan's vision into a more homogeneous Benedictine project, and they helped to articulate a vision of a highly standardized style of Benedictine monasticism that they dreamed of instituting in all the minsters of England.

Members of the reform party defended their ideas about monasticism by invoking a dramatically reimagined past. Unsurprisingly, they disparaged the immediate past, as revolutionaries often do, and they portrayed the Church of the ninth and early tenth centuries as having been hijacked by degenerate clerics. At the same time, they fashioned an understanding, based on Bede's *Ecclesiastical History*, of the seventh and eighth centuries as a Benedictine 'Golden Age'. When Bede used the word *monasterium*, they understood him to be describing a Benedictine monastery, although, of course, he was doing no such thing. But because of their (mis)understanding, it became the reformers' ambition to return minsters to their 'original', Benedictine purity. The reformers, who insisted that monasteries across the length and breadth of the newly unified kingdom of England should live under the Benedictine Rule, were also helping to further the centralizing ambitions of the king, who grew to be the Benedictine monks' most fervent supporter. This particular vision of monasticism, with the approval of King Edgar, was described and codified, perhaps as early as the mid-960s, by, among others, Saints Dunstan and Æthelwold, in a document known as the *Regularis Concordia*, or 'The Monastic Agreement', tenth-century England's elaboration of St Benedict's Rule. The reform that followed in the wake of this document led to the refoundation of a number of minsters as strict Benedictine communities.

The reformers had King Edgar's full support, and together the king and the monks worked hard to found or refound an impressive number of strictly Benedictine houses, many of which accrued massive endowments, thanks to the generosity of the king and of his greatest allies. We find Bishop Æthelwold, for example, refounding the minster at Ely, expelling a community of secular clergy he found there and replacing them with monks living under the Benedictine Rule. In the years that followed, both the king and the local nobility heaped gifts of land and money on Ely Abbey, rapidly transforming it into one of the most important landholding institutions in eastern England and one of the wealthiest monasteries in the kingdom. Because so many of England's key reformers were bishops, they not only refounded ancient minsters, but transformed many episcopal households into communities of monks as well, a distinctive feature of the English Church in the tenth and eleventh centuries. Most of the monastic communities founded or reconstituted during this period were in southern or eastern England, and, although different varieties of religious life would grow fashionable in the eleventh century, the bulk of these tenth-century foundations remained among the wealthiest and most influential religious communities in the kingdom for centuries.

In the decades that followed the deaths of Dunstan, Oswald and Æthelwold a new generation of reformers came to the fore, the most famous of whom were the monks Wulfstan, archbishop of York († 1023), and Ælfric, abbot of Eynsham († c. 1010). These men, living in a kingdom filled with reformed houses, turned their attention to the laity, and they worked hard to provide them with well-trained priests and decent pastoral care. At the same time they moved aggressively to shape the moral lives of laypeople. As all these generations of reformers strove to remake monasticism, they came to underscore the differences between laypeople and monks. We find them mandating that monks be celibate, that they busy themselves with complex daily liturgies and renounce privately held property. Many of the reform party's jaundiced opinions about both the laity and clerics centred on anxieties surrounding sexuality, and reforming monks in the period noisily agitated not only for clerical celibacy, but for restricted lay sexuality as well. In this way, English reformers were quite different from reformers elsewhere in the British Isles. The Céli Dé, reformers originating in eighth-century Ireland, but whose movement had spread into Scotland and probably Wales as well, called for individual monks to lead lives of extreme asceticism and self-denial, never goals of England's Benedictine reformers. The Céli Dé, though, sometimes worked beside married clerics, who probably concerned themselves with the cure of lay souls. At the same time as the ascetic life proposed by the Céli Dé was spreading, both Ireland and Wales continued to have powerful clerical dynasties, and many of the highest Church offices in both places were passed from father to son. For obvious reasons, members of these dynasties found neither the Céli

Dé's nor the English Benedictine reformers' arguments concerning clerical celibacy particularly persuasive.

In any event, ecclesiastical reformers and reform movements, although not always in agreement, could be found working and agitating across Britain during this period. Nonetheless, English reformers were distinct from reformers elsewhere in Britain. Most bishops, by the time of the millennium, were reform-backing monks, and they and the abbots who led England's newly reformed houses had come to be some of the most influential of the English kings' advisers. From King Edgar's reign onwards, it was these men who helped wrap English kingship in sacred trappings, and they developed and officiated over solemn ceremonies in which they anointed kings like priests. High-placed Benedictine reformers in England were not only reshaping monasticism; they were reformulating political discourse and secular politics as well.

But what effect did reformers and their royal partners have on religious communities themselves and on the people already living in them? And how can we characterize the spiritual lives of laypeople living through this period? To begin to answer these questions, we need to leave kings and famous monk-reformers behind, and turn our attention, instead, to a single minster community, Eynsham, in Oxfordshire, because it is here that archaeologists have uncovered compelling evidence that elucidates the impact of the English Benedictine reform on one of the ancient religious communities they transformed.

A handful of early texts suggest that a minster had been established at Eynsham sometime in the late seventh or early eighth century, a period when enthusiastic laymen founded a whole series of religious communities in the Upper Thames Valley. If, as has been argued, two stray charters describe a couple of its early gifts, it was originally a double-minster, ruled by an abbess. Like neighbouring churches, Eynsham's may have contained the body of a special saint; and like other early houses, it looks as if the community, at the time of its foundation, sat at the heart of a 300-hide endowment. Its early endowment would then have been a large, tribute-producing territory, and the minster was probably one of the wealthiest in England.

Excavations at Eynsham support the notion that the early minster was wealthy. The best evidence for this is the extravagant food eaten by its inmates. Although fasts and restrictive diets were hallmarks of early medieval religious life, feasting and drinking nonetheless remained important social activities. According to the penitential ascribed to Archbishop Theodore, a monk made ill from drink had to perform forty days of penance, unless, that is, he had become drunk 'for gladness at Christmas or Easter or for any festival of a saint'. Because dozens of saints' days were celebrated each year, there must have been many a justified hangover. Such occasions would have included elaborate feasting as well as drinking. A series of large outdoor hearths were uncovered during Eynsham's excavation, and this may be where copious amounts of food were cooked for members of the community. Near the hearths, archaeologists discovered a rubbish pit filled with the remains of exotic fare. Not only were fine cuts of meat on the menu, but so too were spoils of the hunt, including roe deer, partridge and crane. Ray and oysters were recovered from the same pit, and these salt-water delicacies had been transported more than 150 kilometres. The people living at Eynsham also ate grapes and figs, rarities in this period. Together, these finds, along with a small quantity of Ipswich ware, and three eighth-century coins and a fourth dated to the ninth century, point to the community's participation in trans-regional trade. The fact that Eynsham lay near a fording point on the River Thames would have facilitated exchange of its surpluses for luxury goods. So Eynsham, like monasteries across Britain in this period, was a high-status community engaged in trade, and its inmates sometimes consumed the same delicacies as their cousins living in secular households.

By the early ninth century, though, lay enthusiasm for monasticism had begun to fade, and the community faced more difficult times. By this period, the king had come to control the minster and its lands, and he had given away the bulk of its extensive early endowment either to more favoured religious houses or to his most important lay followers. Still, Eynsham continued as an ecclesiastical community, no longer one with nuns, but still staffed by priests; and it must have served as the mother church of a *parochia*, for all intents and purposes a large proto-parish. Despite the diminution of its endowment, Eynsham's priests still had access to resources, and sometime in the late ninth or the early tenth century they embarked on an ambitious building programme. Evidence for this is found in the excavated remains of a large domestic structure. This was a relatively grand plank-built building with fancy plastered interior walls. It sat in the middle of a fenced enclosure, one of a number on the site, each probably with a similar timber hall and bounded yard, and all radiating out from Eynsham's church. These are probably the remains of the living accommodation used by Eynsham's minster-priests, each with his own roomy hall and enclosure, and each perhaps with his own wife and children. It is the size of the excavated hall which suggests that these were family accommodation. The hall offered around 88 square metres of floor space, spacious in comparison with those little halls at seventh-century Hartlepool we examined earlier, which averaged only 9.5 square metres. Similar living arrangements have been uncovered at other ecclesiastical sites, including North Elmham, in Norfolk, where the bishop of East Anglia and his *familia* lived until the later ninth century in individual halls set in private enclosures. The remains of a sparrowhawk dating to this period were also recovered at Eynsham, the bird of choice among those with enough leisure time to engage in falconry, despite the fact that ecclesiastical reformers and synods periodically admonished priests not to indulge in hawking. So, although Eynsham's landed endowment diminished, members of the community continued to live in comfort. Archaeologists have also recovered a very fine buckle dating to the late ninth century, decorated with a Maltese cross and made somewhere within the Irish Sea zone: perhaps it once adorned the belt of one of Eynsham's comfortably accommodated priests, whose status, economic well-being and livelihood would have depended on whatever landed endowment Eynsham had left, and on the business of pastoral care, which allowed priests to collect both traditional dues and newer tithes, shared out among the community's members.

Although no texts survive to detail the work of Eynsham's priests before the community's Benedictine refoundation, it is likely that they said Mass and sang the Office every day, and that they performed the occasional baptism and burial. They would have blessed marriages, visited the sick, overseen confession and supervised penance as well. Some of these activities generated income, which, by this period, was often split between a minster's priests. Eynsham's financial arrangements may have mirrored those found at the minster at Twynham, in Hampshire. The pastoral duties and income of Twynham minster's dean and twenty-four priests were described in some detail around the turn of the twelfth century:

All offerings at the morrow mass and the high mass went to Godric [the dean] as his own property, without anyone else taking a share, whereas they divided equally between themselves the other offerings, made before and after masses and up to vespers ... Furthermore, a canon celebrating a mass took all the offerings at that mass, between taking off his cope and putting it on again, without anyone else sharing them.

Eynsham's priests, given their separate domestic quarters, were probably similarly supported from the income generated by individual chapels controlled by the community, but divided and bundled into something like later prebends which would have been used to support each of the community's priests. Most must have been sufficiently well off to live in some style, if the plastered hall, hawks and fancy belt buckle are anything to go by. Again, there is supporting evidence for such individual income, not from Eynsham, but from a minster at Lambourn, in Berkshire. At Lambourn we have an eleventh-century accounting of the dues collected by a single (and perhaps the only) priest at that minster over the course of a year. The king's land at Lambourn, in whose manor the minster lay, rendered tithes to the priest of grain and young animals, cheese, firewood and pennies, and the priest was allowed to pasture an impressive collection of his own livestock – oxen, cows, bulls, pigs and horses – on the king's estate. Tenants on the estate, both free farmers and thegns, also had to pay up, giving the priest tithes in the form of cereal crops and cash. Although tenth-century reformers thought the holding of private property by professional religious a modern innovation, this was not the case: an early eighth-century monk at the monastery of Wenlock, in Shropshire, had owned half a slave girl, and even Bede himself had a little cache of valuables, which he gave away on his deathbed. The kind of bounty described in the Lambourn text was certainly enough for a priest, his wife and their children to live as well as any free farmer or lesser thegn, and it would have been an income worth inheriting. Indeed, at yet another minster, this one at Plympton, in Devonshire, priest-sons can be seen regularly succeeding priest-fathers:

Ælfheah was one of the priests of Plympton. He had in his prebend and his commons the chapel of St Andrew of 'Sutton' and its parish, and the chapel was hitherto of timber. Ælfheah's son was Sladda the priest, and he held the said church of Plympton, and after him Ælfnoth the priest, and after Ælfnoth his son Dunprust ...

The job of priest as well as the possession of particular prebends and customary dues were more or less hereditary at Plympton, and this would have been a common state of affairs during this period at minsters across Britain, including Eynsham.

The arrangements found at Eynsham – which had been organized not only to provide pastoral care to laypeople, but to support more or less hereditary, property-holding clerics and their families – were loathed by the Benedictine reformers, so it is no surprise that these practices were swept away in 1005, when the community was refounded as a Benedictine abbey. By this time the community and what was left of its landed estates had fallen into the hands of a nobleman called Æthelmær the Fat, a cultured man and one deeply involved in reformed monasticism. As a matter of fact, Æthelmær had already refounded another monastery. He also planned to retire to Eynsham, 'busying himself', so he says in Eynsham's foundation charter, 'in a father's role and living communally among them'. He quadrupled the minster's landholdings, but mandated that its clergy should be replaced by monks and that its abbot should be Ælfric of Eynsham, a monk, friend of the family, leading intellectual and Benedictine reformer.

The changes which ensued are witnessed by the Eynsham excavation. At the time of its refoundation, those in charge knocked down the private domestic structures, and they radically reconfigured the community's accommodation to facilitate the particular version of communal living mandated by the Rule of St Benedict. Most of the new buildings on the site, and not just the church, were now constructed from stone, and the domestic structures were built for communal living: masons, for example, put up a common refectory and kitchen as well as a cloister for the monks. In this, Eynsham was following the architectural programme articulated by the *Regularis Concordia*. There must have been a new communal dormitory there as well, but it has not been found. Along with this complex of very Benedictine structures, archaeologists uncovered another new building, probably timber, which served as a centre for craft production. Eynsham, after its refoundation, would have participated in the renaissance of religious art and texts unleashed by monastic reform. A roughed-out, half-carved walrus-ivory saint was found here, as was a fragment of an elephant-ivory panel, delicately carved with arches and saints. Both may have been made to adorn book covers or reliquaries. So relic-shrines and books were probably produced at the monastery, hardly surprising now that it was headed by one of the most renowned intellectuals in the kingdom.

What happened to Eynsham's old minster-priests, though, is something of a mystery. Highly partisan texts written by members of the reformed party often speak of the driving out of these men and their wives when monasteries were refounded, but there are hints that many remained in a number of reconstituted communities, continuing to work as pastoral-care specialists. There is clear evidence for this at the reformed community at Worcester, and this may well have happened at Eynsham, too. Ælfric himself, while abbot of Eynsham, wrote a monastic customary, a detailed description of the annual cycle of liturgy for which the monks were responsible. The text begins with a preface explaining that 'because you have recently been ordained to the monastic habit at Æthelmær's request, you need to be instructed in monastic customs'. So perhaps the members of the old community who were unmarried had been remade into monks.

The changes found at Eynsham were dramatic and may echo similar revolutions taking place at other reformed minsters. But only around three dozen out of what must have been hundreds of minsters were refounded as Benedictine houses in the second half of the tenth and the early eleventh centuries; so the vast majority simply carried on with their fellowships of secular priests and continued to operate as the centres of mother parishes and as the overseers of pastoral care. Indeed, the rights of ancient, unreformed minster-communities were protected throughout the tenth and eleventh centuries by English kings, who frequently legislated to enforce their ancient fiscal dues. The most important of these were church-scot, an annual render of grain given over in the autumn on the feast of St Martin; and soul-scot, a fee for burial by a priest or in a consecrated cemetery. These dues were probably paid to particular minster-priests whose job it was to minister to the needs of particular rural communities. Certainly, we know that soul-scot was sometimes paid 'at the open grave', which sounds like a payment made to the priest himself, rather than his community. That soul-scot was lucrative is suggested by the complaints of a Church reformer, writing in the period: 'Some priests are glad when men die and they flock to the corpse like greedy ravens when they see a carcass . . .' In the tenth century, much more burdensome tithe obligations were added to the older dues of church-scot and soul-scot, and their payment was mandated by royal legislation. Still, minster-priests and their communities, long stripped of the bulk of their endowments, were now beginning to lose some of their ecclesiastical income, too, especially because lay lords were putting up their own churches and cemeteries. When this happened, as it often did now, especially in eastern England, minsters lost tithes and burial fees.

Nonetheless, many minsters managed to hold on to their rights of burial. Indeed, laws issued around the turn of the millennium mandated that a dead man's survivors were to pay soul-scot to the minster in whose *parochia* he had died, even if the body had been buried at another church. The minster at Bampton, in Oxfordshire, is notable for the success with which it maintained its burial rights, and its activities allow us to see how this was done. Burial in the cemetery next to the minster was probably reserved for the community's own clergy, for wealthy lay patrons and perhaps for some of the better-off farmers living in the area, whose families, at some expense, would have carted the corpses of loved ones to Bampton's church for burial. As a matter of fact, well-to-do laypeople in the late tenth and the eleventh centuries were coming to organize themselves into gilds centred on their local minsters for just this purpose. We know quite a lot about the one operating at Abbotsbury, in Dorset, in the second quarter of the eleventh century. Members of the Abbotsbury gild not only ate, drank and prayed together at special times throughout the year, but also brought the bodies of their dead fellows to the minster-church at Abbotsbury for burial. Gilds at Abbotsbury and elsewhere also paid for commemorative Masses for their dead members, and we can see that thegns in the eleventh century could now provide themselves with the same commemorative and intercessory services that had once been the preserve of the royal and noble patrons of early minsters. It would not be surprising if landholders living around Bampton belonged to a similar dining-and-burial club.

Bampton's cemetery has not been excavated, but a portion of another cemetery laid out next to the important early minster-church at Wing, in Buckinghamshire, has. The graves dug here in the ninth, tenth and eleventh centuries were found in neat rows aligned with the church, each one with its corpse lying supine in the grave. In the excavated part of the cemetery – a zone its excavators posit was reserved for lay patrons – it looks as if existing graves were sometimes reopened within a few years of the initial burial and another body inserted, usually a member of the opposite sex or a person belonging to a different generation, and it may be that spouses or parents and children who died at different dates were buried in the same graves so that they might wait for the Second Coming together. Some of the bodies had also been buried in wooden coffins, a mark of some status. Wing's church had a famous early relic-crypt, so its possession of holy relics may account for the cemetery's popularity among locally prominent families.

Not everyone, however, was prosperous enough to bury their dead at a minster cemetery or belong to a minster gild. Poorer people, even those living within a minster's *parochia*, would have had neither the money to pay for such exalted carryings and buryings, nor enough social cachet to warrant a minster funeral. This seems to be the case at Bampton. There was, however, a cemetery at Chimney, 5 kilometres down the road, which people like these probably used instead. Given this cemetery's proximity to Bampton, and the fact that it lay within the bounds of Bampton's pre-Conquest estate, the site was probably controlled by the minster, which was vigilant in maintaining its monopoly over burial. Indeed, we know that the church at Bampton was still insisting on it in the fourteenth century. Although archaeologists have only excavated part of the cemetery at Chimney, it is clear from radiocarbon dating that the people buried there died in the tenth and eleventh centuries. Many of the cemetery's later graves cut into earlier ones, a classic sign of a heavily used, multi-generation cemetery, and it has been estimated that it contains the remains of somewhere between 1,500 and 2,000 bodies. We have textual evidence for yet another cemetery that catered specially to the low-status dead. Better-off people living near the minster at Christchurch, in Hampshire, were expected to bring their dead to the minster itself for burial, but low-status peasants and slaves, 'who were so poor that they did not have enough resources from which they could be carried to Christchurch', were buried at Boldre, where the minster controlled an auxiliary chapel and burial ground. Whatever the social status of the dead, local minsters wanted control over burial and burial fees, and they fought hard to maintain them. The most lurid example of this is found in a legal case heard by King William soon after the Norman Conquest. When the priests of the minster at Steyning, in Sussex, learned that the tenants of a local nobleman were being buried at the cemetery next to the lord's manorial church, they sued him and won. The lord was ordered to exhume all the bodies and cart them to the church at Steyning for reburial.

THE PROLIFERATION OF CHURCHES

At the same time that King Edgar was actively supporting and refounding Benedictine monasteries – each practising religious life in the ways laid out by the *Regularis Concordia*, each under the special protection of the king or his wife and each participating in a daily cycle of prayers designed to bring divine favour to the West Saxon dynasty – other benefactors, from England's most powerful families, were also founding or refounding Benedictine houses. Some, like Æthelmær the Fat and a nobleman called Athelwine 'Friend of God', threw their support behind the reform efforts and gave significant portions of their own patrimonies to Benedictine establishments. In much the same way, in the seventh and eighth centuries kings and their most important supporters shared an enthusiasm for similar kinds of religious foundations. A king's lay followers mimicked their lord's pattern of endowments, both in the seventh century and in the tenth, to flatter and support their king, but they also emulated their king's pious benefactions to prove to others that they, too, were great men.

By the eleventh century, although kings and their courtiers still supported Benedictine communities, many were increasingly drawn to newer forms of communal religious life, not so much the kind found at traditional minsters, but a more properly regular style of living, under one of the rules for canons that had come out of the Carolingian and post-Carolingian Church. The community of this kind that we know most about is the one we have already encountered at Waltham Holy Cross, in Essex, an establishment lavishly supported by Earl Harold Godwineson. An important Scandinavian follower of King Cnut had originally built the church at Waltham to house a miraculous cross found on one of his estates, and he staffed the place with a priest and a few clerics. When Harold refounded the community a generation later, he modernized it, transforming it into a proper college of secular priests with a dean, a master and an apostolic twelve canons. This community would have had little in common with those old-fashioned minstercommunities we examined earlier. Rather, it took its inspiration from the reformed houses of canons thick on the ground across the Channel in the lands between the Rhine and the Maas rivers. Harold had come of age in England's royal household, which was staffed by a number of well-educated clerics who had trained in this region. He was also a widely travelled man and had visited many such communities during his times abroad. These communities were not simply models of clerical probity, following a way of life prescribed by some combination of the Rule for canons penned by the great eighth-century Carolingian reformer Chrodegang and a ninth-century work known as the *Rule of Aachen*; they were also vibrant centres of new learning, and places in which clerics could be trained for public service and secular administration. The utility of this learning would have appealed to a nobleman like Harold, who as earl of Wessex had burdensome administrative responsibilities. Indeed, one of the reasons behind Harold's refoundation at Waltham seems to have been his interest in creating a school to train priests who would be active in the world. After the refoundation, he appointed Adelard – a native of Liège and a physician who had studied at Utrecht – as master of his new school. One of the reasons Harold appointed Adelard was because he expected him to 'establish in the church at Waltham the rules, ordinances and customs, both ecclesiastical and secular, of the churches in which he, himself, had been educated'. Adelard's intellectual credentials were impeccable, but he had a son, so at least some of Waltham's priests were married.

Men like these, although living (at least in theory) more in the world than Benedictine monks did, nonetheless pursued a life of religion and spirituality *within* the world. The Rule probably used to regulate the lives of a group of priests at St Paul's cathedral in London, thoughtfully mused on the life of a secular priest: 'There are some who can wear a worldly habit, and yet not have a worldly mind ... Reflect on that when you cannot give up all those things which are of the world: do well what you have to do outside in the world, but let your zeal be within, impatient for the things that are eternal.' Harold's canons, whether married or not, ate in a common refectory, and their food allowances were lovingly detailed in a little twelfth-century chronicle written by a member of the community:

Each canon's portion was divided up each week as follows: from Saturday to Saturday, each day two loaves of the purest white bread, a third loaf not so white (these loaves when divided carefully being certainly sufficient for six persons at one meal). Six bowls of ale (these were quite sufficient for ten persons at one meal). Every ordinary day there were six dishes of food, each one of a different kind, but on feast days of primary importance each man had three pittances of food, two on feast days of secondary importance, and one on feast days of third rank of importance. There were the following additional allowances for each of the canons: from Michaelmas to the beginning of Lent a choice of twelve blackbirds, two plovers, two partridges or one pheasant. For the rest of the year they could have either geese or chickens. At the main festivals of the year, namely Christmas, Easter, Pentecost and the two feast days of the Holy Cross, each canon was allowed wine and mead. In addition to these allowances, payments of forty shillings were made to each canon for the provision of clothes ... Furthermore a sum of forty shillings by way of commons was granted to each canon from altar offerings and tithes.

Although some of these rations would have gone towards feeding the poor, the food provided to Waltham's priests tells us that this was a luxurious establishment, and the generosity of its table would not only have made life very pleasant here, but it would have reflected well on Waltham's great patron, Earl Harold.

Waltham has the feel of a private establishment, used for the moral improvement and edification of its founder and his household. Indeed, Harold had a hunting lodge nearby, and his common-law wife and their children often resided in the neighbourhood, so he must have been a regular visitor. When in residence, Harold doubtless took the opportunity to venerate the relics in his vast, personal collection which he kept in Waltham's church. We also know that the church could be locked, another sign of its status as a private place. We learn this by chance, because sometime in the eleventh century thieves tunnelled into Waltham's church in order to steal some of its treasures, and when they were caught the sole cleric in the robber band was branded on the face with the key of the church.

For the richest man in England, the founding and funding of such an extravagant establishment was not only possible, but necessary; and Harold's extraordinary benefactions would have signalled his matchless wealth, sophistication and social position to both allies and competitors. Even the king himself might have difficulty building and endowing a church so sumptuously. It is hard to believe that a sheep-farming West Country thegn with a single estate or a five-hide man in the Yorkshire Dales would have been refined enough to know he even wanted a poetry-writing schoolmaster, much less a school for administrators. Nonetheless thegns like these were also building churches during this period, and we can see them using their churches and priests as a means of both enhancing their social position and administering their estates. Some thegns, for example, who had their own churches, used their priests as reeves: we know this because the practice was roundly denounced by high-ranking ecclesiastics. We also know that when a middling thegn, who built a church in Hampshire just after the Norman Conquest, arranged for a member of a nearby minster-community to serve as the priest of his new church, he insisted that the priest come to Sunday dinner each week and that he serve as a one-man entourage when the thegn attended meetings of the local hundred court. A priest like this must have been seen as a cut above the rest of the rural population and not only deemed proper company for a thegn and his family, but proof of his household's elevated social status.

In spite of their much more limited resources and lack of courtly sophistication, hundreds of landholding families, particularly in eastern England, founded churches during the tenth and eleventh centuries, in part because they, too, wanted to monumentalize their piety and enhance their reputations. Ordinary thegns, much like Earl Harold himself, often built their churches close to their halls. Many probably did so so that they might attend religious services alongside their slaves and other dependent workers. The Mass, baptisms, funerals and other religious celebrations held in manorial churches constituted important moments for lords in whose churches they took place to remind peasants just who was boss. Indeed, the weekly ritual reminder of the social order must have been an increasingly important tool in the exercise of lordship, because legal thinkers were coming to see the possession of a church as one of a handful of things that was required of a thegn. The placement of many eleventh-century churches in relation to local manor houses also emphasized their role as instruments of lordship. Churches often lay just outside the manorial enclosures in which local lords' domestic quarters sat, adding to the architectural dignity of thegnly seats. Church-yards, however, were usually separate from the manorial enclosure itself, and this would have allowed peasants to enter the church without infringing upon their lords' private enclosures, probably something they were not allowed to do except by invitation.

There is some evidence to suggest that low-status people, both as good Christians and as manorial tenants, were coming to be obliged to attend a particular church. Many of the new churches' proprietors were doubtless interested in the revenues their churches could generate – a share of the tithes and, if they were able to establish cemeteries, soul-scot as well – and so they probably insisted that their rural workers attend their churches in the same way that they would have insisted that their peasants use their mills. So it is hardly surprising that thegns are sometimes described as owning churches in much the same way that we are told they owned mills. In mid-eleventh-century Kent, for example, a man named Blæcmann had his estate in the village of Blackmanstone, where he had a church known locally as 'Blæcmann's church'. Black-manstone, in short, was Blæcmann Ltd., and the church operated as just another part of Blæcmann's enterprise.

The development of the church at Raunds Furnells, in Northampton-shire, helps us to establish a chronology for the building and elabor-ation of such churches. A fine timber hall at Raunds, which served as the living quarters for the estate's thegnly proprietor, predates the church by a decade or two, and it is likely that hall-building came first on many estates, and was only followed a generation or two later by church-building. The proprietor of Raunds first built his church around 950. Its dimensions were a minute 4.5 by 3 metres, but, in spite of the fact that the building would have held no more than two dozen standing adults at any one time, it had some pretensions: not only was it built of stone, but it may have been plastered inside and out, and its doorjamb and windows were modestly embellished with carved decorations. The tiny church at Raunds was a status building, put up to enhance the reputa-tion of the village's leading family and to make the compound in which it lived more imposing. Around the turn of the millennium, Raunds' proprietor added a timber bell-cote and a chancel, transforming the church from a one- to a two-cell structure. Although the new addition provided no more room for villagers than the old church, it must have lent solemnity to the religious services held there, since the priest could now celebrate Mass in the new, roomy chancel. It was only after the church was transformed into a two-cell structure that people began burying in the churchyard at Raunds, and it seems that cemeteries, not just at Raunds, but in many other places, were added a generation or two after the initial building of a church. There was a special plot in the cemetery at Raunds for its leading family, and some of the graves within it were marked with elaborate and expensive stone markers. Thus, even in death, members of Raund's thegnly family could be distinguished from everyone else. The rows of low-status dead buried within the churchyard also remind us of the income Raunds' lord now collected from church dues and burial fees.

The church at Raunds, like most thegnly churches, embodied the worldly ambitions of its thegnly proprietor. Its construction on a ridge and its possession of a bell-cote meant that people travelling through the area could not only see the church from some distance; they could hear it as well, so the proprietor's exalted status was broadcast throughout the neighbourhood. Its church bell could also be used to organize workers, and help the thegn or his reeve discipline their labour. Similarly, the chancel extension, although it provided no more space for the congregants, added dignity to the services and would have impressed visiting thegns.

There are also hints, though, of deep devotion at Raunds. Both the permanence of stone churches like this and their ubiquity are evidence of their builders' religious enthusiasm, and suggest that church-building families were coming to subscribe to a notion of good lordship that required them to do what they could to help their dependants meet their religious obligations. Crosses were also a prominent feature within the cemetery at Raunds, marking the graves of the village's most important dead. Their use reflects the growing popularity of the cult of the cross in this period, and shows how pious laypeople, who were often admonished by churchmen to invoke the cross, actually did so. Practical charms of the period, which would have been familiar to the agricultural workers living at Raunds, and which they would have used with the aid of their priest, often invoked the cross. One prescribed the carving of a cross on a sick horse's forehead. Another called upon the cross after livestock had been rustled:

> One should say this when someone has stolen his cattle. Before he speaks any other words, say: 'Bethlehem is the name of the city in which Christ was born; it is famed throughout the world. So may this deed become famous among men, through the cross of Christ.' And then pray three times to the east and say, 'May the cross of Christ bring it back from the east.' And three times to the west and say, 'May the cross of Christ bring it back from the west.' And three times to the south and say, 'May the cross of

Christ bring it back from the south.' And three times to the north and say, 'The cross of Christ was hidden and is found.' The Jews hanged Christ, did to him the worst of deeds; they hid what they could not hide. So may this deed never be hidden, through the cross of Christ.

Thegns' churches and graveyards during their official consecrations were also sanctified in a ritual which appealed to the cross, and we know from excavation that the church at Raunds itself had been consecrated. Someone, moreover, had buried a baby under the chancel arch of the church, very near the altar. This was the only grave found within the church, and its placement must reflect the hopes of parents (doubtless members of the church's founding family) for the eternal salvation of their lost child.

By the eleventh century in many places in England a thegn's manor was coterminous with a village, and the church he built would have been where the whole settlement's population attended services. Still, hundreds of settlements had more than one thegnly family. In places like these, landholders sometimes banded together to build a church for the entire community. This is what happened at Clopton, in Suffolk, where four landholders built a church. At other places, though, each thegn in the village built a church for himself and his tenants, but for no one else. This is the case at Raunds, where two churches sat on opposite sides of the road that ran through the village, each one serving the population of a different manor. One would like to know more about what these two churches actually looked like, and when exactly they were built and improved in relation to one another. Were they sites of intense competition between Raunds' two leading families? When one thegn made improvements to his church, did the other?

A few free farmers also managed to build churches in the eleventh century. Some may have done this in emulation of their social betters, because the building of churches was something that people of means did, especially those hoping to 'thrive to thegnhood', that is, climb their way into thegnly status. Others, though, may have put up churches because there was no room for them and their families in places where lords had built churches only big enough to accommodate their own workers. And yet these local farmers may have wanted to worship and bury next to their cousins and neighbours who were more bound to a local lord than they were. Under such circumstances, freemen apparently sometimes built small, second churches next to thegn-built churches, which often shared the same churchyards. Some of these secondary churches, though, were built abutting older, grander minster-churches that were no longer large enough to accommodate the local population. Domesday Book's account of Thorney, in Suffolk, for example, probably describes just such a church. In 1086 there were two churches in the village. One had a carucate of land (the equivalent of a hide), a sizeable endowment for a village church and a sign that it was an ancient minster. But 9 hectares of this church's carucate 'belonged to a certain chapel which four brothers, freemen ... built on their own land next to the cemetery of the mother church. They lived in the parish of the mother church, [and built the second church] because [the mother church] could not take in the whole of the parish.' Domesday goes on to say that the mother church took half of the burial fees of this chapel. That churches by the middle of the eleventh century were too small for a whole village's population may have been increasingly common in a period of considerable population growth. It may also be that the phenomenon of more than one church in a settlement owes something to the rise of local identities, strengthened by the communal farming practices of open-field agriculture, and by the shared belief of people who lived in the same villages and spent at least part of each week or each season labouring together that they should worship and bury near one another. The four brothers in Thorney were not the only freemen in the eleventh century building churches. Domesday Book describes nine freemen elsewhere in Suffolk who came together to found yet another church.

Many of these second churches, sharing churchyards with older, better endowed churches, were dedicated to the Virgin Mary, and this may give us an insight into the particular religious devotions of farmers on the eve of the Norman Conquest. The Virgin was an especially suitable saint for the sheep-rearing families of East Anglia, where so many of the freemen-built churches can be found. She was fêted on six different days each year, but the most popular of her feasts was the Annunciation, celebrated on 25 March. The feast coincided with the height of lambing season and with the time when farmers moved their animals from winter pastures. Since Mary was the 'mother of the Lamb', she and the Annunciation were linked to some of the most important activities in the agricultural year, and this may explain why her cult was so popular among East Anglia's freemen church-builders.

The men who served as priests in local churches like these were different from both Benedictine monks and the kinds of men who worked out of minster-churches. Church reformers assumed, in their writings, not only that minster-priests would be literate, but that they would have respectable little libraries to draw upon for their ministries: 'a psalter and a book with the epistles, an evangeliary and a missal, songbooks and a manual, a computus and a passional, a penitential and a reading book. These books the priest must needs have, and he cannot be without them, if he wishes to observe his order rightly and to direct correctly the people who belong to him.' Most of the priests who could be found working in churches built by thegns or freemen, however, had been drawn from the peasantry, and some may even have been slaves. Many would have been like the priests an archbishop worried over: 'If one must for necessity ordain a half-educated man, who knows all too little, one is then to do so, if there is great necessity.' Such priests' rough deportment and lack of polish were a constant source of concern for reform-minded bishops, who regularly ordered them to shave, take their weapons off before they entered church, and refrain from getting drunk, singing in taverns or gambling. They were also admonished not to leave their wives for other women. Men like these did not have the dues and fees to support them that minster-priests would have had, but instead lived off whatever their lords gave them; some may have even worked part-time at other occupations, because they were sometimes encouraged by their bishops to learn a craft. It is also clear that priests like these sometimes worked in badly supplied churches. They were instructed, for example, not to celebrate the Mass without wine and that they should have more than one set of clean vestments. They were also to make sure that the interior of their church, particularly around the altar, was kept free of filth, and they were to keep livestock out of the churchyard.

BRITAIN'S NEW CHRISTIANS

The Scandinavians who were fighting, conquering and settling in Britain in the second half of the ninth century not only arrived as pagans, but committed unspeakable acts of violence against Christian holy places. Yet in less than a century most of their descendants were indistinguishable in their religious observances from their Welsh, English and Scottish neighbours. Indeed, Raunds Furnells, whose church we have examined in some detail, fell under viking control in the second half of the ninth century, and the first hall built there was inhabited by people who used Scandinavian-style stirrups and gaming pieces. They may, or so the animal bones found on the site suggest, even have kept a pet buzzard. If they did, we can only imagine what their already fearful English neighbours thought of them. Buzzard or no buzzard, by the middle of the tenth century, the proprietor of Raunds was building and improving his church like every other pious English landholder. Still, the fact of such conversions tells us little about how newcomers were actually made into Christians and what kind of Christians they made.

A couple of texts give us tantalizing glimpses of a few early converts. Archbishop Oda of Canterbury († 958), for example, who was bishop of Ramsbury in the first decades of the tenth century, was the son of one of the warriors who had accompanied the *micel here* to England. According to a monastic chronicle, Oda had left his parents' household in order to take up residence with an English thegn, apparently because he wanted to live with Christians. One of Oda's brothers also became a priest, so Oda was not the only member of his family or his generation to convert. The story of Oda and his brother suggests that the children of men who had transformed themselves from viking warriors into landholders were embracing the religion of their neighbours, and they may have been doing so more rapidly than their foreign-born parents. How they learned about Christianity's tenets and who took responsibility for their religious education remains a mystery; but this story does suggest that they had contact with Christians whom they admired – which can only mean that these were Christians of at least the same social status – and that people like these had the means to get converts baptized.

Other pagan immigrants may have become Christians for more pragmatic reasons. Typically, when viking warlords and their men entered into alliances with Christians, baptism was the price. So, for example, in 926, when a Hiberno-Norse king of York married King Athelstan's sister, he was almost certainly baptized before he was allowed to bed the granddaughter of Alfred the Great. Similarly, other Norse leaders who entered into agreements with English kings – including many who were defeated by them in the first half of the tenth century – would have been baptized as well. Because men seem to have followed their lords in matters of religion, when a leader converted (whatever that conversion might entail) his followers would probably 'become' Christian as well. At other times influential immigrants may have chosen Christianity as a way of differentiating themselves from other elite settlers with whom they were competing. This might have been happening on Orkney in the Brough of Deerness. During the excavation at what was probably a high-status site, archaeologists uncovered both a stone church and, beneath it, an earlier timber chapel, built in Norse fashion, and which was probably in use in the second half of the tenth century. Of course, we cannot judge the orthodoxy of the person who used this chapel; but we do know that people elsewhere on the Orkney Mainland continued to use grave goods in this period, especially on the opposite side of the island from Deerness. It is just possible that the man in charge here found that Christianity was a potent means of signalling his opposition to a competing household, which was itself using its adherence to paganism in exactly the same way.

Large amounts of stone sculpture survive which served in the tenth century as funerary monuments in the cemeteries of the Danelaw, and which marked the graves of some of its most distinguished members. The earliest of these stone funerary monuments in Lincolnshire, made sometime in the first half of the tenth century, are found in the northern part of the county in places with good access to waterways. The most interesting of this group of sculptures is a cross shaft at Crowle which may have been made from a Roman column that a craftsman working in York had found there. Some of the other Lincolnshire sculpture that belongs to this group was carved by craftsmen familiar with decorative motifs being used in contemporary Scandinavia. Both the sculptures themselves and the artistic sensibilities of their makers suggest that people in this part of Lincolnshire in the first half of the tenth century were going to some trouble to procure these monuments, and that they must have had close connections with the Hiberno-Norse clique controlling York as well as with people in Scandinavia. Still, these were Christian sculptures, decorated with Christian designs and presumably used to mark Christian graves in Christian cemeteries. The group of Scandinavian lords who commissioned these pieces, many of whom would have fought against the English armies busy winning back the region, must have already converted to Christianity.

However conversion took place, we have only to look at Domesday Book to see the enthusiasm with which the descendants of Norse pagan immigrants had taken to church-building by the eleventh century. The Danelaw towns of Norwich, Lincoln and York each had more than forty churches; and Domesday Book records that the county of Suffolk had something like 639 churches, Norfolk 730 and Lincolnshire 754. Indeed, in their church-building, the grandchildren and great-grandchildren of pagan warriors showed themselves to be as enthusiastic as people living, at just this time, in Italy and France, who, according to a French chronicler, were building and rebuilding churches with extraordinary fervour: 'It was as if the whole world were shaking itself free, shrugging off the burden of the past, and cladding itself everywhere in a white mantle of churches.'

13

Living and Dying in Early
Medieval Britain: The Fifth
to Eleventh Century

For most of us, the men, women and children who lived fourteen or fifteen centuries ago are mere abstractions, and it is sometimes hard to comprehend that the people early medieval historians study were actually people rather than concepts or faceless automatons pushed across time and space by anonymous, impersonal historical forces. But the evidence of human bones, the subject of this final chapter, helps to re-animate the historical dead. When confronted with the skeletons of a mother and baby who died in childbirth, or the remains of a mutilated man dumped into a shallow grave beside the corpse of a decapitated dog, or a dead child with a cleft palate, we begin to understand that people in early medieval Britain did live and did breathe. Bones, as a matter of fact, enable us to say all sorts of things about the overall health and well-being of people living a millennium before we have any other useful demographic data. Skulls and tibias, for example, can betray dubious water and poor health; tiny bodies, infant mortality; broken-necked corpses, the terrible physical consequences of being found guilty of thievery. While bones permit us to track broad demographic trends that none of the period's texts disclose and while they sometimes graphically reveal social developments, like the growing power of greater men over lesser, the specificity of bones allows for more than this. Skeletons, first and foremost, are the remains of *individuals*, who, while living, had hopes and sorrows all their own. These were people with individually aching knees and their very own sore shoulders. They had private sufferings brought on by infected lungs, poorly mended fractures and dead loved ones. Because of this, their remains can disclose truths about unique beings and singular lives which are absent from our texts.

THREE LIVES

Before looking at broader trends, we shall look in some detail at the lives, and especially the deaths, of three otherwise anonymous women. The first is a young woman whose skeleton was recovered from an early medieval cemetery in present-day Cambridgeshire. In life, Eighteen (as we shall call her, because this is the number archaeologists assigned to her grave) was on the tall side, indeed as tall as some men. Her early childhood had been a healthy one. She had never suffered from chronic anaemia, as almost a fifth of her neighbours had, and as a child she had never experienced serious, growth-stopping malnourishment or infection. In this she was lucky, because the early Middle Ages were hard on sick children, and half of her contemporaries died before their seventeenth year. So although Eighteen managed to avoid fatal bouts of measles or summer diarrhoea, she nonetheless would have seen many babies, toddlers and children die over the course of her own short life. Eighteen was lucky in other ways. She had never fallen so badly that she had broken a limb, a serious, sometimes fatal injury in the period. Still, hers was an early death. Most of the women buried alongside her died after the age of 25, probably because they married late and did not begin succumbing to the complications of pregnancy and childbirth until their mid-twenties. Eighteen, however, did not make it that far; and she died sometime between her eighteenth and her twenty-fourth year.

The community in which Eighteen lived was a little old-fashioned. It was not as hierarchical as some seventh-century communities: certainly, there were no newfangled 'princely burials' in the cemetery where her community laid its dead to rest. Nor were women there, if their graves are anything to go by, wearing much Continental exotica, objects that were wildly popular in other contemporary settlements. Still, some of her community's dead were given more elaborate send-offs than others, and this includes Eighteen herself. She lay next to two high-status men who had been buried with shields and spears; but it was she, not the men, who had the most impressive grave goods in the cemetery. In death, she wore a necklace hung with silver rings, and she had latch-lifters hanging from her belt, accessories reserved for high-ranking women, and she was laid to rest with special things – a small vessel made from maple wood, a weaving batten, an oak bucket and a box full of little treasures, which included a sheep's knuckle and a fossilized sea urchin. The most interesting thing about her grave, though, is that it contained a bed, and hers is one of only a dozen bed burials known in England. The bed served as a kind of inside-out coffin, making it possible for mourners standing around Eighteen's open grave to view her unshrouded, dressed corpse and all its accompanying finery, things that had been carefully arranged by someone who, at some point, must have got into the grave with her to tidy her jewellery and arrange her grave goods just so.

The most astounding thing about Eighteen, though, is not her bed, but her skull. It is the skull of a leper. Given what we know about the disease, she probably contracted it from someone within her own household in her early teens, but its telltale lesions would not have appeared for another three or four years. Although the disease, by the time of her death, had not caused her to lose any fingers or toes, as sometimes happens with leprosy, her lower legs were badly infected, and her face was terribly disfigured. She had lost much of the bone supporting her upper front teeth and nose. Her mouth and nose would have collapsed inward, and her face would have been an infected, discharging horror. Yet, in spite of her deformities, she was treated in death with great respect, buried with considerable wealth and some ceremony in a well-dug grave lying at the heart of a communal cemetery. There is no sign here that Eighteen had led a pariah's life, the way later medieval lepers would. Nor does her grave, given the care and resources put into it, suggest that her death was viewed by those who buried her as a 'bad death'. Indeed, in the years after she died, people returned to her grave, choosing to bury others – a child and two adults – in graves that cut into hers, something that happened nowhere else in the cemetery.

The remains of the second and third women were found in a contemporary cemetery in the north of England, at a place called Sewerby, in Yorkshire. The two women, as a matter of fact, were buried on the same day in the same grave, one on top of the other. Once the two women had been put in the ground, those who buried them constructed a large cairn – the only one in the cemetery – to mark the spot, probably from chalk they hauled up the cliffs from a nearby beach. The woman at the bottom of the grave (number Forty-Nine, as she was dubbed by Sewerby's excavator), and the one, therefore, placed first in the ground, was a young woman about the same age as the leper, Eighteen. Forty-Nine, though, was not buried on a bed, but rather in a large wooden coffin, a rarity in both the period and the cemetery, and something used to denote high status. Not only was Forty-Nine placed in a coffin, but, like Eighteen, she had been given the most impressive grave goods of anyone buried in the cemetery. She had a large, imported bronze cauldron in her coffin along with a piece of meat and a box made from wood and shale. Her body was also adorned with the kinds of objects we associate with young women in the region from striving families – gilded wrist-clasps and bronze girdle-hangers, a pair of long-small brooches and a large, square-headed brooch. She also had a glorious double- or triple-strand necklace strung with more than 200 glass and amber beads. She, her grave goods and her coffin were placed in a grave dug more than a metre deep. A thin layer of soil was then shovelled on top of the coffin.

The skeleton of a second woman, number Forty-One, lay on top of the dirt-covered lid. Forty-One was older, somewhere between 35 and 45, an age that no more than 10 or 15 per cent of all the girls born in the early Middle Ages ever reached. She was about 1.65 metres tall, had suffered from serious anaemia early in life and had a lopsided smile. She, too, had grave goods, although nothing as elaborate as Forty-Nine's. Like many women in the north, she wore a knife on her belt and an annular brooch on each shoulder, and she had a short string of mostly glass beads strung between the two brooches. Unlike every other person in the cemetery, though, she was buried in a peculiar position. She lay on her stomach, with her head twisted towards the left. Both her arms were bent up and out from the rest of her body, and her right fist was clenched. Her knees were doubled up under her, and a heavy stone lay across her lower back. It seems that after Forty-Nine was placed in the ground, Forty-One, not yet dead, was buried alive on top of her coffin. The position of Forty-One's arms and legs suggests that, after being pushed into the grave from behind, she had struggled up onto her knees and forearms, but had fallen back. While she was down, someone heaved a large piece of a broken quernstone on her lower back. It was thrown with enough force to fracture her pelvis, and it seems to have knocked the fight out of her. She was covered with earth and must have been smothered in the ground.

Some have suggested that Forty-One was a slave, a human sacrifice made to keep her mistress company, but this seems unlikely given the fact that her body was adorned with the kinds of personal possessions buried with women of some standing. It seems more likely that hers was a punishment burial, and that members of her community held her in some way responsible for the younger woman's death. She may have been accused of murder, although we know from somewhat later written evidence that killers could pay compensation to surviving kin and suffer no further consequences. So perhaps, instead, those around her accused her of the unamendable offence of sorcery, because they suspected that she had bewitched the other woman. Whatever her alleged crimes, her bones tell us that she was humiliated, tortured and put to death by those who knew her.

The bones of Eighteen, Forty-Nine and Forty-One preserve stories about life and death in early medieval Britain that early medieval texts rarely do – intimate things, the kinds of things that we know from our own experiences make or break individual lives. But these three women are obviously special cases, their remains dramatic in ways that most are not. Eighteen's affliction, for example, a rare, bone-deforming malady, enables information to be learned about her life and death that could never be discovered about the vast majority of early medieval people, even those dug up by archaeologists, because most died as a result of infections that moved so quickly they left no impressions on the bones of their victims. Beyond this, Eighteen's skeleton and the story it tells are meaningful in the end only in the context of the bones and the stories of the rest of her community. Similarly, it is difficult to know what to make of Forty-One's terrifying end, but when we think about it in the context of other anomalous burials we can begin to glimpse the dark undercurrents of hamlet life and uncover the grotesque punishments meted out by those who claimed the right to execute.

HEALTH AND HARDSHIP

Before thinking about the broader implications of individuals and their bones, it is crucial to know something about four skeletal indicators of 'stress', which help archaeologists and historians make determinations about the overall health, morbidity (that is, disease load) and longevity of people living in Britain in the early Middle Ages.

The first indicator of stress is a porous bone lesion, known as porotic hyperostosis (when found in the crown of the skull) or cribra orbitalia (when manifest in the orbits of the eyes). It is formed as a result of iron-deficiency anaemia suffered between the ages of six months and about twelve years. When anaemic, a child's body increases the bone tissue that creates red blood cells at the expense of outer, non-blood-cell-producing bone, and it is this reaction that creates the tell-tale lesion. Although developed early in life, it is permanently inscribed on the skull, and thus in adult skeletons these lesions preserve information about serious bouts of childhood anaemia. Anaemia's effects include exhaustion and decreased learning ability, both of which can have a major effect on the well-being of communities. It can also result in the late onset of sexual maturity; and severe maternal anaemia can lead to underweight new-borns and premature births: these, in turn, can have a significant impact on birth rates and infant mortality. Most importantly, however, although anaemia can be caused by starvation, poor diet or scurvy, it is much more commonly the result either of chronic blood loss (often due to diarrhoeal diseases, caused by parasites), or of bacterial or viral infections. Anaemia is, therefore, typically an adaptation to poor environmental conditions such as appalling sanitation or high levels of pathogens. As a result, the prevalence of hyperostosis and cribra orbitalia in any given burial community tells us much about the overall health and living conditions of that population.

The second skeletal manifestation of stress is dental enamel hypoplasia, a condition that typically presents itself as horizontal lines etched across the external surfaces of teeth. Dental enamel hypoplasia is generally caused by stress-induced interruptions of tooth growth during childhood, and brought on by, among other things, an episode of disease, malnourishment, low birthweight or parasitic infection. Since tooth tissue is not remoulded during life, and the tooth one has at 7 is still the tooth one has at 30, dental enamel hypoplasia is a permanent record of early childhood trauma.

The third indicator of stress is delayed or stunted growth. Patterns of growth in a population are a good measure of a community's overall health and nutrition. Skeletal evidence makes it clear that medieval children were much smaller than their modern counterparts, and so subject to stresses that the latter are not. Harris lines are horizontal lines of increased bone density, most frequently found in long bones and detected through X-ray. They are formed when a child's growth has ground to a halt, and thus they can signal periods of childhood illness or malnutrition.

The fourth and final stress marker is periostitis, an inflammatory response to infection or injury that manifests itself in the formation of bony plaques on the outer surface of bones. Unlike our previous three stress markers, periosteal reactions can occur in adulthood as well as childhood. The lesions can be found throughout a skeleton, or they can be highly localized. In early medieval British populations, periostitis is often confined to the shin bone, a site of poor circulation, and thus an excellent home for bacteria. Shin bones, moreover, have little padding, and bruising along the shin promotes bacterial proliferation at the bone. Periostitis of the tibia was probably sometimes accompanied by leg ulcers.

That said, those whose skeletons and teeth are marked by these signs of stress were not necessarily the sickest members of their communities. After all, they were strong enough to survive whatever ailed them, long enough for their teeth or bones to be marked by stress. Those who succumbed to their ailments swiftly, on the other hand, did not live long enough to undergo such changes. This conundrum constitutes the famous 'osteological paradox': skeletons marked by stress sometimes represent healthier people than the healthy-looking ones. Nonetheless, broad studies comparing trends across cemetery populations do show, on average, that those whose skeletons exhibit signs of stress had shorter lives.

So, how did bone- and teeth-remodelling conditions like poor sanitation, bad diet and disease affect the lives of early medieval people? One of the most striking things that come from studying the bones of the fifth-, sixth- and seventh-century dead is that some communities were lucky and others were not. Nearly 40 per cent of the skeletons excavated from the sixth-century cemetery at Oakington, in Cambridgeshire, for example, show signs of serious stress. A toddler there, dead before its second birthday, suffered from chronic anaemia. A dead 11-year-old in the same cemetery had teeth marked with dental enamel hypoplasia. Skeleton after skeleton at Oakington exhibits related pathologies – just over a third with cribra orbitalia and just under a third with dental enamel hypoplasia. Similarly, over half the people buried in another sixth-century cemetery, this one at Norton, in Cleveland, had hypoplastic teeth, as did *every* juvenile buried in the eighth century at the cemetery at Nazeingbury. At Mill Hill, near Deal, Kent, on the other hand, only about 5 per cent of the population show signs of hypoplasia. Clearly misfortune struck different places in different ways; but a community that had lost most of its children would have had a grimmer future than one in which they had all been spared.

Differences in communities' fortunes can also be seen in the quite different mortality rates of men and women. At Mill Hill, half of all the girls who survived to the age of 15 were dead by the age of 25, and 65 per cent were dead by 35. On the other hand, at the cemetery where our leper, Eighteen, was laid to rest, just under two-thirds of all the women survived to the age of 25, and more than a quarter lived to 35 or more. And at a cemetery in Barton-on-Humber, only a quarter of the women were dead by 25, and over half lived past the age of 35. Behind these dry statistics lay real communities, some full of sick babies and motherless children, and others with adolescents and grown women in every household. In the early medieval period, in particular in the sixth century, when individuals and families were scrambling for resources and social position, households with long-lived wives, middle-aged men and adult children must have fared better and had a better chance of moving up the social hierarchy than households comprised of widowers, parentless children and childless parents. The quality of life, communal sociability, the commonness of orphans and the competition between young men and older men for wives were dictated in important ways by local demographic differences, which could vary markedly depending on the luck of a community or a generation.

Still, in spite of their variability from one cemetery to the next, the statistics for men's and women's mortality tell broadly similar stories: women were much more likely, in the early Middle Ages, to die before men. The relentless and uneven nature of these numbers shaped individual lives and communities in profound ways. At Raunds Furnells, for example, 44 per cent of the women who reached the age of 17 died by the age of 25, but only 22 per cent of the men did. By the age of 35, 71 per cent of the women were dead, but only 46 per cent of the men were. What happened to all of these dead women's households? Their children? How did people in Raunds clothe themselves, with female labour in such short supply? What chance did a 20-year-old man have of finding a wife, with so many older, more established widowers on the prowl? Were 35-year-old women lonely because most of the girls they had grown up with were already dead? The dearth of adult female labour, so clearly manifest in burial populations, may help to explain some of the broad economic and social transformations we have already examined; for example, why peasant families were increasingly drawn to nucleated settlements in the ninth, tenth and eleventh centuries, and why places with mills became such powerful attractors of peasant populations. One of the answers to these questions may be: because there were so few adult women.

In spite of the inequalities in life expectancy between the sexes, though, the news was not good for either sex. At Raunds and Mill Hill, 28 per cent of the boys born there survived to see their thirty-fifth year, while at Berinsfield, in Oxfordshire, and Barrington A only about 20 per cent did. In contrast, twenty-first-century Britons' life expectancy at birth is four times greater. The expectation of such extraordinary and commonplace longevity is transformative. How different life must have looked to the seventh-century people digging graves or tending babies whose mothers had just died!

What about child mortality? It is usually impossible to determine, since children, especially those under 2, are missing from most early medieval cemeteries. Only three cemeteries – the fifth- and sixth-century cemetery at Great Chesterford, in Essex, the tenth- and eleventh-century cemetery at Raunds Furnells, in Northamptonshire, and the somewhat later twelfth- to sixteenth-century cemetery at Wharram Percy, in Yorkshire – seem to contain all the children they should, so it is only here that we can estimate the prevalence of child mortality. In spite of their chronological and geographical range, these cemeteries do tell a consistent story. Very nearly half the individuals buried in each of these three cemeteries were children under the age of 17, a figure that closely matches levels of child mortality both for eighteenth-century London and for undeveloped and developing parts of the world in the twentieth century before the onslaught of AIDS. A closer look at our three cemeteries makes it clear that the first two years of life were the most lethal. Of all those who died at Raunds, for example, 6 per cent died at birth, another 15 per cent died during their first year, and another 3 per cent in their second. At Great Chesterford, although overall child mortality rates were the same, more 1- and 2-year-olds died: 84 per cent of all those who died there before the age of 15 died as babies or toddlers.

This rate of child mortality makes it clear that children on the whole were unhealthy, a fact borne out by the skeletons found not only in these three cemeteries, but in many others. At St Helen-on-the-Walls, a post-Conquest parish cemetery in York, the baby teeth of many of the youngest children buried there are marked by dental enamel hypoplasia. Hypoplastic lesions on baby teeth form *in utero*; thus we know that these children's mothers had been sick or malnourished while pregnant. These children, then, had been born stressed, and they must have been especially vulnerable to disease. At St Andrew, Fishergate, another York cemetery, three-quarters of all those who died before the age of 20 had hypoplastic lesions: a quarter of these had had at least three episodes and a few had had as many as seven. Or again, at Wharram Percy, more children dying between the ages of 6 and 11 suffered from periostitis than any other age group, which strongly suggests not only that these children were the victims of low-level, systemic infections, but that their ability to fight other diseases was compromised by their underlying ill health. The babies, children and adolescents who were buried at Raunds, Wharram Percy, St Helen's and St Andrew, Fishergate, all exhibit high levels of stress. Sick children and dead babies, then, were part of everyone's life.

Although adults buried in medieval cemeteries were as tall, on average, as mid-twentieth-century Britons, their anaemic, parasite-ridden children were not. One-year-olds at Raunds were the same size as modern babies, but by early adolescence many lagged behind twentieth-century children by as much as four years. The same is true for Wharram Percy. Fourteen-year-olds there were the same height as modern 10-year-olds. Still, undersize children grew to their more or less genetically programmed adult heights in the Middle Ages; it just took them longer. Modern children finish growing at about 18, but in the nineteenth century, a period for which we have good data, we know that the working classes continued to grow, on average, until the age of 29, and it looks as if something similar was taking place among medieval populations. This simple fact has profound economic and social implications. This was a world in which human muscle power was in chronic short supply. As we have seen, many people, by the tenth and eleventh centuries, practised communal farming, which centred around the whole village's participation in heavy ploughing with large teams of oxen. It was very hard work, and some of its associated tasks required full-grown male labour. Yet about half the people living in this period were under the age of 18, and 16-year-old boys were the size of today's 12-year-olds, so most could not have done a man's work. It is little wonder, then, that food was so often a worry. And it is of no surprise that conspicuous consumption and the public squandering of food were the best ways for nobles to show the world how rich they were. Hardwired into the demography of this world, then – a world where about half of all people were undersized children – was the predisposition towards poverty, chronic labour shortages, hunger and probably violence.

Town life in the tenth and eleventh centuries may have been even more lethal than life in the countryside. Certainly, periostitis, dental enamel hypoplasia and cribra orbitalia were more prevalent among townspeople than among those being buried in many rural cemeteries, and this suggests that townspeople suffered more from parasites and pathogens. For example, both cribra orbitalia and periostitis were twice as prevalent among those buried at the post-Conquest urban cemetery of St Helen-on-the-Walls as they were among those buried 30 kilometres down the road in the rural cemetery of Wharram Percy. There are a number of reasons for this. An individual's immunity is influenced, in important ways, by living and sanitary conditions. In urban communities, both were more degraded than they were in small-scale settlements. Towns, with their large populations, their access to new immigrants and their seriously compromised drinking water, were environments in which diseases tended to linger longer, kill more and indeed settle in and become endemic. Immigrants from rural communities arriving in late adolescence would have suffered very high mortality rates in towns, because they did not have the immunity to urban diseases that those who had grown up with them did. And, because urban communities had comparatively large and vulnerable populations, they had enough people to serve as permanent human reservoirs for slow-moving killers like leprosy and tuberculosis. Many an excavated rural cemetery has disgorged a leper or two, but it was only in towns, and probably only from the twelfth century on, that leprosy became a serious scourge. The cemetery attached to St John Timberhill, in Norwich, for example, used all through the eleventh century, contained something like thirty lepers, a number never seen in rural cemeteries. Rural cemeteries often contain one or two victims of tuberculosis as well, but this disease, and, indeed, a nastier form of it, was far more prevalent in towns, where it had larger numbers of hosts, and, therefore, higher levels of infection. Other, faster-moving killers – smallpox, mumps, influenza and cholera – were unable to persist in small, rural settlements for any length of time, because they would erupt suddenly and infect all those without immunity. Within a week or two, some would have died, but everyone who had survived gained immunity, so these infections often disappeared as quickly as they had come. Tenth- and eleventh-century towns, however, with their hefty populations and their pools of immigrants ripe for infection, were places where diseases simmered or came back year after year.

Medieval towns were also astonishingly filthy. Houses in York were crawling with bugs, and this was probably true in all pre-Conquest towns. Common house-dwellers at 16–22 Coppergate, a row of York craftsmen's houses built in the Viking Age, include rove and silken fungus beetles, hairy cellar beetles, spider beetles and nocturnal black beetles, as well as the less euphemized fleas, body lice, flies and sheep keds, which all found conducive environments indoors. Latrines and cesspits, too, were homes to enormous populations of insects; the total number estimated for the cesspits at 16–22 Coppergate alone is on the order of ten million. Cesspits and heaps of rotting, carelessly dumped rubbish were omnipresent in tenth- and eleventh-century York, and they were fatally near wells. They acted as reservoirs for intestinal parasites, in particular whipworm and maw worm, which frequently show up in latrine fills and in excavated faecal material. Flies, fleas, lice and beetles also acted as vectors for pathogenic micro-organisms, including poliomyelitis, salmonella and summer diarrhoea. This terrible combination of insects, micro-organisms and filth must lie behind much of the human misery etched on the bones of the urban dead.

The insalubriousness of urban life was exacerbated, before the later twelfth century, by the fact that so little was built in or covered by stone. Romano-British towns were cleaner, in part, because so much within them was constructed from inorganic materials like brick, tile, cobbles and stone; and, as a result, they had much less surface build-up of organic, rotting, insect-friendly, pathogen-loving waste. It was only from the late twelfth century onwards that York and other English towns began using inorganic building material as a matter of course, especially for cellars, foundations and stone-clad wells, and because of this they probably became healthier places.

When the prevalence of stress indicators like cribra orbitalia in urban cemeteries is compared with their prevalence in early rural cemeteries, it seems that early rural populations were considerably less stressed than later urban ones, and they were probably healthier. In many rural cemeteries, for example, well under 20 per cent of the population exhibited signs of cribra orbitalia, but in urban cemeteries the number is often closer to 30 per cent. Similarly, in many early rural cemeteries, under 10 per cent of the population exhibited signs of periostitis, but in urban cemeteries it was often double this. Nonetheless, peasants living in the relatively large, densely settled, nucleated villages established from the ninth century onwards were also less healthy than their early progenitors, who had generally lived in smaller, more dispersed, drifting settlements. This suggests that life in tenth- and eleventh-century nucleated villages – with their larger populations, greater settlement densities and permanent locations – was hard on the health of cultivators. It is a public-health truism that in pre-industrial societies the larger and the more sedentary the group, the greater the frequency of chronic disease, tuberculosis, intestinal infections and parasites; so it follows that large, compact villages were less healthful than small, scattered hamlets. In other historical contexts, moreover, it is clear that taxing states and aggressive landlords, both of which, as we have seen, were ubiquitous in tenth- and eleventh-century England, were hazardous to peasants' health. Stature in Britain, for example, increased after the Roman empire's collapse, which suggests that many people had healthier childhoods once urbanization, taxation and galloping social inequalities had disappeared. We should not, therefore, look for broad improvements of mortality and morbidity across whole populations as we move forward in time.

Nonetheless, there are hints at the very end of our period that those living economically and socially privileged lives were beginning to live longer and healthier lives as well. In the sixth and seventh centuries it does not look as if there was enough physical and social distance between people of high and low status for the former to enjoy more favourable levels of mortality and morbidity than the latter. Certainly, those buried with rich collections of grave goods often had bones marked by stress. So wealth and social status did not stop the privileged few from breathing the same air and drinking the same, bad, water as their less fortunate dependants. There is, however, some evidence that from the twelfth century onwards, professional religious were living longer than other people, and this may reflect lower mortality rates among all people of means. By the twelfth century, cemeteries of ecclesiastical communities (which did not just contain professional religious, but sometimes also wealthy patrons) often have larger numbers of older individuals than do other cemeteries. Among the clergy buried at St Andrew, Fishergate, for example, it seems that two-thirds died after the age of 40, which is astonishing, considering the mortality rates found in cemeteries used by peasants and the urban poor. A condition, moreover, known as diffuse idiopathic skeletal hyperostosis, or DISH, is particularly prevalent in monastic cemeteries. In modern populations, DISH is closely associated with ageing, with late-onset diabetes and with obesity. Its prevalence among monks is suggestive both of their high living and their long lives. Economic privilege, carefully designed water systems, organized waste disposal, and construction in stone were beginning, at the very end of our period, to contribute to the increasing longevity of professional religious, and these factors may well have been operating in aristocratic households, too.

WORKING, EATING AND MOVING

Interesting inferences about the working lives of individuals can occasionally be made from skeletal remains. We know, for example, that women living in the early medieval period spent long hours on their haunches, because their ankles are often marked with tell-tale 'squatting facets'. This common bone modification, in turn, suggests that many women habitually worked close to the ground while performing tasks like grinding grain. Occasionally, however, particular labours and stresses do more than witness trends across whole populations: they change particular bodies in ways that are dramatic enough for us view the working lives of individuals. Take, for example, the extraordinary body of an old man from a Norse-period cemetery in Orkney. His skeleton describes a life oriented towards the sea and dominated by back-breaking work. Both because of the way his bones developed during adolescence and because of the patterns of arthritis and cartilage loss he accrued as an adult, it seems that our man habitually rowed boats – from boyhood to old age – with his back to the bow, and that he had often participated in the desperately hard work of pulling boats upstream or dragging them across land from one navigable stretch of river to the next. Such labours must have often ruined the day of Norse traders, raiders and mercenaries. These bone-wearying tasks concerned neither the vikings' monastic victims nor their saga-writing admirers and are not, therefore, part of written culture, but they must have preoccupied the Orkney boatman, with his bad knees, arthritic shoulders, malformed arms and wrenched wrist.

Isotopes found in the Orkney boatman's bones, moreover, tell us that he consumed huge amounts of fish. Indeed, it turns out that a variety of isotopes found in skeletal remains can provide information about an individual's diet, origins and mobility. It is from the application of this knowledge that we learn, for example, that a woman buried in what has been called a viking family cemetery in Cnip, on the Isle of Lewis, and who lived sometime in the ninth or tenth century, had been laid to rest next to adults who had spent their childhoods in Norway and babies and children who had been born in the Hebrides; in short, in a cemetery used by a little group of Norse colonists and their native-born children. But the woman in whom we are interested hailed from neither Scandinavia nor the Scottish Isles: she had spent her childhood in England, in either the South Downs or the Yorkshire Wolds. How did an English-woman end up living at the centre of a vast, Norse-colonial, North Atlantic world with a group of grave-goods-using Norse settlers? The most likely explanation is that viking slavers derailed her life in some unrecorded raid, and, as a consequence of it, she spent her final years among foreigners who owned her.

SOCIAL CONTROL

A relatively large number of burials from the early medieval period can be labelled 'deviant', and this class of burials preserves interesting information about the ways people across the early Middle Ages controlled and marked individuals they deemed to be outcasts or criminals. Archaeologists, while investigating Stonehenge in the late 1920s, for example, came across one such deviant burial at the centre of the complex. They assumed that it dated, like the megaliths themselves, to the Neolithic period, but later radiocarbon dating showed that it most probably dates to the eighth century. The remains were of a short, adult male about 30 years of age. He had something called Schmorl's nodes on his vertebrae, a lesion common in people who perform hard, physical labour as children. The muscle insertions for his upper limbs suggest that he was powerfully built and provide further evidence that this was a man who had done back-breaking work. He had periostitis, too, so he had suffered from some kind of chronic, low-grade infection. In short, we have a small, muscled, not very healthy man, who had worked hard most of his life. He died, however, neither from disease nor exhaustion, but because he had been decapitated with a single sword blow from behind. He was probably kneeling when it happened: it looks like an execution.

This man's burial is clearly anomalous, not least because it lay at the centre of the largest, most uncanny site in Britain; but it deviated from standard burial customs in other ways. The vast majority of people in eighth-century Britain were buried with their kith and kin, in well-dug graves, and they were placed in the ground with care. Our man, however, lay alone in this eerie landscape, having been dumped into an indecently shallow, indecently short hole in the ground. Clearly, those who buried the dead man's body treated it with disrespect. Indeed, his ribs may have been broken *post mortem*, when those who disposed of his corpse were stuffing it into its inadequate grave. The burial, moreover, took place in a kind of no man's land. Stonehenge, by the eleventh century, lay on the border of two administrative districts known as hundreds, and many have argued that it marked an early and important territorial boundary. It would have been a site known to everyone in the region, but inhabited by no one.

Other anomalous burials dating to the seventh and eighth centuries have something of the look and feel of this one. Take, for example, a solitary grave found in north Wiltshire, near Broad Town. Here, another man had been put in the ground without grave goods and buried in an isolated, shallow grave. Like the Stonehenge burial, this one lay on the boundary of two hundreds; and, although it was nowhere near a stone circle, it sat next to a crossroads. Like Stonehenge, this spot could be seen from afar, and, like Stonehenge, it lay far from human habitation or a proper cemetery. This skeleton was poorly preserved, so it is uncertain how the man died, but the archaeologist who undertook the excavation thinks that this man, too, was executed.

There are striking differences between the burials of these two men and that of the woman Forty-One, with whom we began this chapter. Forty-One, as we have seen, was probably put to death by members of her own community in a space well used and often visited by the people who knew her. And, although she may have been killed for some deviant behaviour, she was, nonetheless, buried where local people were always buried. Her death, moreover, although extraordinary, was not unique. Many early cemeteries have produced an anomalous burial or two – some hinting at acts of stoning, amputation or beheading – and the stories that stand behind them may be tales of communal violence acted out against local outcasts: group killings committed after an agreement struck between local heads of households. Indeed, the occasional punishment burial found in early communal cemeteries suggests that members of local settlements did away with deviants on their own, without the aid or encouragement of outsiders. The killings of the two men found at Stonehenge and Broad Town, however, feel different. Their two dramas played themselves out far from settlements and communal cemeteries, in isolated spots lying on the boundaries of territories, rather than at their cores. The two men's graves were also placed in dramatic landscapes, and their execution places would have been visible from afar. The punishing forces here also look less cosily communal, and more like groups of powerful men, even kings or their surrogates, in charge of whole regions; people who claimed for themselves the rights to keep the peace and punish wrongdoers living within their *regiones*, and who executed and buried such people on the borders of the territories they controlled. This habit of more distant authorities killing outcasts on the margins of territories is one of the earliest archaeologically visible manifestations of the arrogation of the power of families and neighbours to regulate their own communities by elite men working hard to monopolize violence for themselves. This move took centuries to effect, but by the tenth century state-sponsored executions on boundaries had become a standard feature of the landscape and a commonplace of royal power.

As early as the eighth century, it seems that particular places had become designated sites of judicial killing. The cemetery surrounding the Sutton Hoo ship burial provides us with the most dramatic example of this. When Sutton Hoo was systematically re-excavated in the 1980s, archaeologists found that the famous ship mound was surrounded by other graves, some contemporary and others not; some elaborate and others downright grotesque. Seventeen people in the cemetery had been laid to rest under great mounds of earth with extraordinary grave goods and doubtless awesome ceremonies as well. There were, however, thirty-nine others buried at Sutton Hoo who had been given neither grave goods nor burial mounds. All but one died at least a century after the locals had ceased to use the cemetery for elite burial, and the deaths of most probably date to the tenth and eleventh centuries. Corpses in the acidic soil of East Anglia, where Sutton Hoo lies, survive not as skeletons, but as 'sand bodies'. Most of the late sand bodies preserve the shadowy outlines of people who had been decapitated, hanged or mutilated in other ways, and then buried in weirdly staged tableaux. A number, moreover, shared their graves with two or three others. One burial, for example, contained two decapitated men, one on top of the other. Another, this one a triple burial, held a decapitated man lying on his back and two women whose bodies had been thrown on top of his. The position of other sand bodies suggests that some are the remains of people killed while kneeling in their graves. About half of Sutton Hoo's anomalous burials radiated out from a single seventh-century, high-status mound; the rest lay on the eastern edge of the cemetery near the remains of what had, at one time, been an enormous tree. It fell down sometime in the early Middle Ages, only to be replaced by a set of posts which probably supported a gallows. Many of the people found here had had their necks broken and were lying with their hands behind their backs, which suggests that they had bound wrists. It looks as if they were hanged.

Sutton Hoo is not the only pagan-period cemetery reused in later centuries for execution. Similar sites have been found from Sussex to Yorkshire. A run-of-the-mill sixth-century cemetery at Guildown, on a summit overlooking Guildford in Surrey, has produced just under forty burials of men, women and children with all the usual grave goods – spears, brooches, buckets and glass beakers. But almost 200 later bodies also lay buried here, mostly dating from the tenth and eleventh centuries. Like the anomalous burials at Sutton Hoo, many of the later Guildown burials were found in double, triple or even quadruple graves. Large numbers of those buried, moreover, had been mutilated. One triple grave, for example, contained two people who had had their legs cut off at the knees and a third skeleton had its arms, head and feet removed. Some of the bodies were prone, and many look as if their wrists had been tied behind their backs.

At Sutton Hoo, Guildown and at many other places – Stockbridge

Down, in Hampshire, and South Acre, in Norfolk, to name but two – it seems that people buried in graves like these suffered horrendous deaths. Occasionally, moreover, it looks as if executed corpses were further mutilated. One man, found at a cemetery at Roche Court Down, in Wiltshire, for example, had been decapitated. Then, after he was quite dead, the people presiding over his execution smashed his skull and buried it separately from the rest of his body, surrounding it with a ring of flints. Another man, whose skeleton was excavated at Meon Hill, in Hampshire, was placed in his grave on his stomach, and for good measure those who buried him weighed down his corpse with a heavy boulder. Yet another headless man, this one found at Stockbridge Down, in Hampshire, was treated with the ultimate disrespect: his corpse shared its grave with a decapitated dog. Here is evidence for horrific crimes, for the breaching of dangerous taboos and for appalling acts of brutality. All of these bodies not only point to gut-wrenching violence, but smack of ritualistic behaviour, and even, perhaps, to a niggling fear that the reluctant dead might not lay quietly in their graves, and that steps sometimes had to be taken to ensure that they would not rise again. At the turn of the millennium, the monk and homilist Ælfric of Eynsham described how witches consorted at 'heathen burial sites with their dark rites, and call upon the Devil, and he arrives in the form of the person who lies buried there, as if he had risen from death'. No wonder people were uneasy.

As we might expect from reading the law codes promulgated by ninth-, tenth- and eleventh-century kings, most of the skeletons found in execution cemeteries are those of adults. King Athelstan had stipulated in the early tenth century that execution was proper only for those 12 years of age or older. Still, a handful of children have been found in these terrible places: the execution cemetery at Staines, in Middlesex, for example, includes a 10-year-old. Most, though, were men. Given the evidence of the law codes, with so many capital sentences levied against the commonplace crimes of men – cattle rustling, housebreaking, treachery – this is not a surprise. Nonetheless, there is some evidence to suggest that women were put to death differently than men, and this might explain their small numbers in execution cemeteries. We know, for example, that women were sometimes drowned rather than hanged, especially when suspected of witchcraft. One such killing is described in a charter: 'And a widow and her son had previously forfeited the land at Ailsworth because they drove iron pins into [a wax image of] Wulfstan's father, Ælfsige. And it was detected and the murderous instrument dragged from her chamber; and the woman was seized, and drowned at London Bridge, and her son escaped and became an outlaw.' There is no archaeological evidence for the judicial drowning of women, but, as we have seen, during the excavation of the ancient banks of the River Thames at Bull Wharf Lane in London, archaeologists uncovered the skeleton of a woman who had been killed by a blow to the head and then staked to the riverbank. Was her strange grave meant to serve as a warning to those who saw it?

If we look at the placement of the score or so of execution cemeteries now identified within the landscape, several telling patterns emerge. First, they are located on the boundaries of shires or hundreds, the territories harnessed by kings in the tenth and eleventh centuries to maintain the peace. Judicial courts were held by both hundreds and shires: they oversaw the judicial ordeal and they decided the rights and wrongs of legal cases. It is hardly surprising, then, to find that the men who presided over such courts were executing those they found guilty of capital offences at the boundaries of their jurisdictions. The later execution sites also share another common feature: they are located next to prehistoric monuments and earthworks or early pagan cemeteries. Many in the tenth and eleventh centuries believed that devils and demons haunted such places. It seems that criminals were deliberately executed and buried at sites with pagan associations, to drive home the point that crimes were also sins, and that condemned criminals were being not only put to death, but sent to hell, since their bodies lay next to the pagan dead.

What can we learn from these broken bodies and desecrating burials? In the sixth century, punishment killings like the one at Sewerby seem to have happened now and again, performed by members of local communities. As elites and kingdoms formed, however, executions came to be the business of kings and their surrogates. These judicial killings, judging from the graves of the executed, were highly ritualized. Criminals were mutilated and subjected to hair-raising physical tortures, and they were killed and buried in carefully choreographed ways. By the tenth and eleventh centuries Christian ideology had also permeated these gruesome killings. Thus it came to be seen as fitting to execute the condemned and bury them in sites that were perceived as pagan. The unlucky dead were not only denied burial in consecrated ground; their bodies were abandoned in places long claimed by the damned.

So, what, in the end, do the bones of people, both those who died in their beds and those who died on the gibbet, tell us about living and dying in early medieval Britain? First they suggest that numbers matter. It is not enough to say that women died in childbirth, that infant mortality must have been high or that people were often ill. It is only when we look at the statistics provided by the bones of the early medieval dead that we come face to face with just how dire life in this period was; how sick, how sad and how short. With the cold, hard numbers in our heads we can see that one out of every two babies born in Raunds Furnells was dead by 18; that nine out of ten baby girls born there would be dead by 35; that most first-time 17- or 18-year-old mothers' own mothers were dead; that every village must have had a sad little gang of orphans. Secondly, the specificity of bones matters. Narrative sources, again particularly those written before 1100, do not allow us to see the leg ulcers that plagued so many; the swarms of disease-carrying flies; the constant discomfort caused by a gut full of parasites; the scrawny, undersized, 14-year-old boys. Yet these were fundamental, bodily aspects of most people's lives in early medieval Britain. Thirdly, bones betray the human cost of things usually written about by historians as impersonal and faceless trends. The story of the rise of urban communities was clearly, when we look at cemeteries, about more than the birth of the commercial economy. For many, it was about sick children, fast-moving illnesses and early death. The genesis of nucleated villages and interventionist landlords did more than change the look of the landscape and the pace of the economy; farmers lived less healthy lives because of it. And the rise of the state did more than organize taxation and create a well-regulated currency; it led to the institutionalization of terrible killing places, places where the power of the state was cloaked in Christian ideology and then performed in shocking ways. The human costs of some of the period's grand trends, then, can sometimes be recovered if we look at bones; and with them we can begin to discern just how high a price some people did, in fact, pay. Finally, our texts, for the most part, tell us about men, about monks, about the holders of land, about the people who lived after *c.* 700 and about the English; yet the vast majority of people in early medieval Britain could be placed in none of these categories. If we limited ourselves to texts we would never know about the likes of Eighteen, Forty-One or the little man buried at Stonehenge. Yet these people's bones allow us to recover specific, personal and significant details of their otherwise forgotten lives. In the end, they allow us to recuperate some of the lives of flesh-and-blood people never described in texts, who lived and died in early medieval Britain.

Further Reading

INTRODUCTION

Basic Readings on the Political Narrative of the Period

J. Campbell, E. John and P. Wormald (eds.), *The Anglo-Saxons* (Harmondsworth, Middlesex, 1991).

T. Charles-Edwards (ed.), *After Rome* (Oxford, 2003).

B. E. Crawford, *Scandinavian Scotland* (Leicester, 1987).

W. Davies (ed.), *From the Vikings to the Normans* (Oxford, 2003).

—— *Wales in the Early Middle Ages* (London, 1982).

A. S. Esmonde Cleary, *The Ending of Roman Britain* (London, 1989).

P. Hunter Blair, *An Introduction to Anglo-Saxon England*, 3rd edn. (Cambridge, 2003).

E. James, *Britain in the First Millennium* (Oxford, 2001).

D. P. Kirby, *The Earliest English Kings*, rev. edn. (London, 2000).

M. Lapidge, J. Blair, S. Keynes and D. Scragg (eds.), *The Blackwell Encyclopedia of Anglo-Saxon England* (Oxford, 1999).

R. McKitterick, *The New Cambridge Medieval History*, vol. 2: *c. 700–c. 900* (Cambridge, 1995).

T. Reuter, *The New Cambridge Medieval History*, vol. 3: *c. 900–c. 1024* (Cambridge, 2000).

J. D. Richards, *Viking Age England*, 2nd edn. (Stroud, 2004).

P. Stafford, *A Companion to the Early Middle Ages: Britain and Ireland c.500–1100* (London, 2009).

—— *Unification and Conquest: A Political and Social History of England in the Tenth and Eleventh Centuries* (London, 1989).

A. Woolf, *From Pictland to Alba: Scotland, 789 to 1070* (Edinburgh, 2007).

B. Yorke, *The Anglo-Saxons* (Stroud, 1999).

—— *Kings and Kingdoms of Early Anglo-Saxon England* (London, 1990).

Basic Books that Treat Major Themes
Important in the Period

S. R. Bassett (ed.), *The Origins of Anglo-Saxon Kingdoms* (London, 1989).

J. Blair, *The Church in Anglo-Saxon Society* (Oxford, 2006).

—— and R. Sharpe (eds.), *Pastoral Care before the Parish* (Leicester, 1992).

C. Dyer, *Making a Living in the Middle Ages: The People of Britain 850–1520* (New Haven, 2002).

R. Faith, *The English Peasantry and the Growth of Lordship* (London, 1997).

S. Foot, *Monastic Life in Anglo-Saxon England, c. 600–900* (Cambridge, 2006).

P. Fowler, *Farming in the First Millennium AD: British Agriculture between Julius Caesar and William the Conqueror* (Cambridge, 2002).

J. Graham-Campbell and C. E. Batey, *Vikings in Scotland: An Archaeological Survey* (Edinburgh, 1998).

D. M. Hadley, *The Vikings in England: Settlement, Society and Culture* (Manchester, 2006).

H. Mayr-Harting, *The Coming of Christianity to Anglo-Saxon England*, 3rd edn. (London, 1991).

T. F. X. Noble and J. M. H. Smith (eds.), *The Cambridge History of Christianity: Early Medieval Christianities, c. 600–c. 1100* (Cambridge, 2008).

D. M. Palliser (ed.), *The Cambridge Urban History of Britain*, vol. 1: 600–1540 (Cambridge, 2000).

M. Redknap, *Vikings in Wales: An Archaeological Quest* (Cardiff, 2000).

S. Reynolds, *Kingdoms and Communities in Western Europe, 900–1300* (Oxford, 1984).

A. Thacker and R. Sharpe (eds.), *Local Saints and Local Churches in the Early Medieval West* (Oxford, 2002).

D. Wilson, *Anglo-Saxon Paganism* (London, 1992).

B. Yorke, *The Conversion of Britain: Religion, Politics and Society in Britain c. 600–800* (London, 2006).

Books and Articles on Specific Classes of Evidence

H. Hamerow, *Early Medieval Settlements: The Archaeology of Rural Communities in Northwest Europe, 400–900* (Oxford, 2002).

S. Jones, *The Archaeology of Ethnicity: Constructing Identities in the Past and Present* (London, 1997).

K. Leahy, *Anglo-Saxon Crafts* (Stroud, 2003).

S. J. Lucy, *The Anglo-Saxon Way of Death: Burial Rites in Early England* (Stroud, 2000).

S. Mays, *The Archaeology of Human Bones* (London, 1998).

G. R. Owen-Crocker, *Dress in Anglo-Saxon England*, 2nd edn. (Woodbridge, 2004).

M. Parker Pearson, *The Archaeology of Death and Burial* (Stroud, 1999).

A. Reynolds, *Anglo-Saxon Deviant Burial Customs* (Oxford, 2009).

C. A. Roberts and M. Cox, *Health and Disease in Britain from Prehistory to the Present Day* (Stroud, 2003).

T. Waldron, *Counting the Dead: The Epidemiology of Skeletal Populations* (Chichester, 1994).

P. Walton Rogers, *Cloth and Clothing in Early Anglo-Saxon England*, CBA, Research Report, 145 (York, 2007).

H. Williams, *Death and Memory in Early Medieval Britain* (Cambridge, 2006).

T. Williamson, *Shaping Medieval Landscapes: Settlement, Society, Environment* (Macclesfield, 2003).

General Reading on Material Culture

L. R. Baumgarten, 'Leather Stockings and Hunting Shirts', in T. J. Schlereth (ed.), *Material Culture Studies in America* (Nashville, 1982), 251–76.

J. Deetz, *In Small Things Forgotten: An Archaeology of Early American Life*, 2nd edn. (New York, 1995).

J.-C. Dupont, 'The Meaning of Objects: The Poker', in G. L. Pocius (ed.), *Living in a Material World*, Institute of Social and Economic Research, Social and Economic Papers, 19 (St John's, Newfoundland, 1991), 1–18.

E. McC. Fleming, 'Artifact Study: A Proposed Model', in T. J. Schlereth (ed.), *Material Culture Studies in America* (Nashville, 1982), 162–73.

A. J. Frantzen and J. Hines (eds.), *Cædmon's Hymn and Material Culture in the World of Bede: Six Essays* (Morgantown, W. Va., 2007).

C. Hills, 'History and Archaeology: The State of Play in Early Medieval Europe', *Antiquity*, 81 (2007), 191–200.

D. A. Hinton, *Gold and Gilt, Pots and Pins: Possessions and People in Medieval Britain* (Oxford, 2005).

A. S. Martin and J. R. Garrison, 'Shaping the Field: The Multidisciplinary Perspectives of Material Culture', in A. Smart Martin and J. R. Garrison (eds.), *American Material Culture: The Shape of the Field* (Knoxville, Tenn., 1997), 1–20.

C. Martin, 'The Four Lives of a Micmac Copper Pot', *Ethnohistory*, 22 (1975), 111–33.

A. Mason, A. Arceo and R. Fleming, 'Buckets, Monasteries and Crannógs: Material Culture and the Rewriting of Early Medieval British History', *Haskins Society Journal*, 20 (2009), 1–27.

J. D. Prown, 'Material/culture: Can the Farmer and the Cowman still be Friends?', in J. D. Prown (ed.), *Art as Evidence: Writings on Art and Material Culture* (New Haven, 2002), 235–42.

—— 'Mind in Matter: An Introduction to Material Culture Theory and Method', in J. D. Prown (ed.), *Art as Evidence: Writings on Art and Material Culture* (New Haven, 2002), 69–95.

Ten Books that are Good to Think With

P. Booth, A. Dodd, M. Robinson and A. Smith, *The Thames through Time: The Archaeology of the Gravel Terraces of the Upper and Middle Thames. The Early Historical Period: AD 1–1000* Oxford Archaeology Thames Valley Landscapes Monographs, 27 (Oxford, 2007).

D. Bowsher, T. Dyson, N. Holder and I. Howell, *The London Guildhall: An Archaeological History of a Neighbourhood from Early Medieval to Modern Times,* 2 vols., MoLAS Monograph, 36 (London, 2007).

E. Campbell, *Continental and Mediterranean Imports to Atlantic Britain and Ireland, AD 400–800,* CBA, Research Report, 157 (York, 2007).

M. O. H. Carver, C. Hills and J. Scheschkewitz, *Wasperton: A Roman, British and Anglo-Saxon Community in Central England* (Woodbridge, 2009).

R. Faith, *The English Peasantry and the Growth of Lordship* (New York, 1997).

R. Gowland and C. Knüsel (eds.), *The Social Archaeology of Funerary Remains* (Oxford, 2006), 168–78.

A. R. Hall, H. K. Kenward, D. Williams and J. R. A. Greig, *Environment and Living Conditions at Two Anglo-Scandinavian Sites,* Archaeology of York, 14/4 (York, 1983).

M. Henig and P. Lindley (eds.), *Alban and St Albans: Roman and Medieval Architecture, Art and Archaeology* (Leeds, 2001).

C. Loveluck, *Rural Settlement, Lifestyles and Social Change in the Later First Millennium AD: Anglo-Saxon Flixborough in its Wider Context* (Oxford, 2007).

T. Williamson, *Shaping Medieval Landscapes: Settlement, Society, Environment* (Macclesfield, 2003).

Ten Articles that are Good to Think With

J. H. Barrett, A. M. Locker and C. M. Roberts, ' "Dark Age Economics" Revisited: The English Fish Bone Evidence AD 600–1600', *Antiquity,* 78 (2004), 618–36.

J. Blair, 'Anglo-Saxon Pagan Shrines and their Prototypes', *Anglo-Saxon Studies in Archaeology and History,* 8 (1995), 1–28.

P. Blinkhorn, 'Habitus, Social Identity and Anglo-Saxon Pottery', in C. G. Cumberpatch and P. W. Blinkhorn (eds.), *Not So Much a Pot, More a Way of Life: Current Approaches to Artefact Analysis in Archaeology* (Oxford, 1997), 113–24.

R. Bradley, 'Time Regained: The Creation of Continuity', *Journal of the British Archaeological Association*, 140 (1987), 1–17.

P. Budd, A. Millard, C. Chenery, S. Lucy and C. Roberts, 'Investigating Population Movement by Stable Isotope Analysis: A Report from Britain', *Antiquity*, 78 (2004), 127–41.

E. Cambridge, 'The Architecture of the Augustinian Mission', in R. Gameson (ed.), *St Augustine and the Conversion of England* (Stroud, 1999), 202–36.

M. Gardiner, R. Cross, N. MacPherson-Grant, I. Riddler, L. Blackmore, D. Chick, S. Hamilton-Dyer, E. Murray and D. Weir, 'Continental Trade and Non-urban Ports in Mid-Anglo-Saxon England: Excavations at Sandtun, West Hythe, Kent', *Archaeological Journal*, 158 (2001), 161–290.

M. Pitts, A. Bayliss, J. McKinley, A. Boylston, P. Budd, J. Evans, C. Chenery, A. J. Reynolds and S. Semple, 'An Anglo-Saxon Decapitation and Burial at Stonehenge', *Wiltshire Archaeological and Natural History Magazine*, 95 (2002), 131–46.

D. Stocker and P. Everson, 'The Straight and Narrow Way: Fenland Causeways and the Conversion of the Landscape in the Witham Valley, Lincolnshire', in M. O. H. Carver (ed.), *The Cross Goes North: Processes of Conversion in Northern Europe, AD 300–1300* (Woodbridge, 2003), 271–88.

H. Williams, 'Death Warmed Up: The Agency of Bodies and Bones in Early Anglo-Saxon Cremation Rites', *Journal of Material Culture*, 9 (2004), 263–96.

CHAPTER 1. THE RISE AND FALL
OF LATE ANTIQUE BRITAIN

The Fundamental Readings

A. S. Esmonde Cleary, *The Ending of Roman Britain* (London, 1989).

N. Faulkner with R. Reece, 'The Debate about the End: A Review of Evidence and Methods', *Archaeological Journal*, 159 (2002), 59–76.

K. Hopkins, 'Taxes and Trade in the Roman Empire (200 BC–AD 400)', *Journal of Roman Studies*, 70 (1980), 101–25.

M. Millett, *The Romanization of Britain: An Essay in Archaeological Interpretation* (Cambridge, 1990).

M. Todd (ed.), *A Companion to Roman Britain* (Oxford, 2007).

General, Empire-wide Background

P. Brown, *The World of Late Antiquity AD 150–750* (London, 1971).

P. Heather, *The Fall of the Roman Empire: A New History of Rome and the Barbarians* (Oxford, 2007).

A. H. M. Jones, *The Later Roman Empire 284–602*, 2 vols. (Oxford, 1964).

P. Salway, *The Oxford Illustrated History of Roman Britain* (Oxford, 1993).

B. Ward-Perkins, *The Fall of Rome and the End of Civilization* (Oxford, 2005).

C. Wickham, *The Framing of the Early Middle Ages: Europe and the Mediterranean, 400–800* (Oxford, 2007).

Roman Britain

N. Bateman, C. Cowan and R. Wroe-Brown, *London's Roman Amphitheatre: Guildhall Yard, City of London*, MoLAS Monograph, 35 (London, 2008).

P. Booth, A. Dodd, M. Robinson and A. Smith, *Thames through Time: The Archaeology of Gravel Terraces of the Upper and Middle Thames. The Early Historical Period: AD 1–1000*, Oxford Archaeology Thames Valley Landscapes Monographs, 27 (Oxford, 2007).

P. Budd, J. Montgomery, J. Evans and M. Trickett, 'Human Lead Exposure in England from Approximately 5500 BP to the 16th century AD', *The Science of the Total Environment*, 318 (2004), 45–58.

N. Christie, 'Construction and Deconstruction: Reconstructing the Late-Roman Townscape', in T. R. Slater (ed.), *Towns in Decline, AD 100–1600* (Aldershot, 2000), 51–71.

G. Clarke, *The Roman Cemetery at Lankhills* (Oxford, 1979).

H. E. M. Cool, *Eating and Drinking in Roman Britain* (Cambridge, 2006).

A. S. Esmonde Cleary, *Extra-mural Areas of Romano-British Towns*, BAR, Brit. Ser., 169 (Oxford, 1987).

D. E. Farwell and T. I. Molleson, *Excavations at Poundbury, Dorchester, Dorset 1966–82: The Cemeteries*, vol. 2 (Dorchester, 1993).

N. Faulkner, 'Later Roman Colchester', *Oxford Journal of Archaeology*, 13 (1994), 93–120.

A. Gardner, *An Archaeology of Identity: Soldiers and Society in Late Roman Britain* (Walnut Creek, Calif., 2007).

C. Gerrard with M. Aston, *The Shapwick Project, Somerset: A Rural Landscape Explored*, Society for Medieval Archaeology Monograph Series, 25 (Leeds, 2007).

J. Hall, 'The Shopkeepers and Craft-Workers of Roman London', in A. Mac Mahon and J. Price (eds.), *Roman Working Lives and Urban Living* (Oxford, 2005), 125–44.

S. Leach, M. Lewis, C. Chenery, G. Müldner and H. Eckardt, 'Migration and Diversity in Roman Britain: A Multidisciplinary Approach to the Identification of Immigrants in Roman York, England', *American Journal of Physical Anthropology*, 140 (2009), 546–61.

P. Marsden and B. West, 'Population Change in Roman London', *Britannia*, 23 (1992), 133–40.

D. Miles, *Archaeology at Barton Court Farm, Abingdon, Oxon: An Investigation of Late Neolithic, Iron Age, Romano-British and Saxon Settlements*, CBA, Research Report, 50 (Oxford, 1986).

P. Murphy, U. Albarella, M. Germany and A. Locker, 'Production, Imports and Status: Biological Remains from a Late Roman Farm at Great Holts Farm, Boreham, Essex, UK', *Environmental Archaeology*, 5 (2000), 35–48.

D. Perring, *Roman London* (London, 1991).

—— 'Spatial Organization and Social Change in Roman Towns', in J. Rich and A. Wallace-Hadrill (eds.), *City and Country in the Ancient World* (London, 1991), 273–93.

—— and T. Brigham, 'Londinium and its Hinterland: The Roman Period', in T. Brigham (ed.), *The Archaeology of Greater London* (London, 2000), 119–70.

R. Philpott, *Burial Practices in Roman Britain: A Survey of Grave Treatment and Furnishing AD 43–410*, BAR, Brit. Ser., 219 (Oxford, 1991).

G. Pucci, 'Pottery and Trade in the Roman Period', in P. Garnsey, K. Hopkins and C. R. Whittaker (eds.), *Trade in the Ancient Economy* (Berkeley, 1983), 105–17.

R. Reece, *Coinage in Roman Britain* (London, 1987).

M. P. Richards, R. E. M. Hedges, T. I. Molleson and J. C. Vogel, 'Stable Isotope Analysis Reveals Variations in Human Diet at the Poundbury Camp Cemetery Site', *Journal of Archaeological Science*, 25 (1998), 1247–52.

K. Seetah, 'Multi-disciplinary Approaches to Romano-British Cattle Butchery', in M. Maltby (ed.), *Ninth ICAZ Conference: Integrating Zooarchaeology* (Oxford, 2006), 109–16.

H. Swain and T. Williams, 'The Population of Roman London', in J. Clark, J. Cotton, J. Hall, R. Sherris and H. Swain (eds.), *Londinium and Beyond: Essays on Roman London and its Hinterland for Harvey Sheldon*, CBA, Research Report, 156 (York, 2008), 3–40.

J. Timby, R. Brown, E. Biddulph, A. Hardy and A. Powell, *A Slice of Rural Essex: Archaeological Discoveries from the A120 between Stansted Airport and Braintree* (Oxford, 2007).

M. Todd (ed.), *Research on Roman Britain 1960–89*, Britannia Monograph Series, 11 (London, 1989).

M. van der Veen, A. Livarda and A. Hill, 'New Plant Foods in Roman Britain – Dispersal and Social Access', *Environmental Archaeology*, 13 (2008), 11–36.

The Fall of Roman Britain

D. A. Brooks, 'A Review of the Evidence for Continuity in British Towns in the Fifth and Sixth Centuries', *Oxford Journal of Archaeology*, 5 (1986), 77–102.

R. Cowie, 'Descent into Darkness: London in the 5th and 6th Centuries', in J. Clark, J. Cotton, J. Hall, R. Sherris and H. Swain (eds.), *Londinium and Beyond: Essays on Roman London and its Hinterland for Harvey Sheldon*, CBA, Research Report, 156 (York, 2008), 49–53.

J. Davey, 'The Environs of South Cadbury in the Late Antique and Early Medieval Period', in R. Collins and J. Gerrard (eds.), *Debating Late Antiquity in Britain AD 300–700*, BAR, Brit. Ser., 365 (Oxford, 2004), 43–54.

N. Faulkner, 'Change and Decline in Late Romano-British Towns', in T. R. Slater (ed.), *Towns in Decline, AD 100–1600* (Aldershot, 2000), 25–50.

—— 'Verulamium: Interpreting Decline', *Archaeological Journal*, 154 (1996), 79–103.

M. G. Fulford and A. S. M. Clarke, 'Silchester and the End of Roman Towns', *Current Archaeology*, 14 (1999), 176–80.

A. F. Pearson, 'Barbarian Piracy and the Saxon Shore: A Reappraisal', *Oxford Journal of Archaeology*, 24 (2005), 73–88.

D. Petts, 'Burial in Western Britain AD 400–800', in R. Collins and J. Gerrard (eds.), *Debating Late Antiquity in Britain AD 300–700*, BAR, Brit. Ser., 365 (Oxford, 2004), 77–87.

CHAPTER 2. LIFE AMONG THE RUINS

The Fundamental Readings

J. Chapman and H. Hamerow (eds.), *Migration and Invasion in Archaeological Explanation*, BAR, Int. Ser., 664 (Oxford, 1997).

R. Collins and J. Gerrard (eds.), *Debating Late Antiquity in Britain AD 300–700*, BAR, Brit. Ser., 365 (Oxford, 2004).

H. Hamerow, *Early Medieval Settlements: The Archaeology of Rural Communities in Northwest Europe*, 400–900 (Oxford, 2002).

S. J. Lucy, *The Anglo-Saxon Way of Death: Burial Rites in Early England* (Stroud, 2000).

T. Wilmott and P. Wilson (eds.), *The Late Roman Transition in the North*, BAR, Brit. Ser., 299 (Oxford, 2000).

B. Yorke, 'Fact or Fiction? The Written Evidence for the Fifth and Sixth Centuries AD', *Anglo-Saxon Studies in Archaeology and History*, 6 (1993), 45–50.

British Communities in the Post-Roman Period

P. Barker, R. White, K. Pretty, H. Bird and M. Corbishley, *The Baths Basilica Wroxeter: Excavations 1966–90*, English Heritage Archaeological Report, 8 (London, 1997).

R. C. Barrowman, C. E. Batey and C. D. Morris, *Excavations at Tintagel Castle, Cornwall 1990–1999* (London, 2007).

S. Bassett, 'Medieval Ecclesiastical Organisation in the Vicinity of Wroxeter and its British Antecedents', *Journal of the British Archaeological Association*, 145 (1992), 1–28.

J. Bintliff and H. Hamerow (eds.), *Europe between Late Antiquity and the Middle Ages*, BAR, Int. Ser., 617 (Oxford, 1995).

P. Booth, 'Late Roman Cemeteries in Oxfordshire: A Review', *Oxoniensia*, 66 (2001), 13–42.

D. A. Brooks, 'A Review of the Evidence for Continuity in British Towns in the Fifth and Sixth Centuries', *Oxford Journal of Archaeology*, 5 (1986), 77–102.

B. C. Burnham, 'Review of Wroxeter: Life and Death of a Roman City', *Britannia*, 30 (1999), 422–4.

E. Campbell, *Continental and Mediterranean Imports to Atlantic Britain and Ireland, AD 400–800*, CBA, Research Report, 157 (York, 2007).

R. Collins, 'Before "the End": Hadrian's Wall in the Fourth Century and After', in R. Collins and J. Gerrard (eds.), *Debating Late Antiquity in Britain AD 300–700*, BAR, Brit. Ser., 365 (Oxford, 2004), 123–32.

H. E. M. Cool, 'The Parts Left Over: Material Culture into the 5th Century', in T. Wilmott and P. Wilson (eds.), *The Late Roman Transition in the North*, BAR, Brit. Ser., 299 (Oxford, 2000), 47–65.

N. J. Cooper, 'Searching for the Blank Generation: Consumer Choice in Roman and Post-Roman Britain', in J. Webster and N. J. Cooper (eds.), *Roman Imperialism and Post-Colonial Perspectives* (Leicester, 1996), 85–98.

A. S. Esmonde Cleary, 'Summing Up', in T. Wilmott and P. Wilson (eds.), *The Late Roman Transition in the North*, BAR, Brit. Ser., 299 (Oxford, 2000), 89–94.

A. Livarda, 'New Temptations? Olive, Cherry and Mulberry in Roman and Medieval Europe', in M. Allen, S. Baker, S. Middle and K. Poole (eds.), *Food and Drink in Archaeology: University of Nottingham Postgraduate Conference 2007* (Totnes, 2008), 73–83.

S. T. Loseby, 'Power and Towns in Late Roman Britain and Early Anglo-Saxon England', in G. Ripoll and J. M. Gurt (eds.), *Sedes regiae (ann. 400–800)* (Barcelona, 2000), 319–70.

D. Miles, *Archaeology at Barton Court Farm, Abingdon, Oxon: An Investigation of Late Neolithic, Iron Age, Romano-British and Saxon Settlements*, CBA, Research Report, 50 (Oxford, 1986).

S. Parry, *Raunds Area Survey* (Oxford, 2006).

P. Rahtz, A. Woodward and I. Burrow, *Cadbury Congresbury 1968–73: A Late/Post-Roman Hilltop Settlement in Somerset*, BAR, Brit. Ser., 223 (Oxford, 1992).

S. Rippon, *Gwent Levels: The Evolution of a Wetland Landscape*, CBA, Research Report, 105 (York, 1996).

C. Whittaker, *Frontiers of the Roman Empire: A Social and Economic Study* (Baltimore, 1994).

T. Wilmott with L. Hird, K. Izard, J. Summerfield and L. Allason-Jones, *Birdoswald: Excavations of a Roman Fort on Hadrian's Wall and its Successor Settlements, 1987–92*, English Heritage Archaeological Report, 14 (London, 1994).

J. M. Wooding, *Communication and Commerce along the Western Sealanes AD 400–800*, BAR, Int. Ser., 654 (Oxford, 1996).

New Immigrants

P. H. Dixon, 'The Anglo-Saxon Settlement at Mucking: An Interpretation', *Anglo-Saxon Studies in Archaeology and History*, 6 (1993), 125–47.

B. Eagles and C. Mortimer, 'Early Anglo-Saxon Artefacts from Hod Hill Dorset', *Antiquaries Journal*, 73 (1994 for 1993), 132–40.

V. I. Evison, *An Anglo-Saxon Cemetery at Alton, Hampshire* (Winchester, 1988).

H. Hamerow, 'Anglo-Saxon Oxfordshire, 400–700', *Oxoniensia*, 64 (1999), 23–38.

—— *Excavations at Mucking II: Anglo-Saxon Settlement*, English Heritage Archaeological Report, 21 (London, 1993).

—— 'Shaping Settlements: Early Medieval Communities in Northwest Europe', in J. Bintliff and H. Hamerow (eds.), *Europe between Late Antiquity and the Middle Ages*, BAR, Int. Ser., 617 (Oxford, 1995), 8–37.

L. Laing, 'Some Anglo-Saxon Artefacts from Nottinghamshire', *Anglo-Saxon Studies in Archaeology and History*, 13 (2006), 80–96.

J. Murray and T. McDonald, 'Excavations at Station Road, Gamlingay, Cambridgeshire', *Anglo-Saxon Studies in Archaeology and History*, 13 (2006), 173–330.

C. Scull, 'Archaeology, Early Anglo-Saxon Society and the Origins of Anglo-Saxon Kingdoms', *Anglo-Saxon Studies in Archaeology and History*, 6 (1993), 65–82.

M. Welch, 'The Archaeological Evidence for Federate Settlement in Britain within the Fifth Century', in F. Vallet and M. Kazanski (eds.), *L'Armée romaine et les barbares du IIIe au VIIe siècle* (Paris, 1993), 269–78.

—— 'Relating Anglo-Saxon Chronology to Continental Chronologies in the Fifth Century AD', in U. von Freeden, U. Koch and A. Wieczorek (eds.), *Völker an Nord- und Ostsee und die Franken* (Bonn, 1999), 31–8.

Settling In and Assimilation

P. Booth, A. Dodd, M. Robinson and A. Smith, *Thames through Time: The Archaeology of Gravel Terraces of the Upper and Middle Thames. The Early Historical Period: AD 1–1000*, Oxford Archaeology Thames Valley Landscapes Monographs, 27 (Oxford, 2007).

A. Boyle, A. Dodd, D. Miles and A. Mudd, *Two Oxfordshire Anglo-Saxon Cemeteries: Berinsfield and Didcot*, Oxford Archaeology Thames Valley Landscapes Monographs, 8 (Oxford, 1995).

P. Budd, A. Millard, C. Chernery, S. J. Lucy and C. Roberts, 'Investigating Population Movement by Stable Isotope Analysis: A Report from Britain', *Antiquity*, 78 (2004), 127–41.

M. O. H. Carver, C. Hills and J. Scheschkewitz, *Wasperton: A Roman, British and Anglo-Saxon Community in Central England* (Woodbridge, 2009).

R. A. Chambers, 'The Late- and Sub-Roman Cemetery at Queenford Farm, Dorchester-on-Thames, Oxon.', *Oxoniensia*, 52 (1987), 35–69.

V. I. Evison and P. Hill, *Two Anglo-Saxon Cemeteries at Beckford, Hereford and Worcester*, CBA, Research Report, 103 (York, 1996).

H. Geake and J. Kenny (eds.), *Early Deira: Archaeological Studies of the East Riding in the Fourth to the Ninth Centuries AD* (Oxford, 2000).

M. Gelling, *Signposts to the Past: Place-Names and the History of England*, 2nd edn. (Chichester, 1988).

C. M. Hills and T. C. O'Connell, 'New Light on the Anglo-Saxon Succession: Two Cemeteries and their Dates', *Antiquity*, 83 (2009), 1096–1108.

P. Inker, 'Technology as Active Material Culture: The Quoit-Brooch Style', *Medieval Archaeology*, 44 (2000), 25–52.

J. Lloyd-Jones, 'Measuring Biological Affinity among Populations: A Case Study of Romano-British and Anglo-Saxon Populations', in J. Huggett and N. Ryan (eds.), *Computer Applications and Quantitative Methods in Archaeology 1994*, BAR, Int. Ser., 600 (Oxford, 1995), 69–73.

C. Loveluck, 'Archaeological Expressions of the Transition from the Late Roman to Early Anglo-Saxon Period in Lowland East Yorkshire', in P. Halkon and M. Millett, *Rural Settlement and Industry: Studies in the Iron Age and Roman Archaeology of Lowland East Yorkshire*, Yorkshire Archaeological Report, 4 (Leeds, 1999), 228–36.

K. Parfitt and B. Brugmann, *The Anglo-Saxon Cemetery on Mill Hill, Deal, Kent*, Society for Medieval Archaeology Monograph Series, 14 (London, 1997).

G. Taylor, C. Allen, J. Bayley, J. Cowgill, V. Fryer, C. Palmer, B. Precious, J. Rackham, T. Roper and J. Young, 'An Early to Middle Saxon Settlement at Quarrington, Lincolnshire', *Antiquaries Journal*, 83 (2003), 231–80.

B. Ward-Perkins, 'Why Did the Anglo-Saxons Not Become more British?', *English Historical Review*, 115 (2000), 513–33.

R. H. White, *Roman and Celtic Objects from Anglo-Saxon Graves*, BAR, Brit. Ser., 191 (Oxford, 1988).

H. M. R. Williams, 'Identities and Cemeteries in Roman and Early Medieval Britain', in P. Baker, C. Forcey, S. Jundi and R. Witcher (eds.), *TRAC 98: Proceedings of the Eighth Annual Theoretical Roman Archaeology Conference* (Oxford, 1999), 96–107.

CHAPTER 3. MAKING PEOPLES, MAKING CLASS

The Fundamental Readings

D. Anthony, 'Prehistoric Migration as Social Process', in J. Chapman and H. Hamerow (eds.), *Migrations and Invasions in Archaeological Explanation*, BAR, Int. Ser., 664 (Oxford, 1997), 21–32.

D. Austin and J. Thomas, 'The "Proper Study" of Medieval Archaeology: A Case Study', in D. Austin and L. Alcock (eds.), *From the Baltic to the Black Sea: Studies in Medieval Archaeology* (London, 1990), 43–78.

M. O. H. Carver, C. M. Hills and J. Scheschkewitz, *Wasperton: A Roman, British and Anglo-Saxon Community in Central England* (Woodbridge, 2009).

G. Halsall, *Settlement and Social Organization: The Merovingian Region of Metz* (Cambridge, 1995).

Y. Hen, *Roman Barbarians: The Royal Court and Culture in the Early Medieval West* (Basingstoke, 2007).

E. James, 'Burial and Status in the Early Medieval West', *Transactions of the Royal Historical Society*, 5th ser., 39 (1989), 23–40.

R. Jenkins, *Rethinking Ethnicity: Arguments and Explorations* (London, 1997).

S. Jones, *The Archaeology of Ethnicity: Constructing Identities in the Past and Present* (London, 1997).

M. Parker Pearson, *The Archaeology of Death and Burial* (Stroud, 1999).

W. Pohl and H. Reimitz (eds.), *Strategies of Distinction: The Construction of Ethnic Communities, 300–800* (Leiden, 1998).

S. Reynolds, 'Medieval *origines gentium* and the Community of the Realm', *History*, 68 (1983), 375–90.

—— 'What Do We Mean by "Anglo-Saxon" and "Anglo-Saxons"?', *Journal of British Studies*, 24 (1985), 395–414.

Eastern Britain

P. Blinkhorn, 'Habitus, Social Identity and Anglo-Saxon Pottery', in C. G. Cumberpatch and P. W. Blinkhorn (eds.), *Not so Much a Pot, More a Way of Life: Current Approaches to Artefact Analysis in Archaeology* (Oxford, 1997), 113–24.

B. Brugmann, 'The Role of Continental Artefact-Types in Sixth-Century Kentish Chronology', in J. Hines, K. Høilund Nielsen and F. Siegmund (eds.), *The Pace of Change: Studies in Early Medieval Chronology* (Oxford, 1999), 37–64.

S. Chadwick Hawkes and G. Grainger, ed. B. Brugmann, *The Anglo-Saxon Cemetery at Finglesham, Kent* (Oxford, 2006).

S. Crawford, *Childhood in Anglo-Saxon England* (Stroud, 1999).

V. I. Evison, *An Anglo-Saxon Cemetery at Great Chesterford, Essex*, CBA, Research Report, 91 (York, 1994).

W. J. Ford, 'Anglo-Saxon Cemeteries along the Avon Valley', *Birmingham and Warwick Archaeological Society*, 100 (1996), 59–98.

C. M. Hills, 'Who Were the East Anglians?', in J. Gardiner (ed.), *Flatlands and Wetlands: Current Themes in East Anglian Archaeology*, East Anglian Archaeology, 50 (Norwich, 1993), 14–23.

J. Hines, *The Scandinavian Character of Anglian England in the Pre-Viking Period*, BAR, Brit. Ser., 124 (Oxford, 1984).

—— 'The Sixth-Century Transition in Anglian England: An Analysis of Female Graves from Cambridgeshire', in J. Hines, K. Høilund Nielsen and F. Siegmund (eds.), *The Pace of Change: Studies in Early Medieval Chronology* (Oxford, 1999), 65–79.

K. Leahy 'The Anglo-Saxon Settlement of Lindsey', in A. Vince (ed.), *Pre-Viking Lindsey* (Lincoln, 1993), 29–44.

J. Lloyd-Jones, 'Measuring Biological Affinity among Populations: A Case Study of Romano-British and Anglo-Saxon Populations', in J. Huggett and N. Ryan (eds.), *Computer Applications and Quantitative Methods in Archaeology 1994*, BAR, Int. Ser., 600 (Oxford, 1995), 69–73.

F. McCormick, 'The Distribution of Meat in a Hierarchical Society: The Irish Evidence', in P. Miracle and N. Milner (eds.), *Consuming Passions and Patterns of Consumption*, McDonald Institute Monograph (Cambridge, 2002), 25–32.

T. Malim and J. Hines, *The Anglo-Saxon Cemetery at Edix Hill (Barrington A), Cambridgeshire*, CBA, Research Report, 112 (York, 1998).

M. Millett, 'Treasure: Interpreting Roman Hoards', in S. Cottam, D. Dungworth, S. Scott and J. Taylor (eds.), *TRAC 94: Proceedings of the Fourth Annual Theoretical Roman Archaeology Conference* (Oxford, 1994), 99–106.

—— and S. James, 'Excavations at Cowdery's Down, Basingstoke, Hampshire 1978–81', *Archaeological Journal*, 140 (1983), 151–279.

J. Moreland, 'Ethnicity, Power and the English', in W. O. Frazer and A. Tyrrell (eds.), *Social Identity in Early Medieval Britain* (London, 2000), 23–52.

C. O'Brien and R. Miket, 'The Early Medieval Settlement of Thirlings, Northumberland', *Durham Archaeological Journal*, 7 (1991), 57–92.

G. R. Owen-Crocker, *Dress in Anglo-Saxon England*, 2nd edn. (Woodbridge, 2004).

K. Parfitt, 'The Buckland Saxon Cemetery', *Current Archaeology*, 144 (1995), 459–64.

—— and B. Brugmann, *The Anglo-Saxon Cemetery on Mill Hill, Deal, Kent*, Society for Medieval Archaeology Monograph Series, 14 (London, 1997).

K. Penn and B. Brugmann with K. Høilund Nielsen, *Aspects of Anglo-Saxon Inhumation Burial: Morning Thorpe, Spong Hill, Bergh Apton and Westgarth Gardens*, East Anglian Archaeology, 119 (Peterborough, 2007).

K. Steane and A. Vince, 'Post-Roman Lincoln: Archaeological Evidence for Activity in Lincoln in the 5th–9th Centuries', in A. Vince (ed.), *Pre-Viking Lindsey* (Lincoln, 1993), 71–9.

N. Stoodley, *The Spindle and the Spear: A Critical Enquiry into the Construction and Meaning of Gender in the Early Anglo-Saxon Burial Rite*, BAR, Brit. Ser., 288 (Oxford, 1999).

A. Taylor, C. Duhig and J. Hines, 'An Anglo-Saxon Cemetery at Oakington, Cambridgeshire', *Proceedings of the Cambridge Antiquarian Society*, 86 (1997), 57–90.

P. Walton Rogers, *Cloth and Clothing in Early Anglo-Saxon England AD 450–700*, CBA, Research Report, 145 (York, 2007).

R. H. White, *Roman and Celtic Objects from Anglo-Saxon Graves*, BAR, Brit. Ser., 191 (Oxford, 1988).

H. Williams, 'An Ideology of Transformation: Cremation Rites and Animal Sacrifice in Early Anglo-Saxon England', in. N. Price (ed.), *The Archaeology of Shamanism* (London, 2001), 193–212.

Western Britain

R. C. Barrowman, C. E. Batey and C. D. Morris, *Excavations at Tintagel Castle, Cornwall 1990–1999* (London, 2007).

K. S. Brassil, W. G. Owen and W. J. Britnell, 'Prehistoric and Early Medieval Cemeteries at Tandderwen, near Denbigh, Clwyd', *Archaeological Journal*, 148 (1991), 46–97.

E. Campbell, *Continental and Mediterranean Imports to Atlantic Britain and Ireland, AD 400–800*, CBA, Research Report, 157 (York, 2007).

—— 'New Finds of Post-Roman Imported Pottery and Glass from South Wales', *Archaeologia Cambrensis*, 138 (1989), 59–66.

—— and A. Lane, 'Excavations at Longbury Bank, Dyfed and Early Medieval Settlement in South Wales', *Medieval Archaeology*, 37 (1993), 15–77.

—— and P. MacDonald, 'Excavations at Caerwent Vicarage Orchard Garden 1973: An Extra-mural Post-Roman Cemetery', *Archaeologia Cambrensis*, 142 (1993), 74–98.

T. Charles-Edwards, 'Language and Society among the Insular Celts AD 400–1000', in M. J. Green (ed.), *The Celtic World* (London, 1995), 703–36.

W. Davies, *Wales in the Early Middle Ages* (Leicester, 1982).

S. T. Driscoll, 'Discourse on the Frontiers of History: Material Culture and Social Reproduction in Early Scotland', *Historical Archaeology*, 26 (1992), 12–25.

N. Edwards, 'Early-Medieval Inscribed Stones and Stone Sculpture in Wales: Context and Function', *Medieval Archaeology*, 45 (2001), 15–39.

—— (ed.), *Landscape and Settlement in Medieval Wales* (Oxford, 1997).

M. A. Handley, 'The Early Medieval Inscriptions of Western Britain: Function and Sociology', in J. Hill and M. Swan (eds.), *The Community, the Family and the Saint: Patterns of Power in Early Medieval Europe* (Turnhout, 1998), 339–61.

—— 'The Origins of Christian Commemoration in Late Antique Britain', *Early Medieval Europe*, 10 (2001), 177–99.

P. Hill (ed.), *Whithorn and St Ninian: The Excavation of a Monastic Town 1984–1991* (Stroud, 1997).

N. Holbrook and A. Thomas, 'An Early-Medieval Monastic Cemetery at Llandough, Glamorgan: Excavations in 1994', *Medieval Archaeology*, 49 (2005), 1–92.

H. James, 'Early Medieval Cemeteries in Wales', in N. Edwards and A. Lane (eds.), *The Early Church in Wales and the West* (Oxford, 1992), 90–103.

J. Knight, 'Late Roman and Post-Roman Caerwent: Some Evidence from Metalwork', *Archaeologia Cambrensis*, 145 (1996), 35–66.

M. Lapidge and D. N. Dumville, *Gildas: New Approaches* (Woodbridge, 1984).

'Llandough', *Current Archaeology*, 146 (1996), 73–7.

H. Mytum, 'Across the Irish Sea: Romano-British and Irish Settlement in Wales', *Emania*, 13 (1995), 15–22.

D. Petts, 'Christianity and the End of Roman Britain', in P. Baker, C. Forcey, S. Jundi and R. Witcher (eds.), *TRAC 98: Proceedings of the Eighth Annual Theoretical Roman Archaeology Conference* (Oxford, 1999), 86–95.

S. J. Sherlock and M. G. Welch, *An Anglo-Saxon Cemetery at Norton, Cleveland*, CBA, Research Report, 82 (London, 1992).

P. Sims-Williams, 'Gildas and the Anglo-Saxons', *Cambridge Medieval Celtic Studies*, 6 (1983), 1–30.

P. N. Wood, 'On the Little British Kingdom of Craven', *Northern History*, 32 (1996), 1–20.

N. Wright, 'Gildas's Reading: A Survey', *Sacris Erudiri*, 32 (1991), 121–62.

CHAPTER 4. ELITES, KINGDOMS AND A BRAND-NEW PAST

The Fundamental Readings

S. R. Bassett (ed.), *The Origins of Anglo-Saxon Kingdoms* (London, 1989).

R. Bradley, 'Time Regained: The Creation of Continuity', *Journal of the British Archaeological Association*, 140 (1987), 1–17.

T. Charles-Edwards, 'The Making of Nations in Britain and Ireland in the Early Middle Ages', in R. Evans (ed.), *Lordship and Learning: Studies in Memory of Trevor Aston* (Woodbridge, 2004), 11–32.

D. Dumville, 'Kingship, Genealogies and Regnal Lists', in P. Sawyer and I. N. Wood (eds.), *Early Medieval Kingship* (Leeds, 1977), 72–104.

H. Härke, 'Cemeteries as Places of Power', in M. de Jong and F. Theuws with C. van Rhijn (eds.), *Topographies of Power in the Early Middle Ages* (Leiden, 2001), 9–30.

S. Keynes, 'England, 700–900', in R. McKitterick (ed.), *The New Cambridge Medieval History*, vol. 2: *c. 700–c. 900* (Cambridge, 1995), 18–42.

P. Sims-Williams, 'The Settlement of England in Bede and the Chronicle', *Anglo-Saxon England*, 12 (1983), 1–41.

K. Sisam, 'Anglo-Saxon Royal Genealogies', *Proceedings of the British Academy*, 39 (1953), 287–348.

Building a Usable Past

C. M. Antonaccio, *An Archaeology of Ancestors: Tomb Cult and Hero Cult in Early Greece* (London, 1995).

J. Barnatt and J. R. Collis, *Barrows in the Peak District: Recent Research* (Sheffield, 1996).

J. Blair, 'Anglo-Saxon Pagan Shrines and their Prototypes', *Anglo-Saxon Studies in Archaeology and History*, 8 (1995), 1–28.

R. Bradley, *The Significance of Monuments* (London, 1998).

J. Collis, *Wigber Low, Derbyshire: A Bronze Age and Anglian Burial Site in the White Peak* (Sheffield, 1983).

T. M. Dickinson and G. Speake, 'The Seventh-Century Cremation Burial in Asthall Barrow, Oxfordshire: A Reassessment', in M. O. H. Carver (ed.), *The Age of Sutton Hoo: The Seventh Century in North-Western Europe* (Woodbridge, 1992), 95–130.

S. T. Driscoll, 'Picts and Prehistory: Cultural Resource Management in Early Medieval Scotland', *World Archaeology*, 30 (1998), 142–58.

H. Geake, 'Burial Practice in Seventh- and Eighth-Century England', in M. O. H. Carver (ed.), *The Age of Sutton Hoo: The Seventh Century in North-Western Europe* (Woodbridge, 1992), 83–94.

H. Härke, 'Material Culture as Myth: Weapons in Anglo-Saxon Graves', in C. K. Jensen and K. Høilund Nielsen (eds.), *Burial and Society: The Chronological and Social Analysis of Archaeological Burial Data* (Aarhus, 1997), 119–27.

R. Hartridge, 'Excavations at the Prehistoric and Romano-British Site on Slonk Hill, Shoreham, Sussex', *Sussex Archaeological Collections*, 116 (1978), 69–141.

R. Hingley, 'Ancestors and Identity in the Later Pre-history of Atlantic Scotland: The Reuse and Reinvention of Neolithic Monuments and Material Culture', *World Archaeology*, 28 (1996), 231–43.

K. Høilund Nielsen, 'Style II and the Anglo-Saxon Elite', *Anglo-Saxon Studies in Archaeology and History*, 10 (1999), 185–202.

G. Holleyman, 'Harrow Hill Excavations, 1936', *Sussex Archaeological Collections*, 78 (1937), 230–51.

B. Hope-Taylor, *Yeavering: An Anglo-British Centre of Early Northumbria* (London, 1977).

H. James, 'Early Medieval Cemeteries in Wales', in N. Edwards and A. Lane (eds.), *The Early Church in Wales and the West* (Oxford, 1992), 90–104.

A. Meany, 'Bede and Anglo-Saxon Paganism', *Parergon*, new ser., 3 (1985), 1–29.

—— 'Pagan English Sanctuaries, Place-Names and Hundred Meeting-Places', *Anglo-Saxon Studies in Archaeology and History*, 8 (1995), 29–42.

K. Mizoguchi, 'Time in the Reproduction of Mortuary Practices', *World Archaeology*, 25 (1993), 223–35.

K. Murphy, 'Plas Gogerddan, Dyfed: A Multi-period Burial and Ritual Site', *Archaeological Journal*, 149 (1992), 1–38.

M. Parker Pearson, 'The Powerful Dead: Archaeological Relationships between the Living and the Dead', *Cambridge Archaeological Journal*, 3 (1993), 203–29.

—— 'Tombs and Territories: Material Culture and Multiple Interpretation', in I. Hodder, M. Shanks, A. Alexandri, V. Buchli, J. Carman, J. Last and G. Lucas (eds.), *Interpreting Archaeology: Finding Meaning in the Past* (London, 1995), 205–9.

D. Petts, 'Landscape and Cultural Identity in Roman Britain', in M. de Jong and F. Theuws, with C. van Rhijn (eds.), *Topographies of Power in the Early Middle Ages* (Leiden, 2001), 79–94.

M. Ravn, *Death Ritual and Germanic Social Structure (c. AD 200–600)*, BAR, Int. Ser., 1164 (Oxford, 2003).

C. Scull, 'Post-Roman Phase I at Yeavering: A Reconsideration', *Medieval Archaeology*, 35 (1991), 51–63.

S. Semple, 'Burials and Political Boundaries in the Avebury Region, North Wiltshire', *Anglo-Saxon Studies in Archaeology and History*, 12 (2003), 72–91.

—— 'A Fear of the Past: The Place of the Prehistoric Burial Mound in the Ideology of Middle and Later Anglo-Saxon England', *World Archaeology*, 30 (1998), 109–26.

J. Shephard, 'The Social Identity of the Individual in Isolated Barrows and Barrow Cemeteries in Anglo-Saxon England', in B. Burnham and J. Kingsbury (eds.), *Space, Hierarchy and Society: Interdisciplinary Studies in Social Area Analysis*, BAR, Brit. Ser., 59 (Oxford, 1979), 47–79.

G. Speake, *A Saxon Bed Burial on Swallowcliffe Down*, English Heritage Archaeological Report, 10 (London, 1989).

C. Tilley, 'The Powers of Rocks: Topography and Monument Construction on Bodmin Moor', *World Archaeology*, 28 (1996), 161–76.

M. Tingle, *The Vale of the White Horse Survey – The Study of a Changing Landscape in the Clay Lowlands of Southern England from Prehistory to the Present*, BAR, Brit. Ser., 218 (Oxford, 1991).

R. van de Noort, 'The Context of Early Medieval Barrows in Western Europe', *Antiquity*, 67 (1993), 66–73.

H. Williams, 'Ancient Landscapes and the Dead: The Reuse of Prehistoric and Roman Monuments as Early Anglo-Saxon Burial Sites', *Medieval Archaeology*, 41 (1997), 1–31.

—— *Death and Memory in Early Medieval Britain* (Cambridge, 2006).

—— 'Monuments and the Past in Early Anglo-Saxon England', *World Archaeology*, 30 (1998), 90–108.

—— 'Placing the Dead: Investigating the Location of Wealthy Barrow Burials in Seventh-Century England', in M. Rundkvist (ed.), *Grave Matters*, BAR, Int. Ser., 781 (Oxford, 1999), 57–86.

B. Yorke, 'Fact or Fiction? The Written Evidence for the Fifth and Sixth Centuries AD', *Anglo-Saxon Studies in Archaeology and History*, 6 (1993), 45–50.

—— 'The Origins of Anglo-Saxon Kingdoms: The Contribution of Written Sources', *Anglo-Saxon Studies in Archaeology and History*, 10 (1999), 25–9.

Social Aggregates and Early Kingdoms

M. Biddle and B. Kjølbye-Biddle, 'Repton and the Vikings', *Antiquity*, 66 (1992), 36–52.

J. Blair, *Anglo-Saxon Oxfordshire* (Oxford, 1994).

—— *Early Medieval Surrey: Landholding, Church and Settlement before 1300* (Gloucester, 1991).

M. P. Brown and C. A. Farr (eds.), *Mercia: An Anglo-Saxon Kingdom in Europe* (London, 2001).

J. Campbell, 'Bede's Words for Places', in J. Campbell, *Essays in Anglo-Saxon History* (London, 1986), 99–119.

M. O. H. Carver, *Sutton Hoo: A Seventh-Century Princely Burial Ground and its Context* (London, 2005).

P. Combes and M. Lyne, 'Hastings, Haestingaceaster and Haestingaport: A Question of Identity', *Sussex Archaeological Collections*, 133 (1995), 213–24.

W. Davies and H. Vierck, 'The Contexts of Tribal Hidage: Social Aggregates and Settlement Patterns', *Frühmittelalterliche Studien*, 8 (1974), 223–93.

J. McN. Dodgson, 'The Significance of the Distribution of the English Place-Name in *ingas-*, *-inga-* in South-East England', *Medieval Archaeology*, 10 (1966), 1–29.

R. Faith, *The English Peasantry and the Growth of Lordship* (London, 1997).

H. Fox, 'Fragmented Manors and the Customs of the Anglo-Saxons', in S. Keynes and A. P. Smyth (eds.), *Anglo-Saxons: Studies Presented to Cyril Roy Hart* (Dublin, 2006), 78–97.

H. E. Hallam, 'England before the Norman Conquest', in H. E. Hallam (ed.), *The Agrarian History of England and Wales*, vol. 2: *1042–1350* (Cambridge, 1988), 1–44.

H. Hamerow, *Early Medieval Settlements: The Archaeology of Rural Communities in Northwest Europe*, 400–900 (Oxford, 2002).

A. Hardy, B. M. Charles and R. J. Williams, *Death and Taxes: The Archaeology of a Middle Saxon Estate Centre at Higham Ferrers, Northamptonshire* (Oxford, 2007).

P. H. Hase, 'The Church in the Wessex Heartlands', in M. Aston and C. Lewis (eds.), *The Medieval Landscape of Wessex* (Oxford, 1994), 47–81.

C. Loveluck, 'Acculturation, Migration and Exchange: The Formation of an Anglo-Saxon Society in the Peak District 400–700 AD', in J. Bintliff and H. Hamerow (eds.), *Europe between Late Antiquity and the Middle Ages*, BAR, Int. Ser., 617 (Oxford, 1995), 84–98.

—— *Rural Settlement, Lifestyles and Social Change in the Later First Millennium AD: Anglo-Saxon Flixborough in its Wider Context* (Oxford, 2007).

—— and K. Dobney, 'A Match Made in Heaven or a Marriage of Convenience? The Problems and Rewards of Integrating Palaeoecological and Archaeological

Data', in U. Albarella (ed.), *Environmental Archaeology: Meaning and Purpose* (Dordrecht, 2001), 149–75.

C. O'Brien and R. Miket, 'The Early Medieval Settlement of Thirlings, Northumberland', *Durham Archaeological Journal*, 7 (1991), 57–91.

P. Sims-Williams, *Religion and Literature in Western England, 600–800* (Cambridge, 1990).

G. Taylor, C. Allen, J. Bayley, J. Cowgill, V. Fryer, C. Palmer, B. Precious, J. Rackham, T. Roper and J. Young, 'An Early to Middle Saxon Settlement at Quarrington, Lincolnshire', *Antiquaries Journal*, 83 (2003), 231–80.

D. J. Tyler, 'Early Mercia and the Britons', in N. Higham (ed.), *Britons in Anglo-Saxon England* (Woodbridge, 2007), 91–101.

T. Williamson, *Shaping Medieval Landscapes: Settlement, Society, Environment* (Macclesfield, 2003)

Insiders and Outsiders

E. Campbell, *Continental and Mediterranean Imports to Atlantic Britain and Ireland, AD 400–800*, CBA, Research Report, 157 (York, 2007).

—— and A. Lane, 'Celtic and Germanic Interaction in Dalriada: The Seventh-Century Metalworking Site at Dunadd', in R. M. Spearman and J. Higgitt (eds.), *The Age of Migrating Ideas: Early Medieval Art in Northern Britain and Ireland* (Stroud, 1993), 52–63.

A. Lane and E. Campbell, *Dunadd: An Early Dalriadic Capital* (Oxford, 2000), 223–35.

D. O'Cróinín, *The Kings Depart: The Prosopography of Anglo-Saxon Royal Exile in the Sixth and Seventh Centuries*, Quiggin Pamphlets on Sources of Gaelic History, 8 (Cambridge, 2007).

CHAPTER 5. BELIEF AND RITUAL

The Fundamental Readings

M. O. H. Carver (ed.), *The Cross Goes North: Processes of Conversion in Northern Europe, AD 300–1300* (Woodbridge, 2003).

W. Davies, *Wales in the Early Middle Ages* (Leicester, 1982).

R. Gameson (ed.), *St Augustine and the Conversion of England* (Stroud, 1999).

H. Geake, *The Use of Grave-Goods in Conversion-Period England, c. 600–c. 850*, BAR, Brit. Ser., 261 (Oxford, 1997).

S. Lucy, *The Anglo-Saxon Way of Death: Burial Rites in Early England* (Stroud, 2000).

A. L. Meaney, 'Bede and Anglo-Saxon Paganism', *Parergon*, new ser., 3 (1985), 1–29.

A. Thacker and R. Sharpe (eds.), *Local Saints and Local Churches in the Early Medieval West* (Oxford, 2002).

H. Williams, *Death and Memory in Early Medieval Britain* (Cambridge, 2006).

D. Wilson, *Anglo-Saxon Paganism* (London, 1992).

Christians in Western Britain

S. R. Bassett, 'Church and Diocese in the West Midlands: The Transition from British to Anglo-Saxon Control', in J. Blair and R. Sharpe (eds.), *Pastoral Care before the Parish* (Leicester, 1992), 13–40.

—— 'Churches in Worcester before and after the Conversion of the Anglo-Saxons', *Antiquaries Journal*, 69 (1989), 225–56.

M. Biddle and B. Kjølbye-Biddle, 'The Origins of St Albans Abbey: Romano-British Cemetery and Anglo-Saxon Monastery', in M. Henig and P. Lindley (eds.), *Alban and St Albans: Roman and Medieval Architecture, Art and Archaeology*, British Archaeological Association Transactions, 24 (Leeds, 2001), 45–77.

N. Edwards, 'Celtic Saints and Early Medieval Archaeology', in A. Thacker and R. Sharpe (eds.), *Local Saints and Local Churches in the Early Medieval West* (Oxford, 2002), 225–65.

—— 'Identifying the Archaeology of the Early Church in Wales and Cornwall', in J. Blair and C. Pyrah (eds.), *Church Archaeology: Research Directions for the Future*, CBA, Research Report, 104 (York, 1996), 49–62.

B. Gilmour, 'Sub-Roman or Saxon, Pagan or Christian: Who Was Buried in the Early Cemetery at St-Paul-in-the-Bail, Lincoln?', in L. Gilmour (ed.), *Pagans and Christians: From Antiquity to the Middle Ages. Papers in Honour of Martin Henig*, BAR, Int. Ser., 1610 (Oxford, 2007), 229–56.

P. H. Hase, 'The Church in the Wessex Heartlands', in M. Aston and C. Lewis (eds.), *The Medieval Landscape of Wessex* (Oxford, 1994), 47–81.

J. K. Knight, 'Britain's Other Martyrs: Julius, Aaron, and Alban at Caerleon', in M. Henig and P. Lindley (eds.), *Alban and St Albans: Roman and Medieval Architecture, Art and Archaeology*, (Leeds, 2001), 38–44.

—— *The End of Antiquity: Archaeology, Society and Religion* AD 235–700 (Stroud, 1999).

R. Niblett, 'Why *Verulamium*?', in M. Henig and P. Lindley (eds.), *Alban and St Albans: Roman and Medieval Architecture, Art and Archaeology*, (Leeds, 2001), 1–12.

O. J. Padel, 'Local Saints and Place-Names in Cornwall', in A. Thacker and R. Sharpe (eds.), *Local Saints and Local Churches in the Early Medieval West* (Oxford, 2002), 303–60.

D. Petts, 'Burial in Western Britain AD 400–800: Late Antique or Early Medieval?', in R. Collins and J. Gerrard (eds.), *Debating Late Antiquity in Britain AD 300–700*, BAR, Brit. Ser., 365 (Oxford, 2004), 77–87.

H. Pryce, 'Pastoral Care in Early Medieval Wales', in J. Blair and R. Sharpe (eds.), *Pastoral Care before the Parish* (Leicester, 1992), 41–62.

W. Rodwell, 'The Role of the Church in the Development of Roman and Early Anglo-Saxon London', in M. O. H. Carver (ed.), *In Search of Cult* (Woodbridge, 1992), 91–9.

R. Sharpe, 'Martyrs and Local Saints in Late Antique Britain', in A. Thacker and R. Sharpe (eds.), *Local Saints and Local Churches in the Early Medieval West* (Oxford, 2002), 75–154.

P. Sims-Williams, *Religion and Literature in Western England, 600–800* (Cambridge, 1990).

A. Smith, 'The Fate of Pagan Temples in South-East Britain during the Late and Post-Roman Period', in D. Rudling (ed.), *Rural Landscapes of Roman South-East Britain* (Oxford, 2008), 171–90.

C. Sparey Green, *Excavations at Poundbury*, vol 1: *The Settlements*, Dorset Natural History and Archaeology Society Monograph, 7 (Dorchester, 1987).

—— 'Living amongst the Dead: From Roman Cemetery to Post-Roman Monastic Settlement at Poundbury', in R. Collins and J. Gerrard (eds.), *Debating Late Antiquity in Britain AD 300–700*, BAR, Brit. Ser., 365 (Oxford, 2004), 103–11.

C. Stancliffe, 'The British Church and the Mission of Augustine', in R. Gameson (ed.), *St Augustine and the Conversion of England* (Stroud, 1999), 107–51.

Eastern Britain

J. Blair, 'Anglo-Saxon Pagan Shrines and their Prototypes', *Anglo-Saxon Studies in Archaeology and History*, 8 (1995), 1–28.

J. M. Bond, 'Burnt Offerings: Animal Bone in Anglo-Saxon Cremations', *World Archaeology*, 28 (1996), 76–88.

S. Burnell and E. James, 'The Archaeology of Conversion on the Continent in the Sixth and Seventh Centuries: Some Observations and Comparisons with Anglo-Saxon England', in R. Gameson (ed.), *St Augustine and the Conversion of England* (Stroud, 1999), 83–106.

M. O. H. Carver, *Sutton Hoo: A Seventh-Century Princely Burial Ground and its Context* (London, 2005).

S. D. Church, 'Paganism in Conversion-Age Anglo-Saxon England: The Evidence of Bede's *Ecclesiastical History* Reconsidered', *History*, 93 (2008), 162–80.

C. E. Fell, 'Paganism in *Beowulf*: A Semantic Fairy-Tale', in T. Hosfra, L. A. J. R. Houwen and A. A. MacDonald (eds.), *Pagans and Christians: The Interplay between Christian, Latin and Traditional Germanic Cultures in Early Medieval Europe*, Germania Latina II (Groningen, 1995), 9–34.

C. Fern, 'Early Anglo-Saxon Horse Burial of the Fifth to Seventh Centuries AD', *Anglo-Saxon Studies in Archaeology and History*, 14 (2007), 92–109.

W. Filmer-Sankey and T. Pestell, *Snape Anglo-Saxon Cemetery: Excavations and Surveys 1824–1992*, East Anglian Archaeology, 95 (Ipswich, 2002).

R. Gameson (ed.), *St Augustine and the Conversion of England* (Stroud, 1999).

H. Geake, 'Burial Practice in Seventh- and Eighth-Century England', in M. O. H. Carver (ed.), *The Age of Sutton Hoo: The Seventh Century in North-Western Europe* (Woodbridge, 1992), 83–94.

R. Gilchrist and R. Morris, 'Monasteries as Settlements: Religion, Society and Economy, AD 600–1050', in M. O. H. Carver (ed.), *In Search of Cult* (Woodbridge, 1992), 113–18.

J. I. McKinley, *The Anglo-Saxon Cemetery at Spong Hill, North Elmham*, Part 8: *The Cremations*, East Anglian Archaeology, 69 (Dereham, 1994).

A. L. Meaney, *Anglo-Saxon Amulets and Curing Stones*, BAR, Brit. Ser., 96 (Oxford, 1981).

R. I. Page, 'Anglo-Saxon Paganism: The Evidence of Bede', in T. Hosfra, L. A. J. R. Houwen and A. A. MacDonald (eds.), *Pagans and Christians: The Interplay between Christian, Latin and Traditional Germanic Cultures in Early Medieval Europe*, Germania Latina II (Groningen, 1995), 99–130.

K. Penn, *Excavations on the Norwich Southern Bypass, 1989–91*, East Anglian Archaeology, 92 (Dereham, 2000).

R. Samson, 'The Church Lends a Hand', in J. Downes and T. Pollard (eds.), *The Loved Body's Corruption: Archaeological Contributions to the Study of Human Mortality* (Glasgow, 1999), 120–44.

A. Thacker, '*Loca sanctorum*: The Significance of Place in the Study of the Saints', in A. Thacker and R. Sharpe (eds.), *Local Saints and Local Churches in the Early Medieval West* (Oxford, 2002), 1–43.

—— 'The Making of a Local Saint', in A. Thacker and R. Sharpe (eds.), *Local Saints and Local Churches in the Early Medieval West* (Oxford, 2002), 45–73.

A. G. Vince (ed.), *Pre-Viking Lindsey* (Lincoln, 1993).

H. Williams, 'Death Warmed Up: The Agency of Bodies and Bones in Early Anglo-Saxon Cremation Rites', *Journal of Material Culture*, 9 (2004), 263–96.

A. Woodward, *English Heritage Book of Shrines and Sacrifice* (London, 1992).

Continuities

A. Boddington, *Raunds Furnells: The Anglo-Saxon Church and Churchyard*, English Heritage Archaeological Report, 7 (London, 1996).

H. Geake, 'Burial Practice in Seventh- and Eighth-Century England', in M. O. H. Carver (ed.), *The Age of Sutton Hoo: The Seventh Century in North-Western Europe* (Woodbridge, 1992), 83–94.

K. Penn, *Excavations on the Norwich Southern Bypass, 1989–91*, Part II: *The*

Anglo-Saxon Cemetery at Harford Farm, Caistor St Edmund, Norfolk, East Anglian Archaeology, 92 (Dereham, 2000).

CHAPTER 6. MISSIONARIES AND CONVERTS

The Fundamental Readings

L. Abrams, 'Germanic Christianities', in T. F. X. Noble and J. M. H. Smith (eds.), *The Cambridge History of Christianity: Early Medieval Christianities, c. 600–c. 1100* (Cambridge, 2008), 107–29.

J. Blair, *The Church in Anglo-Saxon Society* (Oxford, 2006).

—— and R. Sharpe (eds.), *Pastoral Care before the Parish* (Leicester, 1992).

T. Charles-Edwards, 'Conversion to Christianity', in T. Charles-Edwards (ed.), *After Rome* (Oxford, 2003), 103–39.

S. Foot, *Monastic Life in Anglo-Saxon England, c. 600–900* (Cambridge, 2006).

H. Mayr-Harting, *The Coming of Christianity to Anglo-Saxon England*, 3rd edn. (London, 1991).

A. L. Meaney, 'Anglo-Saxon Idolators and Ecclesiasts from Theodore to Alcuin: A Source Study', *Anglo-Saxon Studies in Archaeology and History*, 5 (1992), 103–25.

B. Yorke, *The Conversion of Britain 600–800* (London, 2006).

The Conversion and the Missionaries

P. A. Barker and A. L. Cubberley, 'Two Burials under the Refectory of Worcester Cathedral', *Medieval Archaeology*, 18 (1974), 146–51.

R. Bryant and C. Heighway, 'Excavations at St Mary de Lode Church, Gloucester, 1978–9', *Transactions of the Bristol and Gloucestershire Archaeological Society*, 121 (2003), 97–178.

D. A. Bullough, 'The Missions to the English and Picts and their Heritage (to c. 800)', in H. Löwe (ed.), *Die Iren und Europa im früheren Mittelalter*, 2 vols. (Stuttgart, 1982), vol. 1, pp. 80–98.

J. Campbell, 'The First Century of Christianity in England', in J. Campbell, *Essays in Anglo-Saxon History* (London, 1986), 49–67.

—— 'Observations on the Conversion of England', in J. Campbell, *Essays in Anglo-Saxon History* (London, 1986), 69–84.

T. Charles-Edwards, 'Bede, the Irish and the Britons', *Celtica*, 15 (1983), 42–52.

M. De Reu, 'The Missionaries: The First Contact between Paganism and Christianity', in Ludo J. R. Milis (ed.), *The Pagan Middle Ages* (Woodbridge, 1998), 13–37.

P. Fouracre, 'Britain, Ireland and Europe, c. 500–c. 750', in P. Stafford (ed.), *A Companion to the Early Middle Ages: Britain and Ireland, c. 500–c. 1100* (London, 2009), 126–42.

R. Gameson (ed.), *St Augustine and the Conversion of England* (Stroud, 1999).

W. Kilbride, 'Why I Feel Cheated by the Term Christianisation', *Archaeological Review from Cambridge*, 17 (2000), 1–17.

C. Stancliffe, 'Kings Who Opted Out', in P. Wormald with D. Bullough and R. Collins (eds.), *Ideal and Reality in Frankish and Anglo-Saxon Society: Studies Presented to J. M. Wallace-Hadrill* (Oxford, 1983), 154–76.

S. Turner, *Making a Christian Landscape: The Countryside in Early Medieval Cornwall, Devon and Wessex* (Exeter, 2006).

D. Tyler, 'Early Mercia and the Britons', in N. Higham (ed.), *Britons in Anglo-Saxon England* (Woodbridge, 2007), 91–101.

I. Wood, 'The Mission of Augustine of Canterbury to the English', *Speculum*, 69 (1994), 1–17.

B. Yorke, *Nunneries and the Anglo-Saxon Royal Houses* (London, 2003).

Non-Monastic Cemeteries

H. Geake, *The Use of Grave-Goods in Conversion-Period England, c. 600–c. 850*, BAR, Brit. Ser., 261 (Oxford, 1997).

B. Gilmour, 'Sub-Roman or Saxon, Pagan or Christian: Who Was Buried in the Early Cemetery at St-Paul-in-the-Bail, Lincoln?', in L. Gilmour (ed.), *Pagans and Christians: From Antiquity to the Middle Ages. Papers in Honour of Martin Henig*, BAR, Int. Ser., 1610 (Oxford, 2007), 229–56.

C. Loveluck, *Rural Settlement, Lifestyles and Social Change in the Later First Millennium AD: Anglo-Saxon Flixborough in its Wider Context* (Oxford, 2007).

S. Marzinzik, *Early Anglo-Saxon Belt Buckles (Late 5th to Early 8th Centuries AD): Their Classification and Context*, BAR, Brit. Ser., 357 (Oxford, 2003).

—— 'Grave-Goods in "Conversion Period" and Later Burials – a Case of Early Medieval Religious Double Standards?', in K. Pollmann (ed.), *Double Standards in the Ancient and Medieval World* (Göttingen, 2000), 149–66.

K. Penn, *Excavations on the Norwich Southern Bypass, 1989–91, Part II: The Anglo-Saxon Cemetery at Harford Farm, Caistor St Edmund, Norfolk*, East Anglian Archaeology, 92 (Dereham, 2000).

P. Rahtz, S. Hirst and S. M. Wright, *Cannington Cemetery*, Britannia Monograph Series, 17 (London, 2000).

H. Williams, *Death and Memory in Early Medieval Britain* (Cambridge, 2006).

Early Religious Communities

K. N. Bascombe, 'Two Charters of King Suebred of Essex', in K. Neale (ed.), *An Essex Tribute* (London, 1987), 85–96.

S. R. Bassett, 'Churches in Worcester before and after the Conversion of the Anglo-Saxons', *Antiquaries Journal*, 69 (1989), 225–56.

J. Blair, 'A Saint for Every Minster? Local Cults in Anglo-Saxon England', in A. Thacker and R. Sharpe (eds.), *Local Saints and Local Churches in the Early Medieval West* (Oxford, 2002), 455–94.

D. R. Brothwell, 'A Possible Case of Mongolism in a Saxon Population', *Annals of Human Genetics*, 24 (1960), 141–50.

R. Cramp, *Wearmouth and Jarrow Monastic Sites*, English Heritage Archaeological Report, 2 vols. (Swindon, 2005–6).

J. Crick, 'Posthumous Obligations and Family Identity', in W. O. Frazer and A. Tyrell (eds.), *Social Identity in Early Medieval Britain* (Leicester, 2000), 193–208.

R. Daniels and C. Loveluck, *Anglo-Saxon Hartlepool and the Foundations of English Christianity: An Archaeology of the Anglo-Saxon Monastery* (Hartlepool, 2007).

H. Hamerow and A. MacGregor (eds.), *Image and Power in the Archaeology of Early Medieval Britain: Essays in Honour of Rosemary Cramp* (Oxford, 2001).

P. Hill, *Whithorn and St Ninian: The Excavation of a Monastic Town, 1984–91* (Stroud, 1997).

P. J. Huggins, 'Excavation of Belgic and Romano-British Farm with Middle Saxon Cemetery and Churches at Nazeingbury, Essex 1975–76', *Essex Archaeology and History*, 10 (1978), 29–117.

—— 'Nazeingbury 20 Years on, or "Where did the Royal Ladies Go?"', *London Archaeologist*, 8 (1996), 105–11.

S. Johnson, *Burgh Castle, Excavations by Charles Green 1958–61*, East Anglian Archaeology, 20 (Dereham, 1983).

C. Loveluck, 'Cædmon's World: Secular and Monastic Lifestyles and Estate Organization in Northern England, AD 650–900', in A. J. Frantzen and J. Hines (eds.), *Cædmon's Hymn and Material Culture in the World of Bede* (Morgantown, W. Va., 2007), 150–90.

T. Pickles, 'Church Organization and Pastoral Care', in P. Stafford (ed.), *A Companion to the Early Middle Ages: Britain and Ireland, c. 500–c. 1100* (London, 2009), 160–76.

H. Pryce, 'Pastoral Care in Early Medieval Wales', in J. Blair and R. Sharpe (eds.), *Pastoral Care before the Parish* (Leicester, 1992), 41–62.

A. Ritchie, *Iona* (London, 1997).

C. Sapin, 'Architecture and Funerary Space in the Early Middle Ages', in C. E. Karkov, K. M. Wickham-Crowley and B. K. Young (eds.), *Spaces of the Living and the Dead: An Archaeological Dialogue* (Oxford, 1999), 39–60.

D. Stocker and P. Everson, 'The Straight and Narrow Way: Fenland Causeways and the Conversion of the Landscape in the Witham Valley, Lincolnshire', in M. O. H. Carver (ed.), *The Cross Goes North: Processes of Conversion in Northern Europe, AD 300–1300* (Woodbridge, 2003), 271–88.

A. Thacker, 'Membra disjecta: The Division of the Body and the Diffusion of the Cult', in C. Stancliffe and E. Cambridge (eds.), Oswald: Northumbrian King to European Saint (Stamford, 1995), 97–127.

—— 'Monks, Preaching and Pastoral Care in Early Anglo-Saxon England', in J. Blair and R. Sharpe (eds.), Pastoral Care before the Parish (Leicester, 1992), 137–70.

Pagan/Christian Interface: Conversion/Christianization

E. G. Armstrong and I. N. Wood (eds.), Christianizing Peoples and Converting Individuals (Turnhout, 2000).

E. Cambridge, 'Archaeology and the Cult of St Oswald in Pre-Conquest England', in C. Stancliffe and E. Cambridge (eds.), Oswald: Northumbrian King to European Saint (Stamford, 1995), 128–63.

T. Charles-Edwards, 'The Penitential of Theodore and the Iudicia Theodori', in M. Lapidge (ed.), Archbishop Theodore: Commemorative Studies on his Life and Influence (Cambridge, 1995), 141–74.

S. D. Church, 'Paganism in Conversion-Age Anglo-Saxon England: The Evidence of Bede's Ecclesiastical History Reconsidered', History, 93 (2008), 162–80.

C. Cubitt, 'Pastoral Care and Conciliar Canons: The Provisions of the 747 Council of Clofesho', in J. Blair and R. Sharpe (eds.), Pastoral Care before the Parish (Leicester, 1992), 193–211.

—— 'Sites and Sanctity: Revisiting the Cult of Murdered and Martyred Anglo-Saxon Royal Saints', Early Medieval Europe, 9 (2000), 53–83.

S. DeGregorio, 'Literary Contexts: Cædmon's Hymn as a Center of Bede's World', in A. J. Frantzen and J. Hines (eds.), Cædmon's Hymn and Material Culture in the World of Bede (Morgantown, W. Va., 2007), 51–79.

A. Dierkens, 'The Evidence of Archaeology', in L. J. R. Milis (ed.), The Pagan Middle Ages (Woodbridge, 1998), 39–64.

—— 'Superstitions, christianisme et paganisme à la fin de l'époque mérovingienne: À propos de l'Indiculus superstitionum et paganiarum', in H. Hasquin (ed.), Magie, sorcellerie, parapsychologie (Brussels, 1984), 9–26.

R. Hill, 'Bede and the Boors', in G. Bonner (ed.), Famulus Christi: Essays in Commemoration of the Thirteenth Centenary of the Birth of the Venerable Bede (London, 1976), 93–105.

J. Hines, 'Changes and Exchanges in Bede's and Cædmon's World', in A. J. Frantzen and J. Hines (eds.), Cædmon's Hymn and Material Culture in the World of Bede (Morgantown, W. Va., 2007), 191–220.

A. Macquarrie, 'Early Christian Religious Houses in Scotland: Foundation and Function', in J. Blair and R. Sharpe (eds.), Pastoral Care before the Parish (Leicester, 1992), 110–33.

A. L. Meaney, 'Old English Legal and Penitential Penalties for "heathenism"', in

S. Keynes and A. P. Smyth (eds.), *Anglo-Saxons: Studies Presented to Cyril Roy Hart* (Dublin, 2006), 127–58.

P. Sims-Williams, *Religion and Literature in Western England, 600–800* (Cambridge, 1990).

D. Tyler, 'Reluctant Kings and Christian Conversion in Seventh-Century England', *History*, 92 (2007), 144–61.

K. Veitch, 'The Columban Church in Northern Britain, 664–717: A Reassessment', *Proceedings of the Society of Antiquaries of Scotland*, 127 (1997), 627–47.

I. N. Wood, 'Pagan Religion and Superstition East of the Rhine from the Fifth to the Ninth Century', in G. Ausunda (ed.), *After Empire* (Woodbridge, 1995), 253–68.

P. Wormald, 'Bede, Beowulf and the Conversion of the Anglo-Saxon Aristocracy', in R. T. Farrell (ed.), *Bede and Anglo-Saxon England*, BAR, Brit. Ser., 46 (Oxford, 1978), 32–95.

B. York, 'The Adaptation of the Anglo-Saxon Royal Courts to Christianity', in M. O. H. Carver, (ed.), *The Cross Goes North: Processes of Conversion in Northern Europe, AD 300–1300* (Woodbridge, 2003), 243–57.

CHAPTER 7. THE REBIRTH OF TRADING COMMUNITIES

The Fundamental Readings

E. Campbell, 'Trade in the Dark-Age West: A Peripheral Activity?', in B. E. Crawford (ed.), *Scotland in Dark Age Britain* (Aberdeen, 1996), 79–91.

R. Fleming, 'Elites, Boats and Foreigners: Rethinking the Rebirth of English Towns', in *Città e campagna prima del mille*, Atti delle Settimane di Studio, 56 (Spoleto, 2009), 393–425.

D. Hill and R. Cowie (eds.), *Wics: The Early Mediaeval Trading Centres of Northern Europe* (Sheffield, 2001).

M. McCormick, *Origins of the European Economy: Communications and Commerce AD 300–900* (Cambridge, 2001).

J. R. Maddicott, 'Prosperity and Power in the Age of Bede and Beowulf', *Proceedings of the British Academy*, 117 (2002), 49–71.

J. Moreland, 'The Significance of Production in Eighth-Century England', in I. L. Hansen and C. Wickham (eds.), *The Long Eighth Century* (Leiden, 2000), 69–104.

P. Ottaway, *Archaeology in British Towns from the Emperor Claudius to the Black Death* (London, 1992).

D. M. Palliser (ed.), *The Cambridge Urban History of Britain*, vol. 1: *600–1540* (Cambridge, 2000).

T. Pestell and K. Ulmschneider (eds.), *Markets in Early Medieval Europe: Trading and 'Productive' Sites 650–850* (Macclesfield, 2003).

C. Scull, 'Urban Centres in Pre-Viking England', in J. Hines (ed.), *The Anglo-Saxons from the Migration Period to the Eighth Century: An Ethnographic Perspective* (Woodbridge, 1997), 269–310.

B. Ward-Perkins, 'Continuitists, Catastrophists, and the Towns of Post-Roman Northern Italy', *Papers of the British School at Rome*, 65 (1997), 157–76.

C. Wickham, 'Overview: Production, Distribution and Demand, II', in I. L. Hansen and C. Wickham (eds.), *The Long Eighth Century* (Leiden, 2000), 346–77.

The Origins of Early Medieval Urban Settlements

M. Anderton, 'Beyond the Emporia', in M. Anderton (ed.), *Anglo-Saxon Trading Centres: Beyond the Emporia* (Glasgow, 1999), 1–3.

G. G. Astill, 'Archaeological Theory and the Origins of English Towns – a Review', *Archaeologia Polona*, 32 (1994), 27–71.

N. Christie and S. T. Loseby (eds.), *Towns in Transition: Urban Evolution in Late Antiquity and the Early Middle Ages* (Aldershot, 1996).

J. Hines, 'North Sea Trade and the Proto-urban Sequence', *Archaeologia Polona*, 32 (1994), 7–26.

D. A. Hinton, 'Decay and Revival: Early Medieval Urban Landscapes', in P. Waller (ed.), *The English Urban Landscape* (Oxford, 2000), 55–74.

S. E. Kelly, 'Trading Privileges from Eighth-Century England', *Early Medieval Europe*, 1 (1992), 3–28.

S. Lebecq, 'England and the Continent in the Sixth and Seventh Centuries', in R. Gameson (ed.), *St Augustine and the Conversion of England* (Stroud, 1999), 50–67.

—— 'On the Use of the Word Frisian', in S. McGrail (ed.), *Maritime Celts, Frisians, and Saxons*, CBA, Research Report, 71 (London, 1990), 85–90.

S. Loseby, 'Power and Towns in Late Roman Britain and Early Anglo-Saxon England', in G. Ripoll and J. M. Gurt (eds.), *Sedes Regiae (ann. 400–800)* (Barcelona, 2000), 319–70.

N. Middleton, 'Early Medieval Port Customs, Tolls, and Controls on Foreign Trade', *Early Medieval Europe*, 13 (2005), 313–58.

J. Naylor, 'Access to International Trade in Middle Saxon England: A Case of Urban Over-emphasis?', in M. Pasquinucci and T. Weski (eds.), *Close Encounters: Sea- and Riverborne Trade, Ports and Hinterlands, Ship Construction and Navigation in Antiquity, the Middle Ages and in Modern Times*, BAR, Int. Ser., 1283 (Oxford, 2004), 139–48.

—— *An Archaeology of Trade in Middle Saxon England*, BAR, Brit. Ser. 376 (Oxford, 2004).

T. O'Connor, 'On the Interpretation of Animal Bone Assemblages from *Wics*', in

D. Hill and R. Cowie (eds.), *Wics: The Early Mediaeval Trading Centres of Northern Europe* (Sheffield, 2001), 54–60.

R. Samson, 'Illusory Emporia and Mad Economic Theories', in M. Anderton (ed.), *Anglo-Saxon Trading Centres: Beyond the Emporia* (Glasgow, 1999), 76–90.

T. Saunders, 'Trade, Towns and States: A Reconsideration of Early Medieval Economics', *Norwegian Archaeological Review*, 28 (1995), 31–53.

C. Scull, 'Scales and Weights in Early Anglo-Saxon England', *Archaeological Journal*, 147 (1990), 183–215.

—— 'Urban Centres in Pre-Viking England?', in J. Hines, *The Anglo-Saxons from the Migration Period to the Eighth Century* (Woodbridge, 1997), 269–98.

W. H. TeBrake, 'Ecology and Economy in Early Medieval Frisia', *Viator*, 9 (1978), 1–29.

K. Ulmschneider, 'Central Places and Metal-Detector Finds: What are the English "Productive Sites"?', in B. Hårdh and L. Larsson (eds.), *Central Places in the Migration and the Merovingian Periods* (Stockholm, 2002), 333–9.

—— 'Settlement, Economy, and the "Productive" Site: Middle Anglo-Saxon Lincolnshire AD 650–780', *Medieval Archaeology*, 44 (2000), 53–79.

A. Vince, 'The Growth of Market Centres and Towns in the Area of the Mercian Hegemony', in M. P. Brown and C. A. Farr (eds.), *Mercia: An Anglo-Saxon Kingdom in Europe* (London, 2001), 183–93.

—— 'Saxon Urban Economies: An Archaeological Perspective', in J. Rackham (ed.), *Environment and Economy in Anglo-Saxon England*, CBA, Research Report, 89 (York, 1994), 108–19.

K. Wade, 'The Urbanization of East Anglia: The Ipswich Perspective', in J. Gardiner (ed.), *Flatlands and Westlands: Current Themes in East Anglian Archaeology*, East Anglian Archaeology, 50 (Norwich, 1993), 141–55.

J. M. Wooding, 'Long-Distance Imports and Archaeological Models for Exchange and Trade in the Celtic West AD 400–800', in G. de Boe and F. Verhaeghe (eds.), *Exchange and Trade in Medieval Europe: Papers of the 'Medieval Europe Brugge 1997' Conference* (Zellik, 1997), vol. 3, pp. 43–50.

Specific Classes of Commodities

L. Blackmore, 'Aspects of Trade and Exchange Evidenced by Recent Work on Saxon and Medieval Pottery from London', *Transactions of the London and Middlesex Archaeological Society*, 50 (1999), 38–54.

P. Blinkhorn, 'Of Cabbages and Kings: Production, Trade, and Consumption in Middle-Saxon England', in M. Anderton (ed.), *Anglo-Saxon Trading Centres: Beyond the Emporia* (Glasgow, 1999), 4–23.

P. J. Crabtree, 'The Wool Trade and the Rise of Urbanism in Middle Saxon England', in B. Wailes (ed.), *Craft Specialization and Social Evolution: In Memory of V. Gordon Childe* (Philadelphia, 1996), 99–105.

D. A. Hinton, 'Metalwork and the Emporia', in M. Anderton (ed.), *Anglo-Saxon Trading Centres: Beyond the Emporia* (Glasgow, 1999), 24–31.

J. W. Huggett, 'Imported Grave Goods and the Early Anglo-Saxon Economy', *Medieval Archaeology*, 32 (1988), 63–96.

K. Leahy, *Anglo-Saxon Crafts* (Stroud, 2003).

D. Whitehouse, '"Things that Travelled": The Surprising Case of Raw Glass', *Early Medieval Europe*, 12 (2003), 301–5.

Boats

M. O. H. Carver, 'Pre-Viking Traffic in the North Sea', in S. McGrail (ed.), *Maritime Celts, Frisians and Saxons*, CBA, Research Report, 71 (London, 1990), 117–25.

O. Crumlin-Pedersen, 'A Note on the Speed of Viking Ships', *International Journal of Nautical Archaeology*, 17 (1988), 270–71.

—— 'Ships as Indicators of Trade in Northern Europe 600–1200', in J. Bill and B. L. Clausen (eds.), *Maritime Topography and the Medieval Town* (Copenhagen, 1999), 11–20.

—— 'Variations on a Theme: Eleventh-Century Ship Types of the North', in C. Beltrame (ed.), *Boats, Ships and Shipyards* (Oxford, 2003), 243–60.

E. Rieth, C. Carrierre-Desbois and V. Serna, *L'Épave de Port Berteau II (Charente-Maritime)* (Paris, 2001).

C. Westerdahl, 'Society and Sail', in O. Crumlin-Pedersen and B. Munch Thye (eds.), *The Ship as Symbol in Prehistoric and Medieval Scandinavia* (Roskilde, 1995), 41–50.

Towns and New-Style Kings

D. Chick, 'The Coinage of Offa in the Light of Recent Discoveries', in D. Hill and M. Worthington (eds.), *Æthelbald and Offa: Two Eighth-Century Kings of Mercia*, BAR, Brit. Ser., 383 (Oxford, 2005), 111–22.

S. E. Kelly, 'Trading Privileges from Eighth-Century England', *Early Medieval Europe*, 1 (1992), 3–28.

S. Keynes, 'England, 700–900', in R. McKitterick (ed.), *The New Cambridge Medieval History*, vol. 2: *c. 700–c. 900* (Cambridge, 1995), 18–42.

—— 'The Kingdom of the Mercians in the Eighth Century', in D. Hill and M. Worthington (eds.), *Æthelbald and Offa: Two Eighth-Century Kings of Mercia*, BAR, Brit. Ser., 383 (Oxford, 2005), 1–26.

J. R. Maddicott, 'London and Droitwich, *c.* 650–750: Trade, Industry and the Rise of Mercia', *Anglo-Saxon England*, 34 (2005), 7–58.

D. M. Metcalf, *Thrymsas and Sceattas in the Ashmolean Museum Oxford*, 2 vols. (London, 1993).

J. Naylor, 'Mercian Hegemony and the Origins of Series J Sceattas: The Case of Lindsey', *British Numismatic Journal*, 76 (2006), 159–70.

D. J. Tyler, 'An Early Mercian Hegemony: Penda and Overkingship in the Seventh Century', *Midland History*, 30 (2005), 1–19.

—— 'Orchestrated Violence and the "Supremacy of the Mercian Kings"', in D. Hill and M. Worthington (eds.), *Æthelbald and Offa: Two Eighth-Century Kings of Mercia*, BAR, Brit. Ser., 383 (Oxford, 2005), 27–34.

G. Williams, 'Military Obligations and the Mercian Supremacy in the Eighth Century', in D. Hill and M. Worthington (eds.), *Æthelbald and Offa: Two Eighth-Century Kings of Mercia*, BAR, Brit. Ser., 383 (Oxford, 2005), 103–10.

B. Yorke, *Kings and Kingdoms of Early Anglo-Saxon England* (London, 1990).

Canterbury

K. Blockley, M. Sparks and T. Tatton-Brown, *Canterbury Cathedral Nave: Archaeology, History and Architecture* (Canterbury, 1997).

—— M. Blockley, P. Blockley and S. S. Frere, *Excavations in the Marlowe Car Park and Surrounding Areas*, Archaeology of Canterbury, 5/1–3 (Canterbury, 1995).

D. A. Brooks, 'The Case for Continuity in Fifth-Century Canterbury Re-examined', *Oxford Journal of Archaeology*, 7 (1988), 99–114.

N. P. Brooks, 'The Anglo-Saxon Cathedral Community, 597–1070', in P. Collinson, N. Ramsay and M. Sparks (eds.), *A History of Canterbury Cathedral* (Oxford, 1995), 1–37.

—— 'Canterbury, Rome and the Construction of English Identity', in J. M. H. Smith (ed.), *Early Medieval Rome and the Christian West* (Leiden, 2000), 221–46.

E. Cambridge, 'The Architecture of the Augustinian Mission', in R. Gameson (ed.), *St Augustine and the Conversion of England* (Stroud, 1999), 202–36.

R. Gameson, 'Augustine of Canterbury: Context and Achievement', in R. Gameson (ed.), *St Augustine and the Conversion of England* (Stroud, 1999), 1–40.

S. E. Kelly, 'Lyminge Minster and its Early Charters', in S. Keynes and A. P. Smyth (eds.), *Anglo-Saxons: Studies Presented to Cyril Roy Hart* (Dublin, 2006), 98–113.

T. Tatton-Brown, 'The Anglo-Saxon Towns of Kent', in D. Hooke (ed.), *Anglo-Saxon Settlements* (Oxford, 1988), 213–32.

—— *Canterbury: History and Guide* (Stroud, 1994).

A. Thacker, 'In Search of Saints: The English Church and the Cult of Roman Apostles and Martyrs in the Seventh and Eighth Centuries', in S. Keynes and A. P. Smyth (eds.), *Anglo-Saxons: Studies Presented to Cyril Roy Hart* (Dublin, 2006), 247–77.

Coddenham and Barham

J. Newman, 'Exceptional Finds, Exceptional Sites? Barham and Coddenham, Suffolk', in T. Pestell and K. Ulmschneider (eds.), *Markets in Early Medieval Europe: Trading and 'Productive' Sites 650–850* (Macclesfield, 2003), 97–109.

S. J. Plunkett, 'Some Recent Metalwork Discoveries from the Area of the Gipping Valley, and the Local Context', in P. Binski and W. Noel (eds.), *New Offerings, Ancient Treasures: Studies in Medieval Art for George Henderson* (Stroud, 2001), 61–87.

J. Watson, 'Laid to Rest: Two Anglo-Saxon Graves Reconstructed', *Research News: Newsletter of the English Heritage Research Department*, 2 (2005–6), 6–9.

S. West, *A Corpus of Anglo-Saxon Material from Suffolk*, East Anglian Archaeology, 84 (Ipswich, 1998).

Sandtun

M. Gardiner, R. Cross, N. MacPherson-Grant, I. Riddler, L. Blackmore, D. Chick, S. Hamilton-Dyer, E. Murray and D. Weir, 'Continental Trade and Non-Urban Ports in Mid-Anglo-Saxon England: Excavations at Sandtun, West Hythe, Kent', *Archaeological Journal*, 158 (2001), 161–290.

Droitwich

D. Hooke, 'The Droitwich Salt Industry: An Examination of the West Midland Charter Evidence', *Anglo-Saxon Studies in Archaeology and History*, 2 (1981), 123–69.

J. D. Hurst, 'The Extent and Development of the Worcestershire Medieval Salt Industry, and its Impact on the Regional Economy', in G. de Boe and F. Verhaeghe (eds.), *Exchange and Trade in Medieval Europe: Papers of the 'Medieval Europe Brugge 1997' Conference* (Zellik, 1997), vol. 3, pp. 139–46.

—— *A Multi-Period Salt Producing Site at Droitwich: Excavations at Upwich*, CBA, Research Report, 107 (York, 1997).

J. R. Maddicott, 'London and Droitwich, c. 650–750: Trade, Industry and the Rise of Mercia', *Anglo-Saxon England*, 34 (2005), 7–58.

Ipswich

P. Blinkhorn, 'Of Cabbages and Kings: Production, Trade, and Consumption in Middle-Saxon England', in M. Anderton (ed.), *Anglo-Saxon Trading Centres: Beyond the Emporia* (Glasgow, 1999), 4–23.

J. Newman, 'The Anglo-Saxon Cemetery at Boss Hall, Ipswich', *Bulletin of the Sutton Hoo Research Committee*, 8 (1993), 32–5.

—— 'The East Anglian Kingdom Survey: South-East Suffolk', *Bulletin of the Sutton Hoo Research Committee*, 8 (1993), 38–31.

—— 'Wics, Trade, and the Hinterlands – the Ipswich Region', in M. Anderton (ed.), *Anglo-Saxon Trading Centres: Beyond the Emporia* (Glasgow, 1999), 32–47.

C. Scull, 'Burials at Emporia in England', in D. Hill and R. Cowie (eds.), *Wics: The Early Mediaeval Trading Centres of Northern Europe* (Sheffield, 2001), 67–74.

—— 'Ipswich: Development and Contexts of an Urban Precursor in the Seventh Century', in B. Hårdh and L. Larsson (eds.), *Central Places in the Migration and the Merovingian Periods* (Stockholm, 2002), 303–16.

—— and A. Bayliss, 'Radiocarbon Dating and Anglo-Saxon Graves', in U. von Freeden, U. Koch and A. Wieczorek (eds.), *Völker an Nord- und Ostsee und die Franken* (Bonn, 1999), 39–50.

K. Wade, 'Ipswich', in R. Hodges and B. Hobley (eds.), *The Rebirth of Towns in the West*, CBA, Research Report, 68 (London, 1988), 93–100.

—— 'The Urbanisation of East Anglia: The Ipswich Perspective', in J. Gardiner (ed.), *Flatlands and Wetlands: Current Themes in East Anglian Archaeology*, East Anglian Archaeology, 50 (Norwich, 1993), 144–51.

S. E. West, *A Corpus of Anglo-Saxon Material from Suffolk*, East Anglian Archaeology, 84 (Ipswich, 1998), 275.

London

L. Blackmore, 'Aspects of Trade and Exchange Evidenced by Recent Work on Saxon and Medieval Pottery from London', *Transactions of the London and Middlesex Archaeological Society*, 50 (1999), 38–54.

—— 'From Beach to Burh: New Clues to Entity and Identity in 7th- to 9th-Century London', in G. de Boe and F. Verhaeghe (eds.), *Urbanism in Medieval Europe: Papers of the 'Medieval Europe Brugge 1997' Conference* (Zellik, 1997), vol. 1, pp. 123–32.

—— 'The Origins and Growth of *Lundenwic*, a Mart of Many Nations', in B. Hårdh and L. Larsson (eds.), *Central Places in the Migration and the Merovingian Periods* (Stockholm, 2002), 273–301.

R. Clark, 'Glass Vessels in Lundenwic: An Illustration of the Contextual Approach to Fragments', *Archaeological Review from Cambridge*, 20 (2005), 82–97.

R. Cowie, 'The Evidence for Royal Sites in Middle Anglo-Saxon London', *Medieval Archaeology*, 48 (2004), 201–9.

—— 'Londinium to Lundenwic: Early and Middle Saxon Archaeology in the London Region', in I. Haynes, H. Sheldon and L. Hannigan (eds.), *London under Ground: The Archaeology of a City* (Oxford, 2000), 175–206.

—— 'Mercian London', in M. P. Brown and C. A. Farr (eds.), *Mercia: An Anglo-Saxon Kingdom in Europe* (London, 2001), 194–209.

—— and R. Whytehead, 'Lundenwic: The Archaeological Evidence for Middle Saxon London', *Antiquity*, 63 (1989), 706–18.

J. Leary, *Tatberht's Lundenwic: Archaeological Investigations in Middle Saxon London* (London, 2004).

G. Malcolm and D. Bowsher, *Middle Saxon London: Excavations at the Royal Opera House 1989–99*, MoLAS Monograph, 15 (London, 2003).

G. Milne, *The Port of Medieval London* (Stroud, 2003).

—— and D. Goodburn, 'The Early Medieval Port of London AD 700–1200', *Antiquity*, 64 (1990), 629–36.

J. Rackham, 'Economy and Environment in Saxon London', in J. Rackham (ed.), *Environment and Economy in Anglo-Saxon England*, CBA, Research Report, 89 (York, 1994), 126–35.

P. Treveil and M. Burch, 'Number 1 Poultry and the Development of Medieval Cheapside', *Transactions of the London and Middlesex Archaeological Society*, 50 (1999), 38–54.

—— and P. Rowsome, 'Number 1 Poultry – the Main Excavation: Late Saxon and Medieval Sequence', *London Archaeologist*, 8 (1998), 283–91.

A. Vince, 'A Tale of Two Cities: Lincoln and London Compared', in J. Gardiner (ed.), *Flatlands and Wetlands: Current Themes in East Anglian Archaeology*, East Anglian Archaeology, 50 (Norwich, 1993), 152–70.

Southampton

P. Andrews, *Excavations at Hamwic*, vol. 2: *Excavations at Six Dials*, CBA, Research Report, 109 (London, 1997).

V. Birkbeck, *Origins of Mid-Saxon Southampton: Excavations at the Friends Provident St Mary's Stadium 1998–2000* (Salisbury, 2005).

J. Bourdillon, 'The Animal Provisioning of Saxon Southampton', in J. Rackham (ed.), *Environment and Economy in Anglo-Saxon England*, CBA, Research Report, 89 (York, 1994), 120–25.

—— 'Countryside and Town: The Animal Resources of Saxon Southampton', in D. Hooke (ed.), *Anglo-Saxon Settlements* (Oxford, 1988), 176–96.

D. A. Hinton, 'Metalwork and the Emporia', in M. Anderton (ed.), *Anglo-Saxon Trading Centres: Beyond the Emporia* (Glasgow, 1999), 24–31.

A. D. Morton, *Excavations at Hamwic*, vol. 1, CBA, Research Report, 984 (London, 1992).

—— 'Hamwic in its Context', in M. Anderton (ed.), *Anglo-Saxon Trading Centres: Beyond the Emporia* (Glasgow, 1999), 48–62.

I. Riddler, 'Spatial Organization of Bone-Working at Hamwic', in D. Hill and R. Cowie (eds.), *Wics: The Early Mediaeval Trading Centres of Northern Europe* (Sheffield, 2001), 61–6.

N. Stoodley, 'The Origins of Hamwic and its Central Role in the 7th Century as

Revealed by Recent Archaeological Discoveries', in B. Hårdh and L. Larsson (eds.), *Central Places in the Migration and the Merovingian Periods* (Stockholm, 2002), 317–31.

Verulamium/St Albans

M. Biddle and B. Kjølbye-Biddle, 'The Origins of St Albans Abbey: Romano-British Cemetery and Anglo-Saxon Monastery', in M. Henig and P. Lindley (eds.), *Alban and St Albans: Roman and Medieval Architecture, Art and Archaeology* (Leeds, 2001), 45–77.

N. Faulkner, 'Change and Decline in Late Romano-British Towns', in T. R. Slater (ed.), *Towns in Decline AD 100–1600* (Aldershot, 2000), 25–50.

—— 'Verulamium: Interpreting Decline', *Archaeological Journal*, 153 (1996), 79–103.

S. S. Frere, *Verulamium Excavations*, 3 vols. (London, 1972–84).

R. Niblett, 'Why Verulamium?', in M. Henig and P. Lindley (eds.), *Alban and St Albans: Roman and Medieval Architecture, Art and Archaeology* (Leeds, 2001), 1–12.

—— and I. Thompson, *Alban's Buried Towns: An Assessment of St Albans' Archaeology up to AD 1600* (Oxford, 2005).

CHAPTER 8. NORSE AND NATIVES

The Fundamental Readings

R. P. Abels, *Alfred the Great: War, Kingship and Culture in Anglo-Saxon England* (London, 1998).

J. H. Barrett (ed.), *Contact, Continuity and Collapse: The Norse Colonization of the North Atlantic* (Turnhout, 2003).

N. P. Brooks, 'England in the Ninth Century: The Crucible of Defeat', *Transactions of the Royal Historical Society*, 5th ser., 29 (1979), 1–20.

B. E. Crawford, 'The Vikings', in W. Davies (ed.), *Short Oxford History of the British Isles: From the Vikings to the Normans* (Oxford, 2003), 41–71.

J. Graham-Campbell and C. E. Batey, *Vikings in Scotland: An Archaeological Survey* (Edinburgh, 1998).

—— R. A. Hall, J. Jesch and D. N. Parsons (eds.), *Vikings and the Danelaw* (Oxford, 2001).

D. M. Hadley and J. D. Richards (eds.), *Cultures in Contact: Scandinavian Settlement in England in the Ninth and Tenth Centuries* (Turnhout, 2000).

J. Hines, A. Lane and M. Redknap, *Land, Sea and Home*, Society for Medieval Archaeology Monograph Series, 20 (Leeds, 2004).

J. D. Richards, *Viking Age England*, 2nd edn. (Stroud, 2004).

P. H. Sawyer, *The Oxford Illustrated History of the Vikings* (Oxford, 1998).

Recent Work on Pre-Viking and Viking Age Scandinavia

J. H. Barrett (ed.), *Contact, Continuity and Collapse: The Norse Colonization of the North Atlantic* (Turnhout, 2003).

W. W. Fitz-Hugh and E. I. Ward (eds.), *Vikings: The North Atlantic Saga* (Washington, DC, 2000).

J. Graham-Campbell (ed.), *Cultural Atlas of the Viking World* (Oxford, 1994).

L. Jørgensen, 'Manor and Market at Lake Tissø in the Sixth to Eleventh Centuries: The Danish "Productive" Sites', in T. Pestell and K. Ulmschneider (eds.), *Markets in Early Medieval Europe: Trading and 'Productive' Sites* (Macclesfield, 2003), 175–207.

B. Myhre, 'The Early Viking Age in Norway', *Acta Archaeologica*, 71 (2000), 35–47.

U. Näsman, 'Raids, Migrations, and Kingdoms – the Danish Case', *Acta Archaeologica*, 71 (2000), 1–7.

F. Svanberg, *Decolonizing the Viking Age*, vol. 1 (Lund, 2003).

J. Ulriksen, 'Danish Sites and Settlements with a Maritime Context, AD 200–1200', *Antiquity*, 68 (1994), 797–811.

Llangorse

P. C. Bartrum, *Early Welsh Genealogical Tracts* (Cardiff, 1966), 14–19.

E. Campbell and A. Lane, 'Llangorse: A Tenth-Century Royal Crannóg in Wales', *Antiquity*, 63 (1989), 675–81.

T. Charles-Edwards, 'Wales and Mercia, 613–918', in M. P. Brown and C. A. Farr (eds.), *Mercia: An Anglo-Saxon Kingdom in Europe* (Leicester, 2001), 89–105.

W. Davies, 'Alfred's Contemporaries: Irish, Welsh, Scots and Breton', in T. Reuter (ed.), *Alfred the Great: Papers from the Eleventh-Centenary Conferences* (Aldershot, 2003), 325–37.

—— *Wales in the Early Middle Ages* (Leicester, 1982).

H. Granger-Taylor and F. Pritchard, 'A Fine Quality Insular Embroidery from Llan-gors Crannóg, near Brecon', in M. Redknap, N. Edwards, S. Youngs, A. Lane and J. Knight (eds.), *Pattern and Purpose in Insular Art* (Oxford, 2001), 91–9.

J. Mulville and A. Powell, 'From Llanmaes to Llangorse: Herding and Hunting in Early Wales', unpublished paper presented at the Association for Environmental Archaeology (2007).

L. Mumford and M. Redknap, 'Worn by a Welsh Queen?', *Amgueddfa/National Museums and Galleries of Wales Yearbook*, 2 (1998/9), 52–4.

M. Redknap, 'Insular Non-Ferrous Metalwork from Wales of the Eighth to Tenth Centuries', in C. Bourke (ed.), *From the Isles of the North: Early Medieval Art in Ireland and Britain* (Belfast, 1995), 59–73.

—— *Vikings in Wales: An Archaeological Quest* (Cardiff, 2000).

—— and A. Lane, 'The Archaeological Importance of Llangorse Lake: An Environmental Perspective', *Aquatic Conservation: Marine and Freshwater Ecosystems*, 9 (1999), 377–90.

—— —— 'The Early Medieval Crannóg at Llangorse, Powys: An Interim Statement of the 1989–1993 Seasons', *International Journal of Nautical Archaeology*, 23 (1994), 189–205.

P. Sims-Williams, 'The Provenance of the Llywarch Hen Poems: A Case for Llangors, Brycheiniog', *Cambrian Medieval Celtic Studies*, 26 (1993), 27–63.

G. Wait, S. Benfield and C. McKewan, 'Rescuing Llangors Crannog', *British Archaeology*, 84 (2005), 37–9.

Repton and Heath Wood

M. Biddle, 'Archaeology, Architecture and the Cult of the Saints in Anglo-Saxon England', in L. A. S. Butler and R. K. Morris (eds.), *The Anglo-Saxon Church: Papers on History, Architecture and Archaeology in Honour of Dr H. M. Taylor*, CBA, Research Report, 60 (London, 1985), 1–31.

—— and B. Kjølbye-Biddle, 'Repton and the "Great Heathen Army", 873–4', in J. Graham-Campbell, R. A. Hall, J. Jesch and D. N. Parsons (eds.), *Vikings and the Danelaw* (Oxford, 2001), 45–96.

—— —— 'The Repton Stone', *Anglo-Saxon England*, 14 (1985), 233–92.

—— —— 'Repton and the Vikings', *Antiquity*, 66 (1992), 36–51.

P. A. Budd, C. Millard, C. Chenery, S. Lucy and C. Roberts, 'Investigating Population Movement by Stable Isotope Analysis: A Report from Britain', *Antiquity*, 78 (2004), 127–41.

J. Graham-Campbell, 'Pagan Scandinavian Burial in the Central and Southern Danelaw', in J. Graham-Campbell, R. A. Hall, J. Jesch and D. N. Parsons (eds.), *Vikings and the Danelaw* (Oxford, 2001), 105–23.

S. Keynes, 'King Alfred and the Mercians', in M. A. S. Blackburn and D. N. Dumville (eds.), *Kings, Currency and Alliance: History and Coinage of Southern England in the Ninth Century* (Woodbridge, 1998), 1–45.

A. L. Meaney, 'Felix's *Life of Guthlac*: History or Hagiography?', in D. Hill and M. Worthington (eds.), *Æthelbald and Offa: Two Eighth-Century Kings of Mercia*, BAR, Brit. Ser., 383 (Oxford, 2005), 75–82.

D. W. Rollason, 'The Cult of Murdered Royal Saints in Anglo-Saxon England', *Anglo-Saxon England*, 11 (1983), 1–22.

J. D. Richards, 'Boundaries and Cult Centres: Viking Burial in Derbyshire', in J. Graham-Campbell, R. A. Hall, J. Jesch and D. N. Parsons (eds.), *Vikings and the Danelaw* (Oxford, 2001), 97–104.

—— P. Beswick, J. Bond, M. Jecock, J. McKinley, S. Rowland and F. Worley, 'Excavations at the Viking Barrow Cemetery at Heath Wood, Ingleby, Derbyshire', *Antiquaries Journal*, 84 (2004), 23–116.

—— M. Jecock, L. Richmond and C. Tuck, 'The Viking Barrow Cemetery at Heath Wood, Ingleby, Derbyshire', *Medieval Archaeology*, 39 (1995), 51–70.

H. M. Taylor, 'St Wystan's Church, Repton, Derbyshire: A Reconstruction Essay', *Archaeological Journal*, 144 (1987), 205–45.

A. Thacker, 'Kings, Saints and Monasteries in Pre-Viking Mercia', *Midland History*, 10 (1985), 1–25.

Orkney

P. J. Ashmore, 'Orkney Burials in the First Millennium AD', in J. Downes and A. Ritchie (eds.), *Sea Change: Orkney and Northern Europe in the Later Iron Age AD 300–800* (Balgavies, Angus, 2003), 35–50.

J. Bäckund, 'War and Peace: The Relations between the Picts and the Norse in Orkney', *Northern Studies*, 36 (2001), 33–48.

J. H. Barrett, 'Beyond War or Peace: The Study of Culture Contact in Viking-Age Scotland', in J. Hines, A. Lane and M. Redknap (eds.), *Land, Sea and Home*, Society for Medieval Archaeology Monograph Series, 20 (Leeds, 2004), 207–17.

—— 'Christian and Pagan Practice during the Conversion of Viking Age Orkney and Shetland', in M. O. H. Carver (ed.), *The Cross Goes North: Processes of Conversion in Northern Europe, AD 300–1300* (Woodbridge, 2003), 207–26.

—— (ed.), *Contact, Continuity and Collapse: The Norse Colonization of the North Atlantic* (Turnhout, 2003).

—— and M. P. Richards, 'Identity, Gender, Religion and Economy: New Isotope and Radiocarbon Evidence for Marine Resource Intensification in Early Historic Orkney, Scotland, UK', *European Journal of Archaeology*, 7 (2004), 249–71.

—— R. P. Beukens and R. A. Nickolson, 'Diet and Ethnicity during the Viking Colonization of Northern Scotland: Evidence from Fish Bones and Stable Carbon Isotopes', *Antiquity*, 75 (2001), 145–54.

—— —— I. Simpson, P. Ashmore, S. Poaps, J. Huntley, 'What Was the Viking Age and When Did it Happen? A View from Orkney', *Norwegian Archaeological Review*, 33 (2000), 1–39.

C. E. Batey, J. Jesch and C. D. Morris (eds.), *The Viking Age in Caithness, Orkney and the North Atlantic: Proceedings of the Eleventh Viking Congress* (Edinburgh, 1993).

J. M. Bond, 'Beyond the Fringe? Recognising Change and Adaptation in Pictish and Norse Orkney', in C. M. Mills and G. Cole (eds.), *Human Settlement and Marginality*, Oxbow Monograph, 100 (Oxford, 1998).

—— 'A Growing Success? Agricultural Intensification and Risk Management in Late Iron Age Orkney', in J. Downes and A. Ritchie (eds.), *Sea Change: Orkney and Northern Europe in the Later Iron Age AD 300–800* (Balgavies, Angus, 2003), 95–104.

—— and J. R. Hunter, 'Flax-Growing in Orkney from the Norse Period to the Eighteenth Century', *Proceedings of the Society of Antiquaries of Scotland*, 117 (1987), 175–81.

D. Broun, 'The Origin of Scottish Identity in its European Context', in B. E. Crawford (ed.), *Scotland in Dark Age Europe* (Fife, 1994), 21–31.

A. J. Dunwell, T. G. Cowie, M. F. Bruce, T. Neighbour and A. R. Rees, 'A Viking Age Cemetery at Cnip, Uig, Isle of Lewis', *Proceedings of the Society of Antiquaries of Scotland*, 125 (1996), 719–52.

G. Fellows-Jensen, 'Viking Settlement in the Northern and Western Isles – Placename Evidence as Seen from Denmark and the Danelaw', in A. Fenton and H. Pálsson (eds.), *The Northern and Western Isles in the Viking World* (Edinburgh, 1984), 148–68.

S. Goodacre, A. Helgason, J. Nicholson, L. Southam, L. Ferguson, E. Hickey, E. Vega, K. Stefánsson, R. Ward and B. Sykes, 'Genetic Evidence for a Family-Based Scandinavian Settlement of Shetland and Orkney during the Viking Periods', *Heredity*, 95 (2005), 129–35.

R. Gowland and C. Knüsel (eds.), *Social Archaeology of Funerary Remains* (Oxford, 2006).

J. Graham-Campbell, *The Viking-Age Gold and Silver of Scotland (AD 850–1100)* (Edinburgh, 1995).

S. J. Grieve and J. Gibson, 'Orkney Viking Period', in J. Downes, S. Foster, C. R. Wickham-Jones and J. Callister (eds.), *The Heart of Neolithic Orkney World Heritage Site Research Agenda* (Edinburgh, 2005), 66–9.

A. Helgason, E. Hickey, S. Goodacre, V. Bosnes, K. Stefánsson, R. Ward and B. Sykes, 'MtDNA and the Islands of the North Atlantic: Estimating the Proportions of Norse and Gaelic Ancestry', *American Journal of Human Genetics*, 68 (2001), 723–37.

J. R. Hunter, 'The Early Norse Period', in K. J. Edwards and I. B. Ralston (eds.), *Scotland After the Ice Age: Environment and Archaeology, 8000 BC–AD 1000* (Edinburgh, 2003), 241–54.

—— 'Pool, Sanday – a Case Study for the Later Iron Age and Viking Periods', in I. Armit (ed.), *Beyond the Brochs* (Edinburgh, 1990), 175–93.

R. Lamb, '"Where Local Knowledge is So Valuable": Nautical Practicalities and the Earliest Viking Age in Orkney', in O. Owen (ed.), *The World of Orkneyinga Saga* (Kirkwall, 2005), 39–53.

J. Montgomery and J. A. Evans, 'Immigrants on the Isle of Lewis – Combining Traditional Funerary and Modern Isotope Evidence to Investigate Social

Differentiation, Migration and Dietary Change in the Outer Hebrides of Scotland', in R. Gowland and C. Knüsel (eds.), *Social Archaeology of Funerary Remains* (Oxford, 2006), 122–42.

—— and T. Neighbour, 'Sr Isotope Evidence for Population Movement within the Hebridean Norse Community of NW Scotland', *Journal of the Geological Society*, 160 (2003), 649–53.

C. D. Morris, 'Viking and Late Norse Orkney: An Update and Bibliography', *Acta Archaeologica*, 62 (1992), 123–50.

D. Ó Corráin, 'The Vikings in Scotland and Ireland in the Ninth Century', *Peritia*, 12 (1998), 296–339.

C. J. Omand, 'The Life of St Findan', in R. J. Berry and H. N. Firth (eds.), *The People of Orkney* (Kirkwall, 1986), 284–7.

O. Owen, 'The Scar Boat Burial – and the Missing Decades of the Early Viking Age in Orkney and Shetland', in J. Adams and K. Holman (eds.), *Scandinavia and Europe 800–1350: Contact, Conflict and Coexistence* (Turnhout, 2004), 3–33.

—— *The Sea Road: A Viking Voyage through Scotland* (Edinburgh, 1999).

—— and Magnar Dalland, *Scar: A Viking Boat Burial on Sanday, Orkney* (Edinburgh, 2001).

M. P. Richards, B. T. Fuller and T. I. Molleson, 'Stable Isotope Palaeodiet Study of Humans and Fauna from the Multi-Period (Iron Age, Viking and Late Medieval) Site of Newark Bay, Orkney', *Journal of Archaeological Science*, 33 (2006), 122–31.

B. J. Sellevold, *Picts and Vikings at Westness: Anthropological Investigations of the Skeletal Material from the Cemetery at Westness, Rousay, Orkney Island*, Norsk Institutt fur Kulturminneforskning, Scientific Report, 10 (Oslo, 1999).

B. Smith, 'The Picts and the Martyrs or Did Vikings Kill the Native Population of Orkney and Shetland?', *Northern Studies*, 36 (2001), 7–32.

W. P. L. Thomson, 'St Findan and the Pictish-Norse Transition', in R. J. Berry and H. N. Firth (eds.), *The People of Orkney* (Kirkwall, 1986), 279–83.

R. D. E. Welander, C. Batey and T. G. Cowie, 'A Viking Burial from Kneep, Uig, Isle of Lewis', *Proceedings of the Society of Antiquaries of Scotland*, 117 (1987), 149–74.

J. F. Wilson, D. A. Weiss, M. Richards, M. G. Thomas, N. Bradman and D. B. Goldstein, 'Genetic Evidence for Different Male and Female Roles during Cultural Transitions in the British Isles', *Proceedings of the National Academy of Sciences*, 98 (2001), 5078–83.

CHAPTER 9. NEW TOWNS

The Fundamental Readings

G. G. Astill, 'Community, Identity and the Later Anglo-Saxon Town: The Case of Southern England', in W. Davies, G. Halsall and A. Reynolds (eds.), *People and Space in the Middle Ages, 300–1300* (Turnhout, 2006), 233–54.

—— 'Towns and Town Hierarchies in Saxon England', *Oxford Journal of Archaeology*, 10 (1991), 95–117.

N. P. Brooks, 'The Administrative Background to the Burghal Hidage', in D. Hill and A. R. Rumble (eds.), *The Defence of Wessex: The Burghal Hidage and Anglo-Saxon Fortifications* (Manchester, 1996), 128–50.

C. Dyer, 'Recent Developments in Early Medieval Urban History and Archaeology in England', in D. Denecke and G. Shaw (eds.), *Urban Historical Geography* (Cambridge, 1988), 69–80.

D. Griffiths, 'Exchange, Trade and Urbanization', in W. Davies (ed.), *From the Vikings to the Normans* (Oxford, 2003), 73–104.

D. M. Palliser (ed.), *The Cambridge Urban History of Britain*, vol. 1: *600–1540* (Cambridge, 2000).

T. Reuter (ed.), *Alfred the Great: Papers from the Eleventh-Centenary Conferences* (London, 2003).

Worcester

N. Baker, H. Dalwood, R. Holt, C. Mundy and G. Taylor, 'From Roman to Medieval Worcester: Development and Planning in the Anglo-Saxon City', *Antiquity*, 66 (1992), 65–74.

N. Baker and R. Holt, 'The City of Worcester in the Tenth Century', in N. P. Brooks and C. Cubitt (eds.), *St Oswald of Worcester: Life and Influence* (London, 1996), 129–46.

—— —— *Urban Growth and the Medieval Church: Gloucester and Worcester* (Aldershot, 2004).

P. Barker, 'Reconstructing Wulfstan's Cathedral', in J. S. Barrow and N. P. Brooks, *St Wulfstan and his World* (Aldershot, 2005), 167–88.

J. S. Barrow, 'The Community of Worcester, 961–c. 1100', in N. P. Brooks and C. Cubitt (eds.), *St Oswald of Worcester: Life and Influence* (London, 1996), 84–99.

—— 'Urban Cemetery Location in the High Middle Ages', in S. R. Bassett (ed.), *Death in Towns: Urban Responses to the Dying and the Dead, 100–1600* (London, 1992), 78–100.

S. R. Bassett, 'Churches in Worcester before and after the Conversion of the Anglo-Saxons', *Antiquaries Journal*, 69 (1989), 225–56.

—— 'The Middle and Late Anglo-Saxon Defences of Western Mercian Towns', *Anglo-Saxon Studies in Archaeology and History*, 15 (2008), 180–239.

H. B. Clarke and C. Dyer, 'Anglo-Saxon and Early Norman Worcester: The Documentary Evidence', *Transactions of the Worcester Archaeological Society*, 3rd ser., 2 (1968–9), 27–33.

C. Dyer, *Lords and Peasants in a Changing Society: The Estates of the Bishopric of Worcester, 680–1540* (Cambridge, 1980).

—— 'St Oswald and 10,000 West Midland Peasants', in N. P. Brooks and C. Cubitt (eds.), *St Oswald of Worcester: Life and Influence* (London, 1996), 174–93.

H. Halwood and R. Edwards, *Excavations at Deansway, Worcester, 1988–89: Romano-British Small Town to Late Medieval City*, CBA, Research Report, 139 (York, 2004).

C. M. Heighway, A. P. Garrod and A. G. Vince, 'Excavations at 1 Westgate Street, Gloucester, 1975', *Medieval Archaeology*, 23 (1979), 159–213.

R. Holt, 'The City of Worcester in the Time of Wulfstan', in J. S. Barrow and N. P. Brooks (eds.), *St Wulfstan and his World* (Aldershot, 2005), 123–36.

G. Hull, 'Barkingwic? Saxon and Medieval Features adjacent to Barking', *Essex Archaeology and History*, 33 (2002), 157–90.

J. R. Maddicott, 'London and Droitwich, c. 650–750: Trade, Industry and the Rise of Mercia', *Anglo-Saxon England*, 34 (2005), 7–58.

P. Sims-Williams, *Religion and Literature in Western England, 600–800* (Cambridge, 1990).

London

J. Ayre and R. Wroe-Brown, 'Æthelred's Hythe to Queenhythe: The Origin of a London Dock', *Medieval Life*, 5 (1996), 14–25.

M. Blackburn, 'The London Mint in the Reign of Alfred', in M. A. S. Blackburn and D. N. Dumville (eds.), *Kings, Currency and Alliances: History and Coinage of Southern England in the Ninth Century* (Woodbridge, 1998), 105–23.

D. Bowsher, T. Dyson, N. Holder and I. Howell, *The London Guildhall: An Archaeological History of a Neighbourhood from Early Medieval to Modern Times*, 2 vols., MoLAS Monograph, 36 (London, 2007).

N. P. Brooks and J. Graham-Campbell, 'Reflections on the Viking-Age Silver Hoard from Croydon, Surrey', in M. A. S. Blackburn (ed.), *Anglo-Saxon Monetary History* (London, 1986), 91–110.

J. Clark, 'King Alfred's London and London's King Alfred', *London Archaeologist*, 9 (1999), 35–8.

—— 'Late Saxon and Norman London Thirty Years On', in I. Haynes, H. Sheldon and L. Hannigan (eds.), *London Under Ground: The Archaeology of a City* (Oxford, 2000), 206–22.

R. Cowie, '*Londinium* to *Lundenwic*: Early and Middle Saxon Archaeology in the London Region', in I. Haynes, H. Sheldon and L. Hannigan (eds.), *London under Ground: The Archaeology of a City* (Oxford, 2000), 175–205.

—— 'Mercian London', in M. P. Brown and C. A. Farr (eds.), *Mercia: An Anglo-Saxon Kingdom in Europe* (London, 2001), 194–209.

—— and C. Harding, 'Saxon Settlement and Economy from the Dark Ages to Domesday', in *The Archaeology of Greater London: An Assessment of*

Archaeological Evidence for Human Presence in the Area Now Covered by Greater London, MoLAS Monograph (London, 2000), 171–206.

O. Crumlin-Pedersen, 'Ships as Indicators of Trade in Northern Europe 600–1200', in J. Bill and B. L. Clausen (eds.), *Maritime Topography and the Medieval Town* (Copenhagen, 1999), 11–20.

T. Dyson, 'King Alfred and the Restoration of London', *London Journal*, 15 (1990), 99–110.

—— 'Two Saxon Land Grants for Queenhithe', in J. Bird, H. Chapman and J. Clark (eds.), *Collectanea Londiniensia: Studies in London Archaeology and History Presented to Ralph Merrifield*, London and Middlesex Archaeological Society, Special Paper, 2 (London, 1978), 200–215.

R. Gilchrist and B. Sloane, *Requiem: The Medieval Monastic Cemetery in Britain* (London, 2005).

D. M. Goodburn, 'Anglo-Saxon Boat Finds from London, are they English?', in C. Westerdahl (ed.), *Cross Roads in Ancient Ship Building* (Oxford, 1994), 97–104.

—— 'Fragments of a 10th-Century Timber Arcade from Vintner's Place on the London Waterfront', *Medieval Archaeology*, 37 (1993), 78–92.

D. A. Hinton, *Gold and Gilt, Pots and Pins: Possessions and People in Medieval Britain* (Oxford, 2005).

V. Horsman, C. Milne and G. Milne, *Aspects of Saxo-Norman London: I Building and Street Development*, London and Middlesex Archaeological Society, Special Paper, 11 (London, 1988).

D. Keene, 'Alfred and London', in T. Reuter (ed.), *Alfred the Great: Papers from the Eleventh-Centenary Conferences* (Aldershot, 2003), 235–49.

—— 'London from the Post-Roman Period to 1300', in D. M. Palliser (ed.), *The Cambridge Urban History of Britain*, vol. 1: 600–1540 (Cambridge, 2000), 187–216.

—— Review of Ken Steedman *et al.*, *Aspects of Saxo-Norman London: III*, *London Journal*, 20 (1995), 107–8.

S. E. Kelly (ed.), *Charters of St Paul's, London* (Oxford, 2004).

—— 'Trading Privileges from Eighth-Century England', *Early Medieval Europe*, 1 (1992), 3–28.

S. Keynes, 'King Alfred and the Mercians', in M. A. S. Blackburn and D. N. Dumville (eds.), *Kings, Currency and Alliances: History and Coinage of Southern England in the Ninth Century* (Woodbridge, 1998), 1–46.

G. Malcolm and D. Bowsher with R. Cowie, *Middle Saxon London: Excavations at the Royal Opera House 1989–99*, MoLAS Monograph, 15 (London, 2003).

G. Milne, *Timber Building Techniques in London c. 900–1400*, London and Middlesex Archaeological Society, Special Paper, 15 (London, 1992).

P. Nightingale, *A Medieval Mercantile Community: The Grocers' Company and the Politics and Trade of London 1000–1485* (New Haven, 1995).

K. Steedman, T. Dyson and J. Schofield, *Aspects of Saxo-Norman London: III The Bridgehead and Billingsgate to 1200*, London and Middlesex Archaeological Society, Special Paper, 14 (London, 1992).

A. Vince (ed.), *Aspects of Saxo-Norman London: II Finds and Environmental Evidence*, London and Middlesex Archaeological Society, Special Paper, 12 (London, 1991).

R. Wroe-Brown, 'Bull Wharf: Queenhithe', *Current Archaeology*, 158 (1998), 75-7.

—— 'The Saxon Origins of Queenhithe', *Transactions of the London and Middlesex Archaeological Society*, 50 (1999), 12-16.

Other Towns and Trading Sites

S. R. Bassett., 'Lincoln and the Anglo-Saxon See of Lindsey', *Anglo-Saxon England*, 18 (1989), 1-32.

E. Cameron and Q. Mould, 'Saxon Shoes, Viking Sheaths? Cultural Identity in Anglo-Scandinavian York', in J. Hines, A. Lane and M. Redknap (eds.), *Land, Sea and Home*, Society for Medieval Archaeology Monograph Series, 20 (Leeds, 2004), 457-66.

C. Dallas, *Excavations in Thetford by B. K. Davison between 1964 and 1970*, East Anglian Archaeology, 62 (Dereham, 1993).

K. Dobney and D. Jaques, 'Avian Signatures for Identity and Status in Anglo-Saxon England', *Acta Zoologica Cracoviensia*, 45 (2002), 7-21.

C. Dyer, 'Towns and Cottages in Eleventh-Century England', in H. Mayr-Harting and R. I. Moore (eds.), *Studies in Medieval History Presented to R. H. C. Davis* (London, 1985), 91-106.

B. J. J. Gilmour and D. A. Stocker, *St Mark's Church and Cemetery*, Archaeology of Lincoln, 13 (London, 1986).

D. Griffiths, R. A. Philpott and G. Egan, *Meols: The Archaeology of the North Wirral Coast*, Oxford University School of Archaeology Monographs, 68 (Oxford, 2007).

R. A. Hall, 'The Five Boroughs of the Danelaw: A Review of Present Knowledge', *Anglo-Saxon England*, 18 (1989), 149-206.

—— D. W. Rollason, M. Blackburn, D. N. Parsons, G. Fellows-Jensen, A. R. Hall, H. K. Kenward, T. P. O'Connor, D. Tweddle, A. J. Mainman and N. S. H. Rogers, *Aspects of Anglo-Scandinavian York*, Archaeology of York, 8/4 (York, 2004).

P. A. Henry, 'Development and Change in Late Saxon Textile Production: An Analysis of the Evidence', *Durham Archaeological Journal*, 14-15 (1999), 69-76.

M. J. Jones, D. Stocker and A. Vince, *The City by the Pool: Assessing the Archaeology of the City of Lincoln* (Oxford, 2003).

K. Poole, 'Living and Eating in Viking-Age Towns and their Hinterlands', in M. Allen, S. Baker, S. Middle and K. Poole (eds.), *Food and Drink in Archaeology: University of Nottingham Postgraduate Conference 2007* (Totnes, 2008), 104–12.

M. Redknap, 'Viking-Age Settlement in Wales and the Evidence from Llanbedrgoch', in J. Hines, A. Lane and M. Redknap (eds.), *Land, Sea and Home*, Society for Medieval Archaeology Monograph Series, 20 (Leeds, 2004), 139–75.

A. Rogerson and C. Dallas, *Excavations in Thetford, 1948–59 and 1973–80*, East Anglian Archaeology, 22 (Dereham, 1984).

N. J. Sykes, 'From *cu* and *sceap* to *beffe* and *motton*', in C. M. Woolgar, D. Serjeantson and T. Waldron (eds.), *Food in Medieval England: Diet and Nutrition* (Oxford, 2006), 56–71.

CHAPTER 10. KINGS AND SURPLUSES
The Fundamental Readings

W. Davies, 'Thinking about the Welsh Environment a Thousand Years Ago', in G. H. Jenkins (ed.), *Cymru a'r Cymry 2000: Wales and the Welsh 2000* (Aberystwyth, 2001), 1–19.

C. Dyer, *Making a Living in the Middle Ages: The People of Britain 850–1520* (New Haven, 2002).

R. Faith, *The English Peasantry and the Growth of Lordship* (New York, 1997).

P. Fowler, *Farming in the First Millennium AD: British Agriculture between Julius Caesar and William the Conqueror* (Cambridge, 2002).

P. Sawyer, 'The Wealth of England in the Eleventh Century', *Transactions of the Royal Historical Society*, 5th ser., 15 (1965), 145–64.

T. Williamson, *Shaping Medieval Landscapes: Settlement, Society, Environment* (Macclesfield, 2003).

The Political Background

R. P. Abels, *Alfred the Great: War, Kingship and Culture in Anglo-Saxon England* (London, 1998).

L. Abrams, 'King Edgar and the Men of the Danelaw', in D. Scragg (ed.), *Edgar, King of the English 959–975: New Interpretations* (Woodbridge, 2008), 171–91.

N. P. Brooks, 'England in the Ninth Century: The Crucible of Defeat', *Transactions of the Royal Historical Society*, 5th ser., 29 (1979), 1–20.

R. A. Hall, 'A Kingdom Too Far: York in the Early Tenth Century', in N. J. Higham and D. H. Hill (eds.), *Edward the Elder 899–924* (London, 2001), 188–99.

D. Hill, 'The Construction of Offa's Dyke', *Antiquaries Journal*, 80 (2000), 195–206.

—— and A. R. Rumble (eds.), *The Defence of Wessex: The Burghal Hidage and Anglo-Saxon Fortifications* (Manchester, 1996).

S. Keynes, 'Edgar, *rex admirabilis*', in D. Scragg (ed.), *Edgar, King of the English 959–975: New Interpretations* (Woodbridge, 2008), 3–59.

—— 'Edward, King of the Anglo-Saxons', in N. J. Higham and D. H. Hill (eds.), *Edward the Elder 899–924* (London, 2001), 40–66.

—— 'A Tale of Two Kings: Alfred the Great and Æthelred the Unready', *Transactions of the Royal Historical Society*, 5th ser., 36 (1986), 195–217.

D. M. Metcalf, 'The Monetary History of England in the Tenth Century Viewed in the Perspective of the Eleventh Century', in M. A. S. Blackburn (ed.), *Anglo-Saxon Monetary History: Essays in Memory of Michael Dolley* (Leicester, 1986), 133–57.

New-Style Landlords

M. Audouy and A. Chapman (eds.), *Raunds: The Origin and Growth of a Midland Village AD 450–1500* (Oxford, 2009).

P. Booth, A. Dodd, M. Robinson and A. Smith, *The Thames through Time: The Archaeology of the Gravel Terraces of the Upper and Middle Thames. The Early Historical Period: AD 1–1000*, Oxford Archaeology Thames Valley Landscapes Monographs, 27 (Oxford, 2007).

M. Costen, 'Settlement in Wessex in the Tenth Century', in M. Aston and C. Lewis (eds.), *The Medieval Landscape of Wessex* (Oxford, 1994), 97–114.

P. Crabtree, 'Production and Consumption in an Early Complex Society: Animal Use in Middle Saxon East Anglia', *World Archaeology*, 28 (1996), 58–75.

C. Crowe, 'Early Medieval Parish Formation in Dumfries and Galloway', in M. O. H. Carver (ed.), *The Cross Goes North: Processes of Conversion in Northern Europe, AD 300–1300* (Woodbridge, 2003), 195–206.

W. Davies, *Wales in the Early Middle Ages* (Leicester, 1982).

K. Dobney, D. Jaques, J. H. Barrett and C. Johnstone, *Farmers, Monks and Aristocrats: The Environmental Archaeology of Anglo-Saxon Flixborough* (Oxford, 2007).

C. Dyer, 'St Oswald and 10,000 West Midland Peasants', in N. P. Brooks and C. Cubitt (eds.), *St Oswald of Worcester: Life and Influence* (London, 1996), 174–93.

R. Faith, 'Cola's *tun*: Rural Social Structure in Late Anglo-Saxon Devon', in R. Evans (ed.), *Lordship and Learning: Studies in Memory of Trevor Aston* (Woodbridge, 2004), 63–78.

C. Gerrard and M. Aston, *The Shapwick Project, Somerset: A Rural Landscape Explored*, Society for Medieval Archaeology Monograph Series, 25 (Leeds, 2007).

G. Hey, *Yarnton: Saxon and Medieval Settlement and Landscape*, Oxford Archaeology Thames Valley Landscapes Monographs, 20 (Oxford, 2004).

D. Hill, '*Sulh* – the Anglo-Saxon Plough c. 1000 AD', *Landscape History*, 22 (2000), 7–19.

D. Hooke (ed.), *Anglo-Saxon Settlements* (Oxford, 1988).

R. Jones and M. Page, 'Characterizing Rural Settlement and Landscape: Whittlewood Forest in the Middle Ages', *Medieval Archaeology*, 47 (2003), 53–83.

—— —— *Medieval Villages in an English Landscape: Beginnings and Ends* (Macclesfield, 2006).

S. R. H. Jones, 'Transaction Costs, Institutional Change and the Emergence of a Market Economy in Later Anglo-Saxon England', *Economic History Review*, 2nd ser., 46 (1993), 658–78.

C. Lewis, P. Mitchell-Fox and C. Dyer, *Village, Hamlet and Field: Changing Medieval Settlements in Central England* (Manchester, 1997), 77–118.

S. Oosthuizen, 'New Light on the Origins of Open-Field Farming', *Medieval Archaeology*, 49 (2005), 165–93.

S. Parry, *Raunds Area Survey: An Archaeological Study of the Landscape of Raunds, Northamptonshire 1984–94* (Oxford, 2006).

A. Reynolds, 'Boundaries and Settlements in Later Sixth to Eleventh Century England', *Anglo-Saxon Studies in Archaeology and History*, 12 (2003), 98–136.

S. Rippon, 'Emerging Regional Variation in Historic Landscape Character: The Possible Significance of the "Long Eighth Century"', in M. F. Gardiner and S. Rippon (eds.), *Medieval Landscapes* (Macclesfield, 2007), 105–21.

—— R. M. Fyfe and A. G. Brown, 'Beyond Villages and Open Fields: The Origins and Development of a Historic Landscape Characterised by Dispersed Settlement in South-West England', *Medieval Archaeology*, 50 (2006), 31–51.

P. Williams and R. Newman, *Market Lavington, Wiltshire: An Anglo-Saxon Cemetery and Settlement*, Wessex Archaeology Report, 19 (Salisbury 2006).

R. Williams, *Pennyland and Hartigans: Two Iron Age and Saxon Sites in Milton Keynes*, Buckinghamshire Archaeological Society Monograph, 4 (Milton Keynes, 1993).

CHAPTER 11. SELLING SURPLUS AND BUYING STATUS

The Fundamental Readings

P. Coss, 'What's in a Construct? The "Gentry" in Anglo-Saxon England', in R. Evans (ed.), *Lordship and Learning: Studies in Memory of Trevor Aston* (Woodbridge, 2004), 95–107.

C. Dyer, *Making a Living in the Middle Ages: The People of Britain 850–1520* (New Haven, 2002).

R. Fleming, 'Lords and Labour', in W. Davies (ed.), *Short Oxford History of the British Isles: From the Vikings to the Normans* (Oxford, 2003), 107–38.

—— 'The New Wealth, the New Rich, and the New Political Style in Late Anglo-Saxon England', *Anglo-Norman Studies*, 22 (2001), 1–22.

M. F. Gardiner, 'Late Saxon Settlement', in H. Hamerow, S. Crawford and D. A. Hinton (eds.), *A Handbook of Anglo-Saxon Archaeology* (Oxford, forthcoming).

J. Gillingham, 'Thegns and Knights in Eleventh-Century England: Who Was Then the Gentleman?', *Transactions of the Royal Historical Society*, 6th ser., 5 (1995), 129–53.

M. R. Godden, 'Money, Power and Morality in Late Anglo-Saxon England', *Anglo-Saxon England*, 19 (1990), 41–65.

C. Loveluck, *Rural Settlement, Lifestyles and Social Change in the Later First Millennium AD: Anglo-Saxon Flixborough in its Wider Context* (Oxford, 2007).

P. H. Sawyer, 'The Wealth of England in the Eleventh Century', *Transactions of the Royal Historical Society*, 5th ser., 15 (1965), 145–64.

The Tenth- and Eleventh-Century Economy

R. H. Britnell, *The Commercialisation of English Society 1000–1500*, 2nd edn. (Cambridge, 1996).

—— 'English Markets and Royal Administration before 1200', *Economic History Review*, 2nd ser., 31 (1987), 183–96.

W. Davies, *An Early Welsh Microcosm: Studies in the Llandaff Charters* (London, 1978).

—— *Wales in the Early Middle Ages* (Leicester, 1982).

H. E. Hallam, 'England before the Norman Conquest', in H. E. Hallam (ed.), *The Agrarian History of England and Wales*, vol. 2: *1042–1350* (Cambridge, 1988), 1–44.

D. A. Hinton, *Archaeology, Economy and Society: England from the Fifth to the Fifteenth Century* (London, 1990), 106–32.

P. Nightingale, 'The Evolution of Weight-Standards and the Creation of New Monetary and Commercial Links in Northern Europe from the Tenth Century to the Twelfth Century', *Economic History Review*, 2nd ser., 38 (1985), 192–209.

High-Status Establishments

M. Audouy and A. Chapman (eds.), *Raunds: The Origin and Growth of a Midland Village AD 450–1500* (Oxford, 2009).

J. Blair, 'Hall and Chamber: English Domestic Planning 1000–1250', in G. Meirion-Jones and M. Jones (eds.), *Manorial Domestic Buildings in England and Northern France* (London, 1993), 1–21.

A. Boddington, *Raunds Furnells: The Anglo-Saxon Church and Churchyard*, English Heritage Archaeological Report, 7 (London, 1996).

P. Booth, A. Dodd, M. Robinson and A. Smith, *The Thames through Time: The Archaeology of the Gravel Terraces of the Upper and Middle Thames. The Early Historical Period: AD 1–1000*, Oxford Archaeology Thames Valley Landscapes Monographs, 27 (Oxford, 2007).

E. Campbell and A. Lane, 'Llangorse: A Tenth-Century Royal Crannóg in Wales', *Antiquity*, 63 (1989), 675–81.

M. Costen, 'Settlement in Wessex in the Tenth Century', in M. Aston and C. Lewis (eds.), *The Medieval Landscape of Wessex* (Oxford, 1994), 97–114.

B. Cunliffe, *Excavations at Portchester Castle: Saxon*, vol. 2, Reports of the Research Committee of the Society of Antiquaries of London, 33 (London, 1976).

W. Davies, *Wales in the Early Middle Ages* (Leicester, 1982).

J. R. Fairbrother, *Faccombe Netherton: Excavations of a Saxon and Medieval Manorial Complex*, 2 vols., British Museum Occasional Papers (London, 1990).

M. F. Gardiner, 'Implements and Utensils in *Gerefa*, and the Organization of Seigneurial Farmsteads in the High Middle Ages', *Medieval Archaeology*, 50 (2006), 260–67.

—— 'The Origins and Persistence of Manor Houses in England', in M. F. Gardiner and S. Rippon (eds.), *Medieval Landscapes* (Macclesfield, 2007), 170–82.

M. Redknap, *Vikings in Wales: An Archaeological Quest* (Cardiff, 2000).

A. Williams, 'A Bell-House and a *burh-geat*: Lordly Residences in England before the Norman Conquest', in C. Harper-Bill and R. Harvey (eds.), *Medieval Knighthood*, 4 (Woodbridge, 1992), 221–40.

P. Williams and R. Newman, *Market Lavington, Wiltshire: An Anglo-Saxon Cemetery and Settlement*, Wessex Archaeology Report, 19 (Salisbury, 2006).

T. Williamson, *Shaping Medieval Landscapes: Settlement, Society, Environment* (Macclesfield, 2003).

Conspicuous Consumption

U. Albarella and R. Thomas, 'They Dined on Crane: Bird Consumption, Wild Fowling and Status in Medieval England', *Acta Zoologica Cracoviensia*, 45 (2002), 23–38.

J. H. Barrett, A. M. Locker and C. M. Roberts, '"Dark Age Economics" Revisited: The English Fish Bone Evidence AD 600–1600', *Antiquity*, 78 (2004), 618–36.

M. Biddle, *Objects and Economy in Medieval Winchester: Artifacts from Medieval Winchester*, 2 vols. (Oxford, 1990).

R. Bruce-Mitford, with P. Ashbee, E. Greenfield, F. Roe and R. J. Taylor, *Mawgan*

Porth: A Settlement of the Late Saxon Period on the North Cornish Coast, English Heritage Archaeological Report, 13 (London, 1997).

W. Davies, 'Thinking about the Welsh Environment a Thousand Years Ago', in G. H. Jenkins (ed.), *Cymru a'r Cymry 2000: Wales and the Welsh 2000* (Aberystwyth, 2001), 1–19.

K. Dobney and D. Jaques, 'Avian Signatures for Identity and Status in Anglo-Saxon England', *Acta Zoologica Cracoviensia*, 45 (2002), 7–21.

C. R. Dodwell, *Anglo-Saxon Art: A New Perspective* (Ithaca, NY, 1982).

C. Dyer, 'The Consumption of Fresh-Water Fish in Medieval England', in M. Aston (ed.), *Medieval Fish, Fisheries and Fishponds in England*, 2 vols., BAR, Brit. Ser., 182 (Oxford, 1988), 27–38.

R. Fleming, 'Acquiring, Flaunting and Destroying Silk in Late Anglo-Saxon England', *Early Medieval Europe*, 15 (2007), 127–58.

—— 'Rural Elites and Urban Communities in Late-Saxon England', *Past and Present*, 141 (1993), 3–37.

H. Granger-Taylor and F. Pritchard, 'A Fine Quality Insular Embroidery from Llan-gors Crannóg, near Brecon', in M. Redknap, N. Edwards, S. Youngs, A. Lane and J. Knight (eds.), *Pattern and Purpose in Insular Art* (Oxford, 2001), 91–9.

P. J. Huggins, 'Excavation of an Eleventh Century Viking Hall and Fourteenth Century Rooms at Waltham Abbey, Essex, 1969–71', *Medieval Archaeology*, 20 (1976), 90–101.

G. Milne, *St Bride's Church London: Archaeological Research 1952–60 and 1992–5*, English Heritage Archaeological Report, 11 (London, 1997).

T. P. O'Connor, *Animal Bones from Flaxengate, Lincoln, c. 870–1500* (Lincoln, 1982).

—— 'Feeding Lincoln in the Eleventh Century – a Speculation', in M. Jones (ed.), *Integrating the Subsistence Economy*, BAR, Int. Ser., 181 (Oxford, 1983), 327–30.

G. R. Owen-Crocker, *Dress in Anglo-Saxon England*, 2nd edn. (Woodbridge, 2004).

A. Powell, 'Animal Bone from Llangorse Crannog 04' (unpublished paper).

H. Pryce, 'Ecclesiastical Wealth in Early Medieval Wales', in N. Edwards and A. Lane (eds.), *The Early Church in Wales and the West: Recent Work in Early Christian Archaeology, History and Placenames* (Oxford, 1992), 22–32.

M. Redknap, 'Viking-Age Settlement in Wales and the Evidence from Llanbedr-goch', in J. Hines, A. Lane and M. Redknap (eds.), *Land, Sea and Home*, Society for Medieval Archaeology Monograph Series, 20 (Leeds, 2004), 139–75.

N. J. Sykes, 'The Dynamics of Status Symbols: Wildfowl Exploitation in England AD 410–1550', *Archaeological Journal*, 161 (2005), 82–105.

P. Wade-Martins, with documentary research by D. Yaxley, *Excavations in North Elmham Park*, East Anglian Archaeology, 9, Norfolk Archaeological Unit (Gressenhall, 1980).

P. Walton Rogers *Textile Production at 16–22 Coppergate*, Archaeology of York, 17/11 (York, 1997).

—— *Textiles, Cordage, and Raw Fiber from 16–22 Coppergate*, Archaeology of York, 17/5 (York, 1989), 374–5.

C. M. Woolgar, D. Serjeantson and T. Waldron (eds.), *Food in Medieval England: Diet and Nutrition* (Oxford, 2006).

The Politics of the Period; Money and the State

J. Campbell, 'Some Agents and Agencies of the Late Anglo-Saxon State', in J. C. Holt (ed.), *Domesday Studies* (Woodbridge, 1987), 201–18.

R. Fleming, *Kings and Lords in Conquest England* (Cambridge, 1991).

J. Gillingham, 'Chronicles and Coins as Evidence for Levels of Tribute and Taxation in Late Tenth- and Early Eleventh-Century England', *English Historical Review*, 105 (1990), 939–50.

—— '"The Most Precious Jewel in the English Crown": Levels of Danegeld and Heregeld in the Early Eleventh Century', *English Historical Review*, 104 (1989), 374–84.

S. Keynes, 'A Tale of Two Kings: Alfred the Great and Æthelred the Unready', *Transactions of the Royal Historical Society*, 5th ser., 36 (1986), 195–217.

M. K. Lawson, 'Danegeld and Heregeld Once More', *English Historical Review*, 105 (1990), 951–61.

—— '"Those Stories Look True": Levels of Taxation in the Reigns of Æthelred II and Cnut', *English Historical Review*, 104 (1989), 385–406.

D. M. Metcalf, 'Inflows of Anglo-Saxon and German Coins into the Northern Lands c. 997–1024: Discerning the Patterns', in B. Cook and G. Williams (eds.), *Coinage and History in the North Sea World, c. AD 500–1250: Essays in Honour of Marion Archibald* (Leiden, 2006), 349–88.

CHAPTER 12. CLERICS, MONKS AND THE LAITY
The Fundamental Readings

J. Blair, *The Church in Anglo-Saxon Society* (Oxford, 2005).

N. P. Brooks and C. Cubitt (eds.), *St Oswald of Worcester: Life and Influence* (London, 1996).

C. Cubitt, 'The Institutional Church', in P. Stafford (ed.), *A Companion to the Early Middle Ages: Britain and Ireland, c. 500–c. 1100* (London, 2009), 376–94.

—— 'The Tenth-Century Benedictine Reform in England', *Early Medieval Europe*, 6 (1997), 77–94.

M. Gretsch, *The Intellectual Foundations of the English Benedictine Reform* (Cambridge, 1999).

N. Ramsay, M. Sparks and T. Tatton-Brown (eds.), *St Dunstan: His Life, Times and Influence* (Woodbridge, 1992).

F. Tinti (ed.), *Pastoral Care in Late Anglo-Saxon England* (Woodbridge, 2005).

B. Yorke (ed.), *Bishop Æthelwold: His Career and Influence* (Woodbridge, 1988).

Unreformed and Reformed Communities

J. S. Barrow, 'The Chronology of Benedictine "Reform"', in D. Scragg (ed.), *Edgar, King of the English 959–975: New Interpretations* (Woodbridge, 2008), 211–23.

—— 'The Community of Worcester, 961–c. 1100', in N. P. Brooks and C. Cubitt (eds.), *St Oswald of Worcester: Life and Influence* (London, 1996), 84–99.

—— 'English Cathedral Communities and Reform in the Late Tenth and Eleventh Centuries', in D. Rollason, M. Harvey and M. Prestwich (eds.), *Anglo-Norman Durham 1093–1193* (Woodbridge, 1994), 25–39.

J. Blair, 'Palaces or Minsters? Northampton and Cheddar Reconsidered', *Anglo-Saxon England*, 25 (1996), 97–121.

—— 'A Saint for Every Minster? Local Cults in Anglo-Saxon England', in A. Thacker and R. Sharpe (eds.), *Local Saints and Local Churches in the Early Medieval West* (Oxford, 2002), 455–94.

P. Booth, A. Dodd, M. Robinson and A. Smith, *The Thames through Time: The Archaeology of the Gravel Terraces of the Upper and Middle Thames. The Early Historical Period: AD 1–1000*, Oxford Archaeology Thames Valley Landscapes Monographs, 27 (Oxford, 2007).

J. Campbell, 'Elements in the Background to the Life of St Cuthbert and his Early Cult', in G. Bonner, D. Rollason and C. Stancliffe (eds.), *St Cuthbert, his Cult and his Community to AD 1200* (Woodbridge, 1989), 3–19.

M. O. H. Carver, *Portmahomack: Monastery of the Picts* (Edinburgh, 2008).

S. Crawford with J. Blair and M. Harman, 'The Anglo-Saxon Cemetery at Chimney, Oxfordshire', *Oxoniensia*, 54 (1989), 45–56.

C. Cubitt, 'Pastoral Care and Religious Belief', in P. Stafford (ed.), *A Companion to the Early Middle Ages: Britain and Ireland, c. 500–c. 1100* (London, 2009), 395–413.

D. Farmer, 'The Monastic Reform of the Tenth Century and Sherborne', in K. Barker, D. A. Hinton. and A. Hunt (eds.), *St Wulfsige and Sherborne* (Oxford, 2005), 24–9.

S. Foot, *Monastic Life in Anglo-Saxon England, c. 600–900* (Cambridge, 2006).

H. Gittos, 'Creating the Sacred: Anglo-Saxon Rites for Consecrating Cemeteries', in S. J. Lucy and A. Reynolds (eds.), *Burial in Early Medieval England and*

Wales, Society for Medieval Archaeology Monograph Series, 17 (Leeds, 2002), 195–208.

A. Hardy, A. Dodd and G. D. Keevil, *Ælfric's Abbey: Excavations at Eynsham Abbey, Oxfordshire 1989–92* (Oxford, 2003).

M. Holmes and A. Chapman (eds.), 'A Middle-Late Saxon and Medieval Cemetery at Wing Church Buckinghamshire', *Records of Buckinghamshire*, 48 (2008), 61–123.

C. A. Jones, *Ælfric's Letter to the Monks of Eynsham* (Cambridge, 1998).

S. E. Kelly, 'An Early Minster at Eynsham, Oxfordshire', in O. J. Padel and D. N. Parsons (eds.), *A Commodity of Good Names* (Donnington, 2008), 79–85.

J. K. Knight, 'From Villa to Monastery: Llandough in Context', *Medieval Archaeology*, 49 (2005), 93–107.

J. Parkhouse, R. Roseff and J. Short, 'A Late Saxon Cemetery at Milton Keynes Village', *Records of Buckinghamshire*, 38 (1996), 199–221.

H. Price, 'The Christianization of Society', in W. Davies (ed.), *From the Vikings to the Normans* (Oxford, 2003), 138–67.

G. Rosser, 'The Anglo-Saxon Gilds', in J. Blair (ed.), *Minsters and Parish Churches: The Local Church in Transition 950–1200* (Oxford, 1988), 31–4.

The Proliferation of Churches

M. Audouy and A. Chapman (eds.), *Raunds: The Origin and Growth of a Midland Village AD 450–1500* (Oxford, 2009).

J. Blair, *Anglo-Saxon Oxfordshire* (Oxford, 1994).

—— 'Churches in the Early English Landscape: *Social* and Cultural Contexts', in J. Blair and C. Pyrah (eds.), *Church Archaeology: Research Directions for the Future*, CBA, Research Report, 104 (York, 1996), 6–18.

A. Boddington, *Raunds Furnells: The Anglo-Saxon Church and Churchyard*, English Heritage Archaeological Report, 7 (London, 1996).

G. Coppack, 'St Lawrence Church, Burnham, South Humberside: The Excavation of a Parochial Chapel', *Lincolnshire History and Archaeology*, 21 (1986), 39–60.

R. Fleming, M. F. Smith and P. Halpin, 'Court and Piety in Late Anglo-Saxon England', *Catholic Historical Review*, 87 (2001), 569–602.

R. Gem, 'The English Parish Church in the Eleventh and Early Twelfth Centuries: A Great Rebuilding?', in J. Blair (ed.), *Minsters and Parish Churches: The Local Church in Transition 950–1200* (Oxford, 1988), 21–30.

P. H. Hase, 'The Mother Churches of Hampshire', in J. Blair (ed.), *Minsters and Parish Churches: The Local Church in Transition 950–1200* (Oxford, 1988), 45–66.

M. Holmes and A. Chapman (eds.), 'A Middle-Late Saxon and Medieval Cemetery at Wing Church, Buckinghamshire', *Records of Buckinghamshire*, 48 (2008), 61–123.

R. M. Liuzza, 'Prayers and/or Charms Addressed to the Cross', in K. L. Jolly, C. E. Karkov and S. L. Keefer (eds.), *Cross and Culture in Anglo-Saxon England: Studies in Honor of George Hardin Brown* (Morgantown, W. Va., 2007), 276–320.

N. Rogers, 'The Waltham Abbey Relic-List', in C. Hicks (ed.), *England in the Eleventh Century: Proceedings of the 1990 Harlaxton Symposium* (Stamford, 1992), 157–81.

P. Warner, 'Shared Churchyards, Freemen Church Builders and the Development of Parishes in Eleventh-Century East Anglia', *Landscape History*, 8 (1986), 39–52.

J. Wilcox, 'Ælfric in Dorset and the Landscape of Pastoral Care', in F. Tinti (ed.), *Pastoral Care in Late Anglo-Saxon England* (Woodbridge, 2005), 52–62.

New Christians

L. Abrams, 'Conversion and Assimilation', in D. M. Hadley and J. D. Richards (eds.), *Cultures in Contact: Scandinavian Settlement in England in the Ninth and Tenth Centuries* (Turnhout, 2000), 135–53.

—— 'The Conversion of the Danelaw', in J. Graham-Campbell, R. A. Hall, J. Jesch and D. N. Parsons (eds.), *Vikings and the Danelaw* (Oxford, 2001), 31–44.

M. Audouy and A. Chapman (eds.), *Raunds: The Origin and Growth of a Midland Village AD 450–1500* (Oxford, 2009).

J. H. Barrett, 'Christian and Pagan Practice during the Conversion of Viking Age Orkney and Shetland', in M. O. H. Carver (ed.), *The Cross Goes North: Processes of Conversion in Northern Europe, AD 300–1300* (Woodbridge, 2003), 207–26.

J. D. Richards, 'The Case of the Missing Vikings: Scandinavian Burial in the Danelaw', in S. J. Lucy and A. Reynolds (eds.), *Burial in Early Medieval England and Wales*, Society for Medieval Archaeology Monograph Series, 17 (Leeds, 2002), 156–70.

D. Stocker and P. Everson, 'Five Towns Funerals: Decoding Diversity in Danelaw Stone Sculpture', in J. Graham-Campbell, R. A. Hall, J. Jesch and D. N. Parsons (eds.), *Vikings and the Danelaw* (Oxford, 2001), 223–43.

CHAPTER 13. LIVING AND DYING IN EARLY MEDIEVAL BRITAIN

Basic and Accessible Introductions to Osteoarchaeology

M. N. Cohen, 'Does Palaeopathology Measure Community Health? A Rebuttal of "the Osteological Paradox" and its Implications for World History', in R. R. Paine (ed.), *Integrating Archaeological Demography: Multidisciplinary*

Approaches to Prehistoric Population, Center for Archaeological Investigations, Occasional Papers, 24 (Carbondale, Ill., 1997), 242–60.

R. Fleming, 'Bones for Historians: Putting the Body Back into Biography', in D. Bates, J. Crick and S. Hamilton (eds.), *Writing Medieval Biography 750–1250: Essays in Honour of Professor Frank Barlow* (Woodbridge, 2006), 29–48.

—— 'Writing Biography on the Edge of History', *American Historical Review*, 114 (2009), 606–14.

R. Gowland and C. Knüsel (eds.), *The Social Archaeology of Funerary Remains* (Oxford, 2006), 168–78.

C. S. Larsen, *Bioarchaeology: Interpreting Human Behavior from the Human Skeleton* (Cambridge, 1997).

S. Mays, *The Archaeology of Human Bones* (London, 1998).

T. Molleson and M. Cox, *The Spitalfields Project*, vol. 2: *The Anthropology: The Middling Sort*, CBA, Research Report, 86 (York, 1993).

D. Ortner, *Identification of Pathological Conditions in Human Skeletal Remains*, 2nd edn. (San Diego, 2003).

C. A. Roberts and M. Cox, *Health and Disease in Britain from Prehistory to the Present Day* (Stroud, 2003).

—— and K. Manchester, *The Archaeology of Disease*, 3rd edn. (Stroud, 2005).

T. Waldron, *Counting the Dead: The Epidemiology of Skeletal Populations* (Chichester, 1994).

J. W. Wood, G. R. Milner, H. C. Harpending and K. M. Weis, 'The Osteological Paradox: Problems of Inferring Prehistoric Health from Skeletal Samples', *Current Anthropology*, 33 (1992), 343–70.

Some Excavation Reports of Cemeteries with Interesting Discussions of Skeletal Material

A. Boddington, *Raunds Furnells: The Anglo-Saxon Church and Churchyard*, English Heritage Archaeological Report, 7 (London, 1996).

A. Boyle, A. Dodd, D. Miles and A. Mudd, *Two Oxfordshire Anglo-Saxon Cemeteries: Berinsfield and Didcot*, Oxford Archaeology Thames Valley Landscapes Monographs, 8 (Oxford, 1995).

J. D. Dawes and J. R. Magilton, *The Cemetery of St Helen-on-the-Walls, Aldwark*, Archaeology of York, 12/1 (York, 1980).

G. Drinkall and M. Foreman, *The Anglo-Saxon Cemetery at Castledyke South, Barton-on-Humber*, Sheffield Excavation Reports, 6 (Sheffield, 1998).

V. I. Evison, *An Anglo-Saxon Cemetery at Great Chesterford, Essex*, CBA, Research Report 91 (York, 1994).

—— *Dover: The Buckland Anglo-Saxon Cemetery* (London, 1987).

P. Hill, *Whithorn and St Ninian: The Excavation of a Monastic Town, 1984–91* (Stroud, 1997).

P. J. Huggins, 'Excavation of Belgic and Romano-British Farm with Middle Saxon Cemetery and Churches at Nazeingbury, Essex 1975–76', *Essex Archaeology and History*, 10 (1978), 29–117.

T. Malim and J. Hines, *The Anglo-Saxon Cemetery at Edix Hill (Barrington A)*, CBA, Research Report, 112 (York, 1998).

K. Parfitt and B. Brugmann, *The Anglo-Saxon Cemetery on Mill Hill, Deal, Kent*, Society for Medieval Archaeology Monograph Series, 14 (London, 1997).

S. J. Sherlock and M. G. Welch, *An Anglo-Saxon Cemetery at Norton, Cleveland*, CBA, Research Report, 82 (London, 1992).

A. Taylor, C. Duhig and J. Hines, 'An Anglo-Saxon Cemetery at Oakington, Cambridgeshire', *Proceedings of the Cambridge Antiquarian Society*, 86 (1997), 57–90.

J. R. Timby, *The Anglo-Saxon Cemetery at Empringham II, Rutland* (Oxford, 1996).

W. White, *Skeletal Remains from the Cemetery of St Nicholas, Shambles, City of London*, London and Middlesex Archaeology Society, Special Papers, 9 (London, 1988).

The Health of Rural and Urban Populations

D. Brothwell, 'On the Possibility of Urban-Rural Contrasts in Human Population Palaeobiology', in A. R. Hall and H. K. Kenward (eds.), *Urban-Rural Connexions: Perspectives from Urban-Rural Archaeology* (Oxford, 1994), 129–36.

A. R. Hall, H. K. Kenward, D. Williams and J. R. A. Greig, *Environment and Living Conditions at Two Anglo-Scandinavian Sites*, Archaeology of York, 14/4 (York, 1983).

M. A. Judd and C. A. Roberts, 'Fracture Trauma in a Medieval British Farming Village', *American Journal of Physical Anthropology*, 109 (1999), 229–43.

H. K. Kenward and E. P. Allison, 'Rural Origins of the Urban Insect Fauna', in A. R. Hall and H. K. Kenward (eds.), *Urban-Rural Connexions: Perspectives from Urban-Rural Archaeology* (Oxford, 1994), 55–77.

—— and A. R. Hall, *Biological Evidence from Anglo-Scandinavian Deposits at 16–22 Coppergate*, Archaeology of York, 14/7 (York, 1995).

—— and F. Large, 'Insects in Urban Waste Pits in Viking York: Another Kind of Seasonality', *Environmental Archaeology (Circaea)*, 3 (1998), 35–53.

D. Klingle, 'Understanding Age, Stature and Nutrition in Cambridgeshire and Bedfordshire during the Roman and Early Anglo-Saxon Periods (AD 43–700)', *Archaeological Review from Cambridge*, 23 (2008), 99–123.

M. Lewis, 'Non-Adult Palaeopathology: Current Status and Future Potential', in M. Cox and S. Mays (eds.), *Human Osteology in Archaeology and Forensic Science* (London, 2000), 39–57.

K. Manchester and C. Roberts, 'The Palaeopathology of Leprosy in Britain: A Review', *World Archaeology*, 21 (1989), 265–72.

S. Mays, 'Linear and Appositional Long Bone Growth in Earlier Human Populations: A Case Study from Medieval England', in R. D. Hoppa and C. M. Fitz-Gerald (eds.), *Human Growth in the Past: Studies from Bones and Teeth* (Cambridge, 1999), 290–312.

P. J. Piper and T. P. O'Connor, 'Urban Small Vertebrate Taphonomy: A Case Study from Anglo-Scandinavian York', *International Journal of Osteoarchaeology*, 11 (2001), 336–44.

I. Ribot and C. Roberts, 'Study of Non-Specific Stress Indicators and Skeletal Growth in Two Mediaeval Subadult Populations', *Journal of Archaeological Science*, 23 (1996), 67–79.

C. A. Roberts, 'The Antiquity of Leprosy in Britain: The Skeletal Evidence', in C. A. Roberts, M. E. Lewis and K. Manchester (eds.), *The Past and Present of Leprosy: Archaeological, Historical, and Palaeopathological and Clinical Approaches*, BAR, Int. Ser., 1054 (Oxford, 2002), 213–21.

J. Rogers and T. Waldron, 'DISH and the Monastic Way of Life', *International Journal of Osteoarchaeology*, 11 (2001), 357–65.

P. K. Stone and D. Walrath, 'The Gendered Skeleton: Anthropological Interpretations of the Bony Pelvis', in R. Gowland and C. Knüsel (eds.), *The Social Archaeology of Funerary Remains* (Oxford, 2006), 168–78.

P. Stuart-Macadam and S. K. Kent (eds.), *Diet, Demography and Disease: Changing Perspectives on Anemia* (New York, 1992).

T. Waldron, 'The Effects of Urbanization on Human Health: The Evidence from Skeletal Remains', in D. Serjeantson and T. Waldron (eds.), *Diet and Crafts in Towns: The Evidence of Animal Remains from the Roman to the Post-Medieval Periods*, BAR, Brit. Ser., 199 (Oxford, 1989), 55–73.

—— 'Nutrition and the Skeleton', in C. M. Woolgar, D. Serjeantson and T. Waldron (eds.), *Food in Medieval England: Diet and Nutrition* (Oxford, 2006), 254–66.

Working, Eating and Moving

J. H. Barrett and M. P. Richards, 'Identity, Gender, Religion and Economy: New Isotope and Radiocarbon Evidence for Marine Resource Intensification in Early Historic Orkney, Scotland, UK', *European Journal of Archaeology*, 7 (2004), 249–71.

P. Budd, A. Millard, C. Chenery, S. J. Lucy and C. Roberts, 'Investigating Population Movement by Stable Isotope Analysis: A Report from Britain', *Antiquity*, 78 (2004), 127–41.

A. J. Dunwell, T. G. Cowie, M. F. Bruce, T. Neighbour and A. R. Rees, 'A Viking Age Cemetery at Cnip, Uig, Isle of Lewis', *Proceedings of the Society of Antiquaries of Scotland*, 125 (1995), 719–52.

B. T. Fuller, T. I. Molleson, D. A. Harris, L. T. Gilmour and R. E. M. Hedges, 'Isotopic Evidence for Breastfeeding and Possible Adult Dietary Differences from Late/Sub-Roman Britain', *American Journal of Physical Anthropology*, 129 (2006), 45–54.

C. Knüsel, 'Bone Adaptation and its Relationship to Physical Activity in the Past', in M. Cox and S. Mays (eds.), *Human Osteology in Archaeology and Forensic Science* (London, 2000), 381–401.

T. Molleson, 'A Norse Age Boatman from Newark Bay', *Papers and Pictures in Honour of Daphne Home Lorimer, MBE*, Orkney Archaeological Trust (2004), http://www.orkneydigs.org.uk/dhl/papers/tm/index.html

J. Montgomery and J. A. Evans, 'Immigrants on the Isle of Lewis – Combining Traditional Funerary and Modern Isotope Evidence to Investigate Social Differentiation, Migration and Dietary Change in the Outer Hebrides of Scotland', in R. Gowland and C. Knüsel (eds.), *The Social Archaeology of Funerary Remains* (Oxford, 2006), 122–42.

K. L. Privat, T. C. O'Connell and M. P. Richards, 'Stable Isotope Analysis of Human and Faunal Remains from the Anglo-Saxon Cemetery at Berinsfield, Oxfordshire: Dietary and Social Implications', *Journal of Archaeological Science*, 29 (2002), 779–90.

Punishment Burials

M. O. H. Carver, *Sutton Hoo: A Seventh-Century Princely Burial Ground and its Context* (London, 2005).

B. Clarke, 'An Early Anglo-Saxon Cross-Roads Burial from Broadtown, North Wiltshire', *Wiltshire Archaeological and Natural History Magazine*, 97 (2004), 89–94.

D. Hamilton, M. Pitts and A. J. Reynolds, 'A Revised Date for the Early Medieval Execution at Stonehenge', *Wiltshire Archaeological and Natural History Magazine*, 100 (2007), 202–3.

G. Hayman and A. Reynolds, 'A Saxon and Saxo-Norman Execution Cemetery at 42–54 London Road, Staines', *Archaeological Journal*, 162 (2005), 215–55.

S. M. Hirst, *An Anglo-Saxon Inhumation Cemetery at Sewerby, East Yorkshire* (York, 1985).

—— 'Death and the Archaeologist', in M. O. H. Carver (ed.), *In Search of Cult: Archaeological Investigations in Honour of Philip Rahtz* (Woodbridge, 1993), 41–3.

M. Pitts, A. Bayliss, J. McKinley, A. Boylston, P. Budd, J. Evans, C. Chenery, A. J. Reynolds and S. Semple, 'An Anglo-Saxon Decapitation and Burial at Stonehenge', *Wiltshire Archaeological and Natural History Magazine*, 95 (2002), 131–46.

A. Reynolds, *Anglo-Saxon Deviant Burial Customs* (Oxford, 2009).

—— *Late Anglo-Saxon England* (Stroud, 1999).

S. Semple, 'A Fear of the Past: The Place of the Prehistoric Burial Mound in the Ideology of Middle and Later Anglo-Saxon England', *World Archaeology*, 30 (1998), 109–26.

J. F. S. Stone, 'Interments of Roche Court Down, Winterslow', *Wiltshire Archaeological and Natural History Magazine*, 45 (1932), 568–82.

M. L. Tildesley, 'The Human Remains from Roche Court Down', *Wiltshire Archaeological and Natural History Magazine*, 45 (1932), 583–99.

R. Wroe-Brown, 'Bull Wharf: Queenhithe', *Current Archaeology*, 158 (1998), 75–7.

Sources

Grateful acknowledgement is given for permission to quote from the following sources:

pp. 25–6: Paulinus of Pella, in H. Isbell, trans., *The Last Poets of Imperial Rome* (Harmondsworth, 1971), 251–60. Reproduced by permission of Penguin Books.

p. 37: Procopius, *Gothic War*, quoted in T. Wilmott with L. Hird, K. Izard, J. Summerfield and L. Allason-Jones, *Birdoswald: Excavations of a Roman Fort on Hadrian's Wall and its Successor Settlements: 1987–92*, English Heritage Archaeological Report, 14 (London, 1994), 225.

p. 61: B. Colgrave and R. A. B. Mynors, eds., *Bede's Ecclesiastical History of the English People* (Oxford, 1969), 51.

pp. 67–8: R. Sharpe, trans., Adomnán of Iona, *Life of St Columba* (London, 1995) 169–70.

p. 91: D. Whitelock with D. C. Douglas and S. I. Tucker, trans., *The Anglo-Saxon Chronicle: A Revised Translation* (New Brunswick, New Jersey, 1961), 11.

p. 98: M. Alexander, trans., *Beowulf* (Harmondsworth, 1995), 73–4. Reproduced by permission of Penguin Books.

p. 114: M. Alexander, trans., *Beowulf* (Harmondsworth, 1995), 111–12. Reproduced by permission of Penguin Books.

pp. 134–5: B. Colgrave and R. A. B. Mynors, eds., *Bede's Ecclesiastical History of the English People* (Oxford, 1969), 183–7.

p. 164: Alcuin quoted in A. L. Meaney, 'Anglo-Saxon Idolators and Ecclesiasts from Theodore to Alcuin: A Source Study', *Anglo-Saxon Studies in Archaeology and History*, 5 (1992), 103–25, at 116.

p. 164: Prayer from an eighth-century Worcester prayer book, quoted in P. Sims-Williams, *Religion and Literature in Western England, 600–800* (Cambridge, 1990), 54.

p. 165: B. Colgrave and R. A. B. Mynors, eds., *Bede's Ecclesiastical History of the English People* (Oxford, 1969), 247.

p. 168: B. Colgrave and R. A. B. Mynors, eds., *Bede's Ecclesiastical History of the English People* (Oxford, 1969), 77–9.

p. 171: 'Bede's letter to Egbert', in D. Whitelock, trans., *English Historical Documents c. 500–1042*, i, 2nd edn. (London, 1979), 800–801.

pp. 171–2: S. DeGregorio, trans., *Bede: On Ezra and Nehemiah* (Liverpool, 2006), 102.

pp. 183–4: 'The Ruin', in S. A. J. Bradley, trans., *Anglo-Saxon Poetry: An Anthology of Old English Poems* (London, 1982), 402.

p. 216: Alfred the Great's translation of Orosius, in M. Swanton, trans., *Anglo-Saxon Prose* (London, 1975), 34.

p. 227: D. Whitelock with D. C. Douglas and S. I. Tucker, trans., *The Anglo-Saxon Chronicle: A Revised Translation* (New Brunswick, New Jersey, 1961), 48.

p. 238: H. Palsson and P. Edwards, trans., *Orkneyinga Saga: The History of the Earls of Orkney* (London, 1981) c. 105.

p. 281: Riddle from the Exeter Book, in K. Crossley-Holland, trans., *The Anglo-Saxon World: An Anthology* (Oxford, 1999), 240.

p. 286: *Rectitudines Singularum Personarum*, in D. C. Douglas and G. W. Greenaway, trans., *English Historical Documents 1042–1189*, ii, 2nd edn (London, 1981), 876.

p. 286: Ælfric's Colloquy, in M. Swanton, trans., *Anglo-Saxon Prose* (London, 1975), 108.

pp. 286–7: *Vita Kenelmi*, in R. C. Love, ed. and trans., *Three Eleventh-Century Anglo-Latin Saints' Lives* (Oxford, 1996), 77.

p. 311: L. Thorpe, trans., Gerald of Wales, *Journey through Wales, The Description of Wales* (Harmondsworth, 1978), 236.

pp. 327–8: Extracts from a Christchurch Priory cartulary, in J. Blair, ed. and trans., *The Church in Anglo-Saxon Society* (Oxford, 2006), 515–16.

p. 328: Extracts from a Plympton Priory cartulary, in J. Blair, ed. and trans., *The Church in Anglo-Saxon Society* (Oxford, 2006), 521.

p. 330: J. Scott, ed. and trans., *The Early History of Glastonbury: An Edition, Translation and Study of William of Malmesbury's* De Antiquitate Glastonie Ecclesie (Woodbridge, Suffolk, 1981), 163.

p. 334: *Registrum Statutorum ... Cathedralis S. Pauli Londiniensis*, ed. W. S.

Simpson (London, 1873), 38, quoted in C. Brooks, *London 800–1216: The Shaping of a City* (London, 1975), 340.

pp. 334–5: L. Watkiss and M. Chibnall, ed. and trans., *The Waltham Chronicle* (Oxford, 1994), 30–31.

pp. 338–9: Charm quoted in R. M. Liuzza, 'Prayers and/or Charms Addressed to the Cross', in K. L. Jolly, C. E. Karkov and S. L. Keefer, eds., *Cross and Culture in Anglo-Saxon England: Studies in Honor of George Hardin Brown* (Morgantown, W. Va., 2007), 276–320, at 293.

p. 341: 'Ælfric's Pastoral Letter for Bishop Wulfsige', in D. Whitelock, M. Brett and C. N. L. Brooke, ed. and trans., *Councils and Synods with Other Documents Relating to the English Church*, I (Oxford, 1981), 206–7.

pp. 363–4: Charter from a twelfth-century cartulary from Peterborough Abbey, in A. J. Robertson, ed. and trans., *Anglo-Saxon Charters* (Cambridge, 1939), 69.

Index